W9-CHO-911

10.
VOLUME TEN

SABUROUTA
PRESENTS
SECRET LOVE AFFAIR
WITH SISTER
特装版

citrus

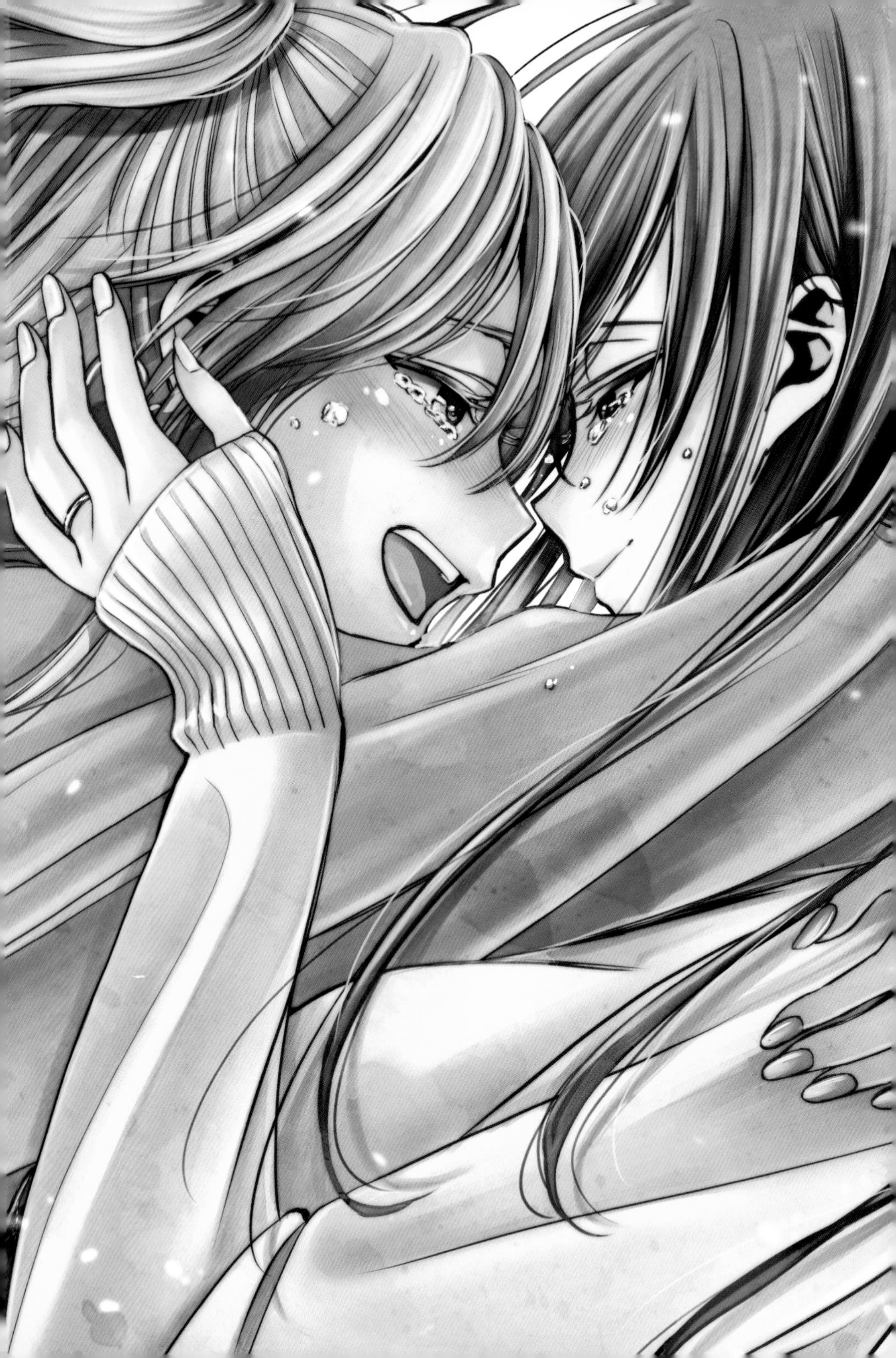

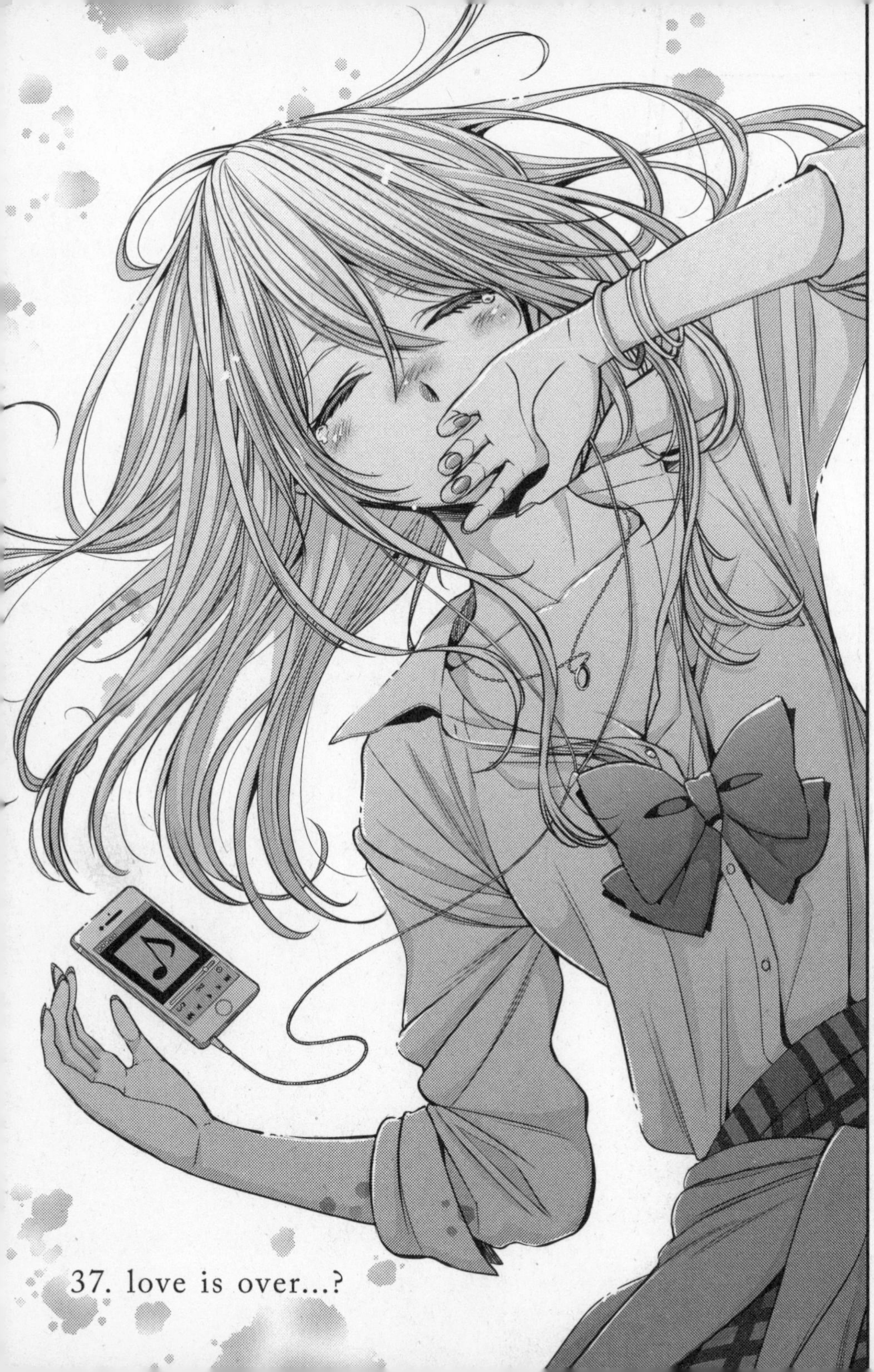

37. love is over...?

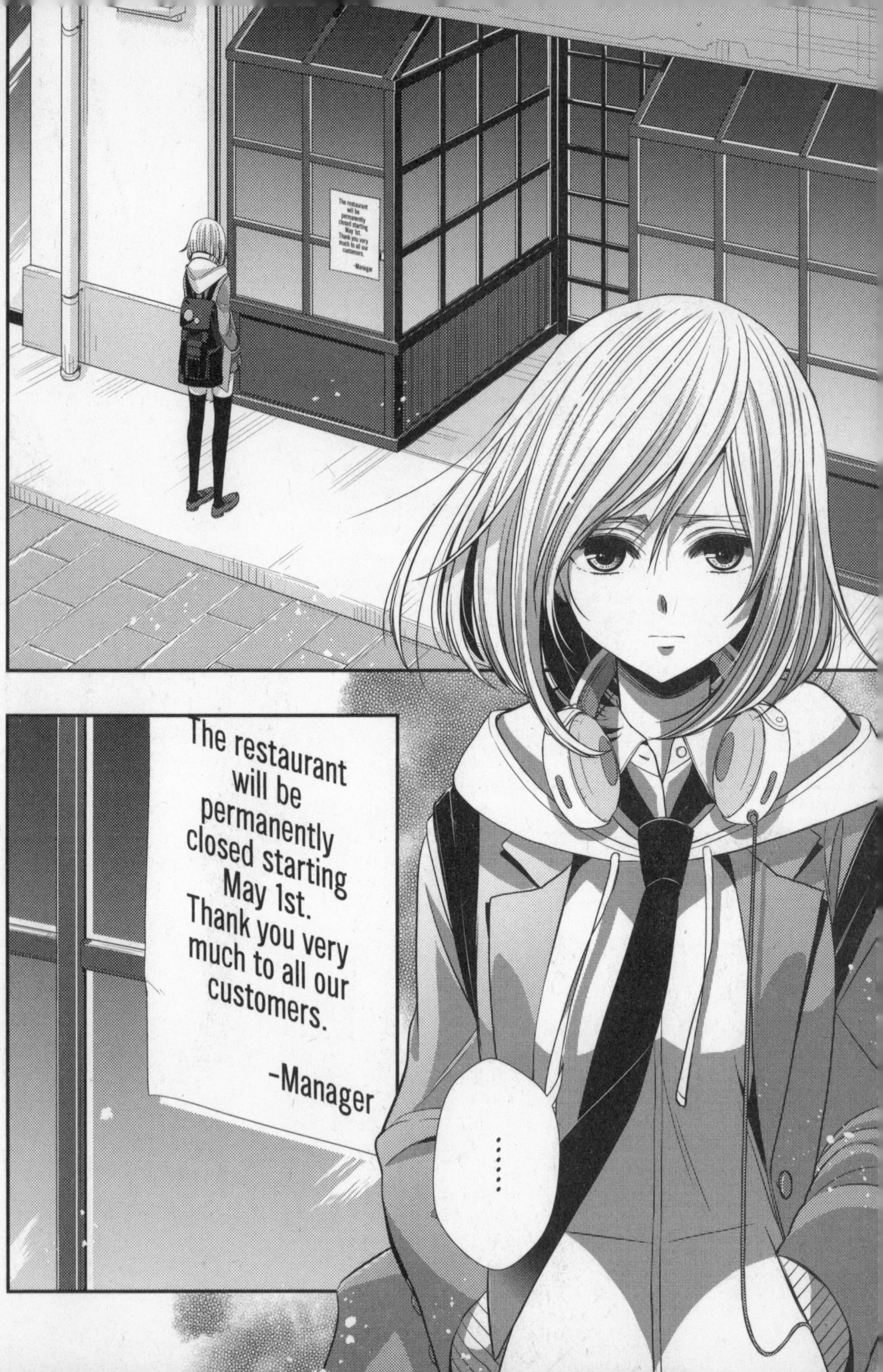
The restaurant will be permanently closed starting May 1st. Thank you very much to all our customers. -Manager
The restaurant will be permanently closed starting May 1st. Thank you very much to all our customers.
-Manager
......

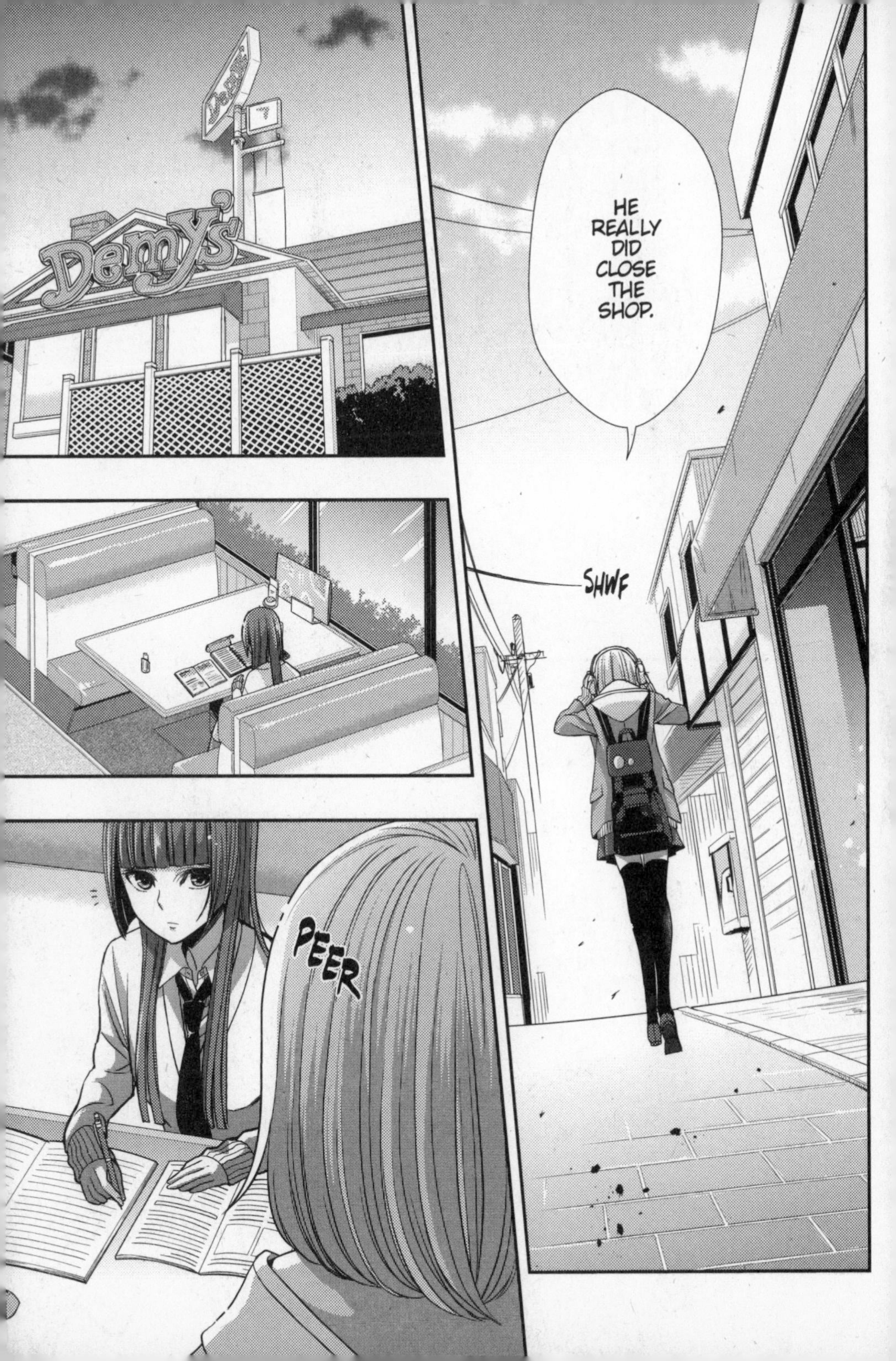
HE REALLY DID CLOSE THE SHOP.
SHWF
Demy's
PEER

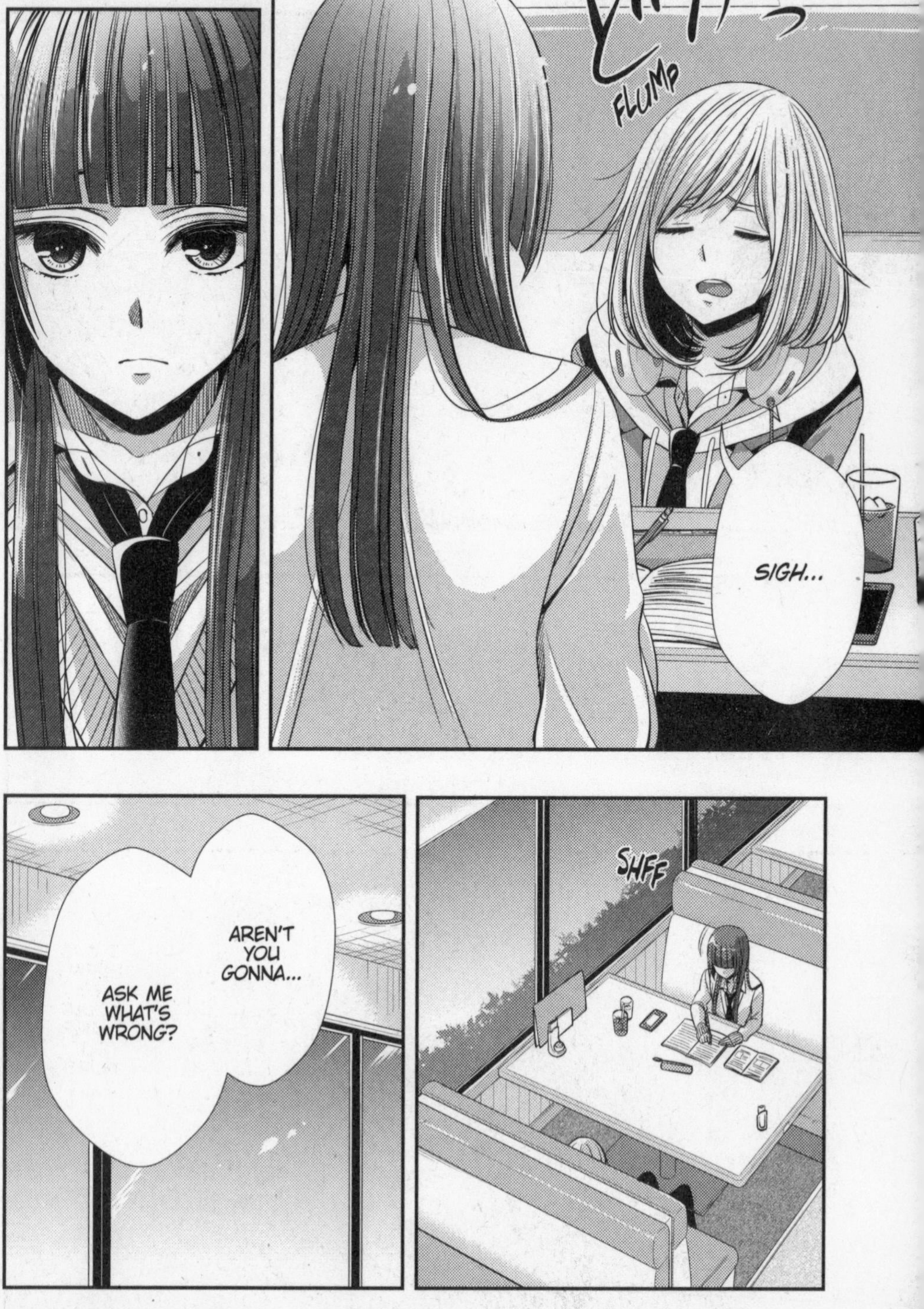
どかっ
FLUMP
SIGH...
SHFF
AREN'T YOU GONNA...
ASK ME WHAT'S WRONG?

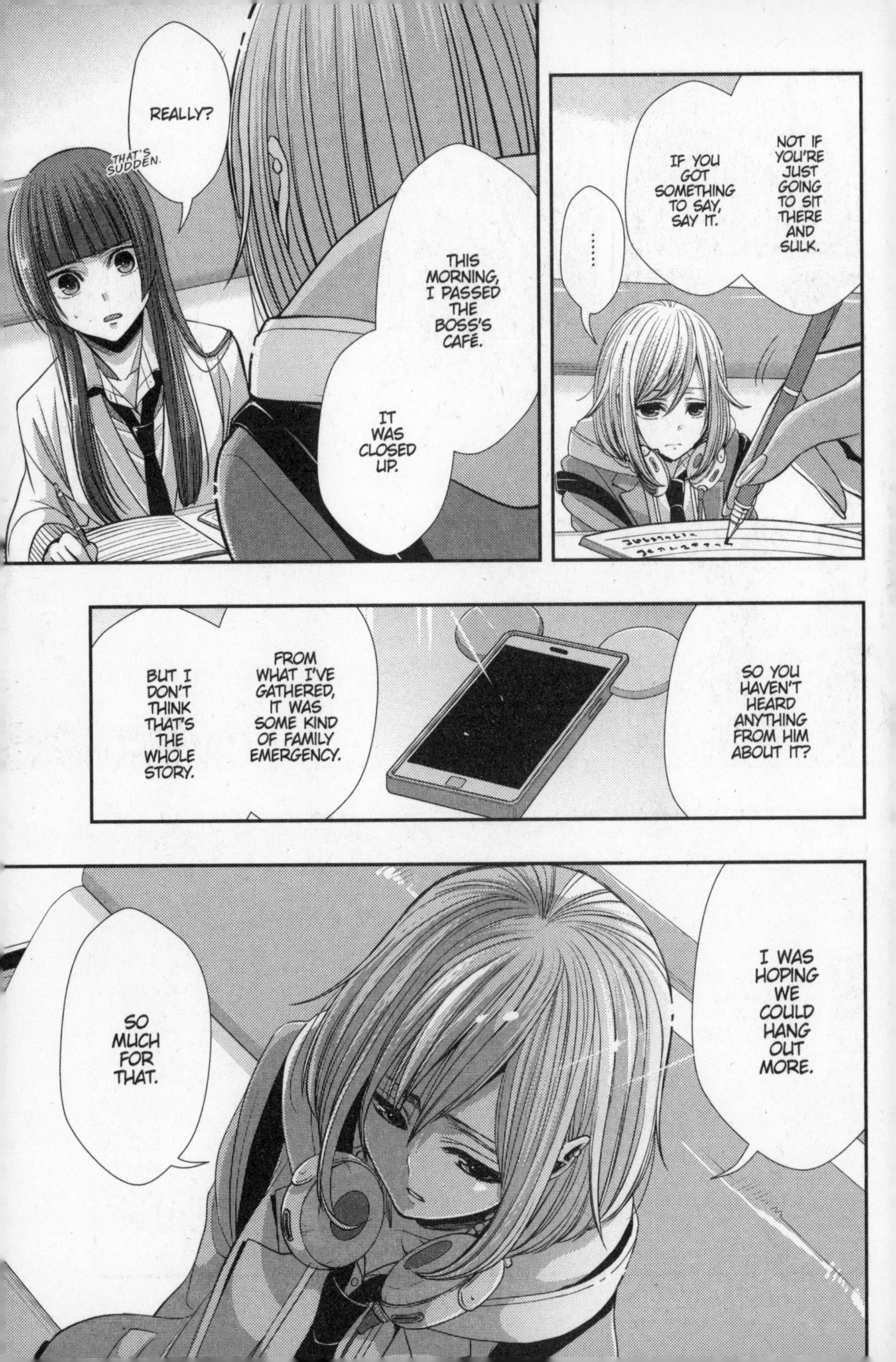
NOT IF YOU'RE JUST GOING TO SIT THERE AND SULK.
IF YOU GOT SOMETHING TO SAY, SAY IT.
......
THIS MORNING, I PASSED THE BOSS'S CAFÉ.
IT WAS CLOSED UP.
REALLY?
THAT'S SUDDEN.
SO YOU HAVEN'T HEARD ANYTHING FROM HIM ABOUT IT?
FROM WHAT I'VE GATHERED, IT WAS SOME KIND OF FAMILY EMERGENCY.
BUT I DON'T THINK THAT'S THE WHOLE STORY.
I WAS HOPING WE COULD HANG OUT MORE.
SO MUCH FOR THAT.

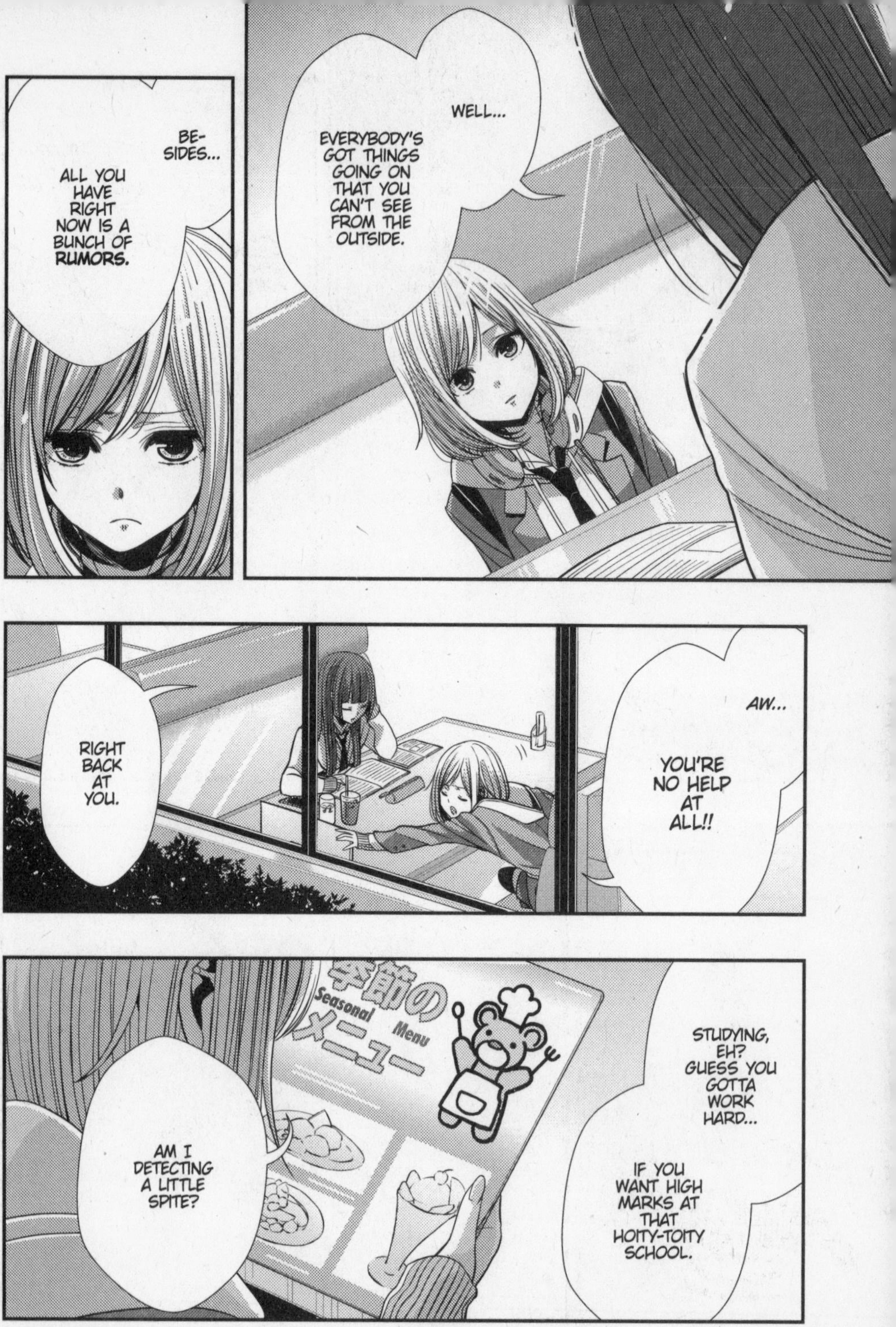
WELL...
EVERYBODY'S GOT THINGS GOING ON THAT YOU CAN'T SEE FROM THE OUTSIDE.
BE-SIDES...
ALL YOU HAVE RIGHT NOW IS A BUNCH OF RUMORS.
AW...
YOU'RE NO HELP AT ALL!!
RIGHT BACK AT YOU.
STUDYING, EH? GUESS YOU GOTTA WORK HARD...
IF YOU WANT HIGH MARKS AT THAT HOITY-TOITY SCHOOL.
季節のメニュー
Seasonal Menu
AM I DETECTING A LITTLE SPITE?

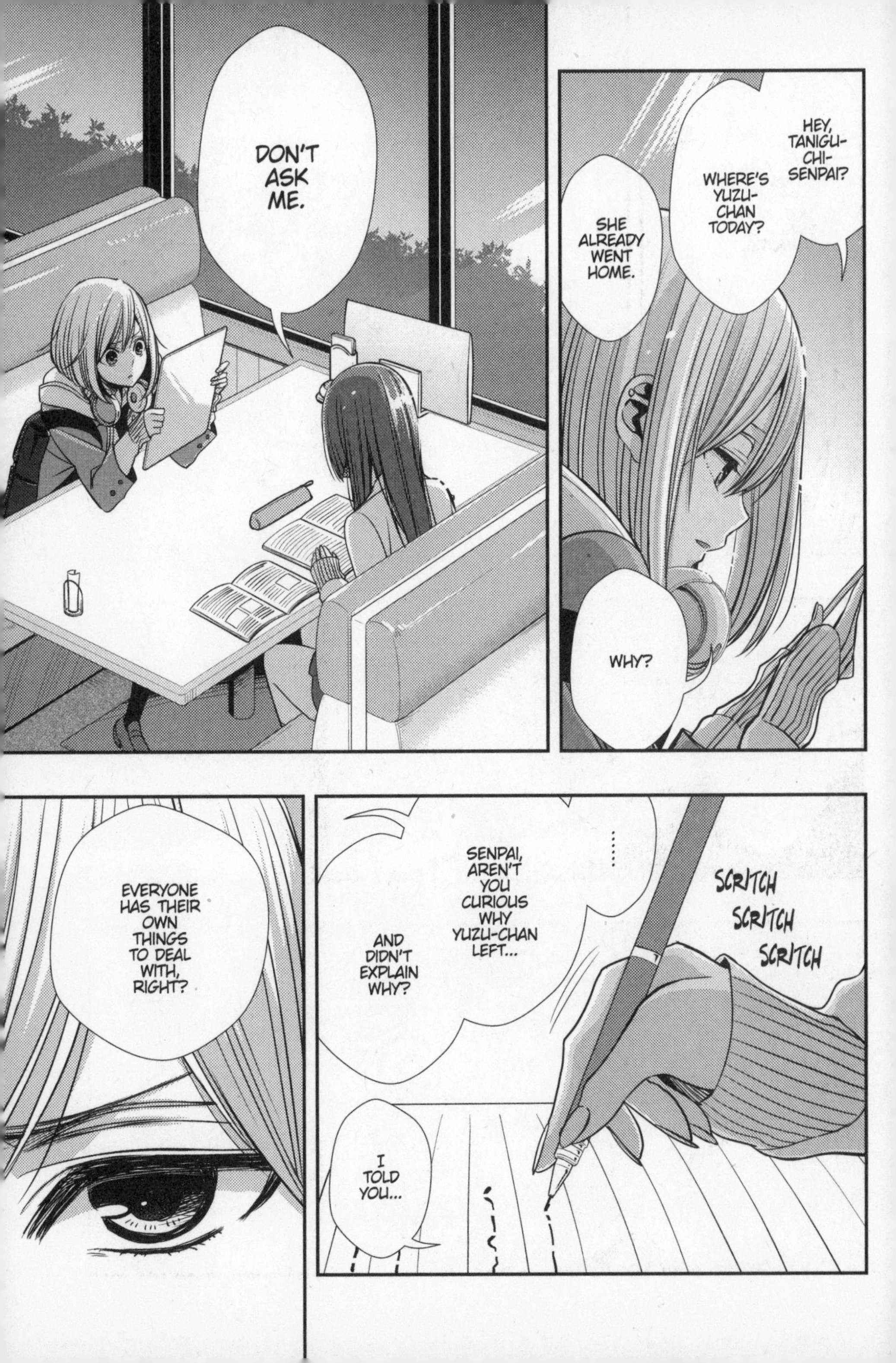

HEY, TANIGUCHI-SENPAI?
WHERE'S YUZU-CHAN TODAY?
SHE ALREADY WENT HOME.
WHY?
DON'T ASK ME.
......
SENPAI, AREN'T YOU CURIOUS WHY YUZU-CHAN LEFT...
AND DIDN'T EXPLAIN WHY?
SCRITCH
SCRITCH
SCRITCH
I TOLD YOU...
EVERYONE HAS THEIR OWN THINGS TO DEAL WITH, RIGHT?

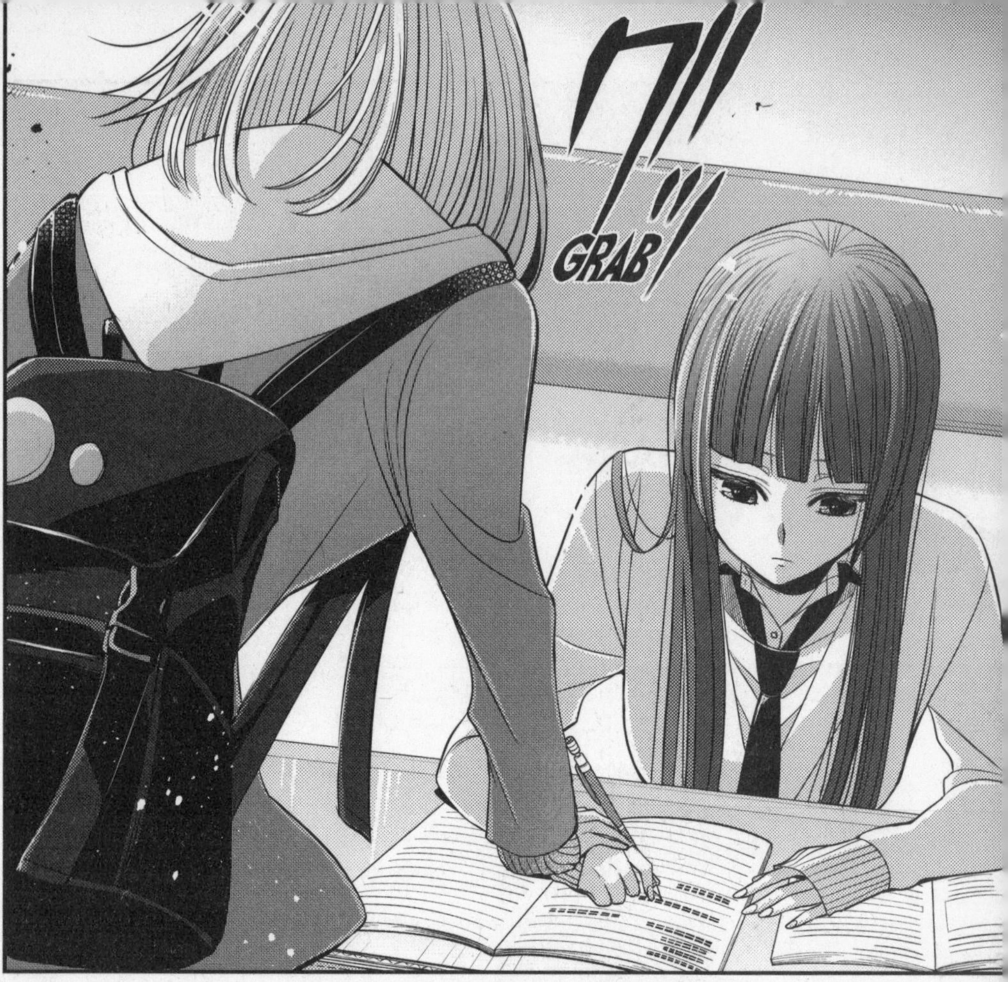
GRAB

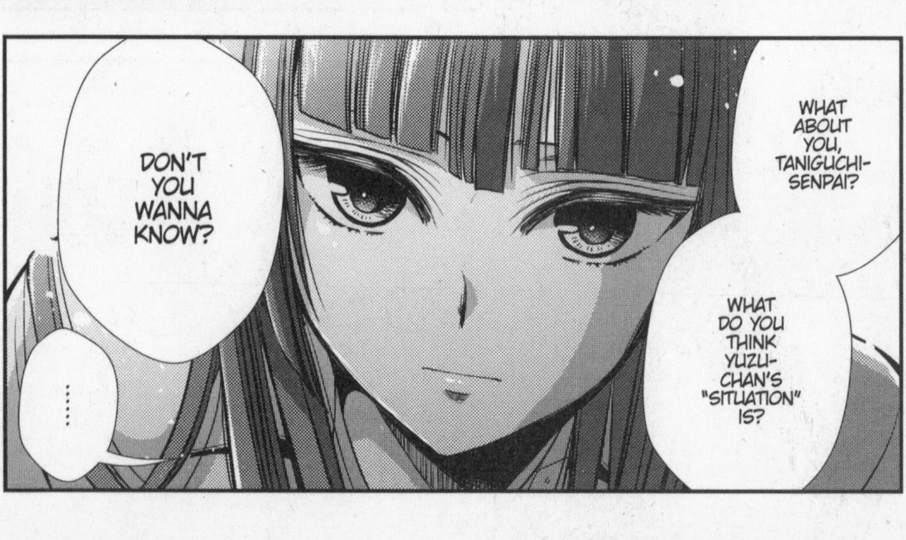
WHAT ABOUT YOU, TANIGUCHI-SENPAI?
WHAT DO YOU THINK YUZU-CHAN'S "SITUATION" IS?
DON'T YOU WANNA KNOW?
......

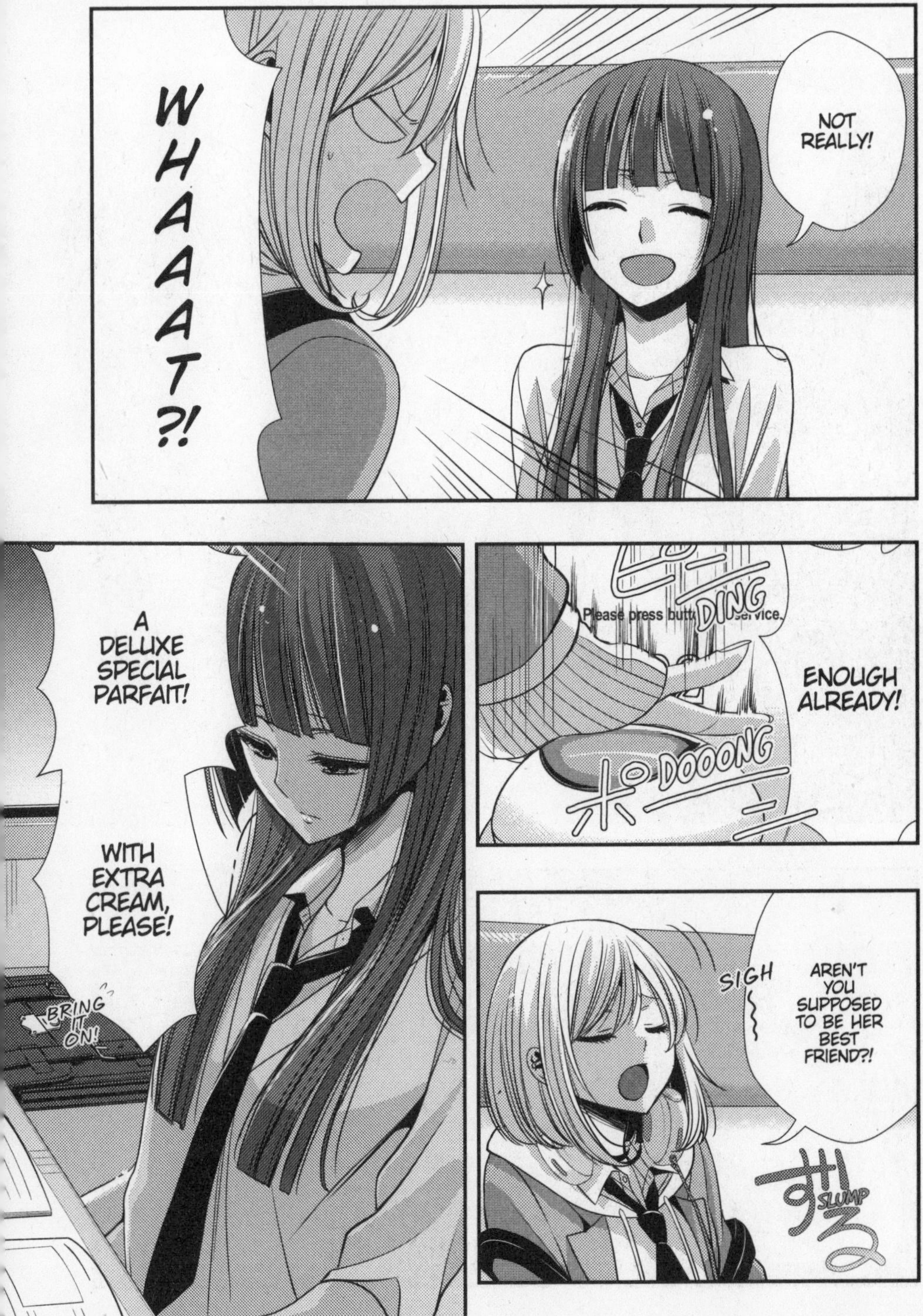
NOT REALLY!
WHAAAT?!
ENOUGH ALREADY!
DING
Please press butt
service.
DOOONG
AREN'T YOU SUPPOSED TO BE HER BEST FRIEND?!
SIGH
SLUMP
A DELUXE SPECIAL PARFAIT!
WITH EXTRA CREAM, PLEASE!
BRING IT ON!

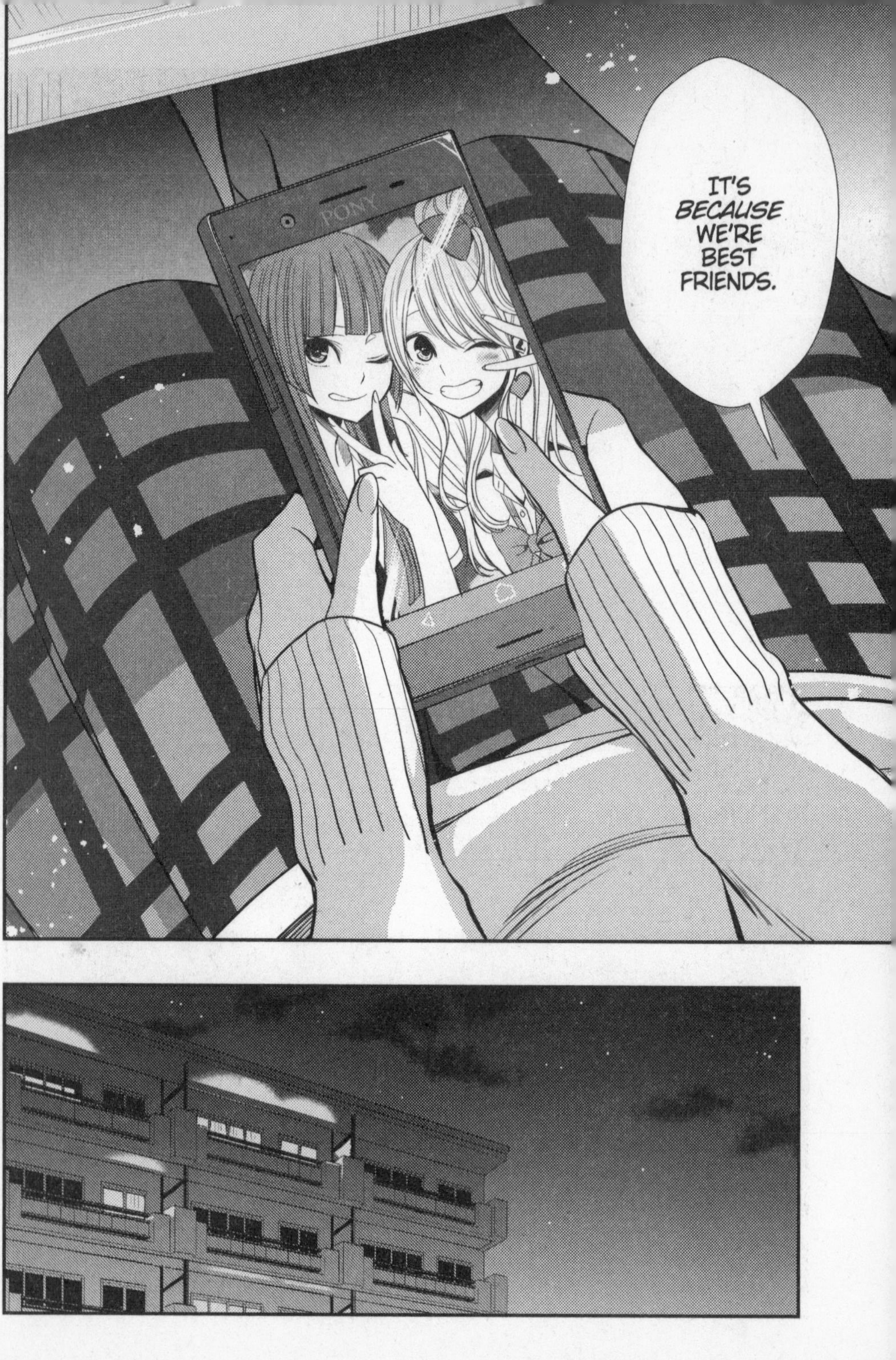
IT'S BECAUSE WE'RE BEST FRIENDS.
PONY

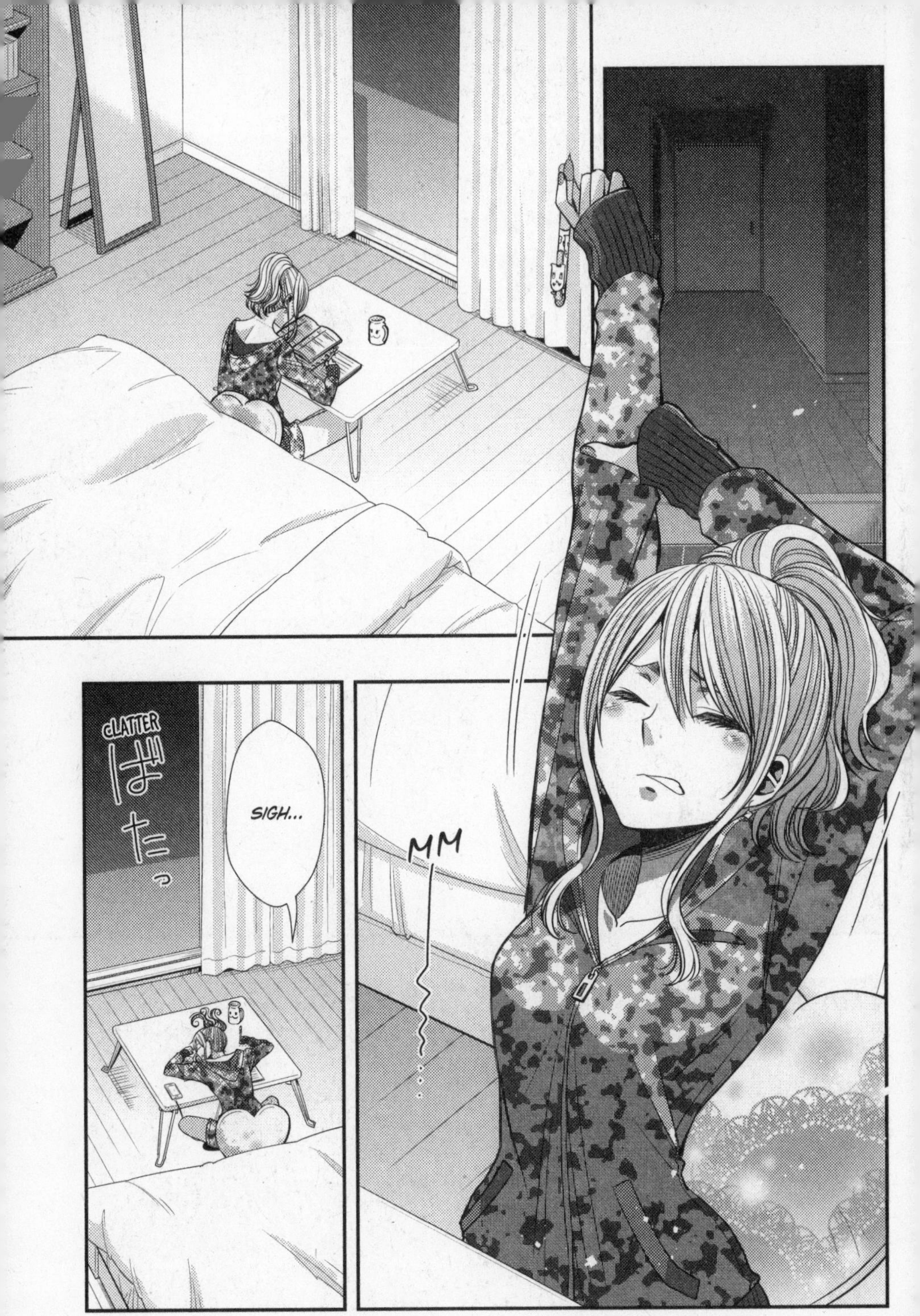
MM
SIGH...
CLATTER
ばたっ

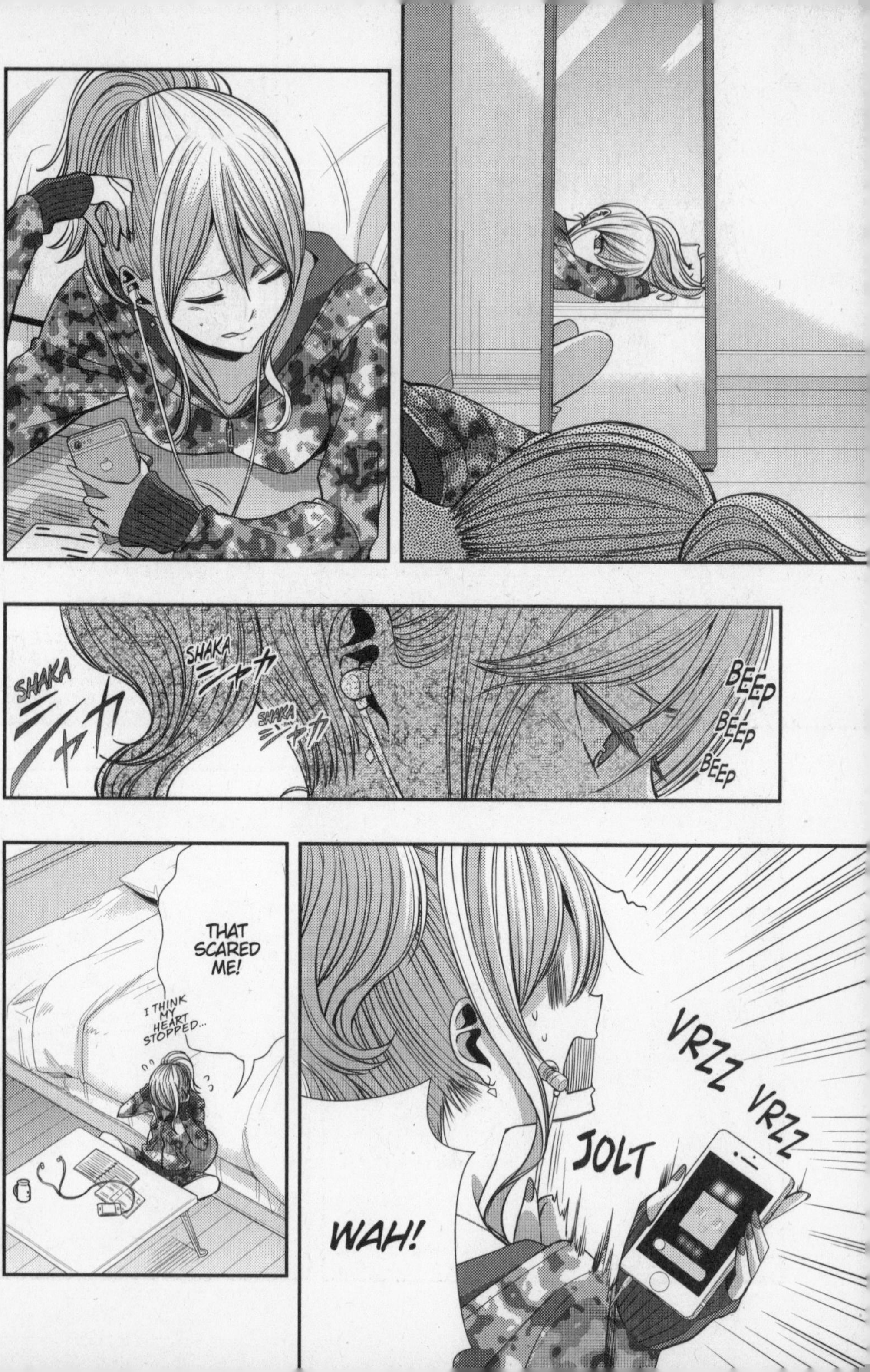
BEEP
BEEP
BEEP
SHAKA
SHAKA
SHAKA
VRZZ VRZZ
JOLT
WAH!
THAT SCARED ME!
I THINK MY HEART STOPPED...

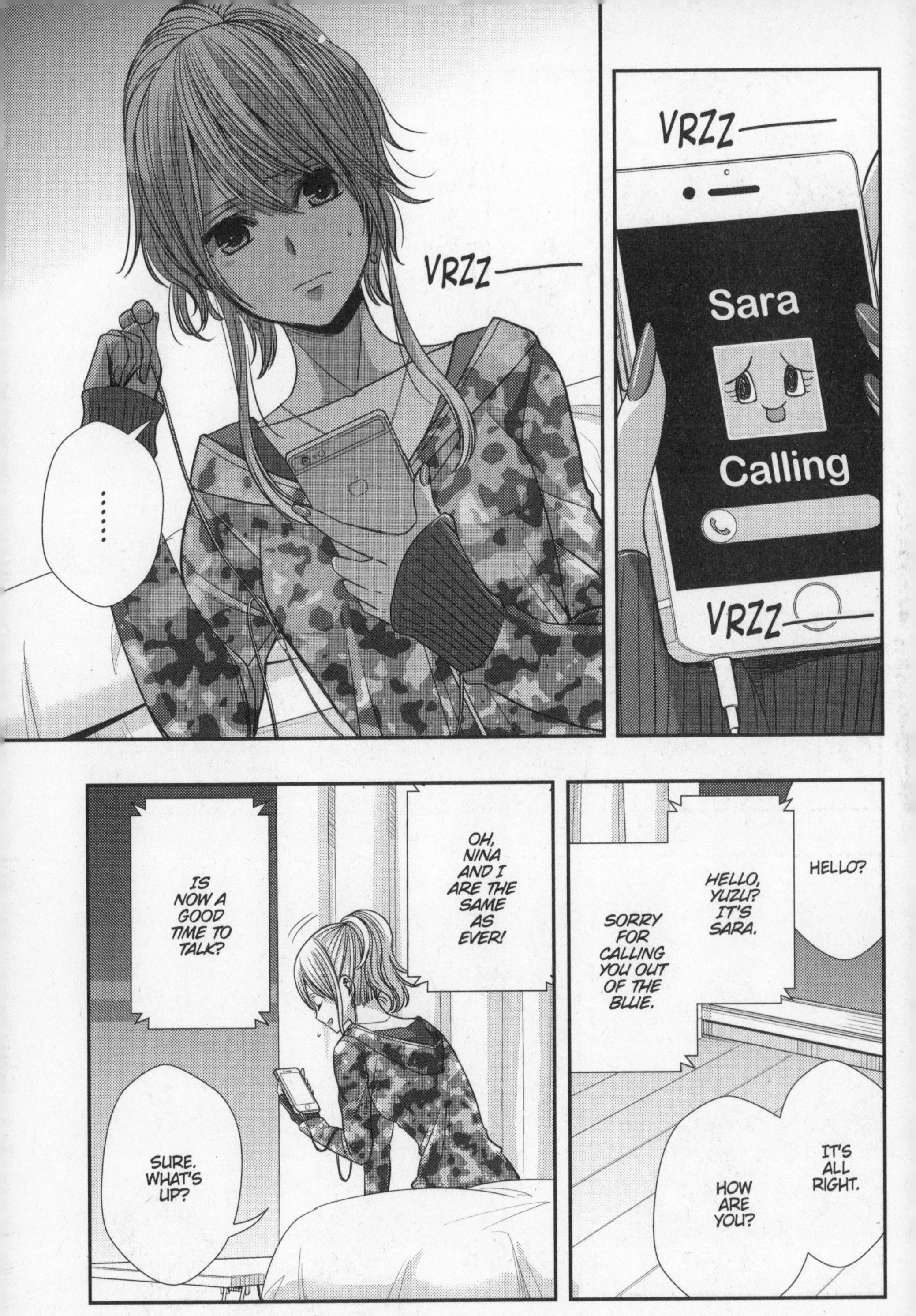
VRZZ
Sara
Calling
VRZZ
VRZZ
……
HELLO?
HELLO, YUZU? IT'S SARA.
SORRY FOR CALLING YOU OUT OF THE BLUE.
IT'S ALL RIGHT.
HOW ARE YOU?
OH, NINA AND I ARE THE SAME AS EVER!
IS NOW A GOOD TIME TO TALK?
SURE. WHAT'S UP?

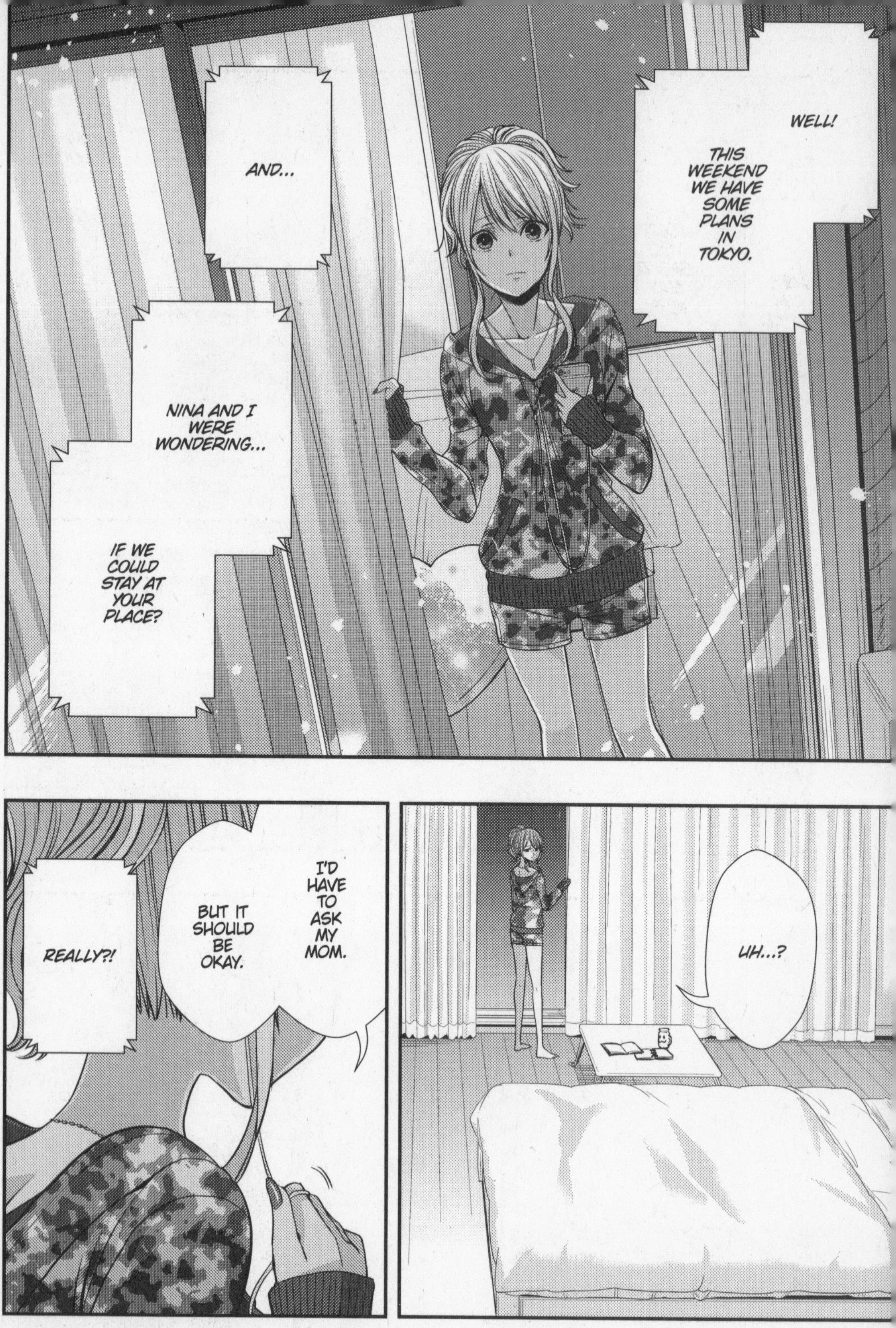
WELL!
THIS WEEKEND WE HAVE SOME PLANS IN TOKYO.
AND...
NINA AND I WERE WONDERING...
IF WE COULD STAY AT YOUR PLACE?
UH...?
I'D HAVE TO ASK MY MOM.
BUT IT SHOULD BE OKAY.
REALLY?!

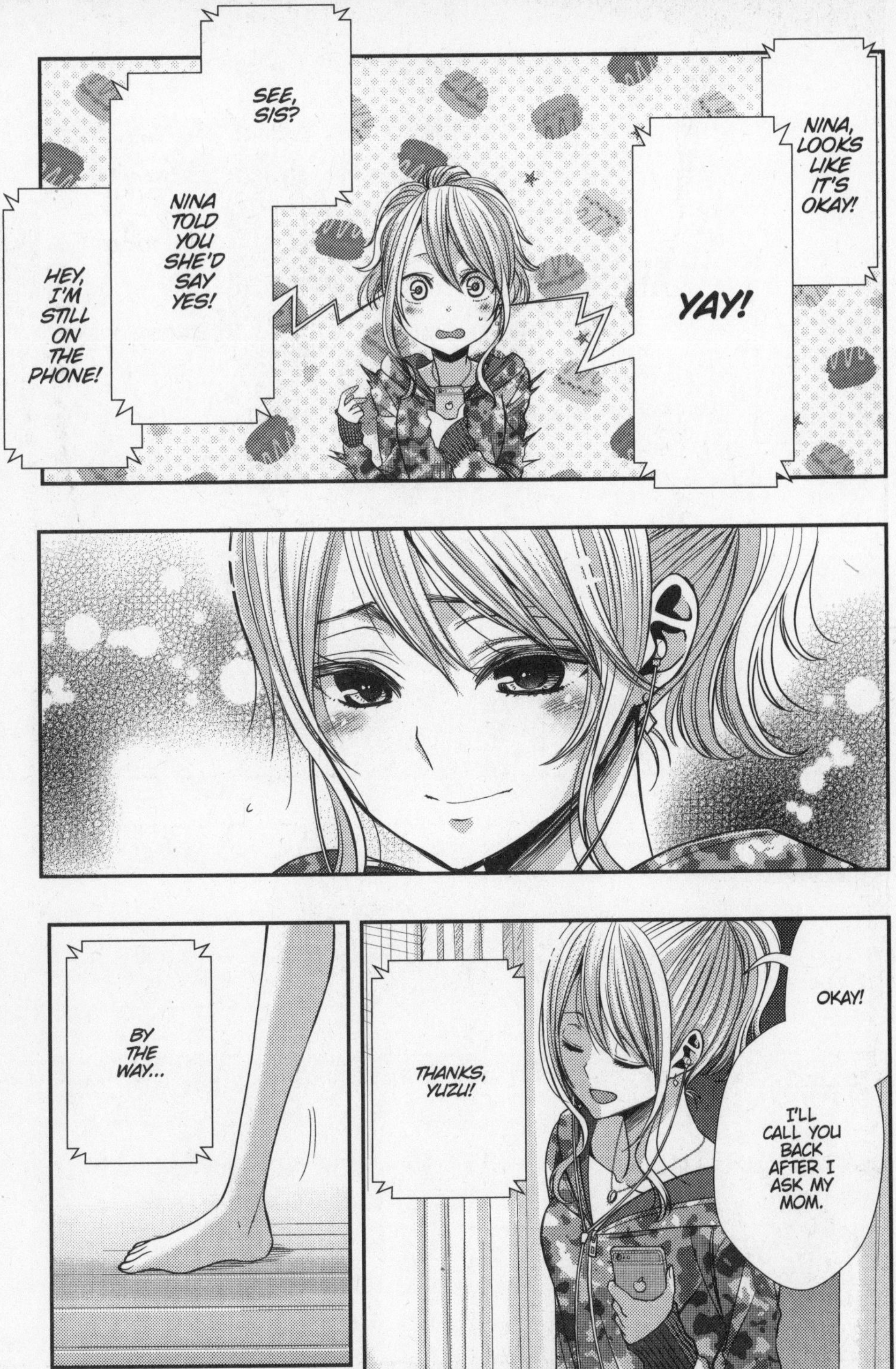
NINA, LOOKS LIKE IT'S OKAY!
YAY!
SEE, SIS?
NINA TOLD YOU SHE'D SAY YES!
HEY, I'M STILL ON THE PHONE!
OKAY!
I'LL CALL YOU BACK AFTER I ASK MY MOM.
THANKS, YUZU!
BY THE WAY...

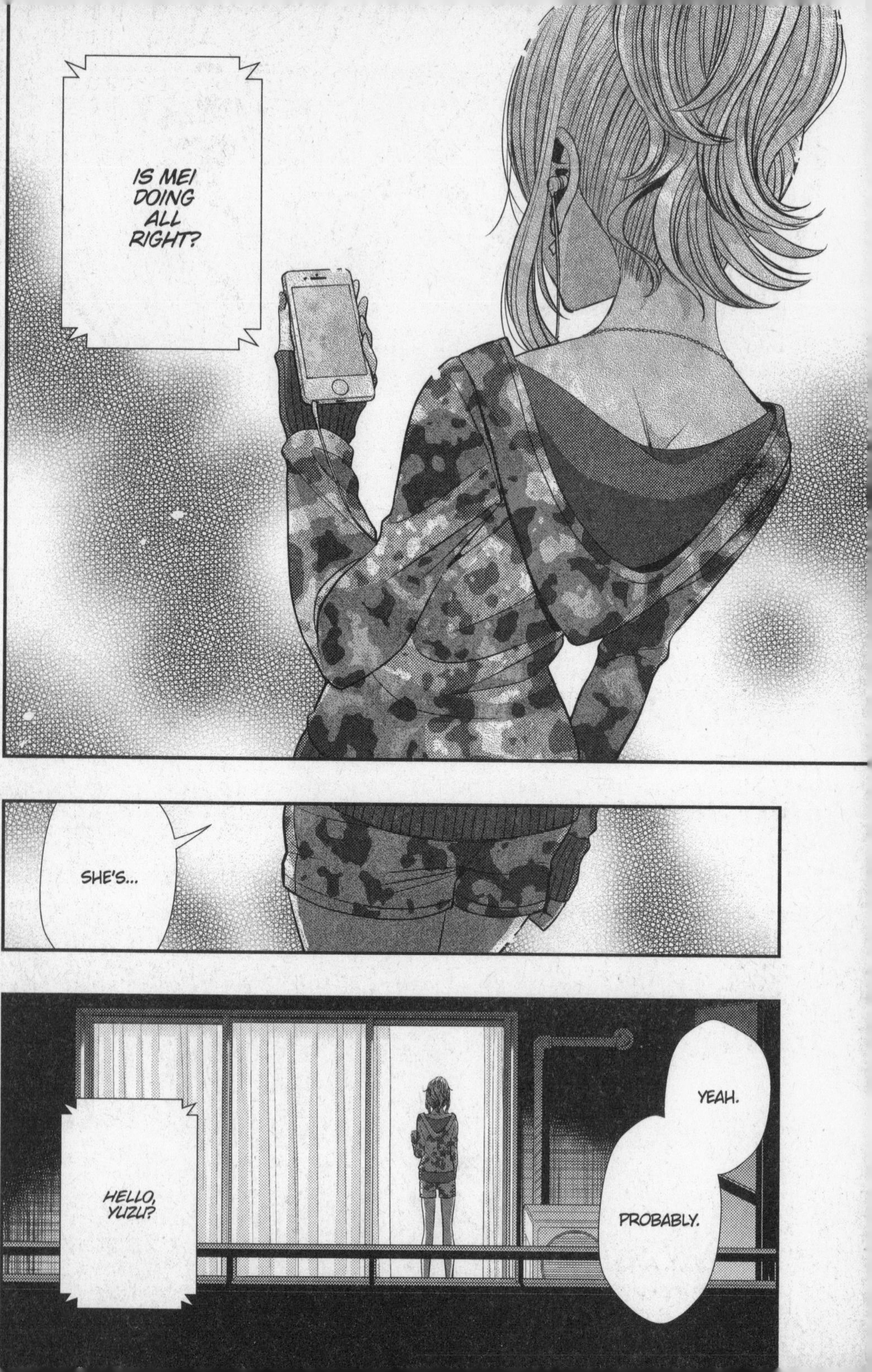
IS MEI DOING ALL RIGHT?
SHE'S...
YEAH.
PROBABLY.
HELLO, YUZU?

38. in love because

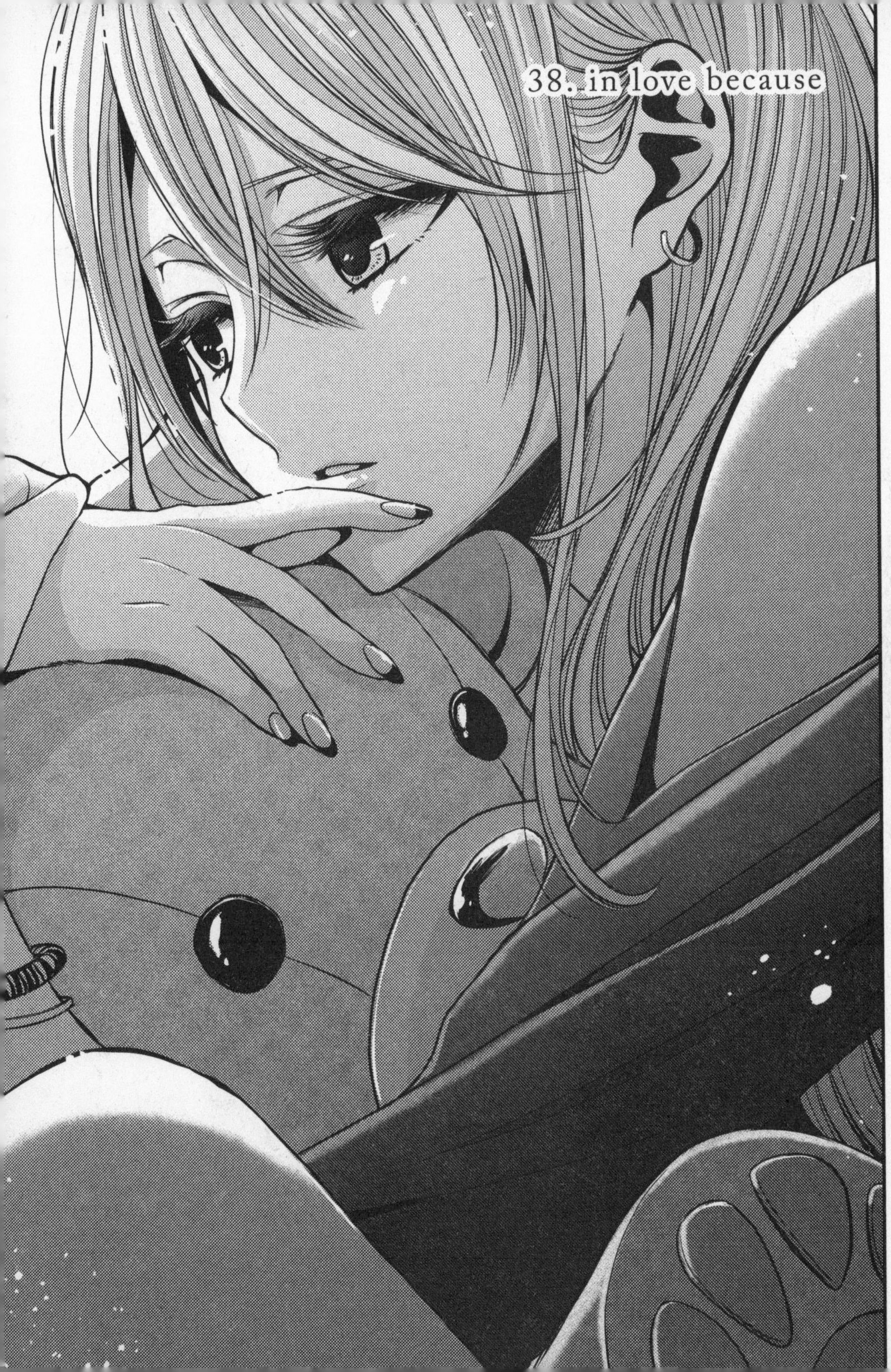

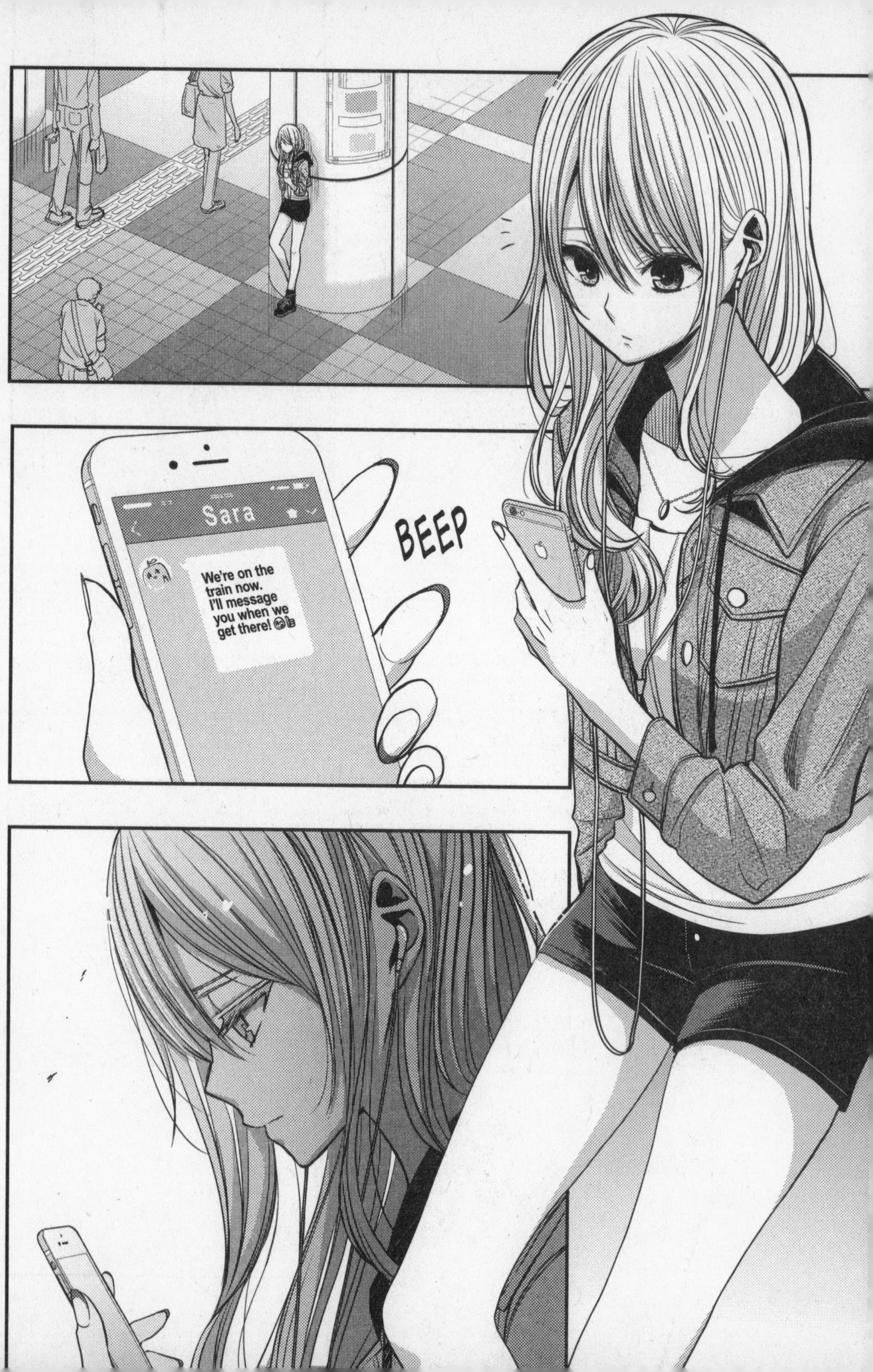
Sara
We're on the train now. I'll message you when we get there!
BEEP

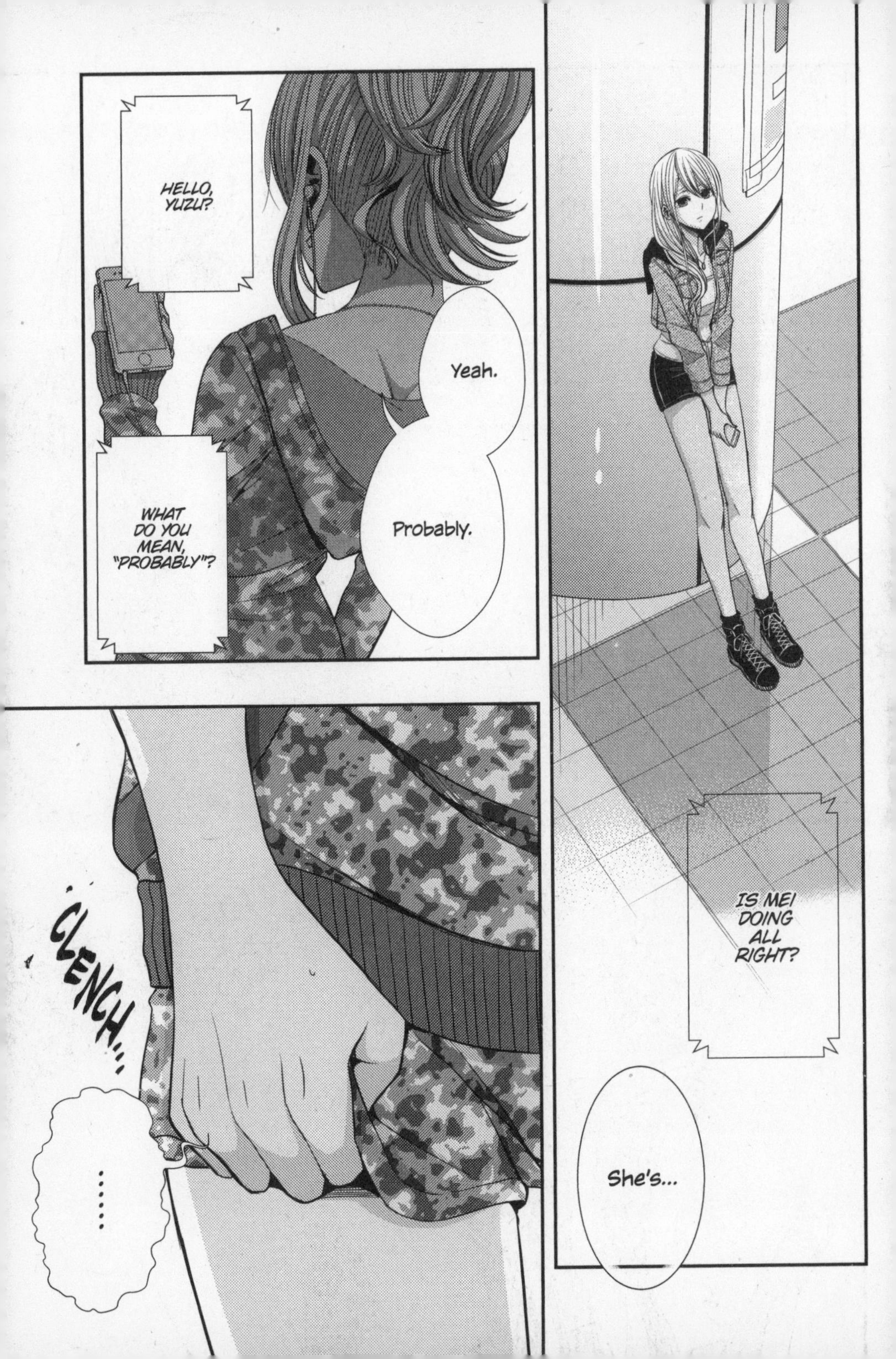
IS MEI DOING ALL RIGHT?
She's...
HELLO, YUZU?
Yeah.
Probably.
WHAT DO YOU MEAN, "PROBABLY"?
CLENCH...
......

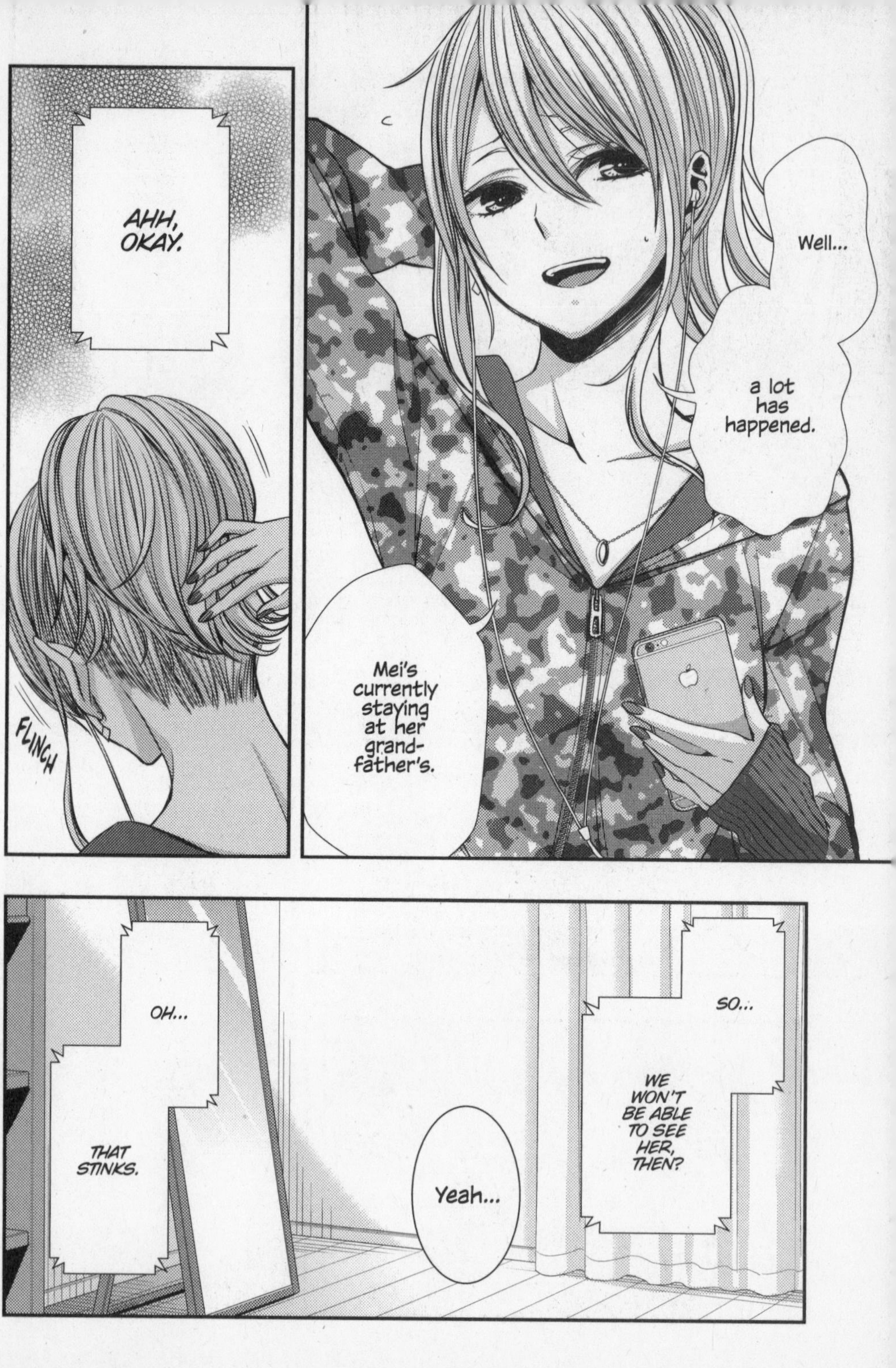
Well...
a lot has happened.
Mei's currently staying at her grand-father's.
AHH, OKAY.
FLINCH
SO...
WE WON'T BE ABLE TO SEE HER, THEN?
Yeah...
OH...
THAT STINKS.

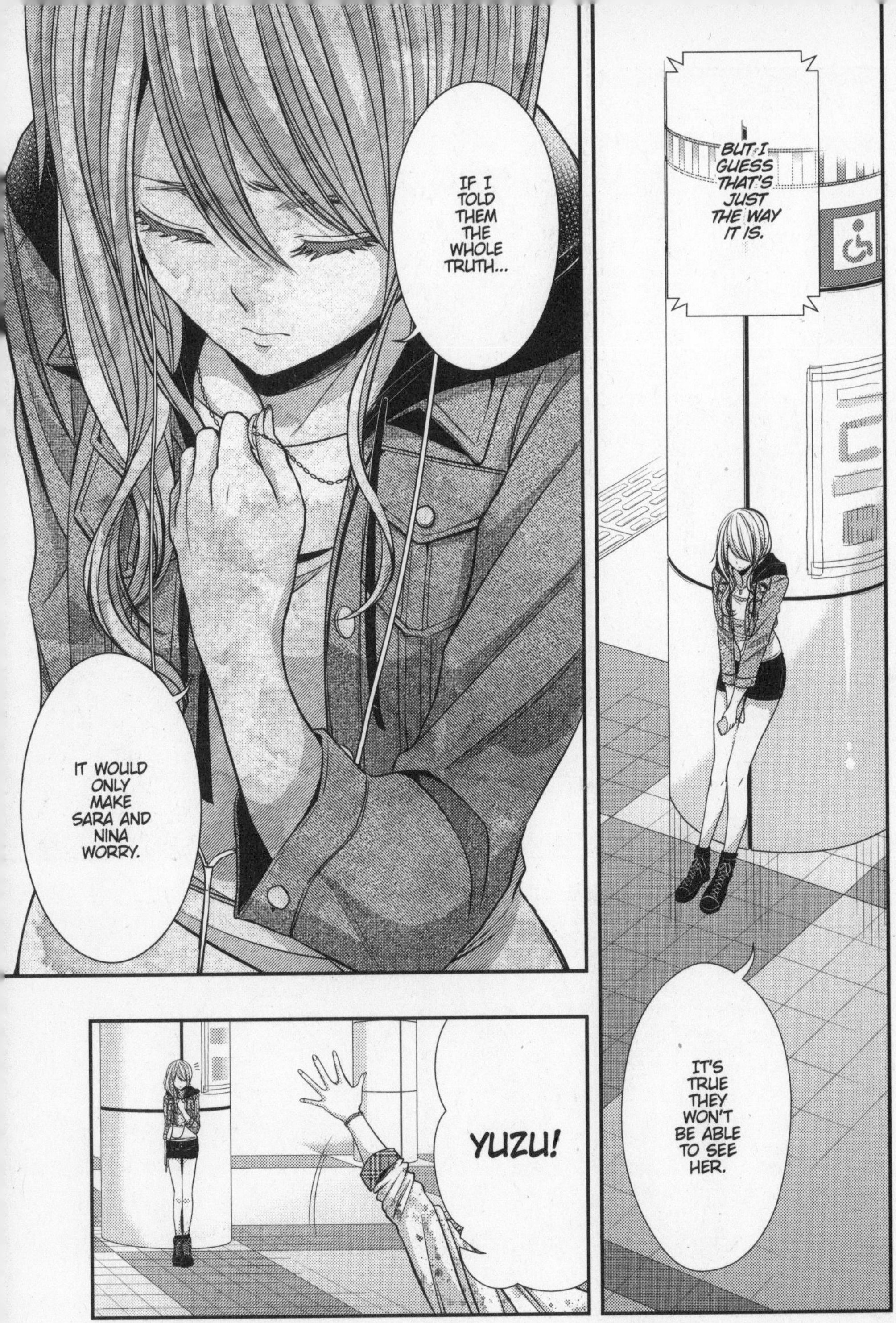
BUT I GUESS THAT'S JUST THE WAY IT IS.
IT'S TRUE THEY WON'T BE ABLE TO SEE HER.
IF I TOLD THEM THE WHOLE TRUTH...
IT WOULD ONLY MAKE SARA AND NINA WORRY.
YUZU!

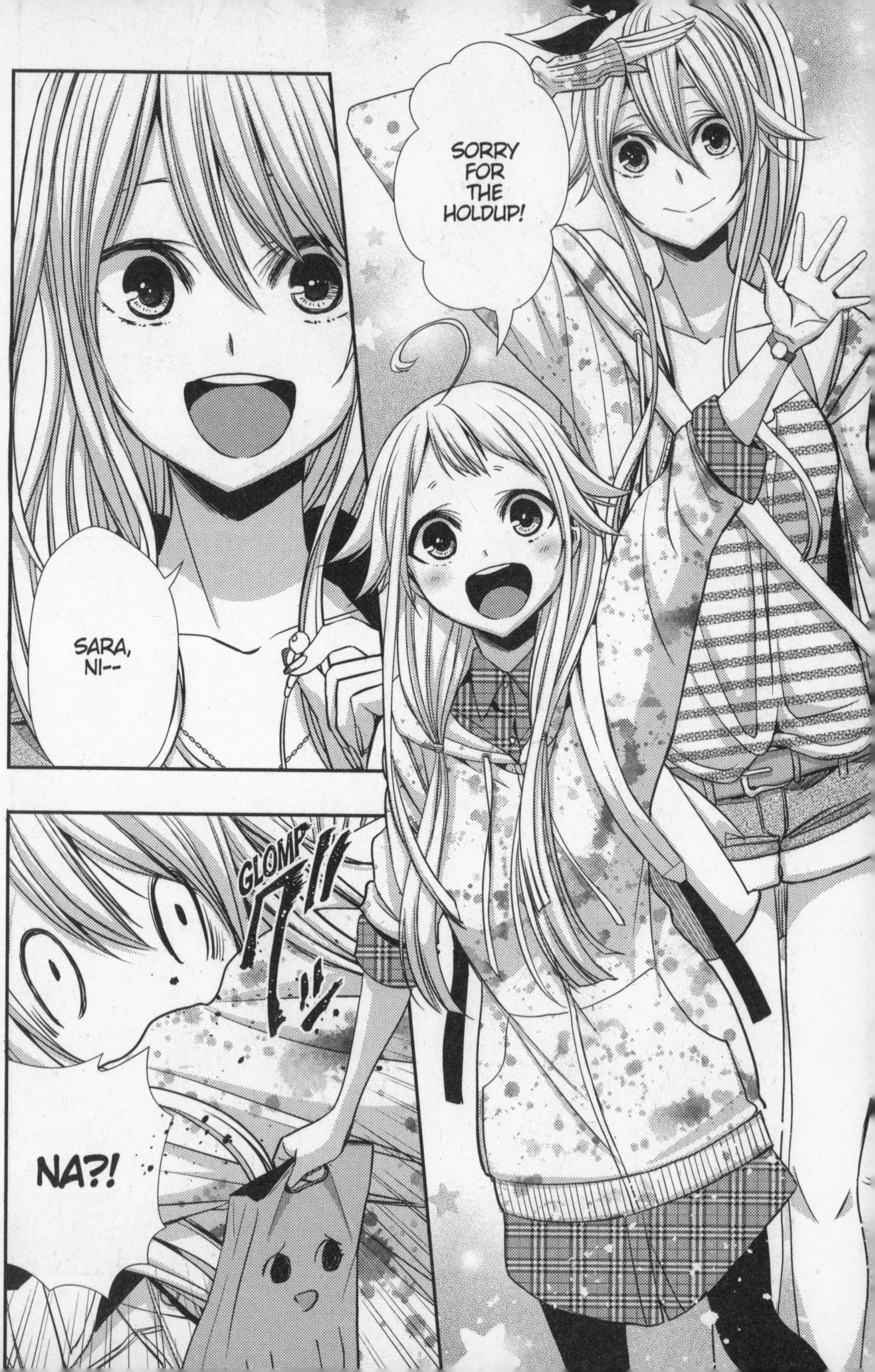
SORRY FOR THE HOLDUP!
SARA, NI--
GLOMP
NA?!

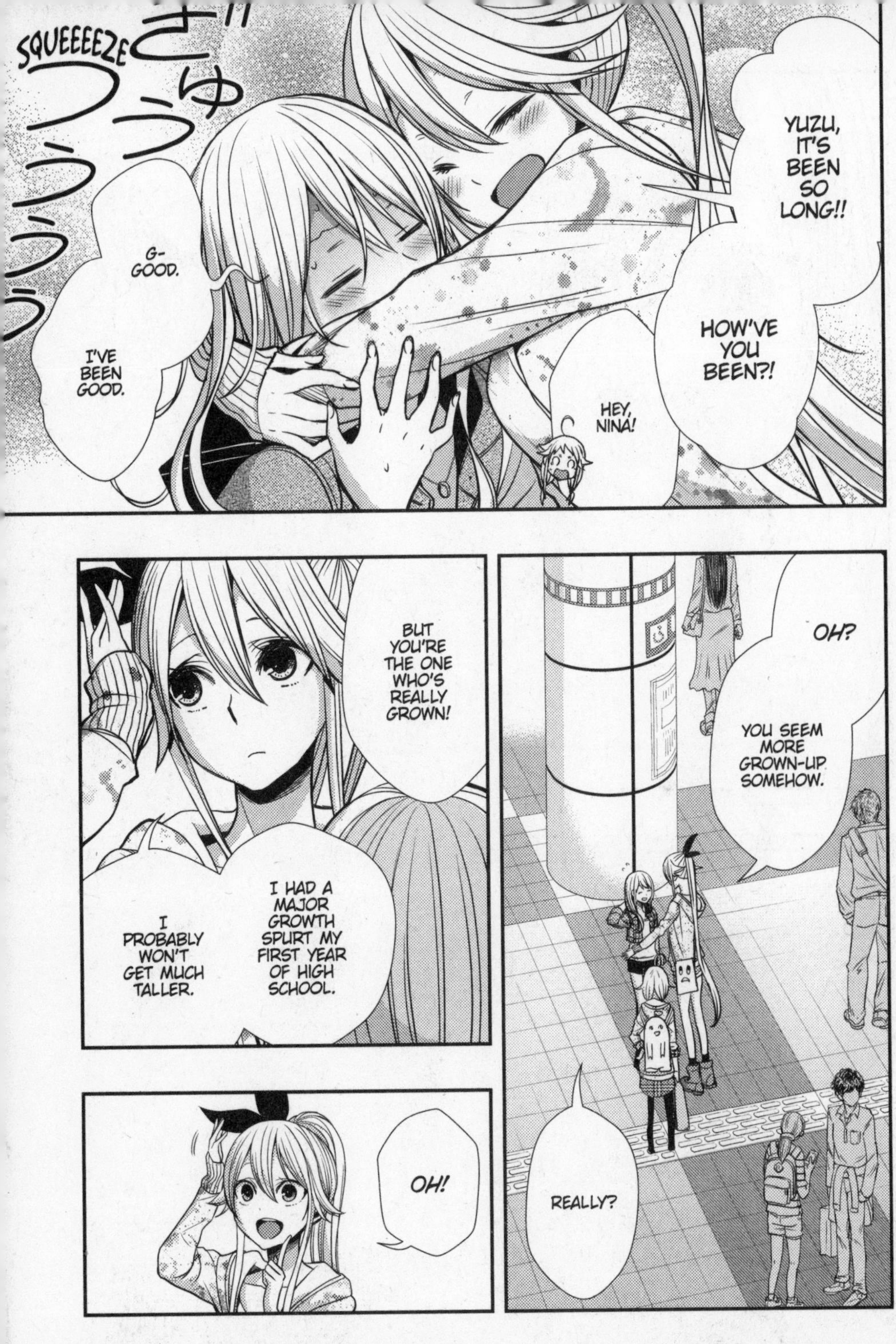
YUZU, IT'S BEEN SO LONG!!
HOW'VE YOU BEEN?!
HEY, NINA!
SQUEEEEZE
G- GOOD.
I'VE BEEN GOOD.
OH?
YOU SEEM MORE GROWN-UP SOMEHOW.
REALLY?
BUT YOU'RE THE ONE WHO'S REALLY GROWN!
I HAD A MAJOR GROWTH SPURT MY FIRST YEAR OF HIGH SCHOOL.
I PROBABLY WON'T GET MUCH TALLER.
OH!

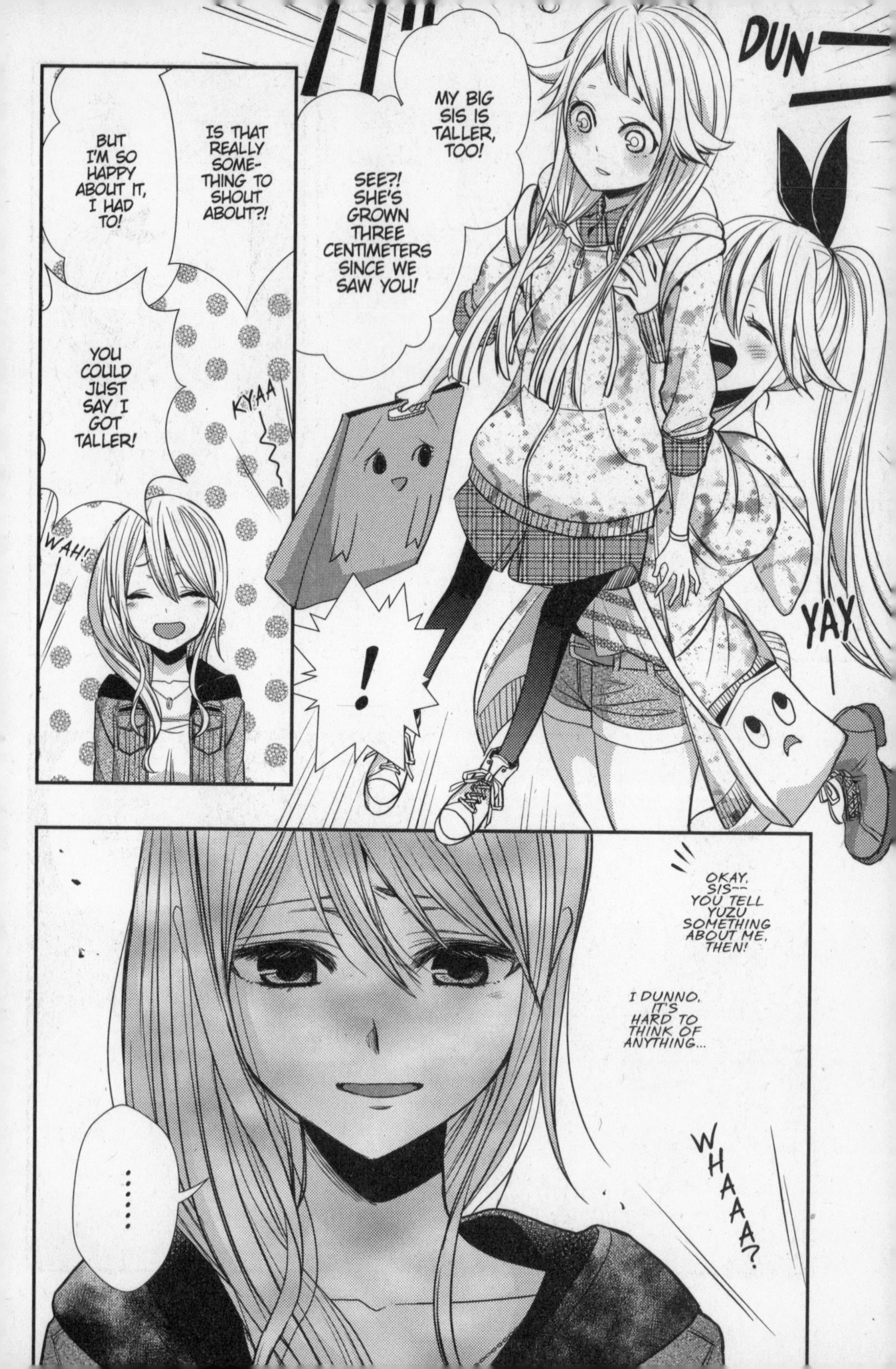
DUN
MY BIG SIS IS TALLER, TOO!
SEE?! SHE'S GROWN THREE CENTIMETERS SINCE WE SAW YOU!
YAY
!
IS THAT REALLY SOME-THING TO SHOUT ABOUT?!
BUT I'M SO HAPPY ABOUT IT, I HAD TO!
KYAA
YOU COULD JUST SAY I GOT TALLER!
WAH!
OKAY, SIS-- YOU TELL YUZU SOMETHING ABOUT ME, THEN!
I DUNNO, IT'S HARD TO THINK OF ANYTHING...
WHAAA?
......

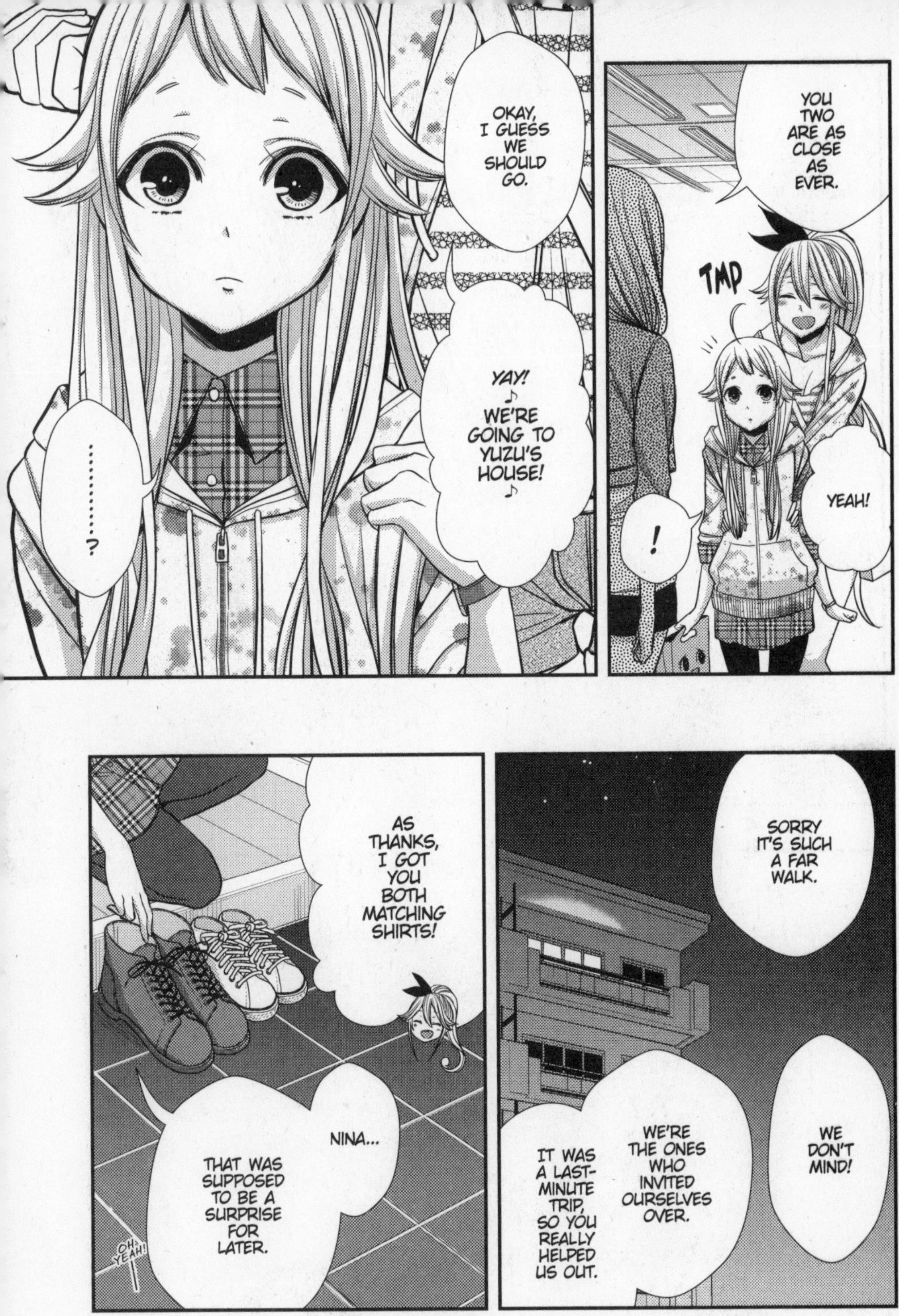
YOU TWO ARE AS CLOSE AS EVER.
TMP
YEAH!
!
OKAY, I GUESS WE SHOULD GO.
YAY! ♪ WE'RE GOING TO YUZU'S HOUSE! ♪
......?
SORRY IT'S SUCH A FAR WALK.
WE DON'T MIND!
WE'RE THE ONES WHO INVITED OURSELVES OVER.
IT WAS A LAST-MINUTE TRIP, SO YOU REALLY HELPED US OUT.
AS THANKS, I GOT YOU BOTH MATCHING SHIRTS!
NINA...
THAT WAS SUPPOSED TO BE A SURPRISE FOR LATER.
OH, YEAH!

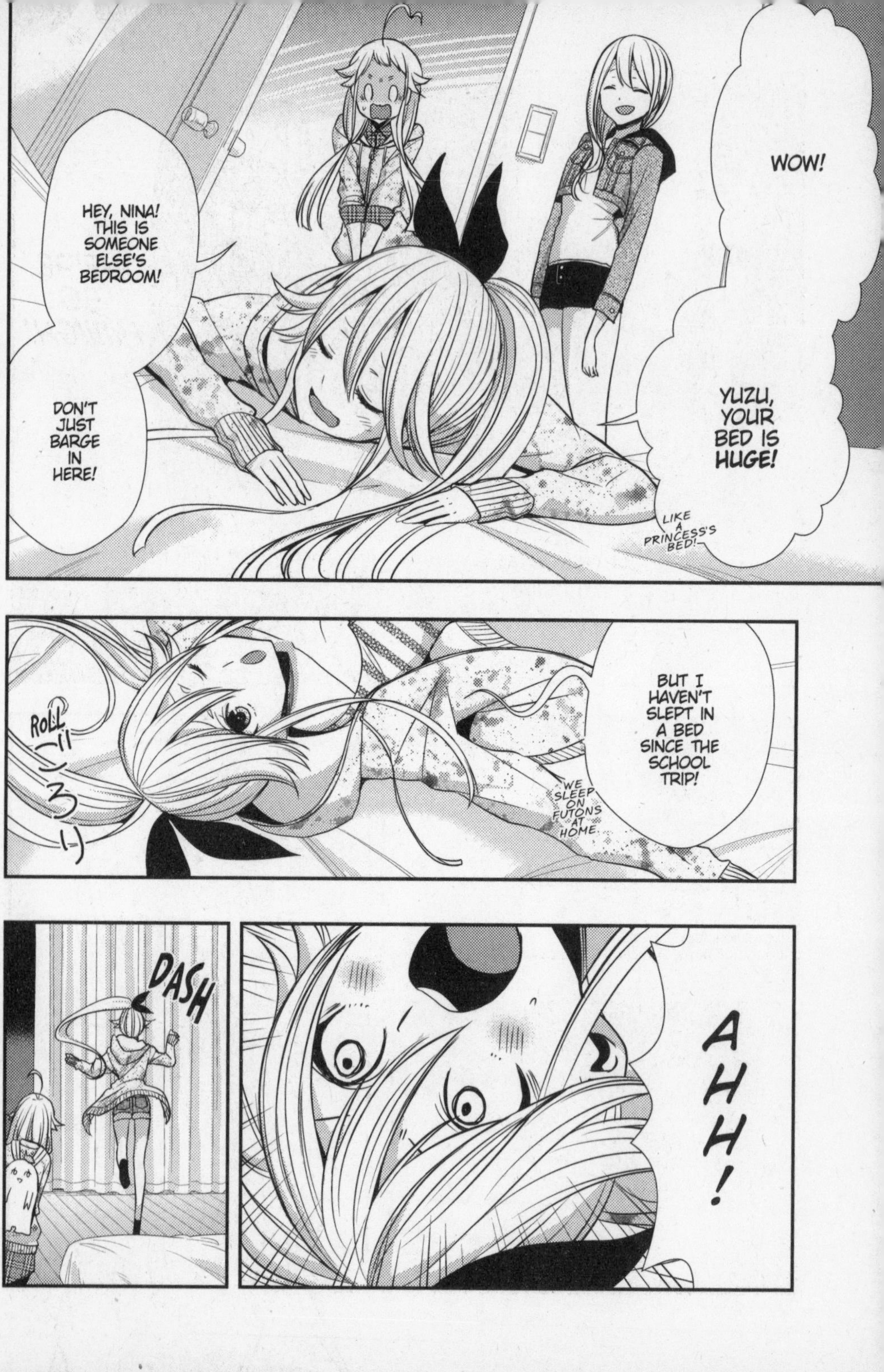

WOW! YUZU, YOUR BED IS HUGE!
LIKE A PRINCESS'S BED!
HEY, NINA! THIS IS SOMEONE ELSE'S BEDROOM!
DON'T JUST BARGE IN HERE!
BUT I HAVEN'T SLEPT IN A BED SINCE THE SCHOOL TRIP!
WE SLEEP ON FUTONS AT HOME.
ROLL
AHH!
DASH

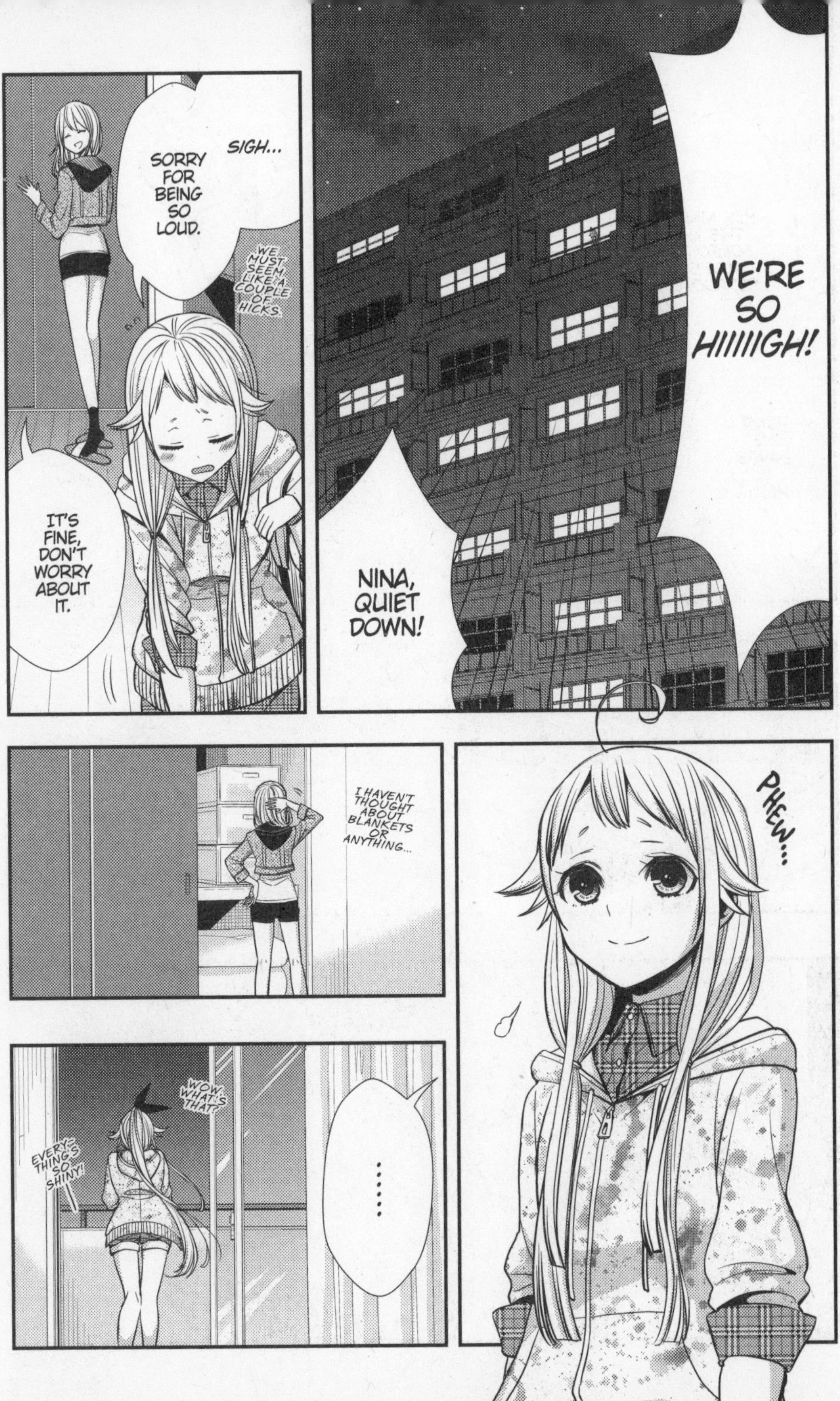
WE'RE SO HIIIIIGH!
NINA, QUIET DOWN!
SIGH...
SORRY FOR BEING SO LOUD.
WE MUST SEEM LIKE A COUPLE OF HICKS.
IT'S FINE, DON'T WORRY ABOUT IT.
PHEW...
I HAVEN'T THOUGHT ABOUT BLANKETS OR ANYTHING...
......
WOW, WHAT'S THAT?
EVERY-THING'S SO SHINY!

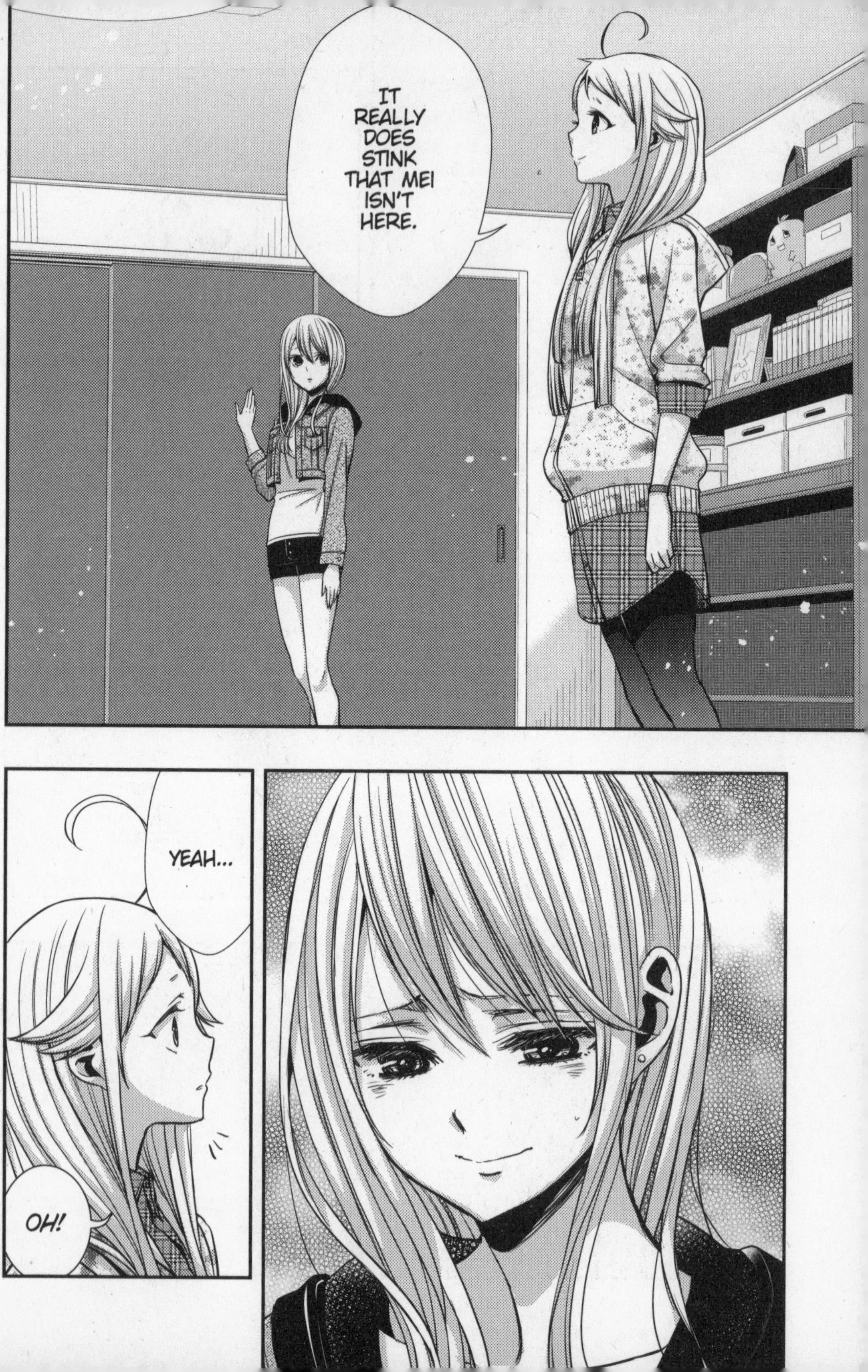
IT REALLY DOES STINK THAT MEI ISN'T HERE.
YEAH...
OH!

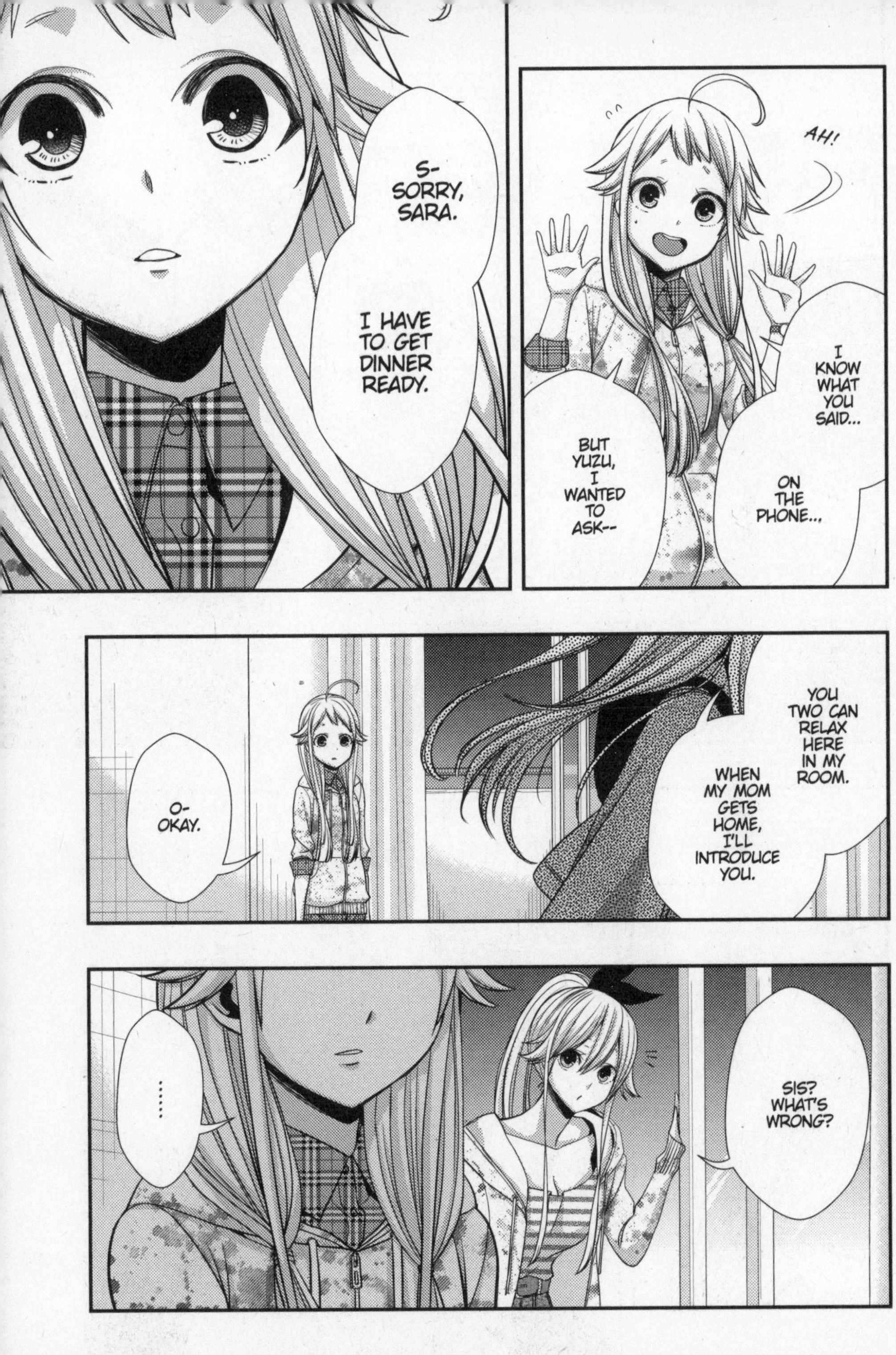
AH!
I KNOW WHAT YOU SAID...
ON THE PHONE...
BUT YUZU, I WANTED TO ASK--
S-SORRY, SARA.
I HAVE TO GET DINNER READY.
YOU TWO CAN RELAX HERE IN MY ROOM.
WHEN MY MOM GETS HOME, I'LL INTRODUCE YOU.
O-OKAY.
SIS? WHAT'S WRONG?
......

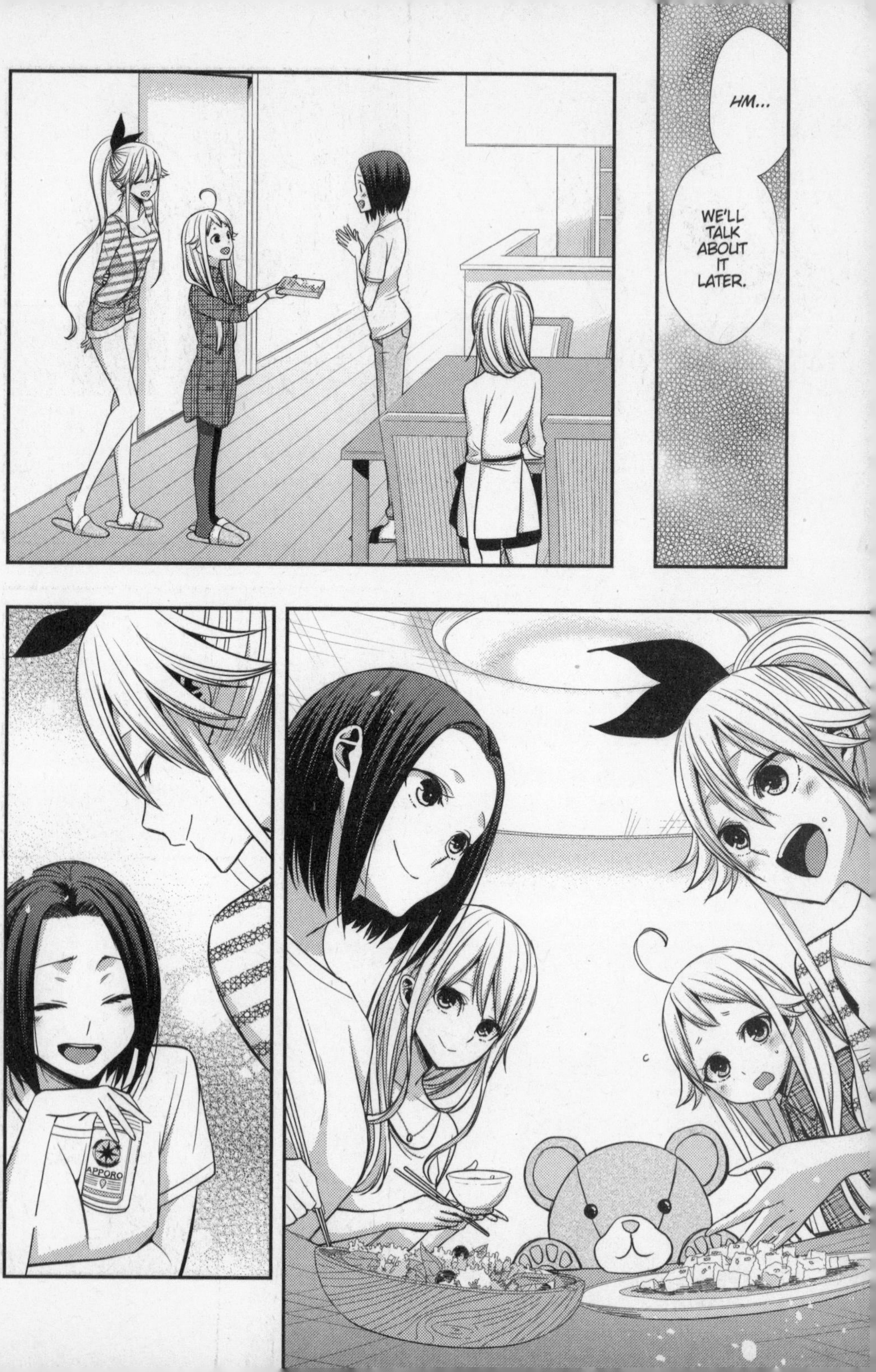
HM...
WE'LL TALK ABOUT IT LATER.

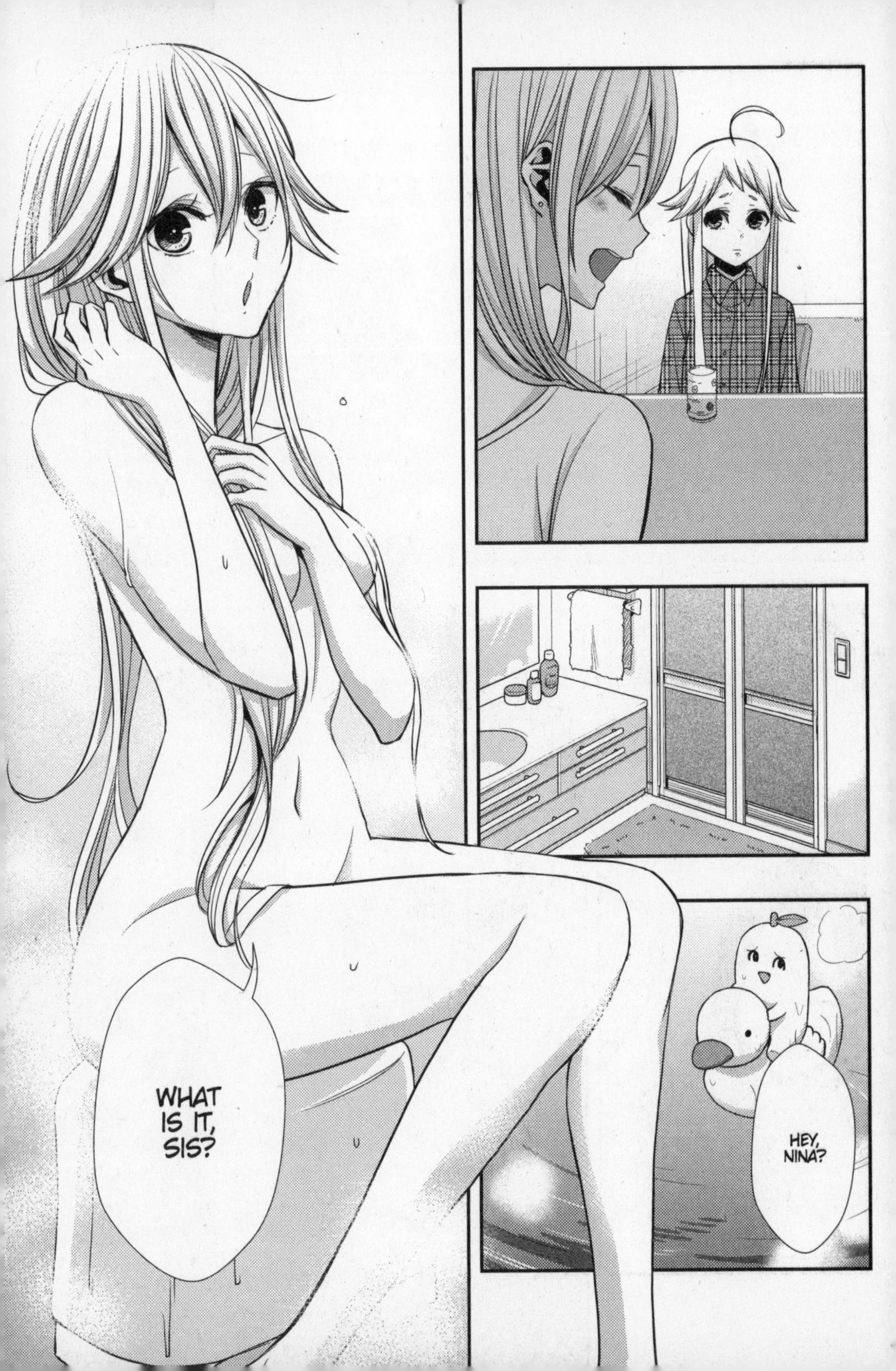
HEY, NINA?
WHAT IS IT, SIS?

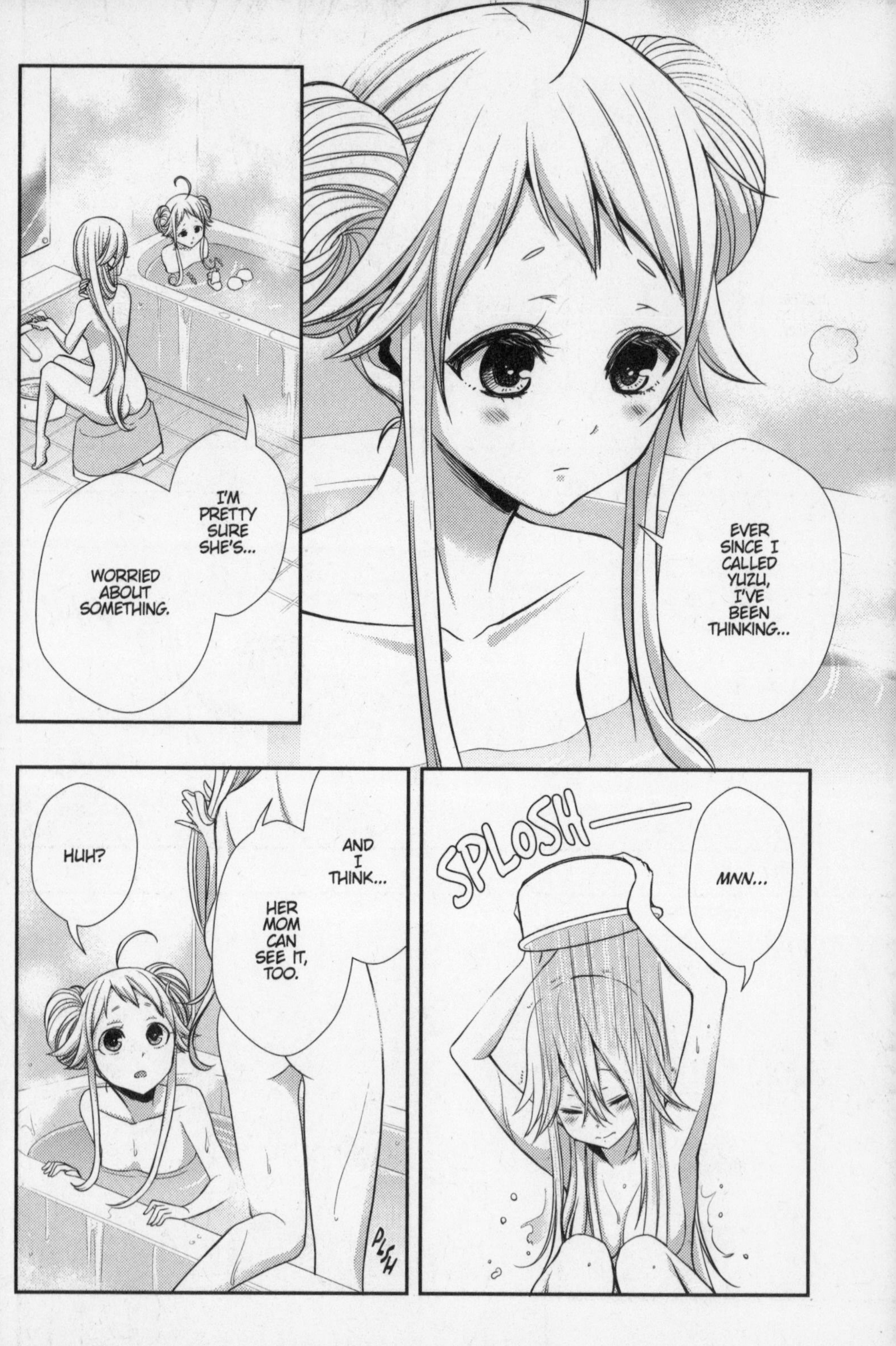
EVER SINCE I CALLED YUZU, I'VE BEEN THINKING...
I'M PRETTY SURE SHE'S...
WORRIED ABOUT SOMETHING.
SPLOSH—
MNN...
AND I THINK...
HER MOM CAN SEE IT, TOO.
HUH?
PLSH

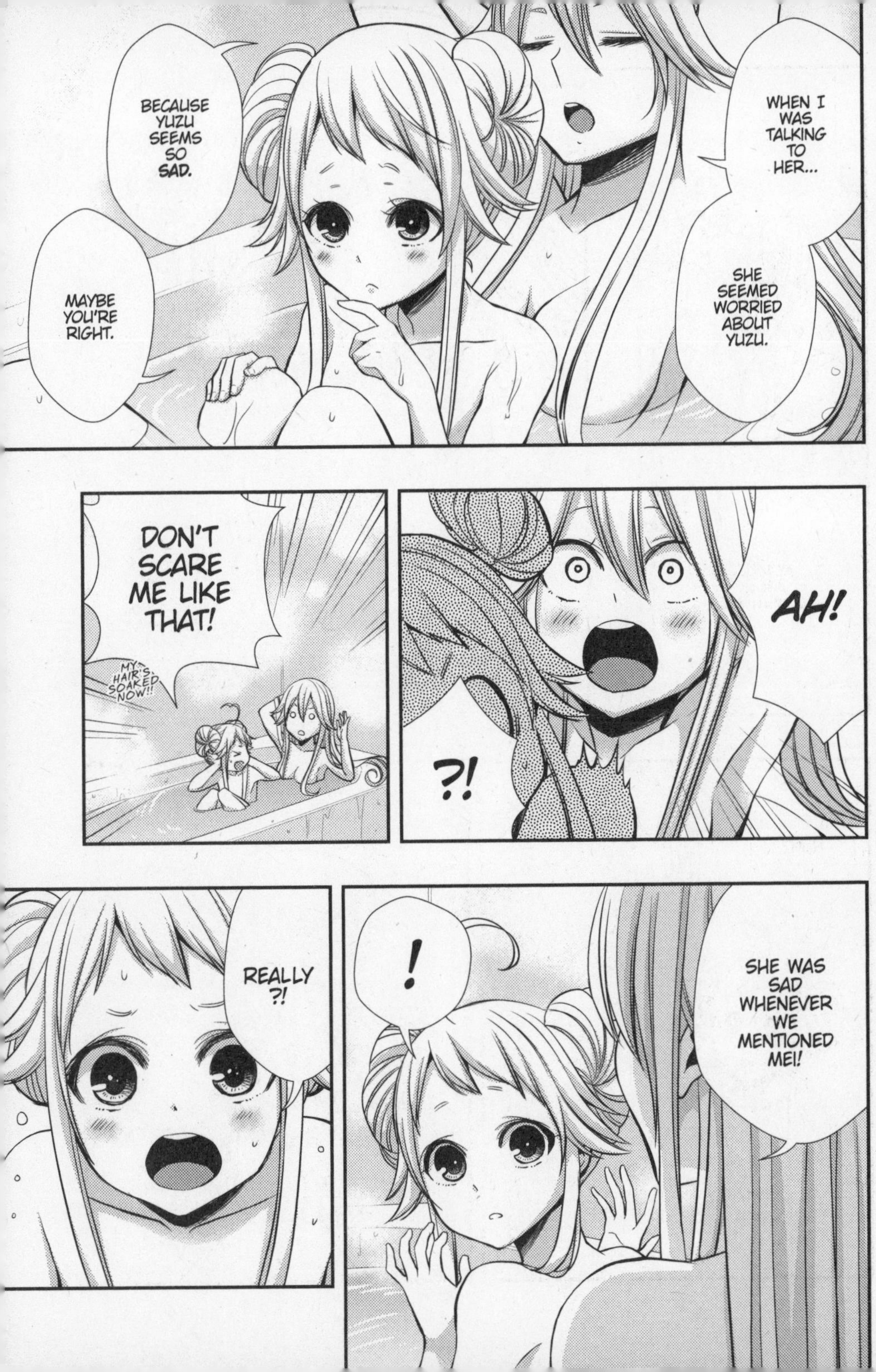

WHEN I WAS TALKING TO HER...
SHE SEEMED WORRIED ABOUT YUZU.
BECAUSE YUZU SEEMS SO SAD.
MAYBE YOU'RE RIGHT.
AH!
?!
DON'T SCARE ME LIKE THAT!
MY HAIR'S SOAKED NOW!!
SHE WAS SAD WHENEVER WE MENTIONED MEI!
!
REALLY ?!

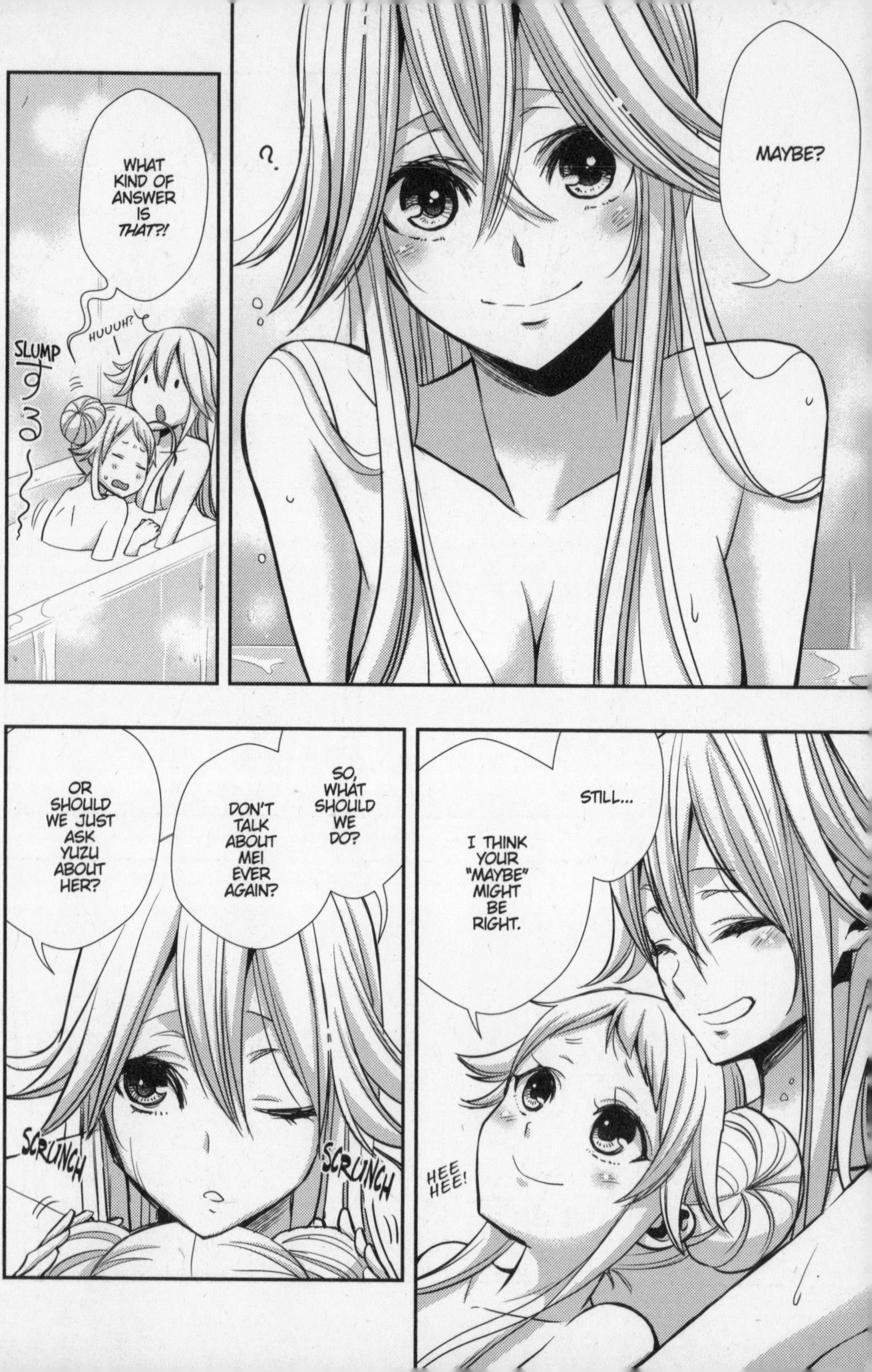
?
MAYBE?
WHAT KIND OF ANSWER IS *THAT?!*
HUUUH?
SLUMP
すぅ〜
STILL...
I THINK YOUR "MAYBE" MIGHT BE RIGHT.
HEE HEE!
SO, WHAT SHOULD WE DO?
DON'T TALK ABOUT MEI EVER AGAIN?
OR SHOULD WE JUST ASK YUZU ABOUT HER?
SCRUNCH
SCRUNCH

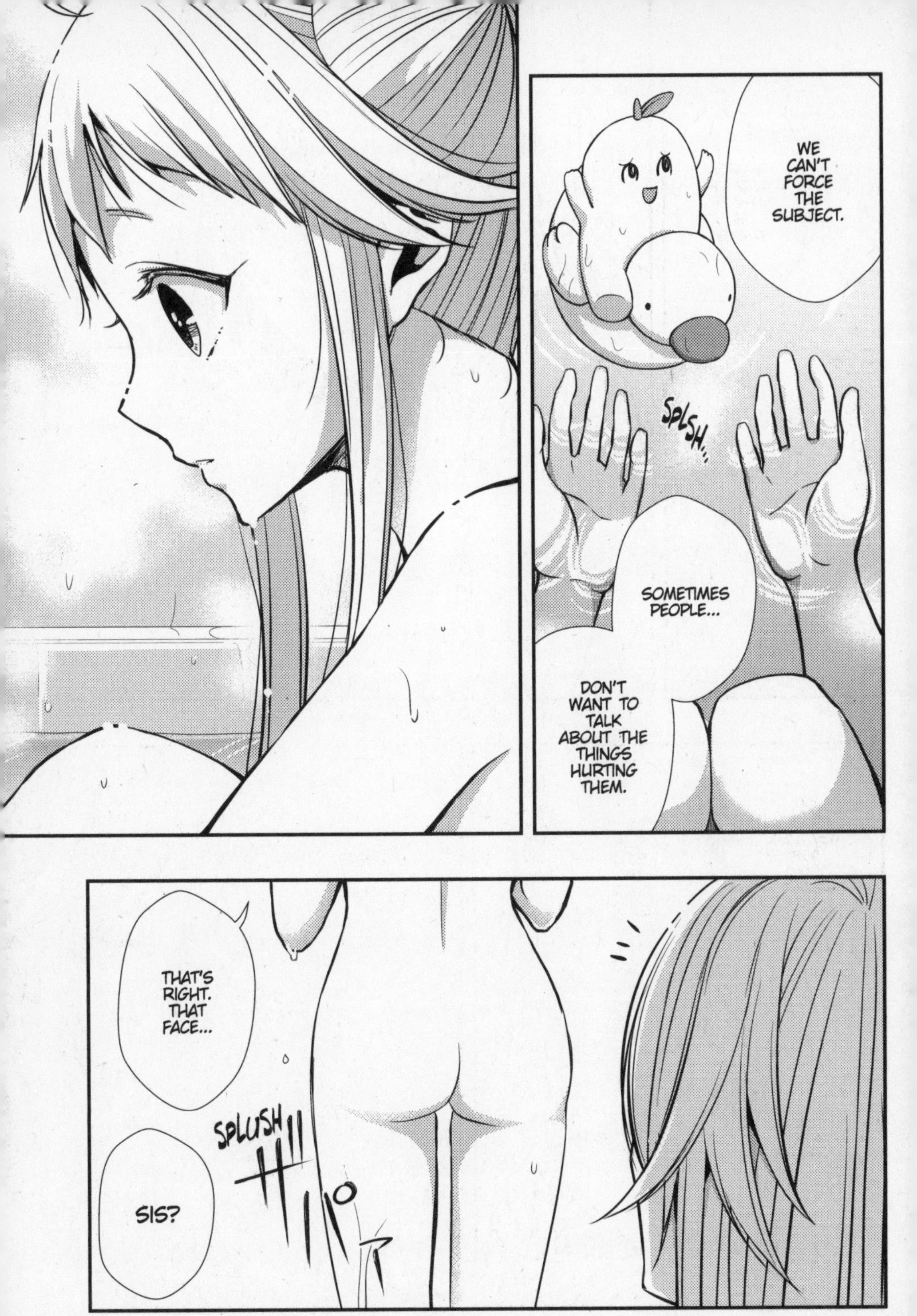
WE CAN'T FORCE THE SUBJECT.
SPLSH...
SOMETIMES PEOPLE...
DON'T WANT TO TALK ABOUT THE THINGS HURTING THEM.
THAT'S RIGHT. THAT FACE...
SPLUSH
SIS?

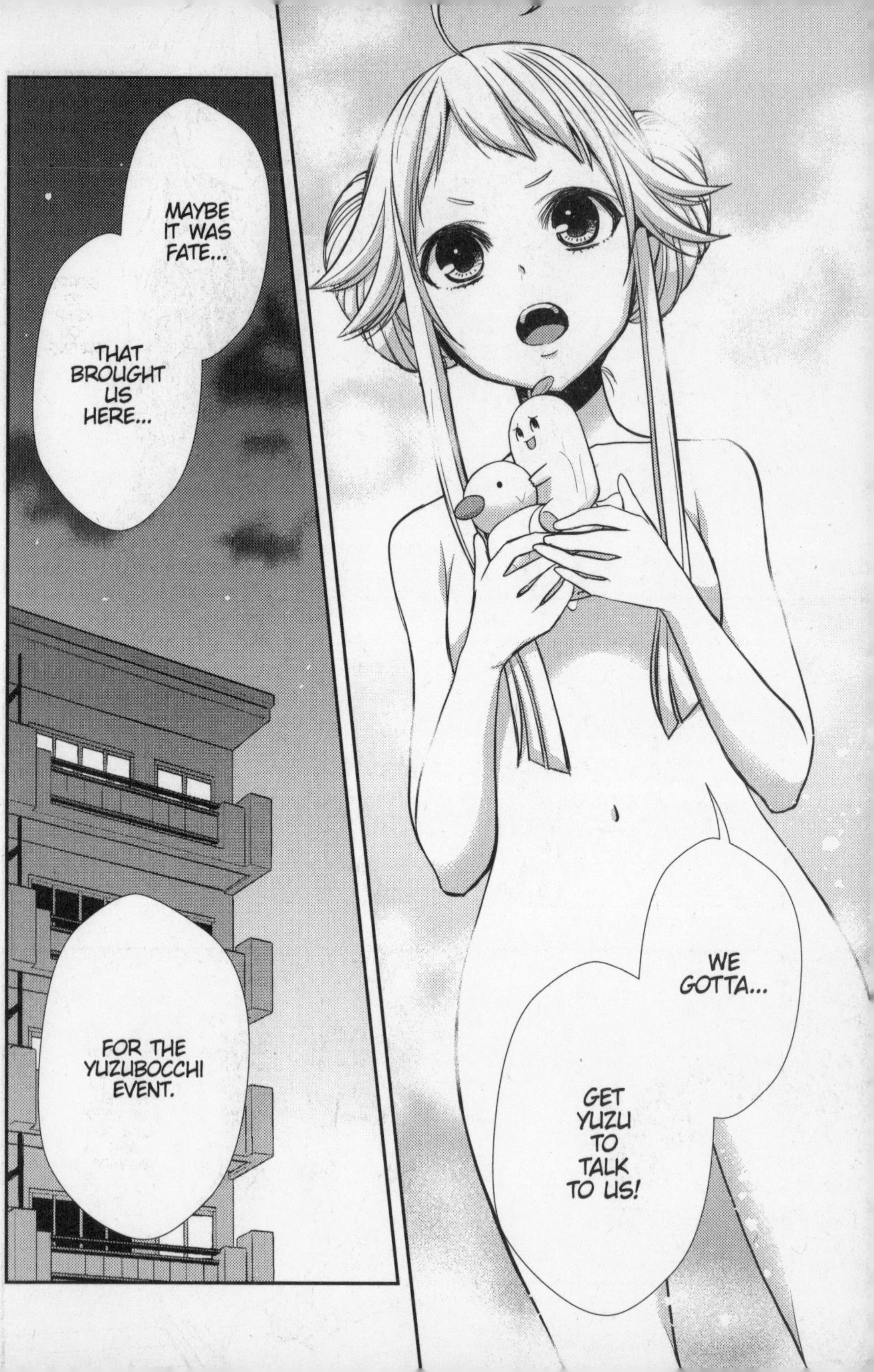
WE GOTTA...
GET YUZU TO TALK TO US!
MAYBE IT WAS FATE...
THAT BROUGHT US HERE...
FOR THE YUZUBOCCHI EVENT.

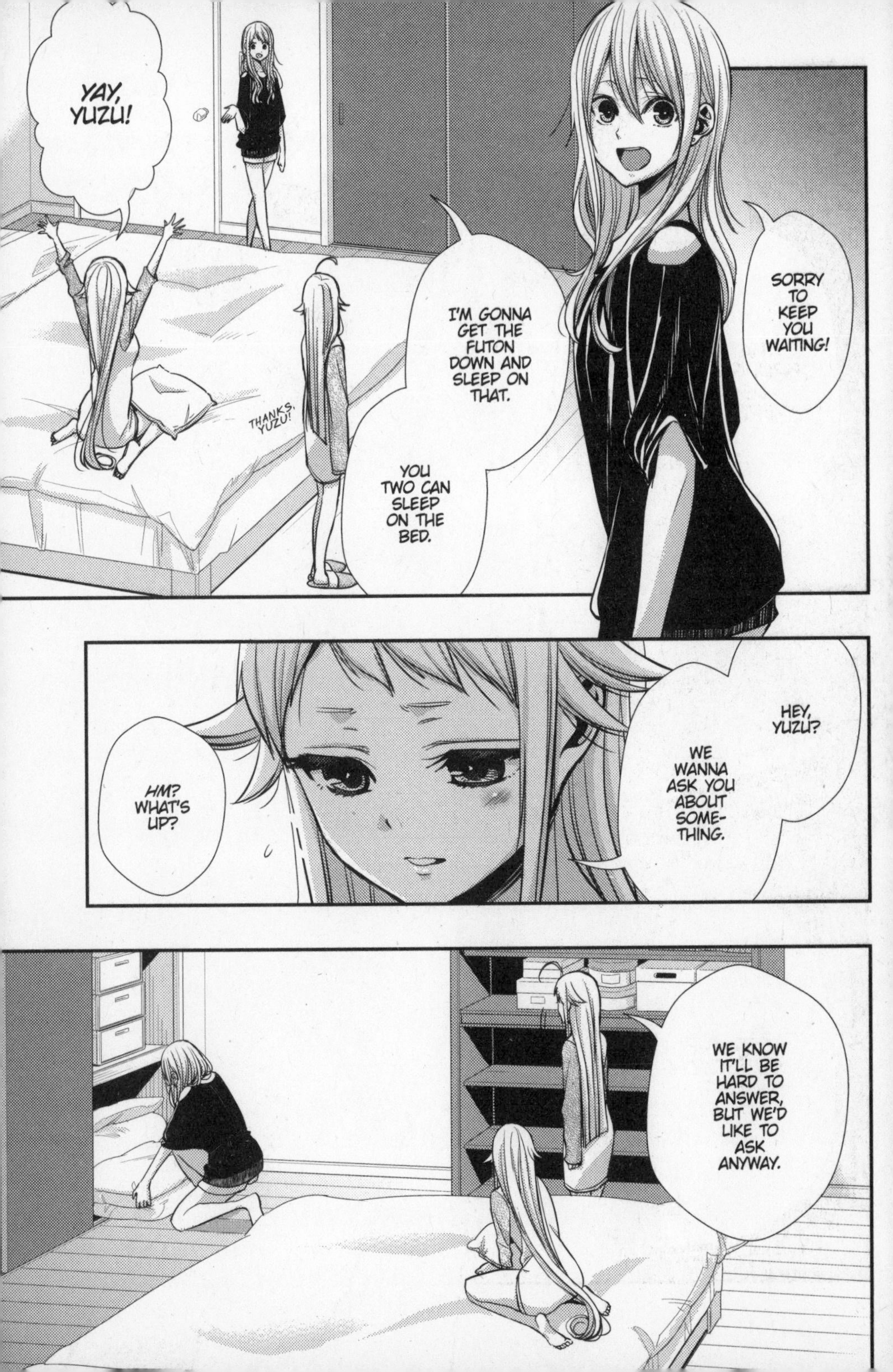
SORRY TO KEEP YOU WAITING!
I'M GONNA GET THE FUTON DOWN AND SLEEP ON THAT.
YOU TWO CAN SLEEP ON THE BED.
THANKS, YUZU!
YAY, YUZU!
HEY, YUZU?
WE WANNA ASK YOU ABOUT SOME-THING.
HM? WHAT'S UP?
WE KNOW IT'LL BE HARD TO ANSWER, BUT WE'D LIKE TO ASK ANYWAY.

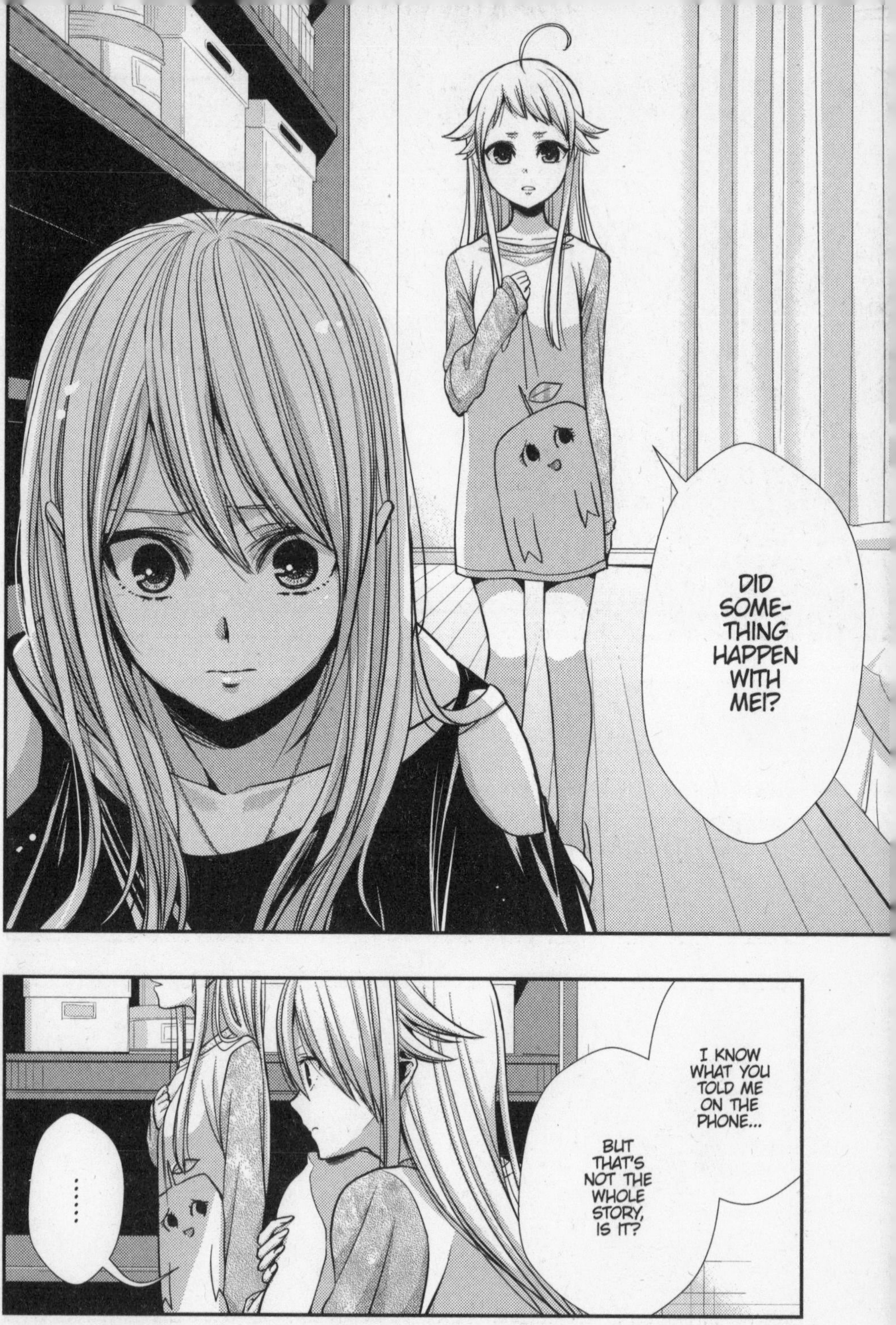
DID SOME-THING HAPPEN WITH MEI?
I KNOW WHAT YOU TOLD ME ON THE PHONE...
BUT THAT'S NOT THE WHOLE STORY, IS IT?
......

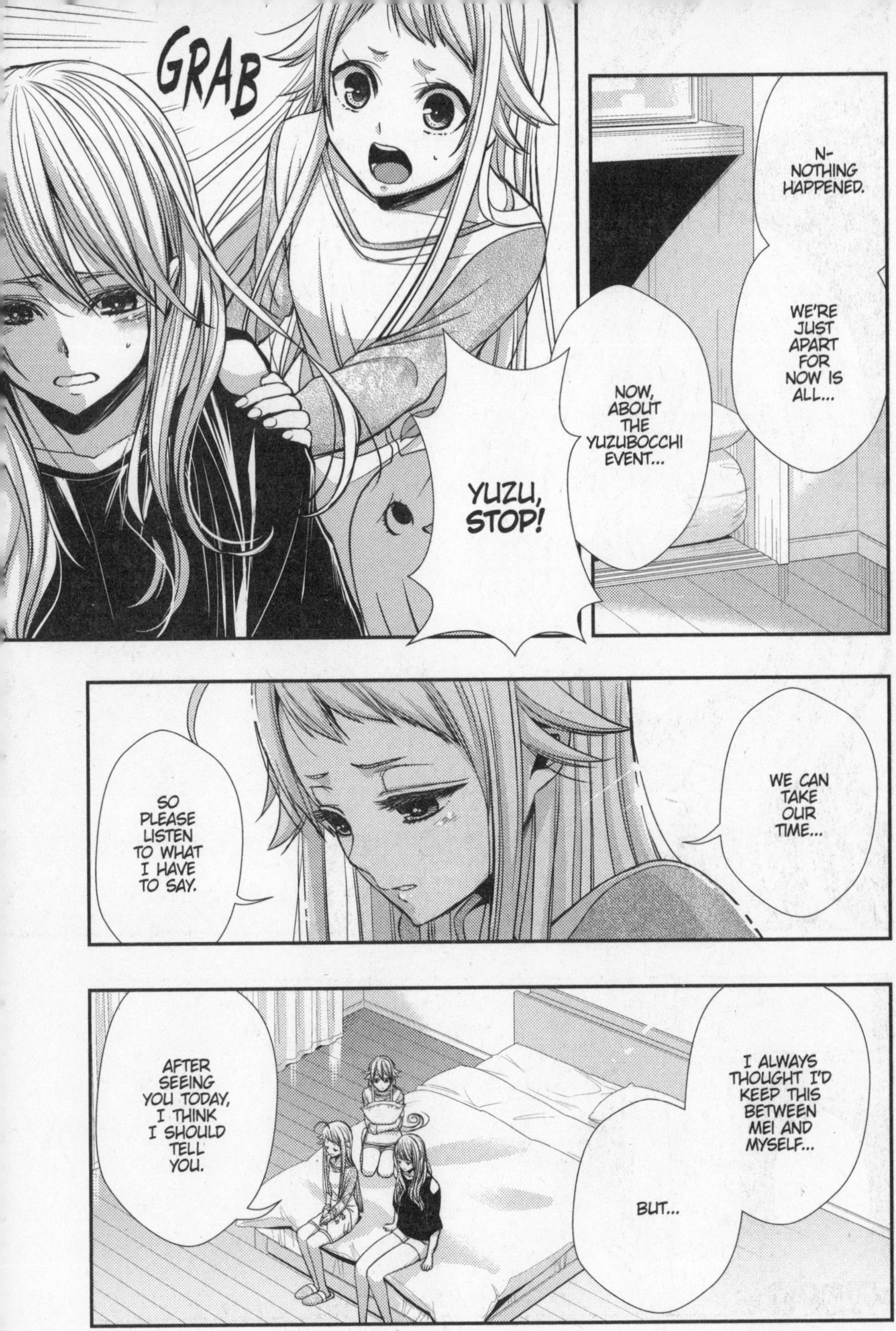
N-NOTHING HAPPENED.
WE'RE JUST APART FOR NOW IS ALL...
NOW, ABOUT THE YUZUBOCCHI EVENT...
GRAB
YUZU, STOP!
WE CAN TAKE OUR TIME...
SO PLEASE LISTEN TO WHAT I HAVE TO SAY.
I ALWAYS THOUGHT I'D KEEP THIS BETWEEN MEI AND MYSELF...
BUT...
AFTER SEEING YOU TODAY, I THINK I SHOULD TELL YOU.

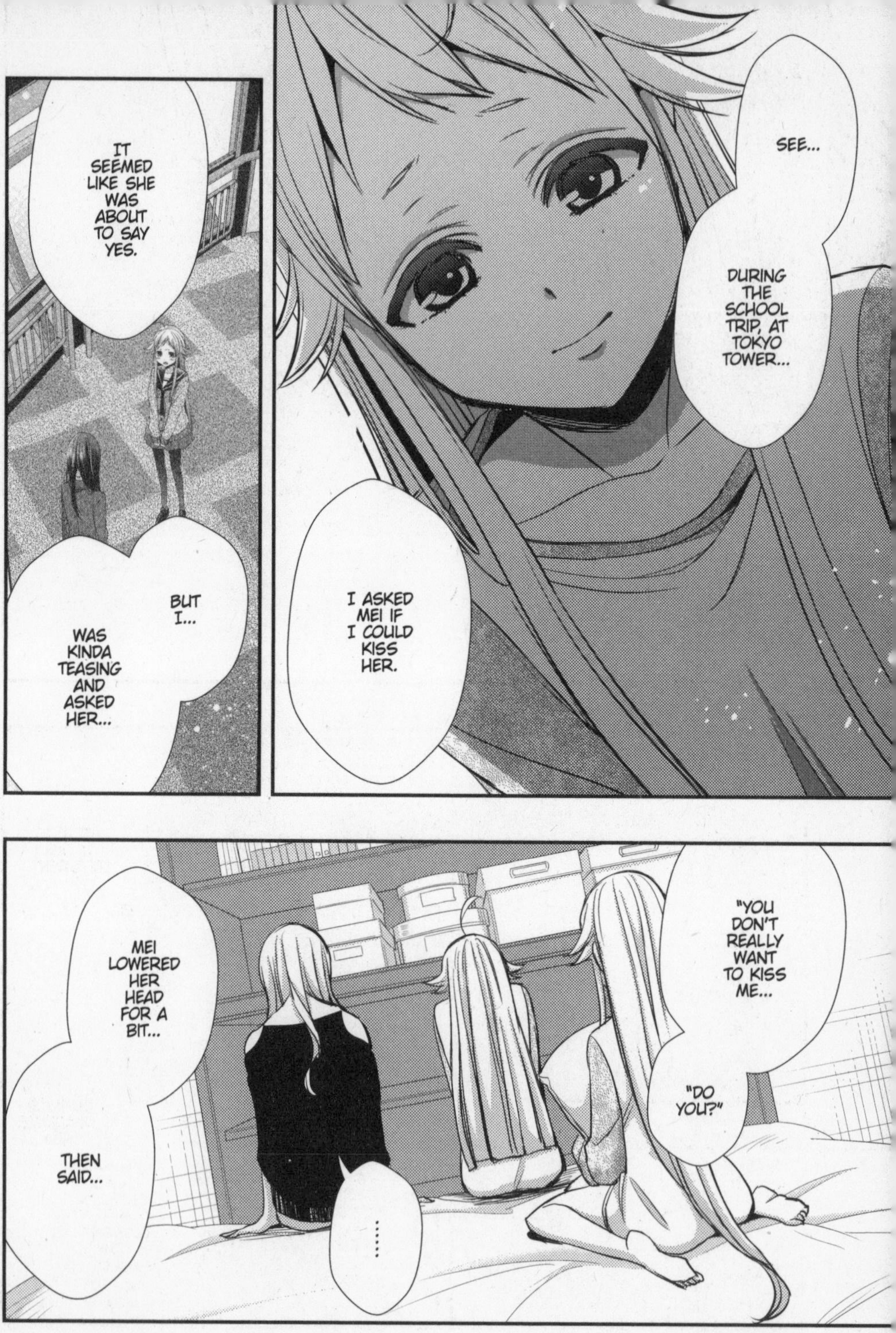
SEE...
DURING THE SCHOOL TRIP, AT TOKYO TOWER...
I ASKED MEI IF I COULD KISS HER.
IT SEEMED LIKE SHE WAS ABOUT TO SAY YES.
BUT I...
WAS KINDA TEASING AND ASKED HER...
"YOU DON'T REALLY WANT TO KISS ME...
"DO YOU?"
......
MEI LOWERED HER HEAD FOR A BIT...
THEN SAID...

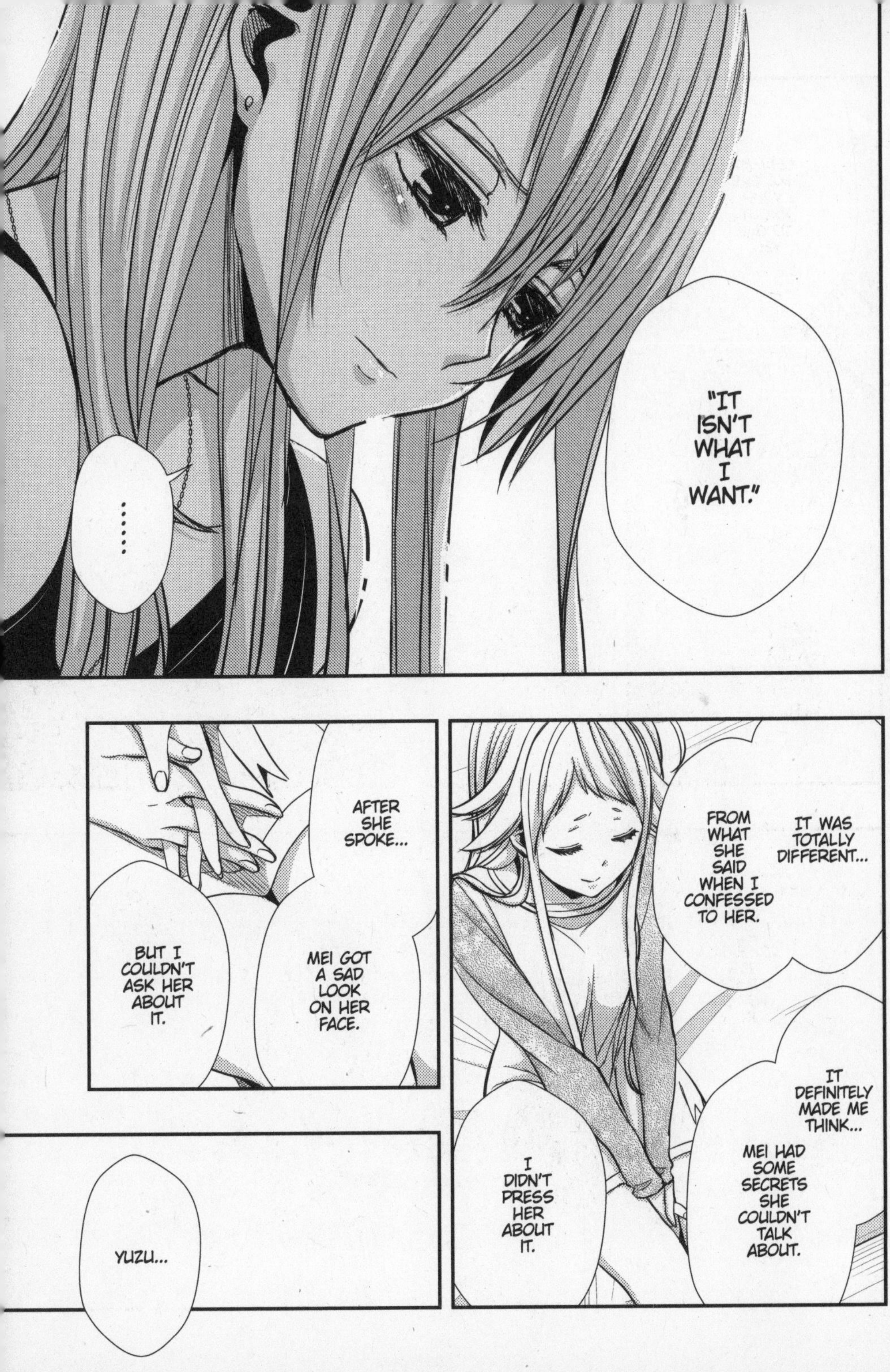
"IT ISN'T WHAT I WANT."
......
IT WAS TOTALLY DIFFERENT...
FROM WHAT SHE SAID WHEN I CONFESSED TO HER.
IT DEFINITELY MADE ME THINK...
MEI HAD SOME SECRETS SHE COULDN'T TALK ABOUT.
I DIDN'T PRESS HER ABOUT IT.
AFTER SHE SPOKE...
MEI GOT A SAD LOOK ON HER FACE.
BUT I COULDN'T ASK HER ABOUT IT.
YUZU...

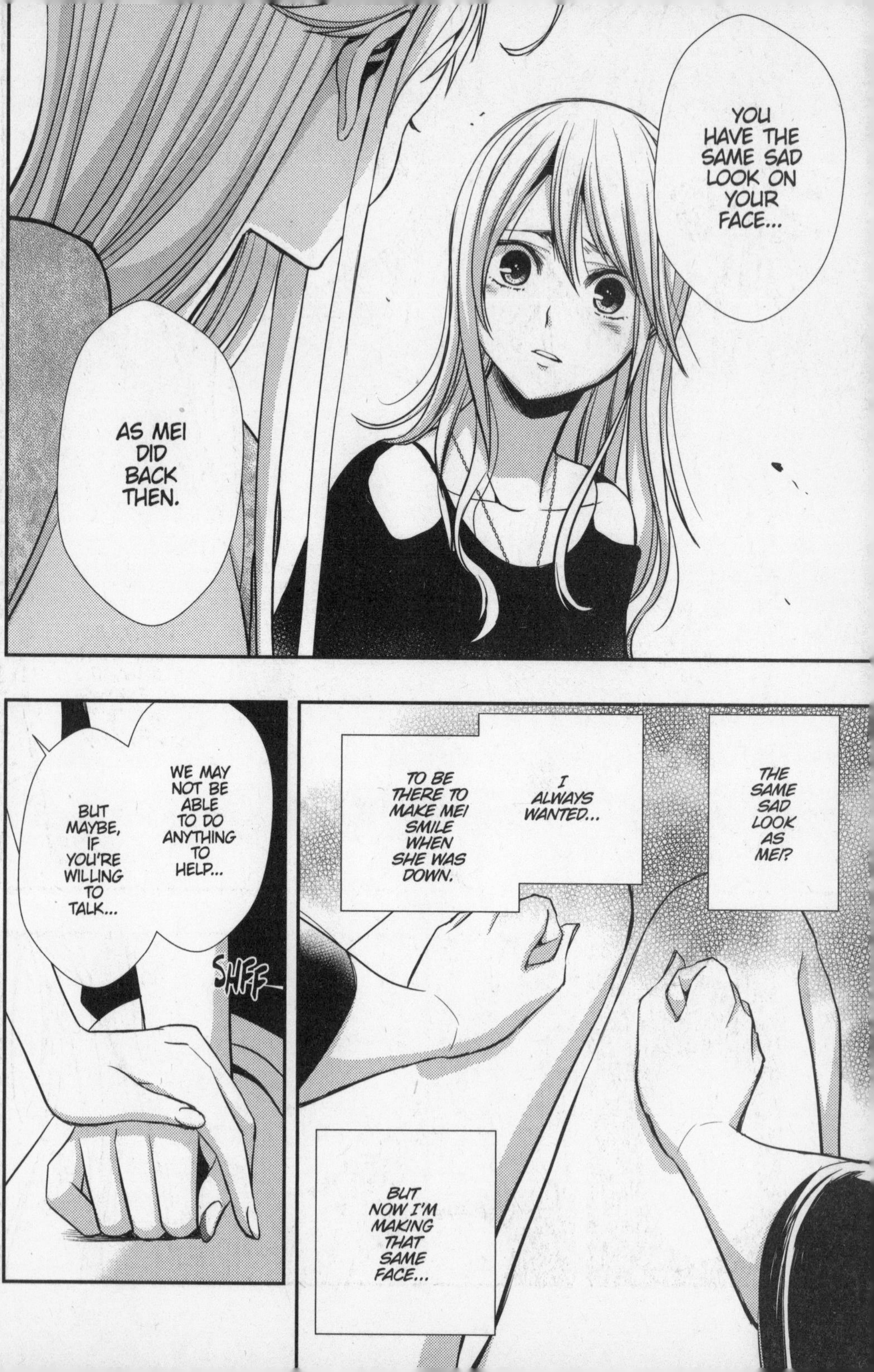
YOU HAVE THE SAME SAD LOOK ON YOUR FACE...
AS MEI DID BACK THEN.
THE SAME SAD LOOK AS MEI?
I ALWAYS WANTED...
TO BE THERE TO MAKE MEI SMILE WHEN SHE WAS DOWN.
BUT NOW I'M MAKING THAT SAME FACE...
WE MAY NOT BE ABLE TO DO ANYTHING TO HELP...
BUT MAYBE, IF YOU'RE WILLING TO TALK...
SHFF

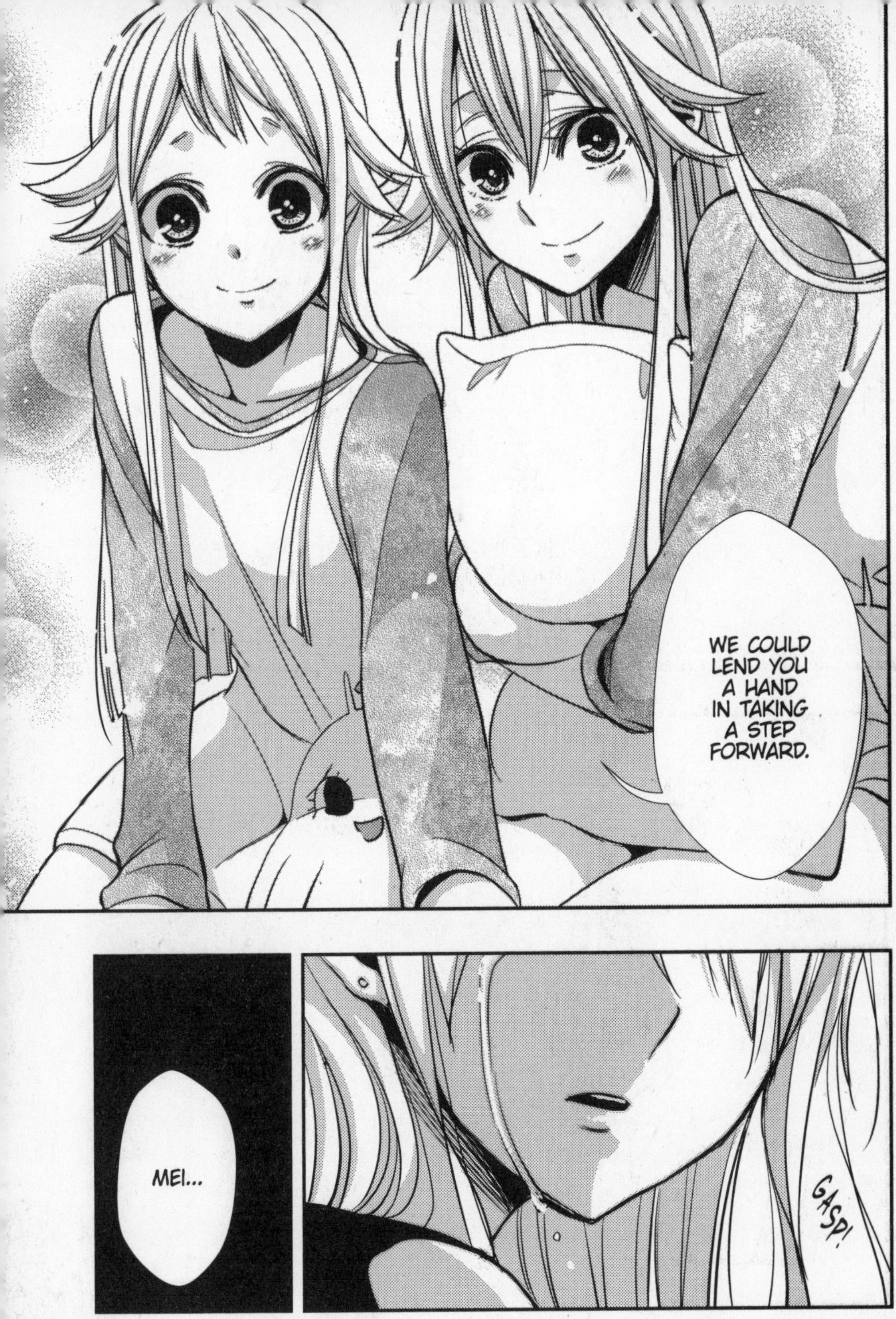
WE COULD LEND YOU A HAND IN TAKING A STEP FORWARD.
GASP!
MEI...

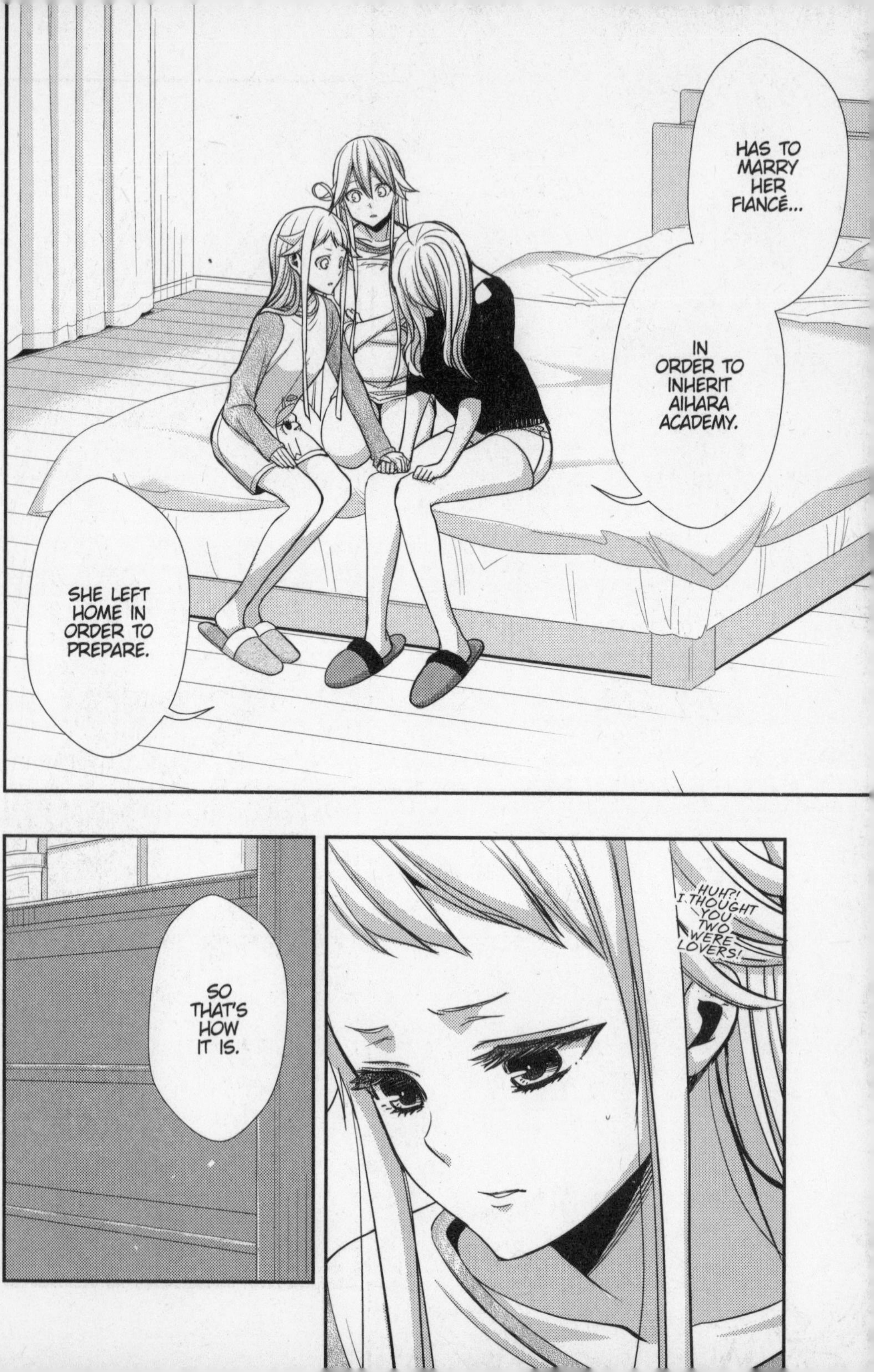
HAS TO MARRY HER FIANCÉ...
IN ORDER TO INHERIT AIHARA ACADEMY.
SHE LEFT HOME IN ORDER TO PREPARE.
HUH?! I THOUGHT YOU TWO WERE LOVERS!
SO THAT'S HOW IT IS.

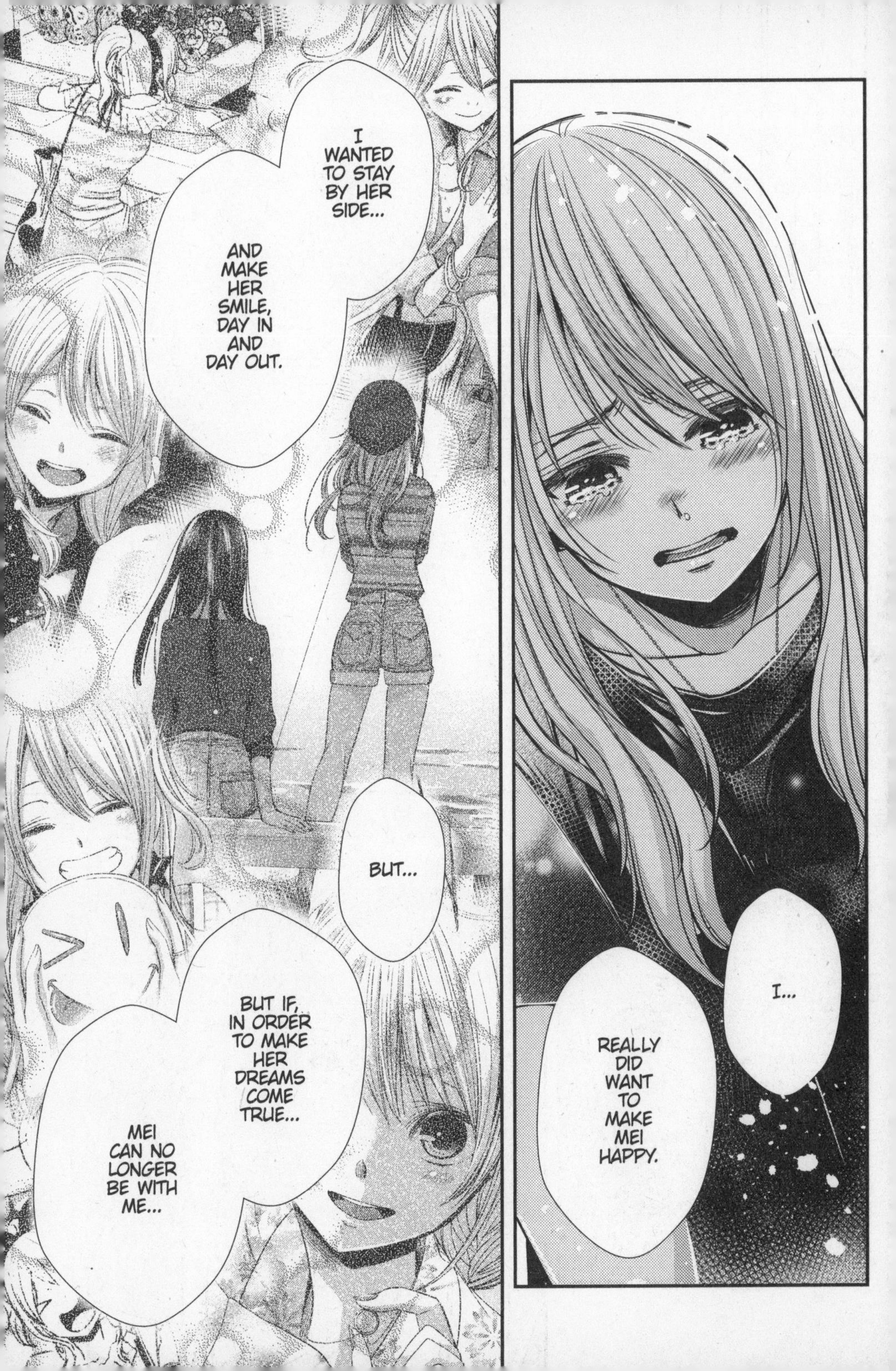
I...
REALLY DID WANT TO MAKE MEI HAPPY.
I WANTED TO STAY BY HER SIDE...
AND MAKE HER SMILE, DAY IN AND DAY OUT.
BUT...
BUT IF, IN ORDER TO MAKE HER DREAMS COME TRUE...
MEI CAN NO LONGER BE WITH ME...

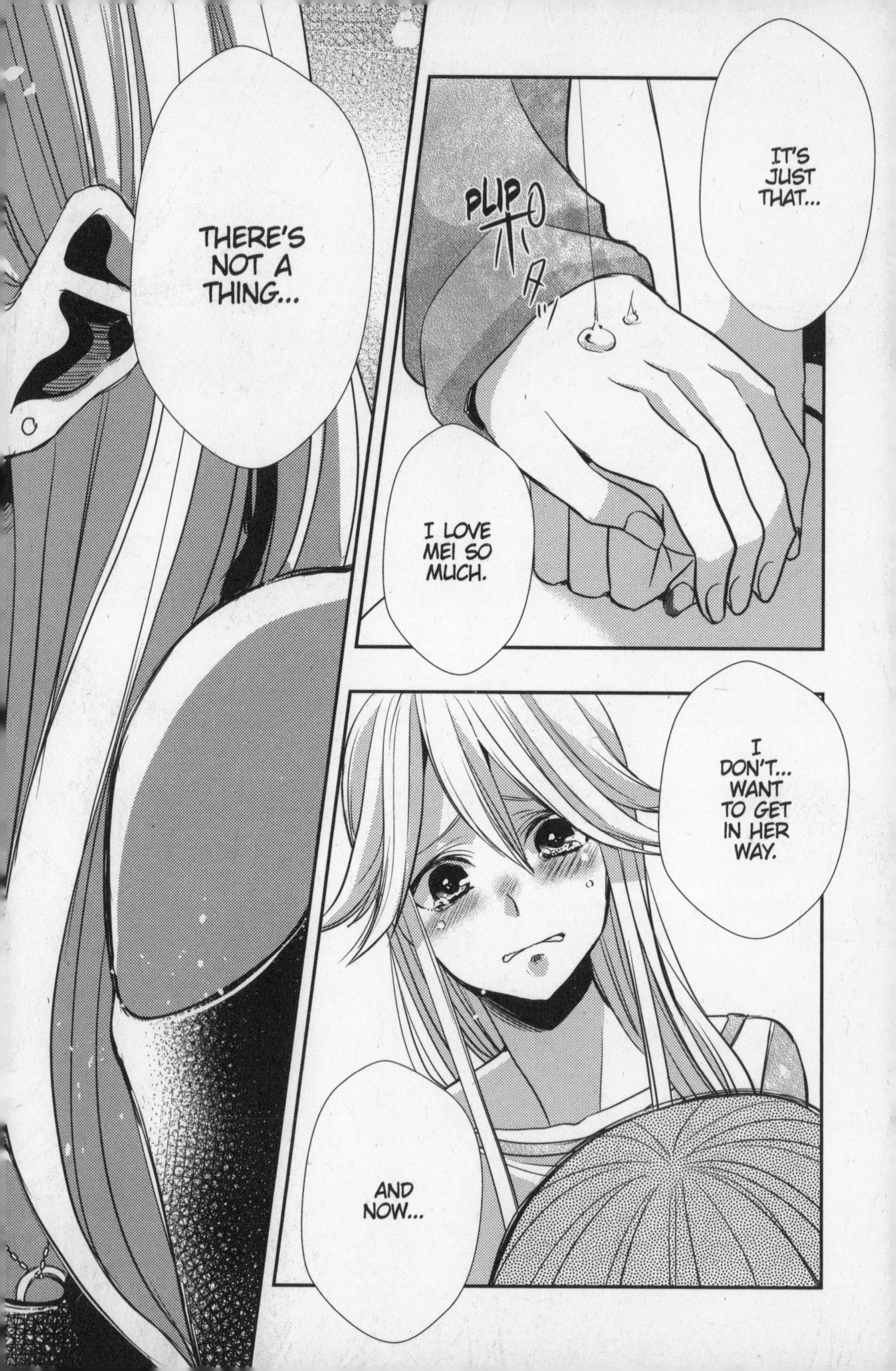
IT'S JUST THAT...
PLIP
I LOVE MEI SO MUCH.
I DON'T... WANT TO GET IN HER WAY.
AND NOW...
THERE'S NOT A THING...

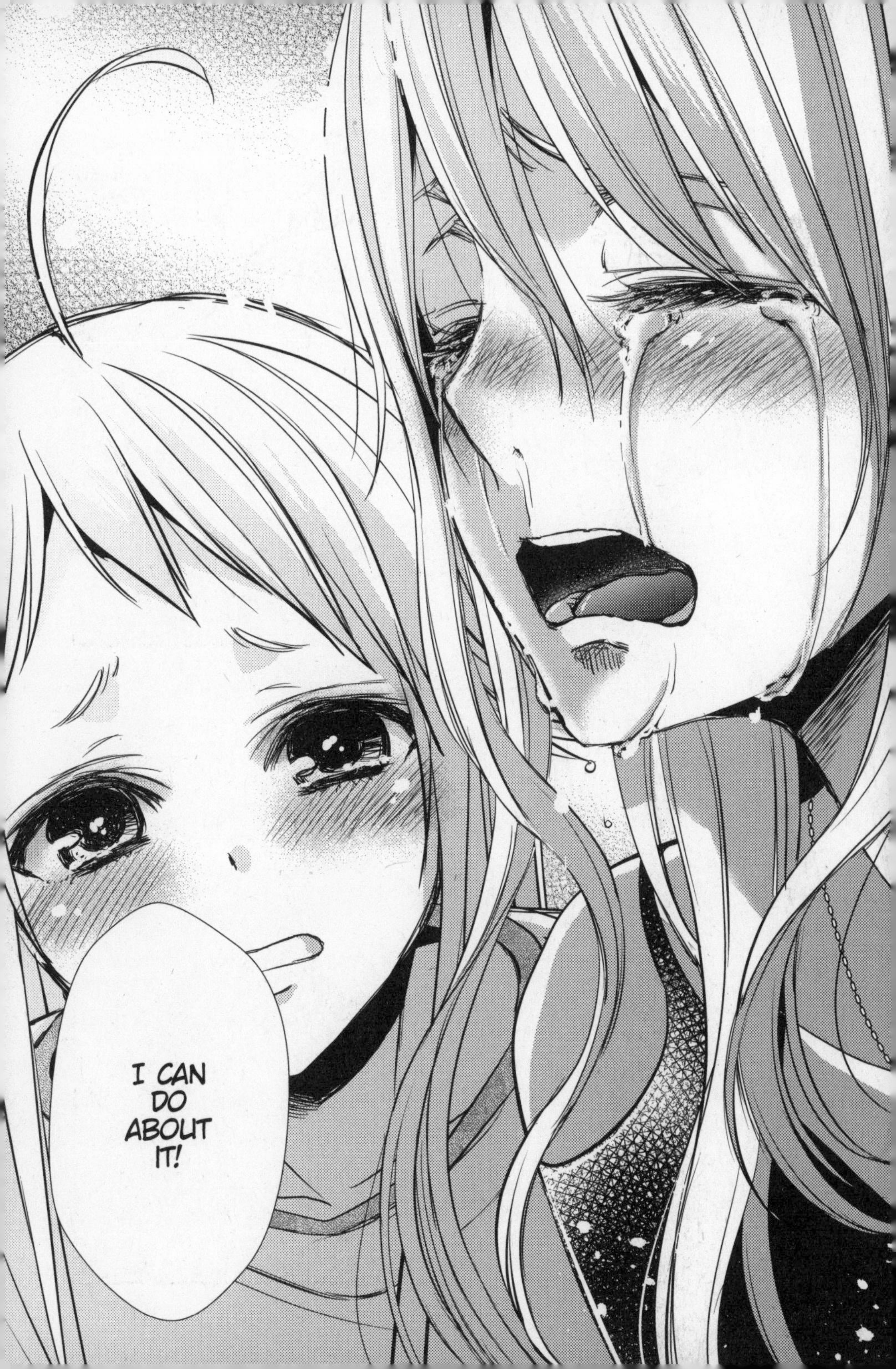
I CAN DO ABOUT IT!

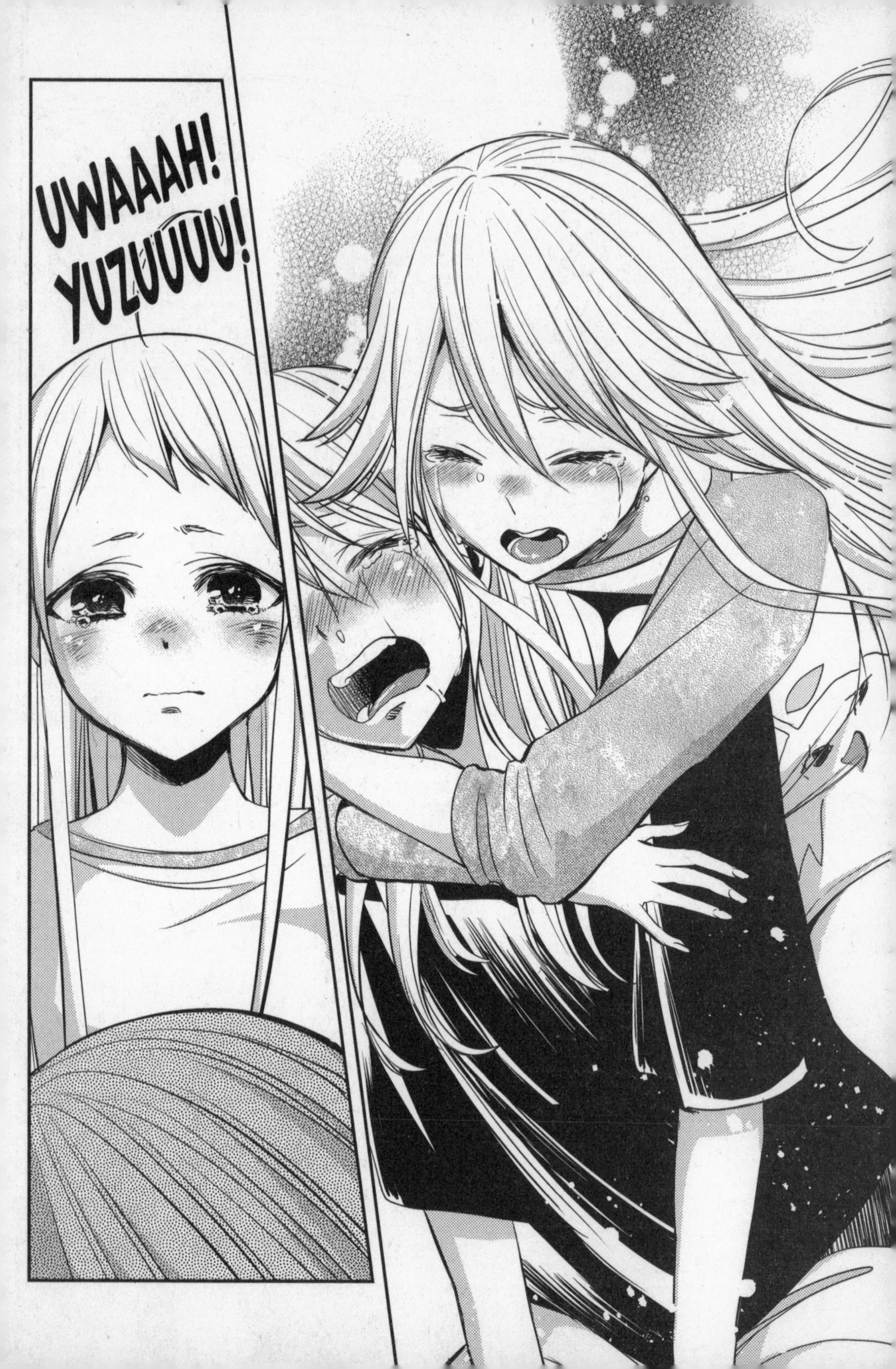
UWAAAH! YUZUUUU!

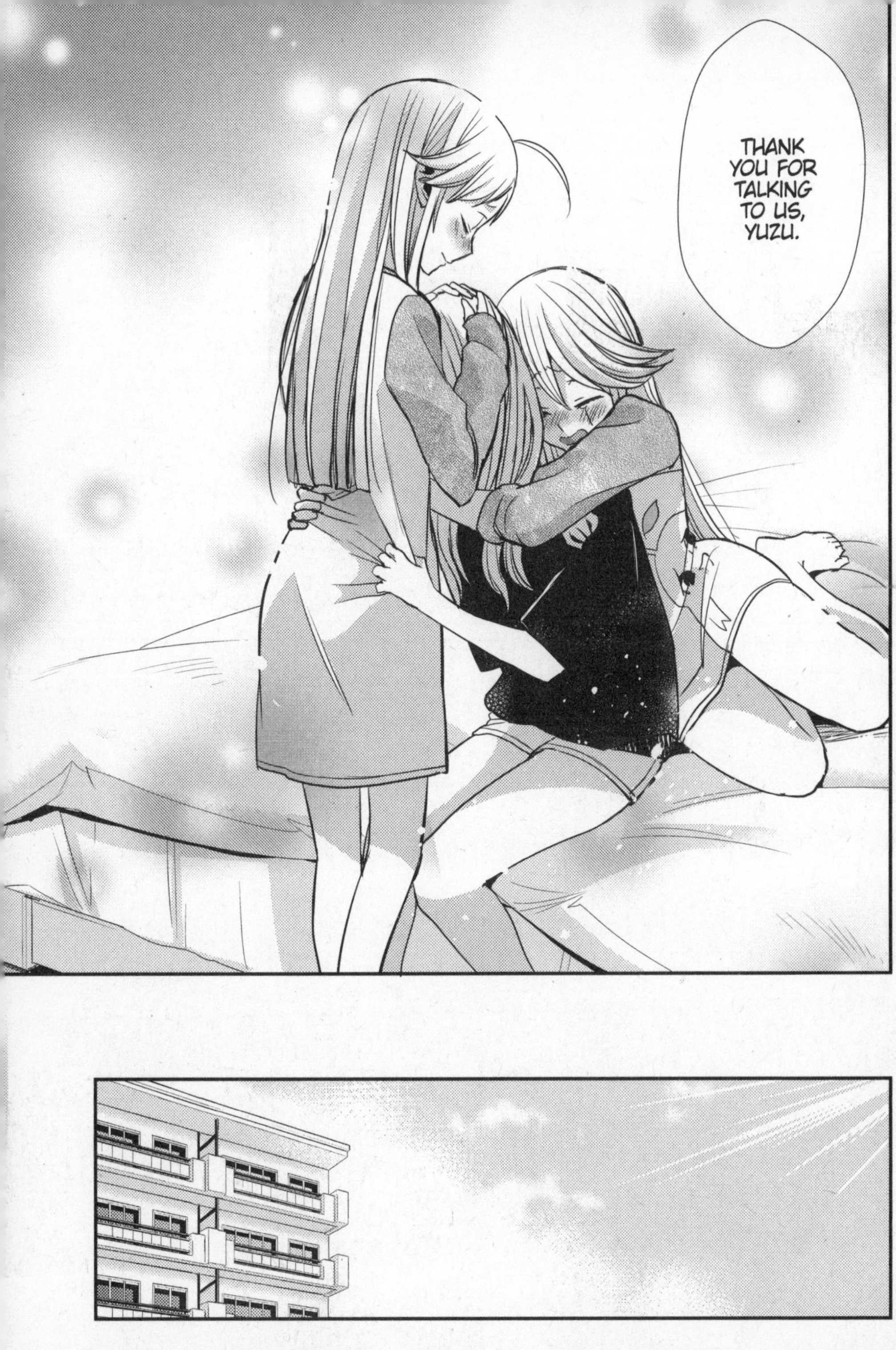
THANK YOU FOR TALKING TO US, YUZU.

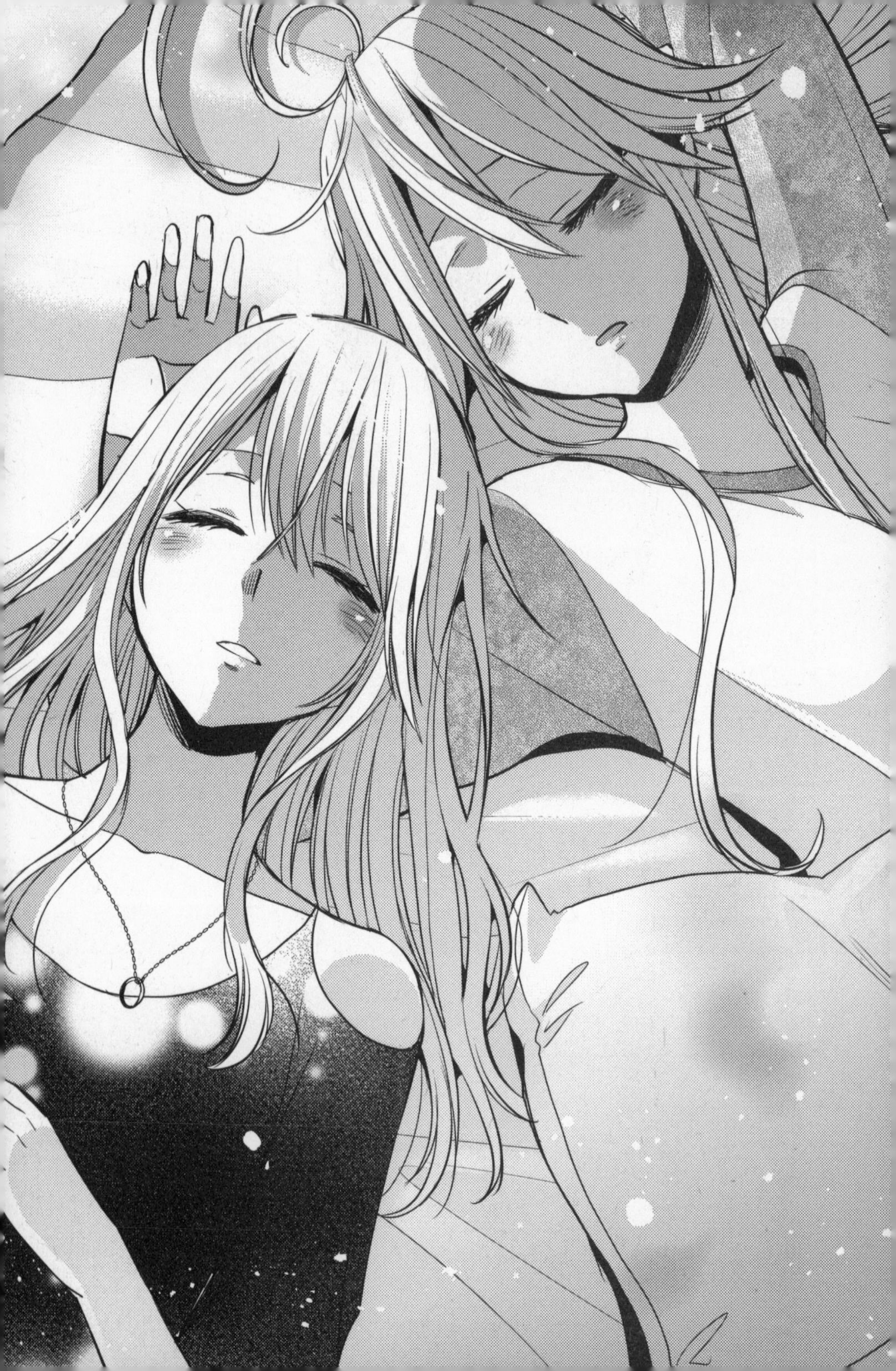

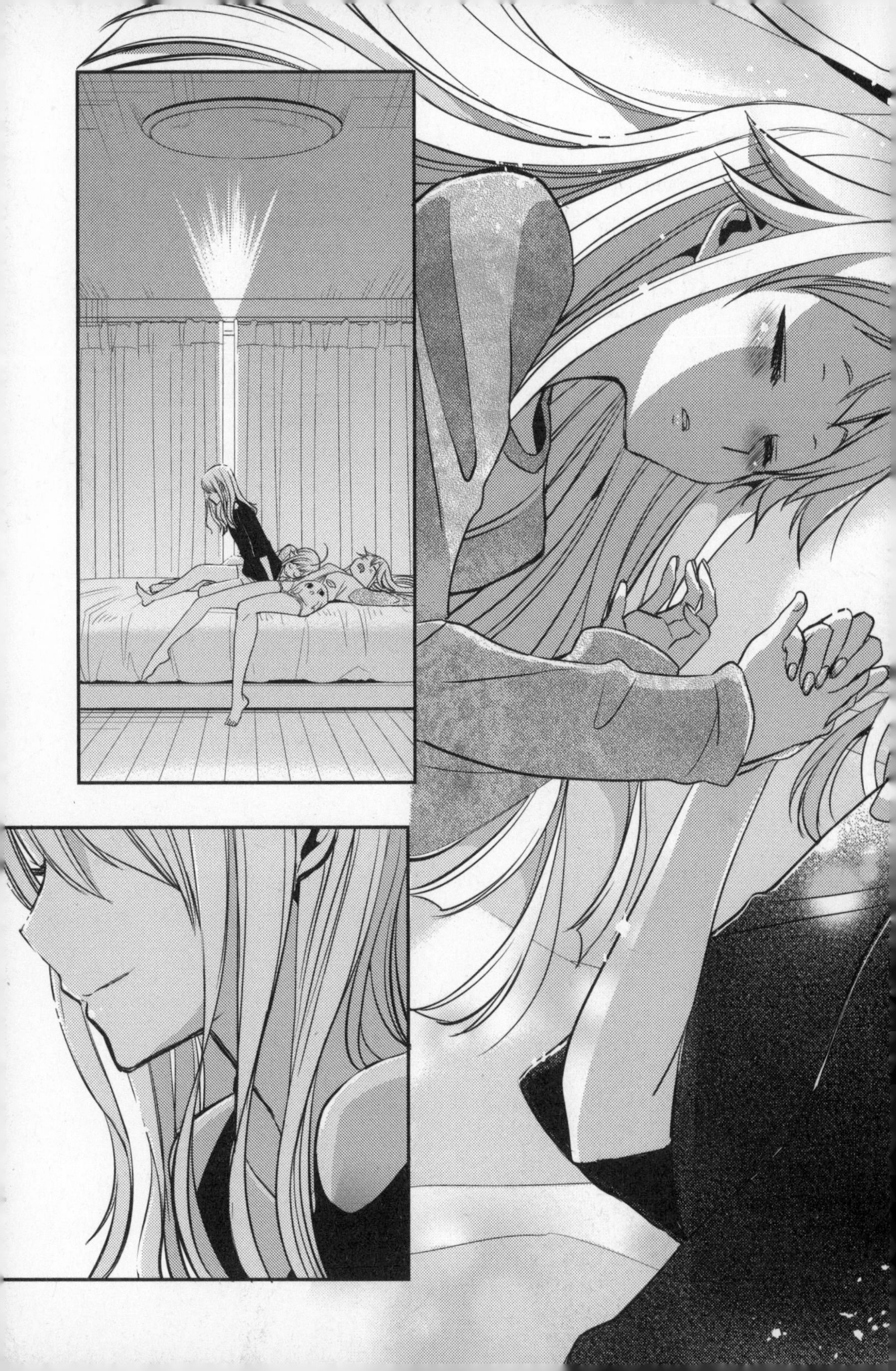

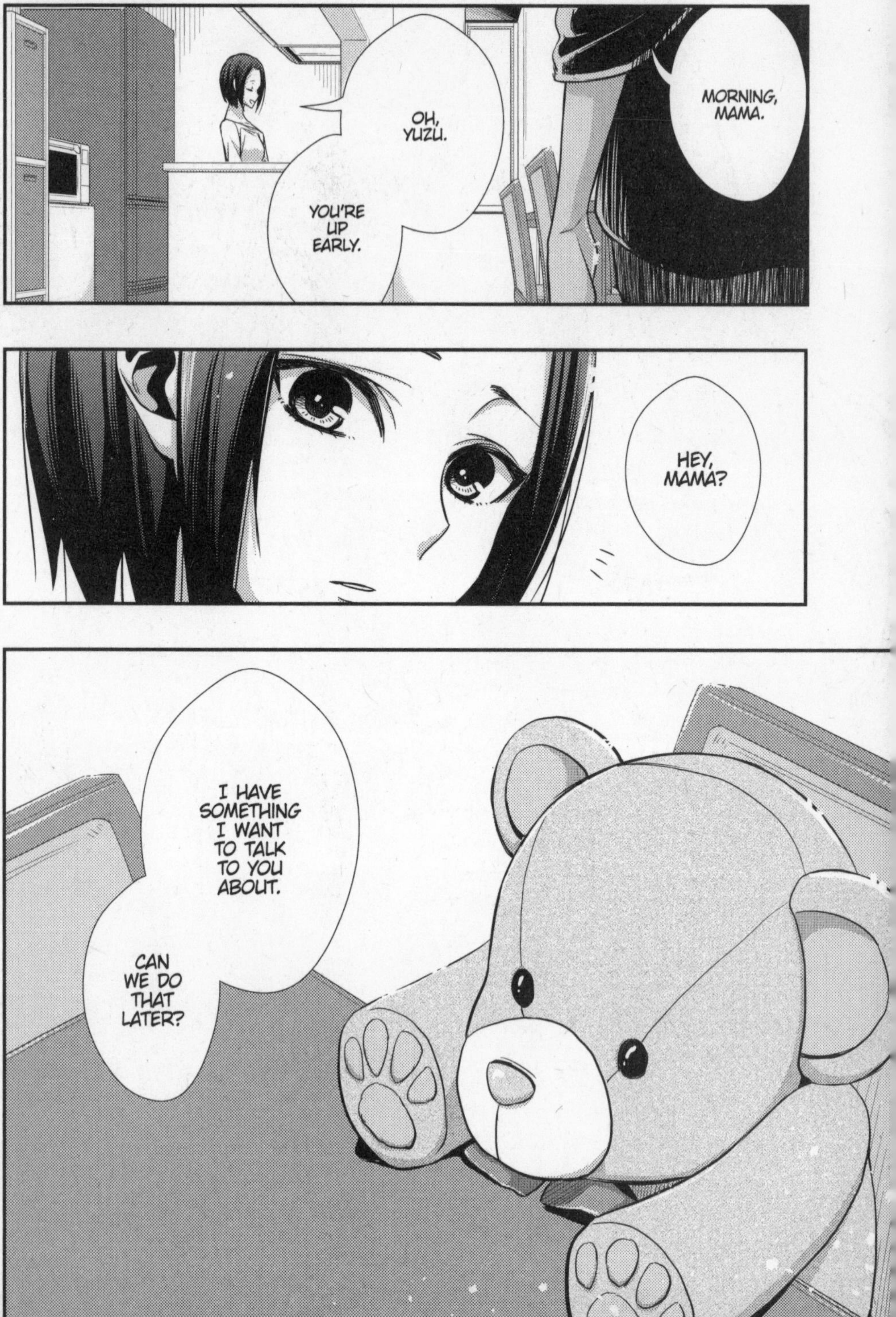
MORNING, MAMA.
OH, YUZU.
YOU'RE UP EARLY.
HEY, MAMA?
I HAVE SOMETHING I WANT TO TALK TO YOU ABOUT.
CAN WE DO THAT LATER?

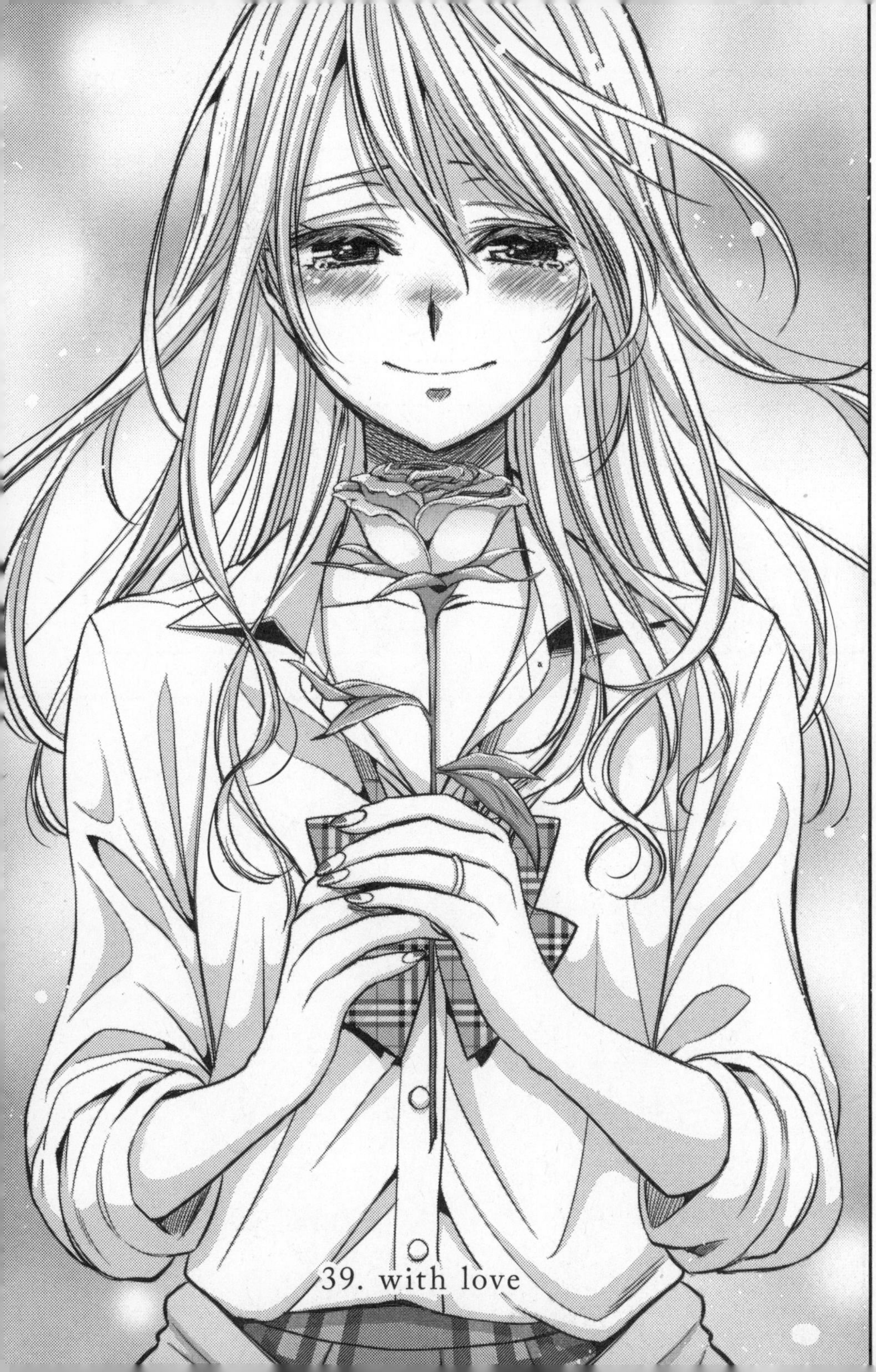

39. with love

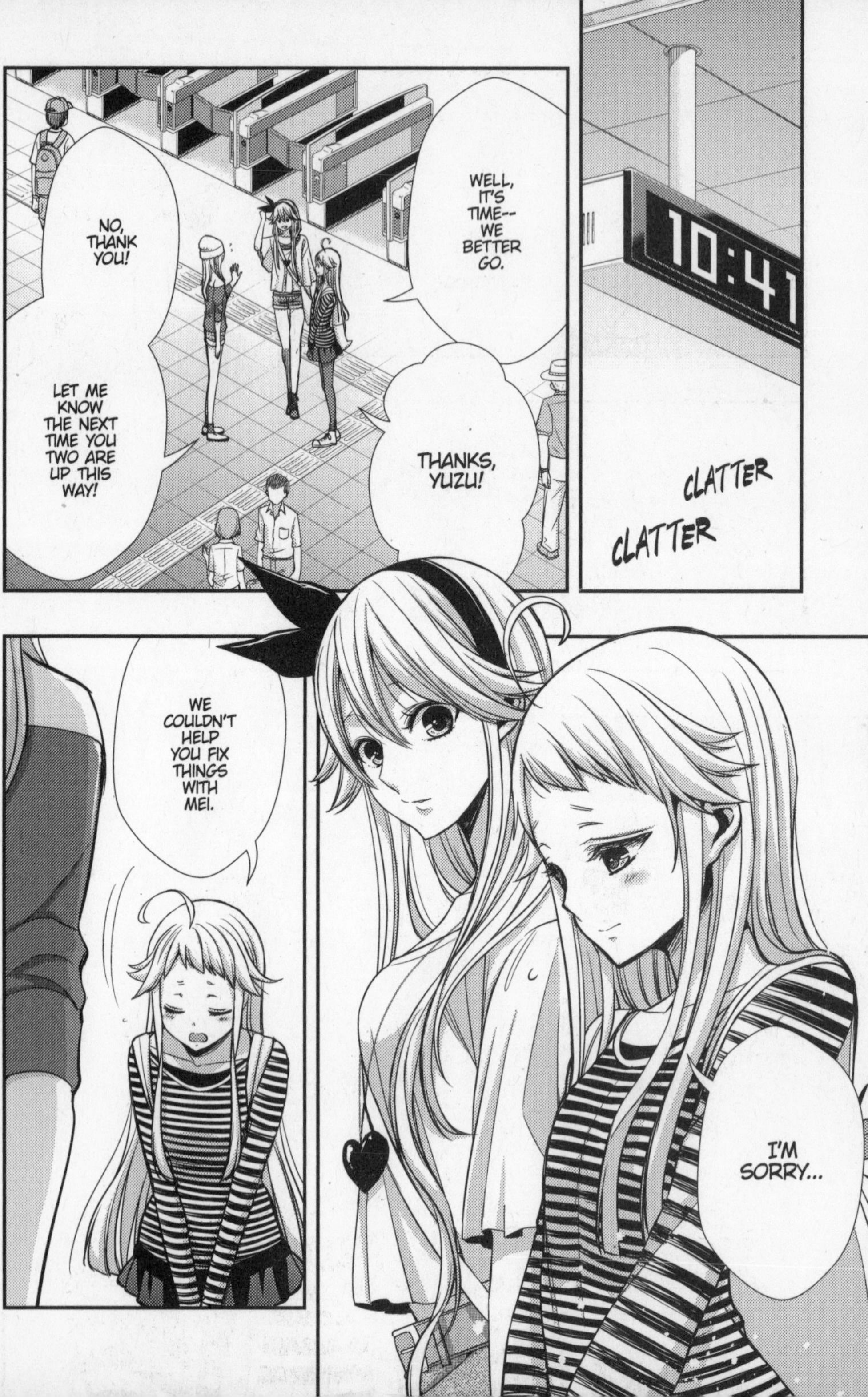
10:41
CLATTER
CLATTER
WELL, IT'S TIME-- WE BETTER GO.
THANKS, YUZU!
NO, THANK YOU!
LET ME KNOW THE NEXT TIME YOU TWO ARE UP THIS WAY!
I'M SORRY...
WE COULDN'T HELP YOU FIX THINGS WITH MEI.

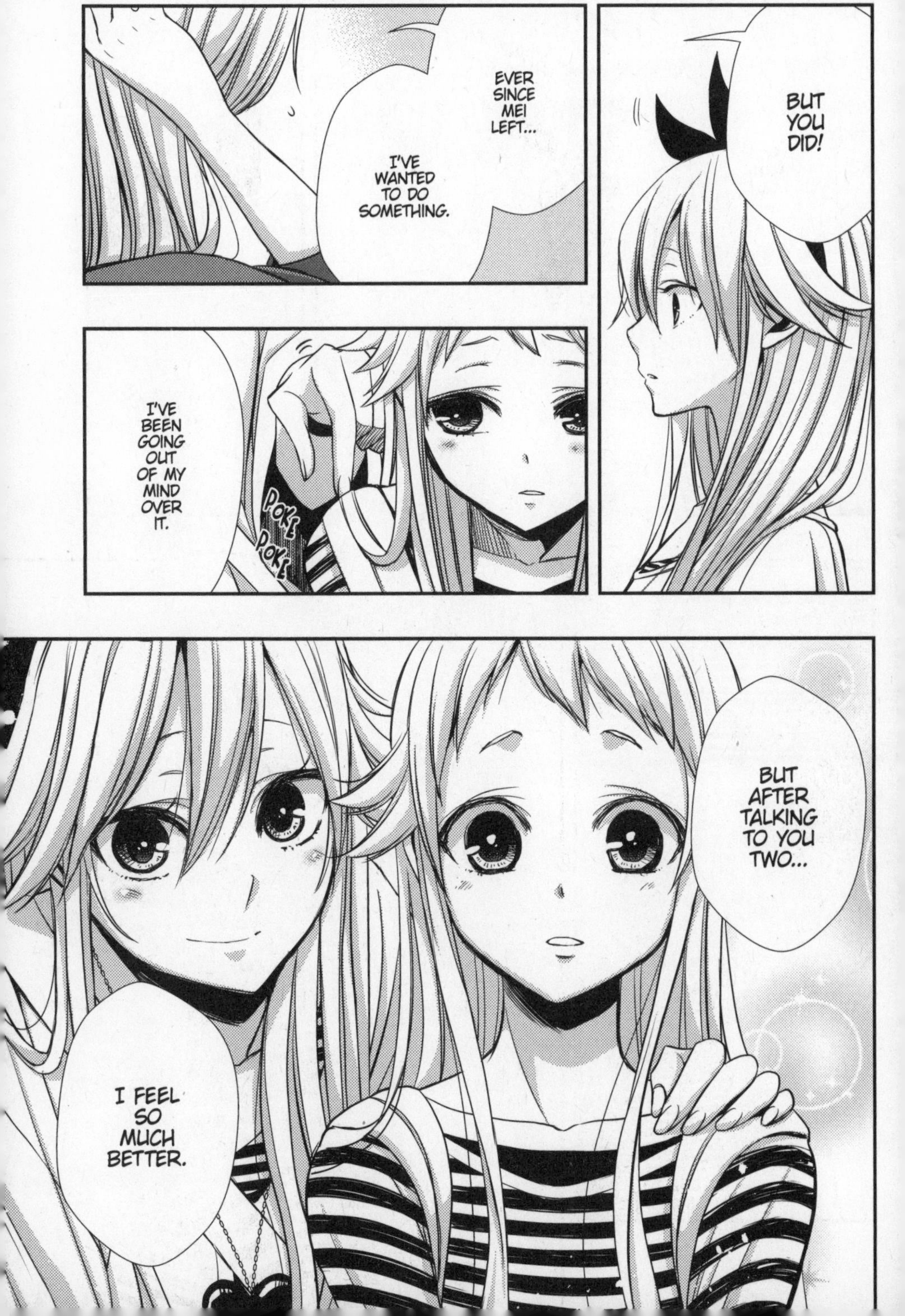
BUT YOU DID!
EVER SINCE MEI LEFT...
I'VE WANTED TO DO SOMETHING.
I'VE BEEN GOING OUT OF MY MIND OVER IT.
POKE POKE
BUT AFTER TALKING TO YOU TWO...
I FEEL SO MUCH BETTER.

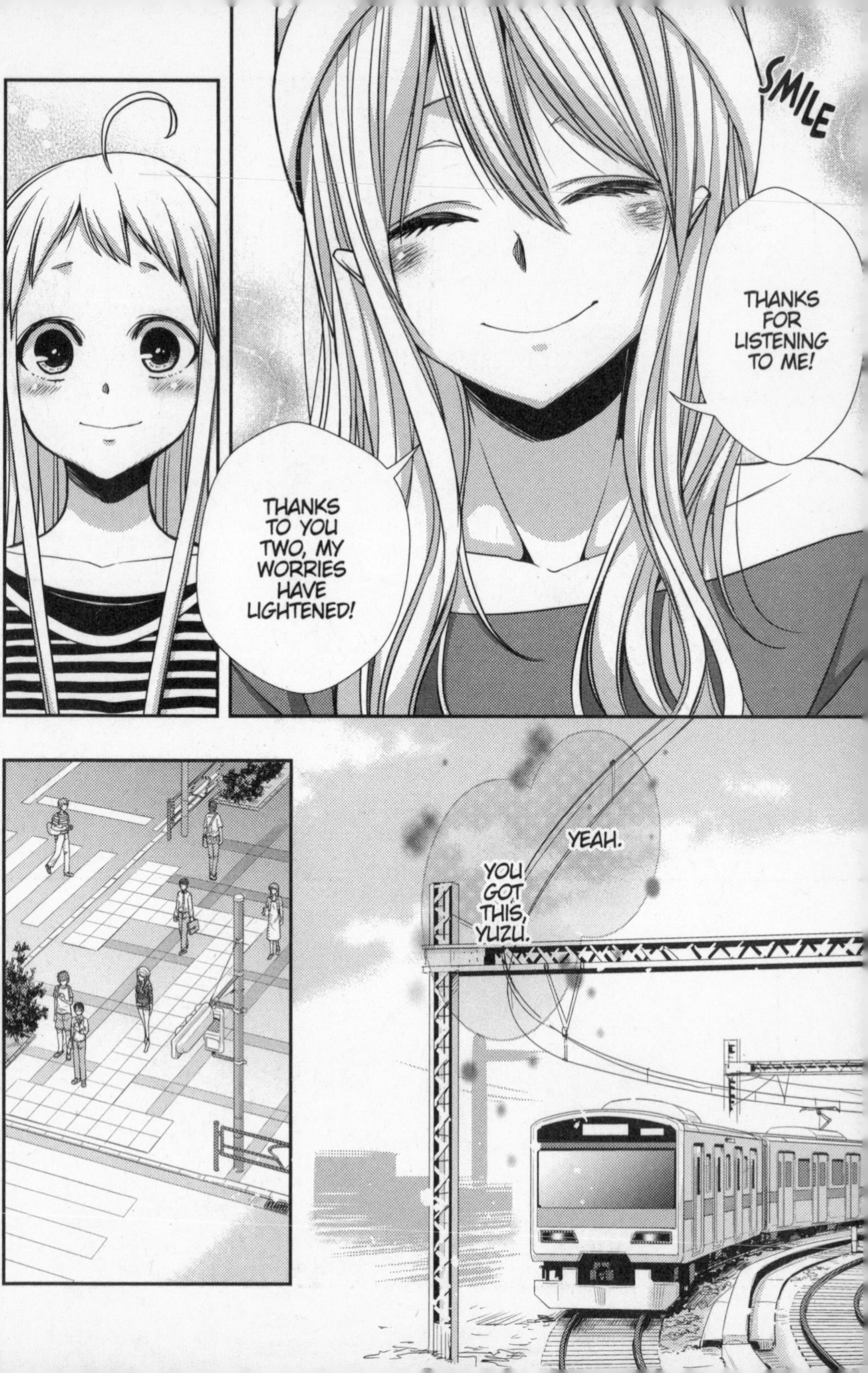
SMILE
THANKS FOR LISTENING TO ME!
THANKS TO YOU TWO, MY WORRIES HAVE LIGHTENED!
YEAH.
YOU GOT THIS, YUZU.

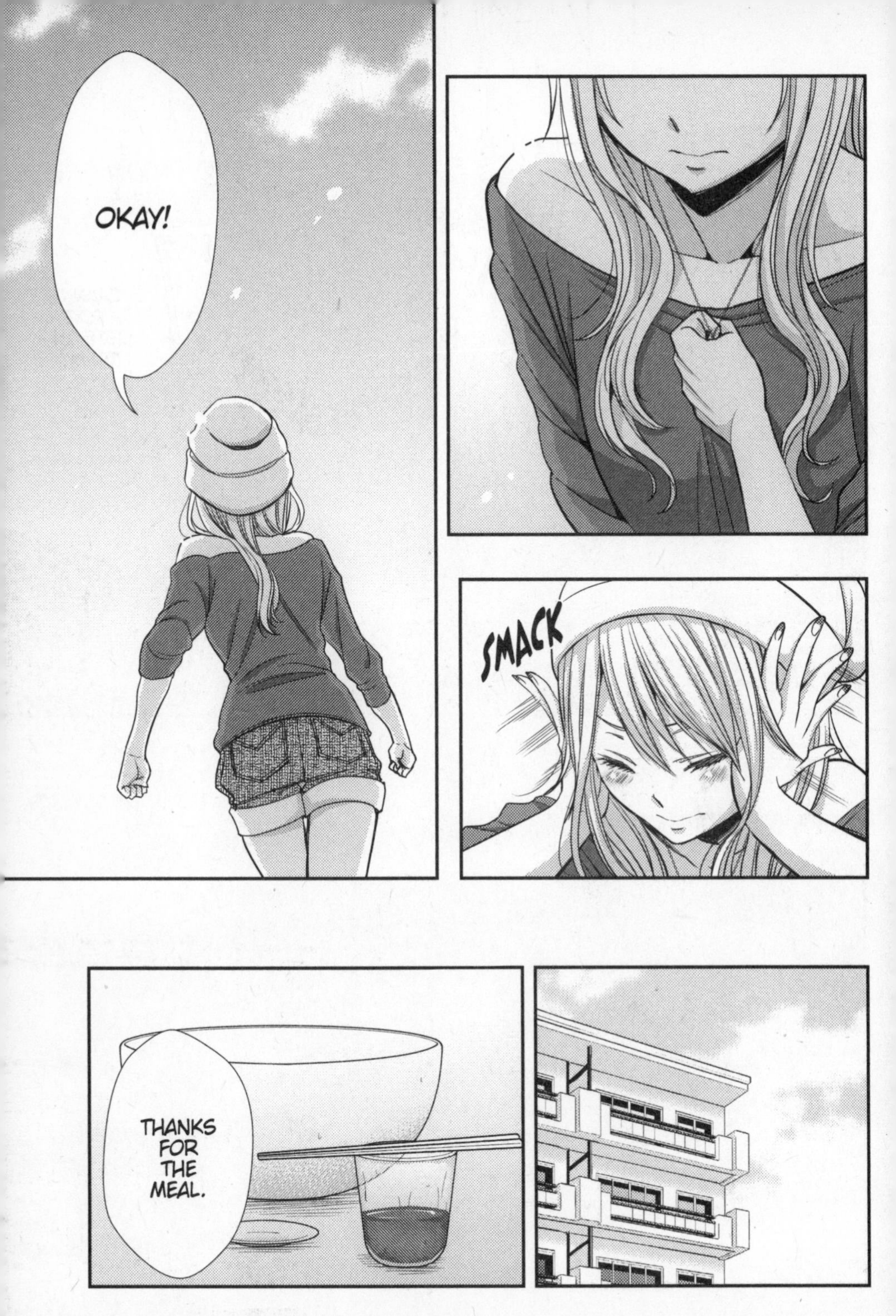
SMACK
OKAY!
THANKS FOR THE MEAL.

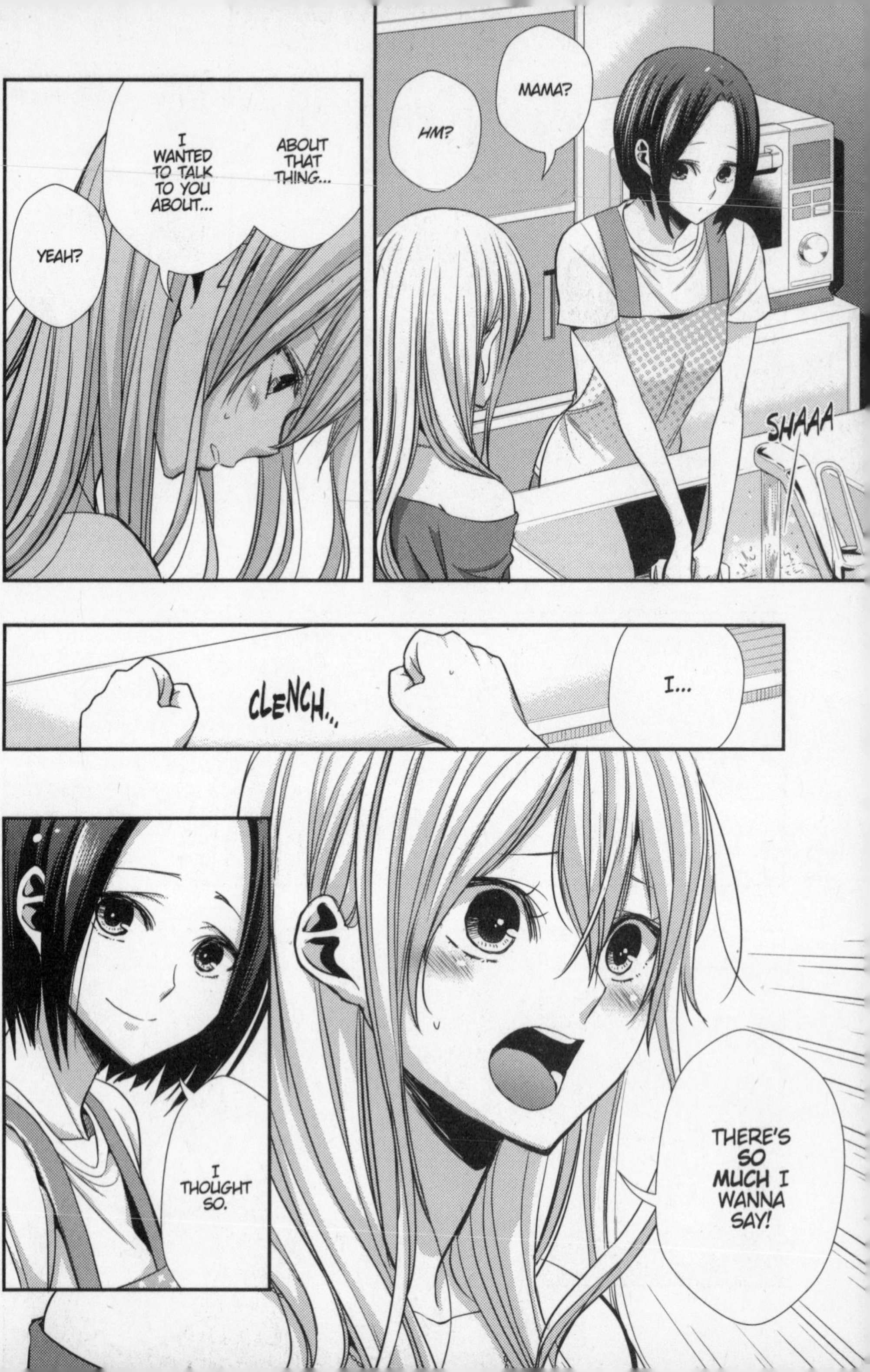
MAMA?
HM?
SHAAA
ABOUT THAT THING...
I WANTED TO TALK TO YOU ABOUT...
YEAH?
I...
CLENCH...
THERE'S SO MUCH I WANNA SAY!
I THOUGHT SO.

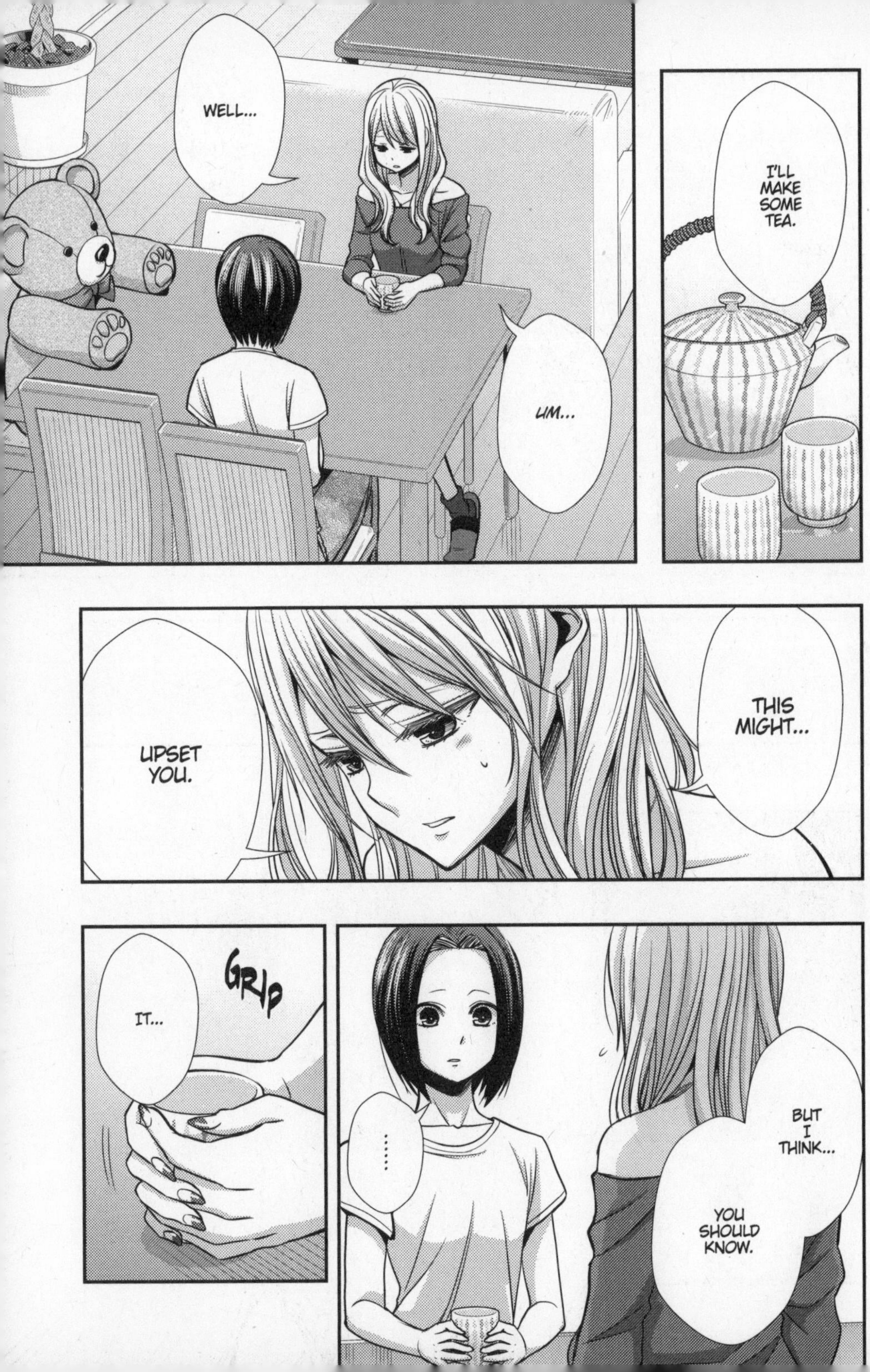

I'LL MAKE SOME TEA.
UM...
WELL...
THIS MIGHT...
UPSET YOU.
BUT I THINK...
YOU SHOULD KNOW.
......
GRIP
IT...

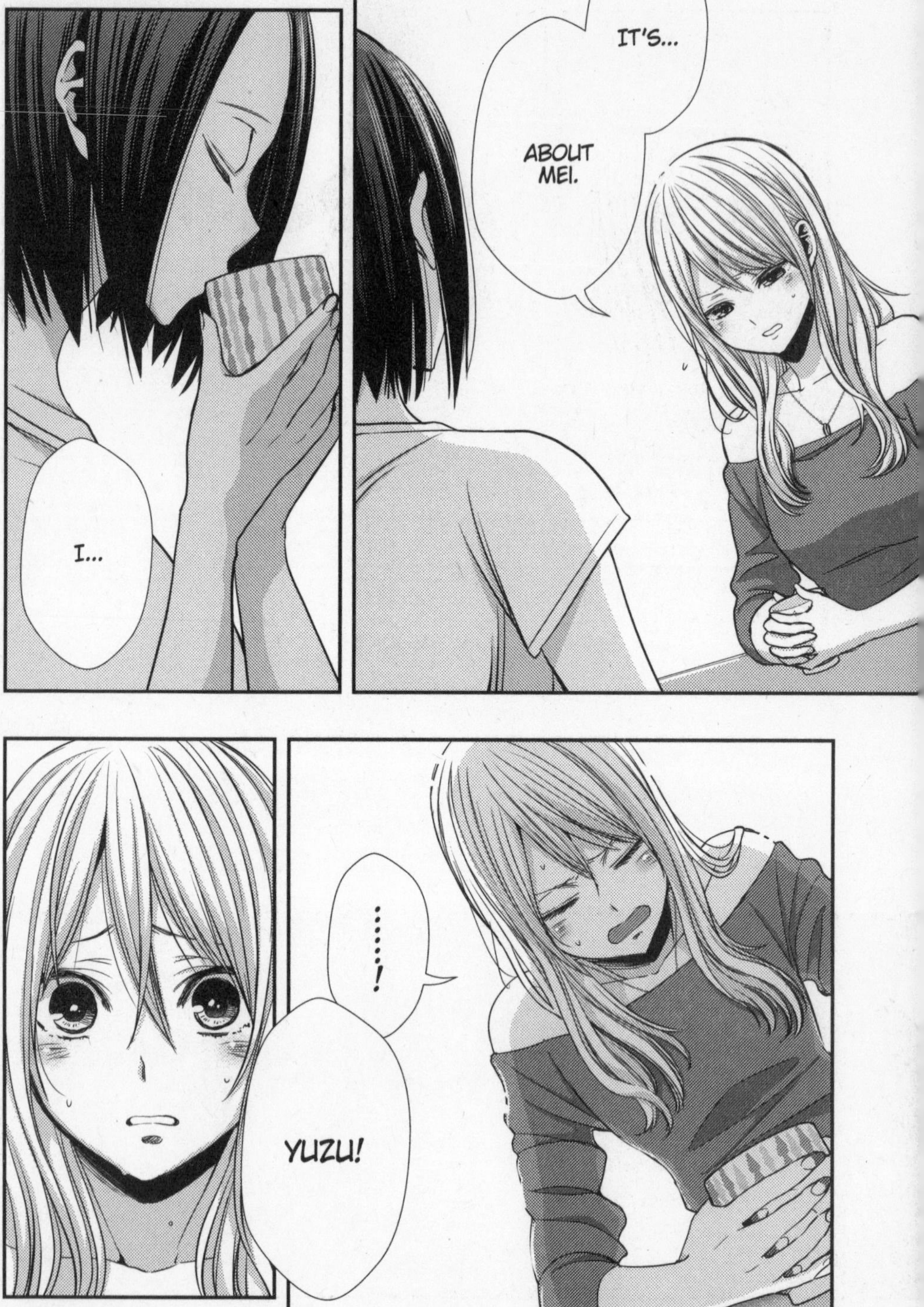
IT'S...
ABOUT MEI.
I...
......!
YUZU!

DON'T FORCE YOURSELF TO GET IT ALL OUT AT ONCE.

TAKE YOUR TIME.

IT'S ALL RIGHT.

OKAY.

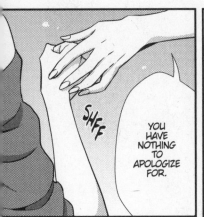

SHFF

YOU HAVE NOTHING TO APOLOGIZE FOR.

I'M SORRY, MAMA...

I SEE...

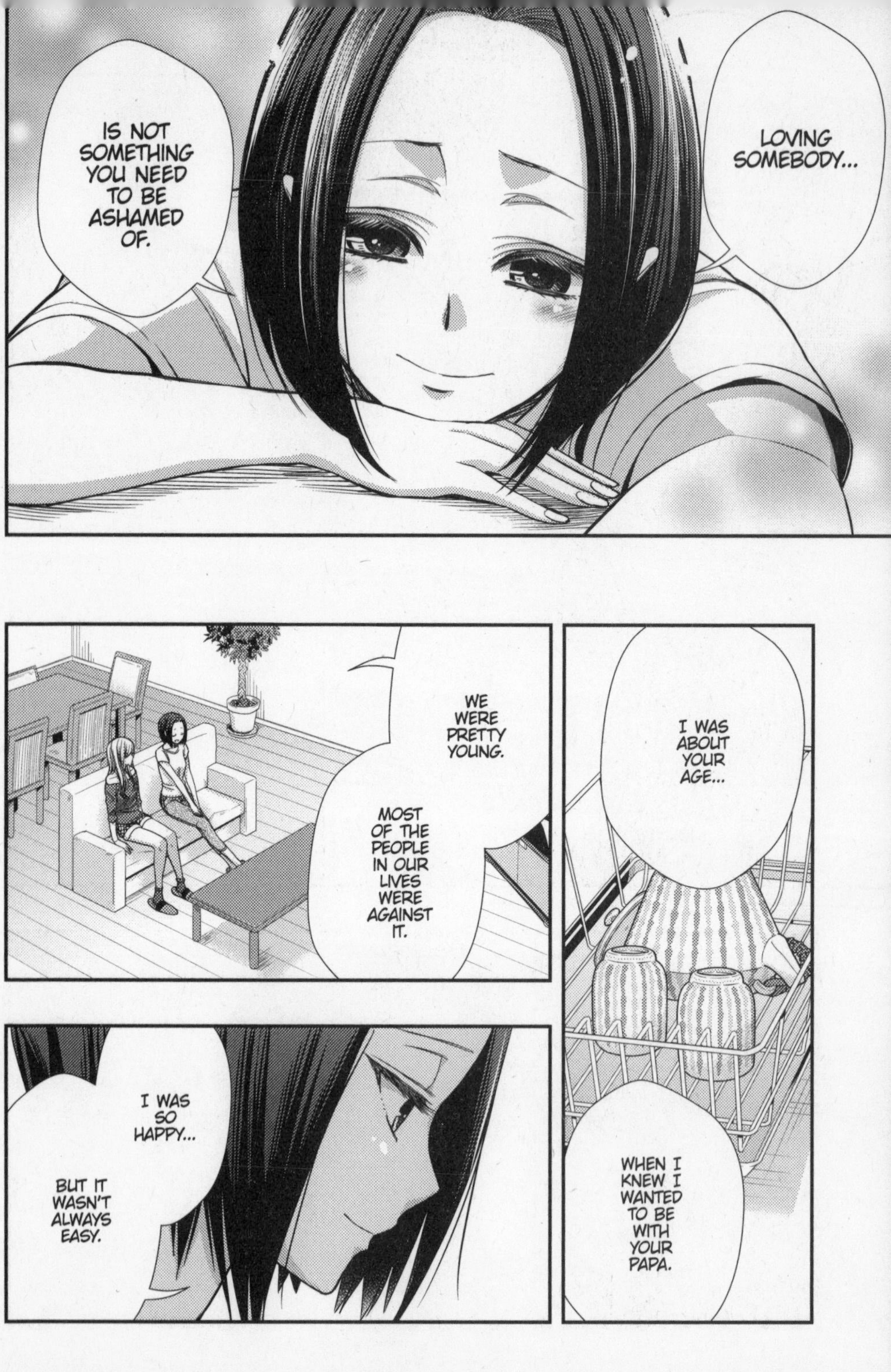
LOVING SOMEBODY...
IS NOT SOMETHING YOU NEED TO BE ASHAMED OF.
I WAS ABOUT YOUR AGE...
WHEN I KNEW I WANTED TO BE WITH YOUR PAPA.
WE WERE PRETTY YOUNG.
MOST OF THE PEOPLE IN OUR LIVES WERE AGAINST IT.
I WAS SO HAPPY...
BUT IT WASN'T ALWAYS EASY.

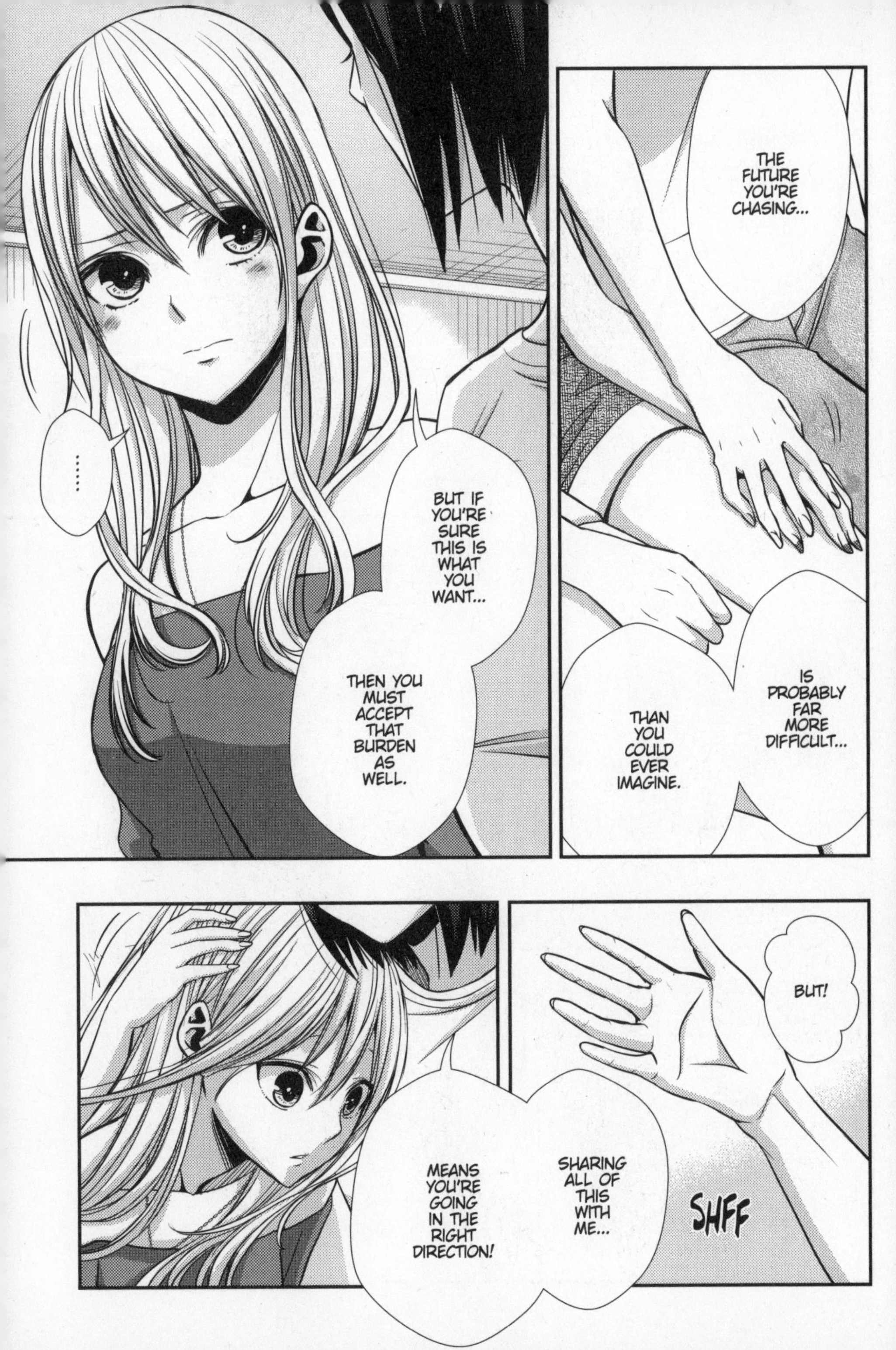
THE FUTURE YOU'RE CHASING...
IS PROBABLY FAR MORE DIFFICULT...
THAN YOU COULD EVER IMAGINE.
BUT IF YOU'RE SURE THIS IS WHAT YOU WANT...
THEN YOU MUST ACCEPT THAT BURDEN AS WELL.
......
BUT!
SHFF
SHARING ALL OF THIS WITH ME...
MEANS YOU'RE GOING IN THE RIGHT DIRECTION!

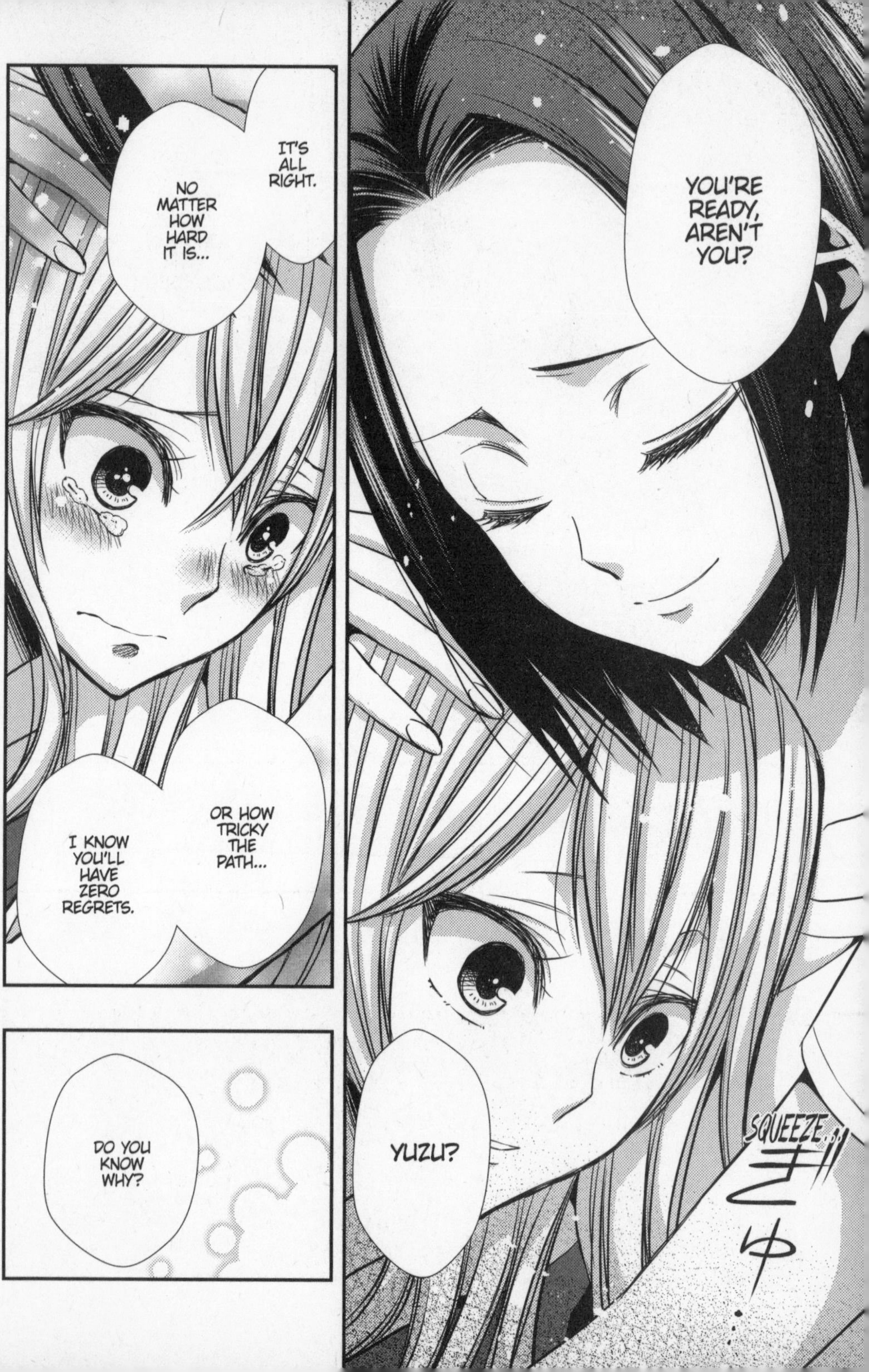
YOU'RE READY, AREN'T YOU?
YUZU?
SQUEEZE
IT'S ALL RIGHT.
NO MATTER HOW HARD IT IS...
OR HOW TRICKY THE PATH...
I KNOW YOU'LL HAVE ZERO REGRETS.
DO YOU KNOW WHY?

BECAUSE IT'S THE FUTURE YOU'VE CHOSEN FOR YOURSELF!

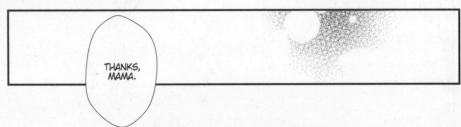

THANKS, MAMA.

AH, IT'S CONNECT-ING...

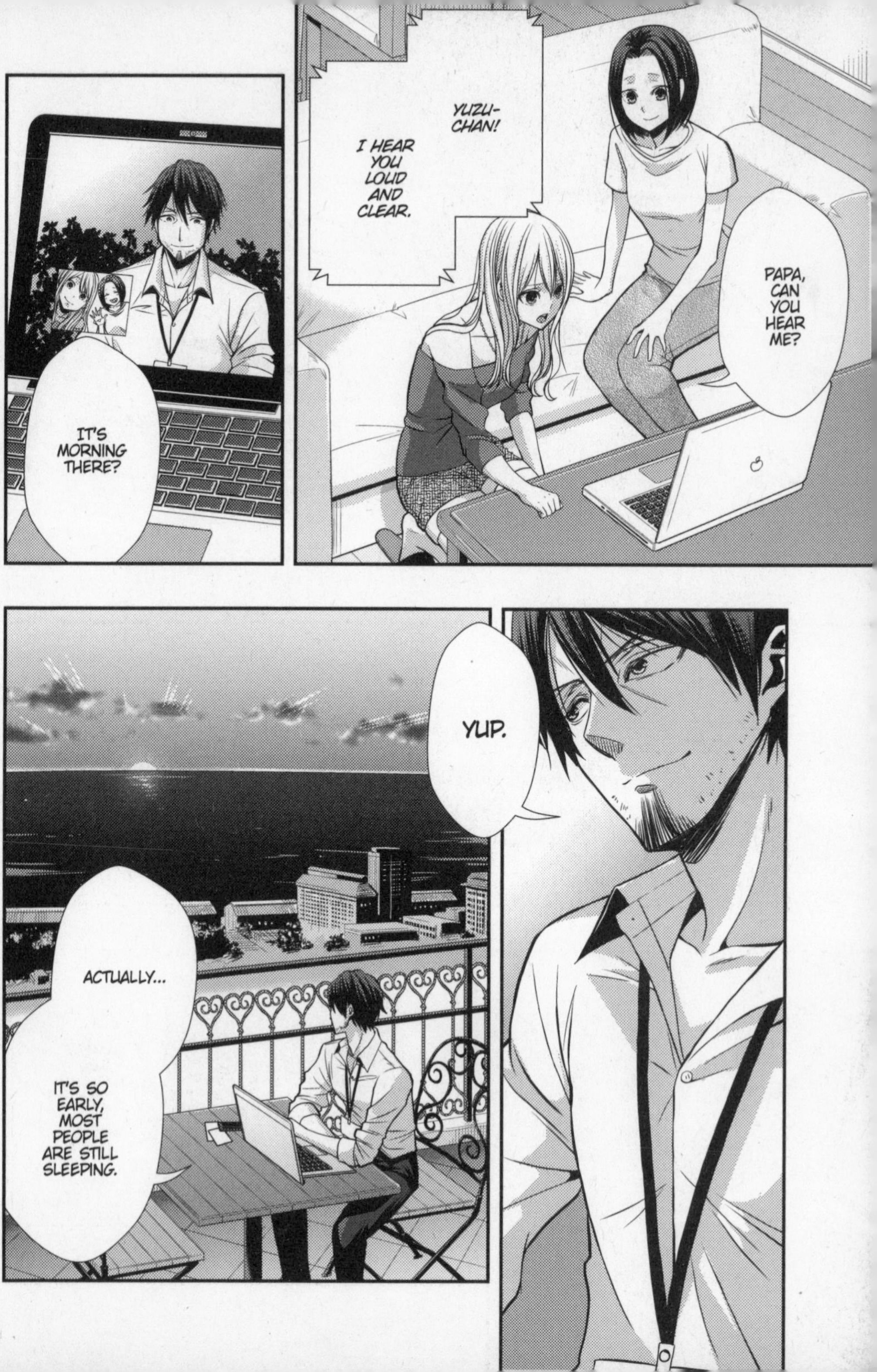
PAPA, CAN YOU HEAR ME?
YUZU-CHAN!
I HEAR YOU LOUD AND CLEAR.
IT'S MORNING THERE?
YUP.
ACTUALLY...
IT'S SO EARLY, MOST PEOPLE ARE STILL SLEEPING.

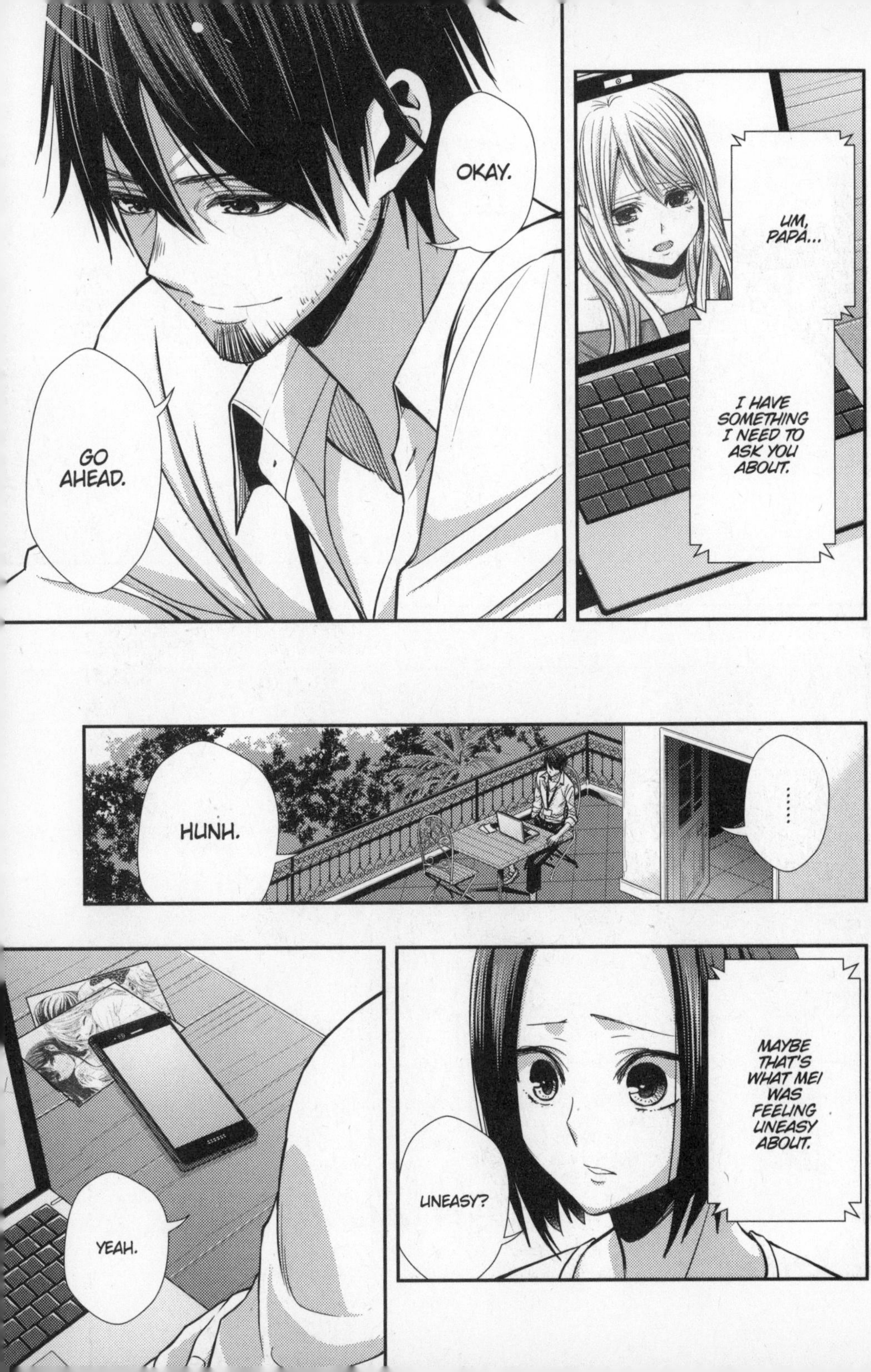
UM, PAPA...
I HAVE SOMETHING I NEED TO ASK YOU ABOUT.
OKAY.
GO AHEAD.
......
HUNH.
MAYBE THAT'S WHAT MEI WAS FEELING UNEASY ABOUT.
UNEASY?
YEAH.

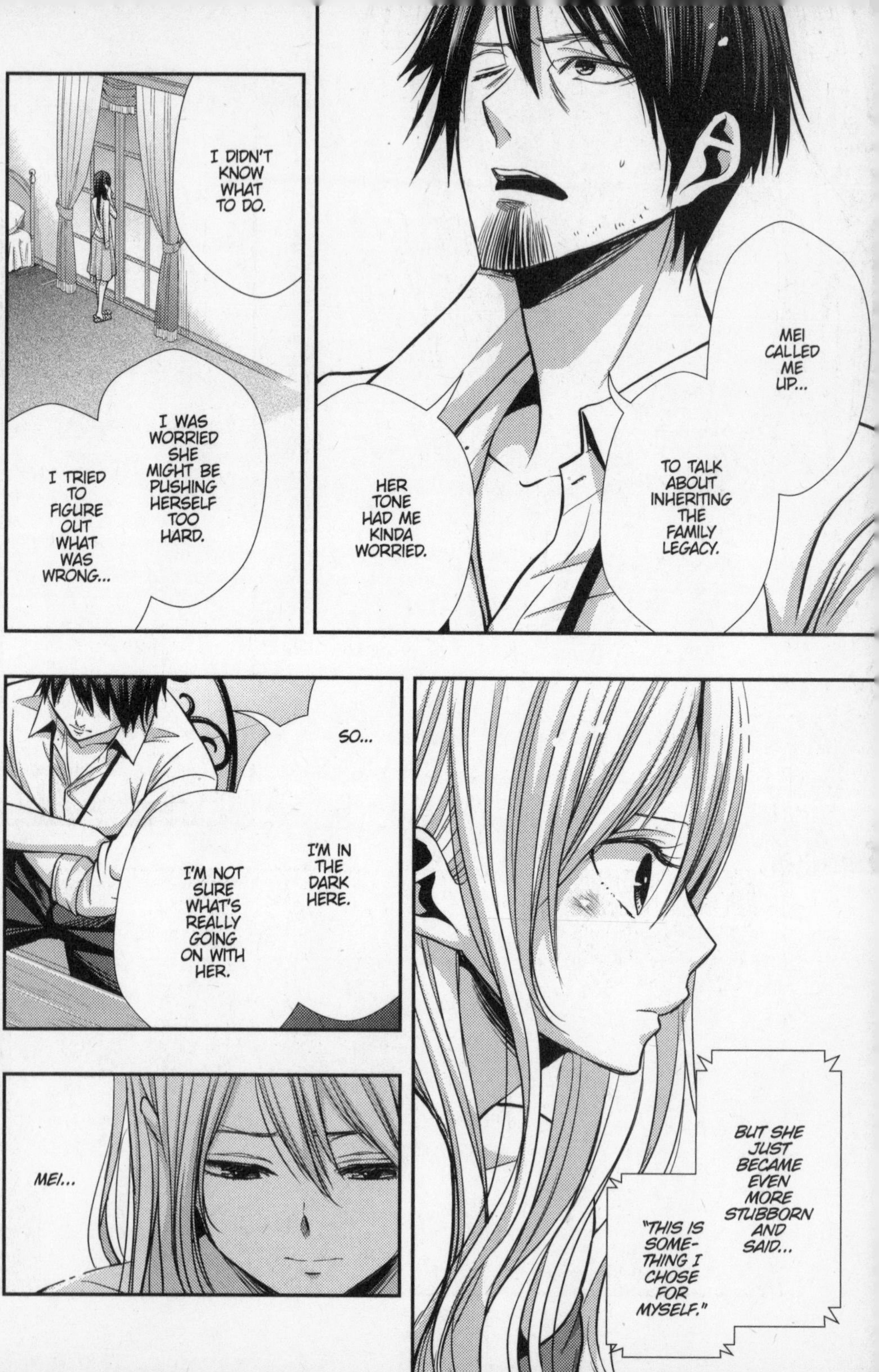
MEI CALLED ME UP...
TO TALK ABOUT INHERITING THE FAMILY LEGACY.
HER TONE HAD ME KINDA WORRIED.
I DIDN'T KNOW WHAT TO DO.
I WAS WORRIED SHE MIGHT BE PUSHING HERSELF TOO HARD.
I TRIED TO FIGURE OUT WHAT WAS WRONG...
BUT SHE JUST BECAME EVEN MORE STUBBORN AND SAID...
"THIS IS SOME-THING I CHOSE FOR MYSELF."
SO...
I'M IN THE DARK HERE.
I'M NOT SURE WHAT'S REALLY GOING ON WITH HER.
MEI...

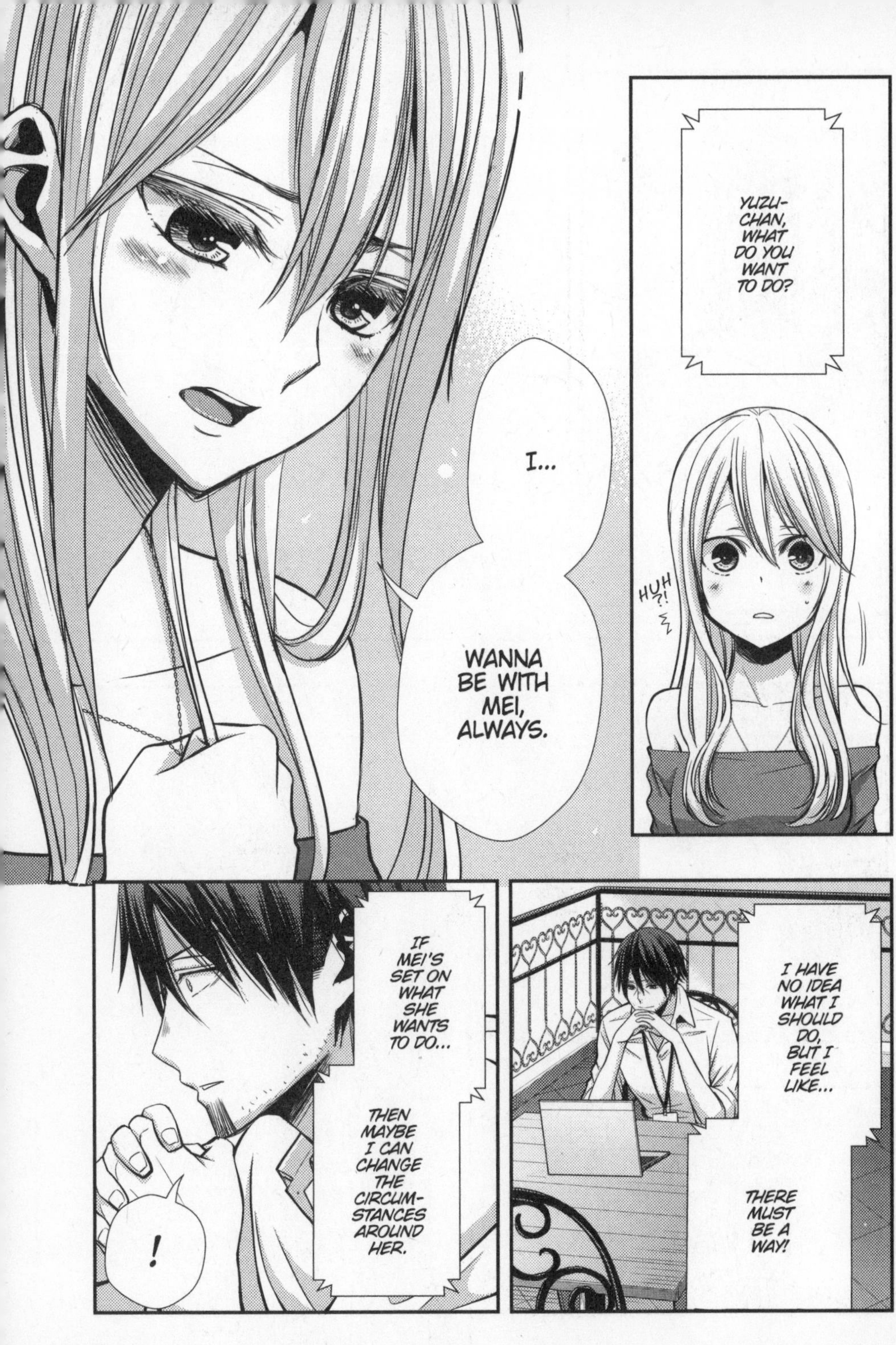
YUZU-CHAN, WHAT DO YOU WANT TO DO?
HUH?!
I...
WANNA BE WITH MEI, ALWAYS.
I HAVE NO IDEA WHAT I SHOULD DO, BUT I FEEL LIKE...
THERE MUST BE A WAY!
IF MEI'S SET ON WHAT SHE WANTS TO DO...
THEN MAYBE I CAN CHANGE THE CIRCUM-STANCES AROUND HER.
!

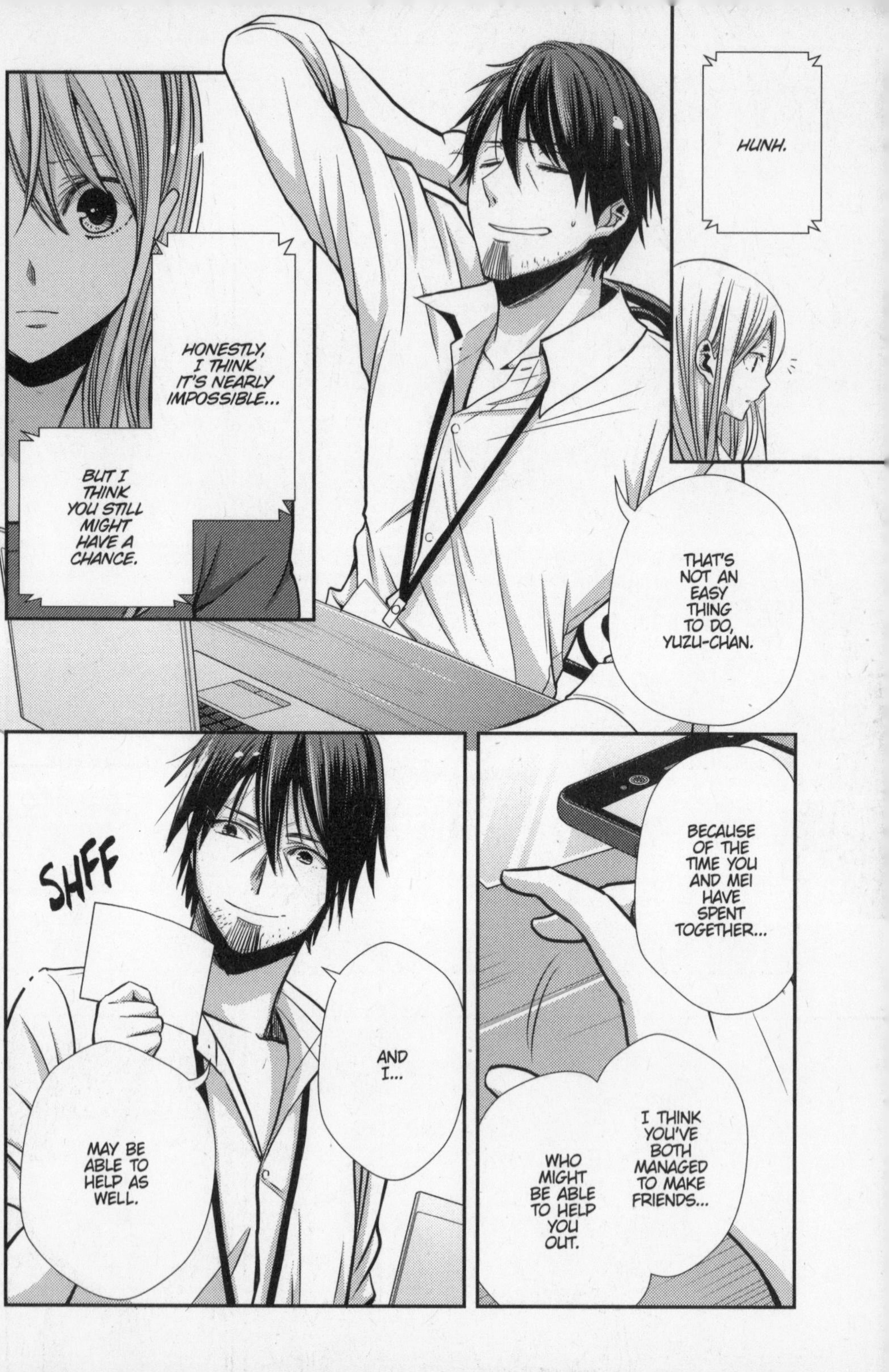
THAT'S NOT AN EASY THING TO DO, YUZU-CHAN.
HONESTLY, I THINK IT'S NEARLY IMPOSSIBLE...
BUT I THINK YOU STILL MIGHT HAVE A CHANCE.
HUNH.
BECAUSE OF THE TIME YOU AND MEI HAVE SPENT TOGETHER...
I THINK YOU'VE BOTH MANAGED TO MAKE FRIENDS...
WHO MIGHT BE ABLE TO HELP YOU OUT.
SHFF
AND I...
MAY BE ABLE TO HELP AS WELL.

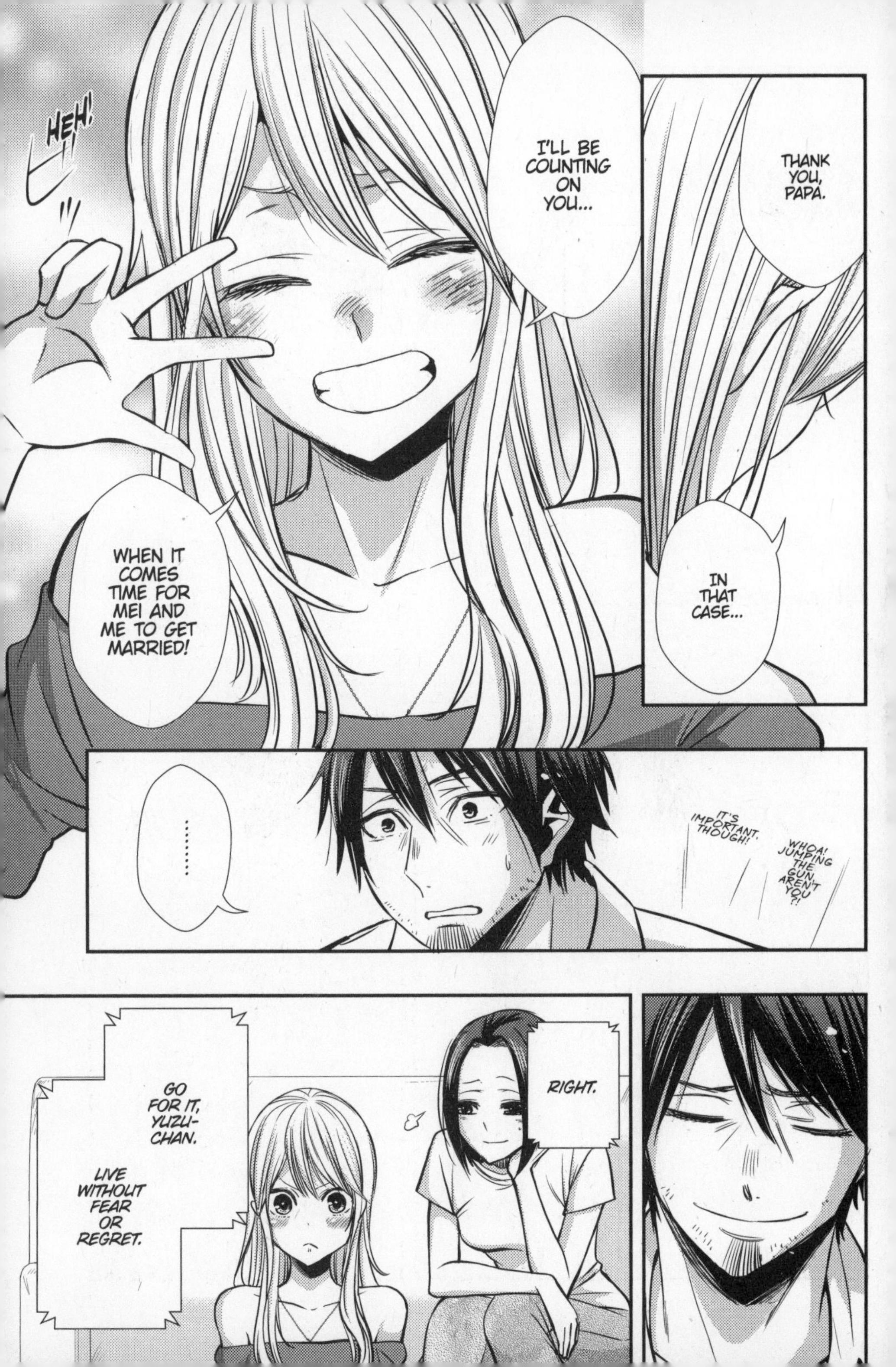
THANK YOU, PAPA.
IN THAT CASE...
I'LL BE COUNTING ON YOU...
HEH!
WHEN IT COMES TIME FOR MEI AND ME TO GET MARRIED!
WHOA! JUMPING THE GUN, AREN'T YOU?!
IT'S IMPORTANT, THOUGH!
......
RIGHT.
GO FOR IT, YUZU-CHAN.
LIVE WITHOUT FEAR OR REGRET.

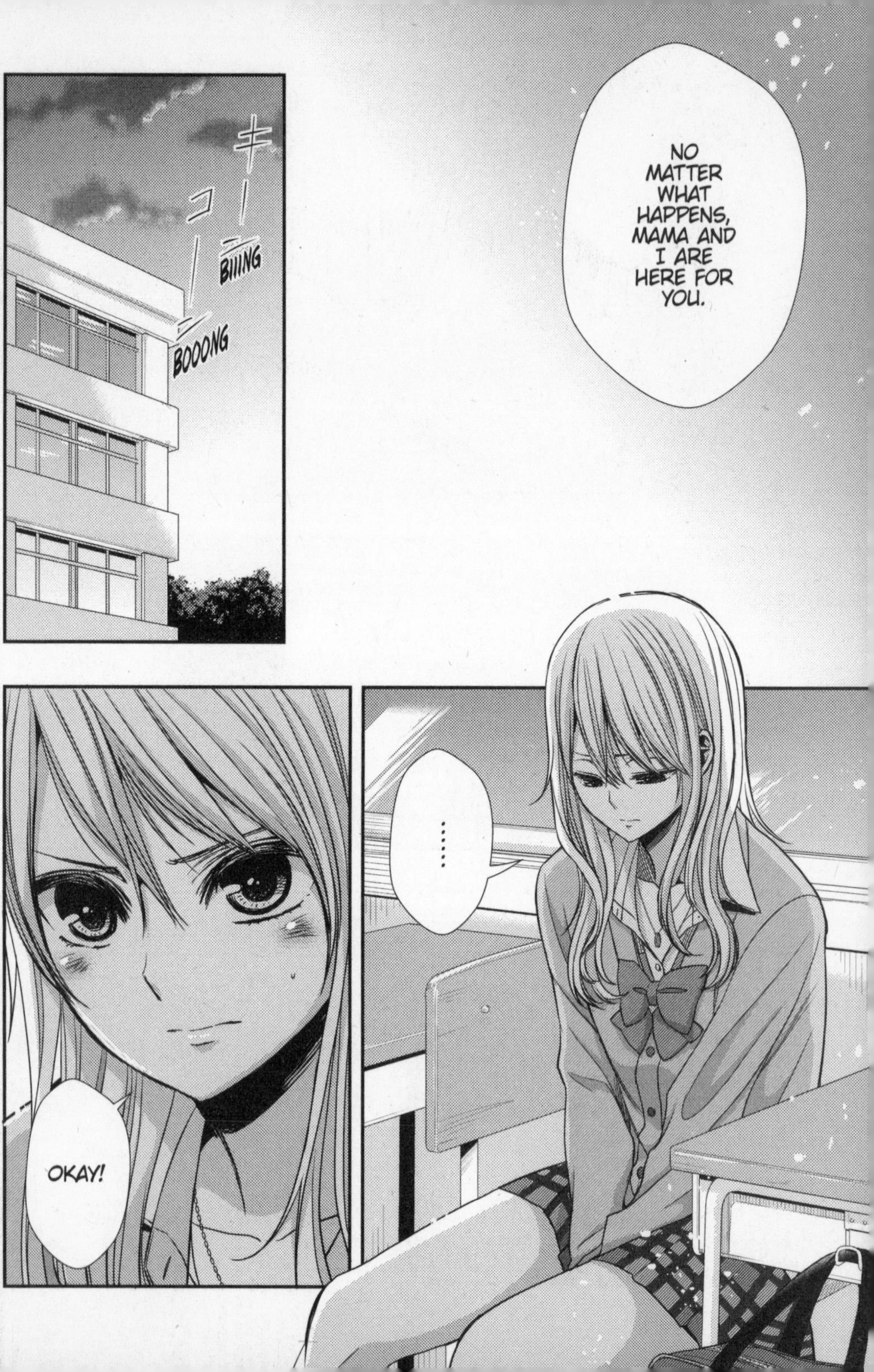
NO MATTER WHAT HAPPENS, MAMA AND I ARE HERE FOR YOU.
BIIING
BOOONG
......
OKAY!

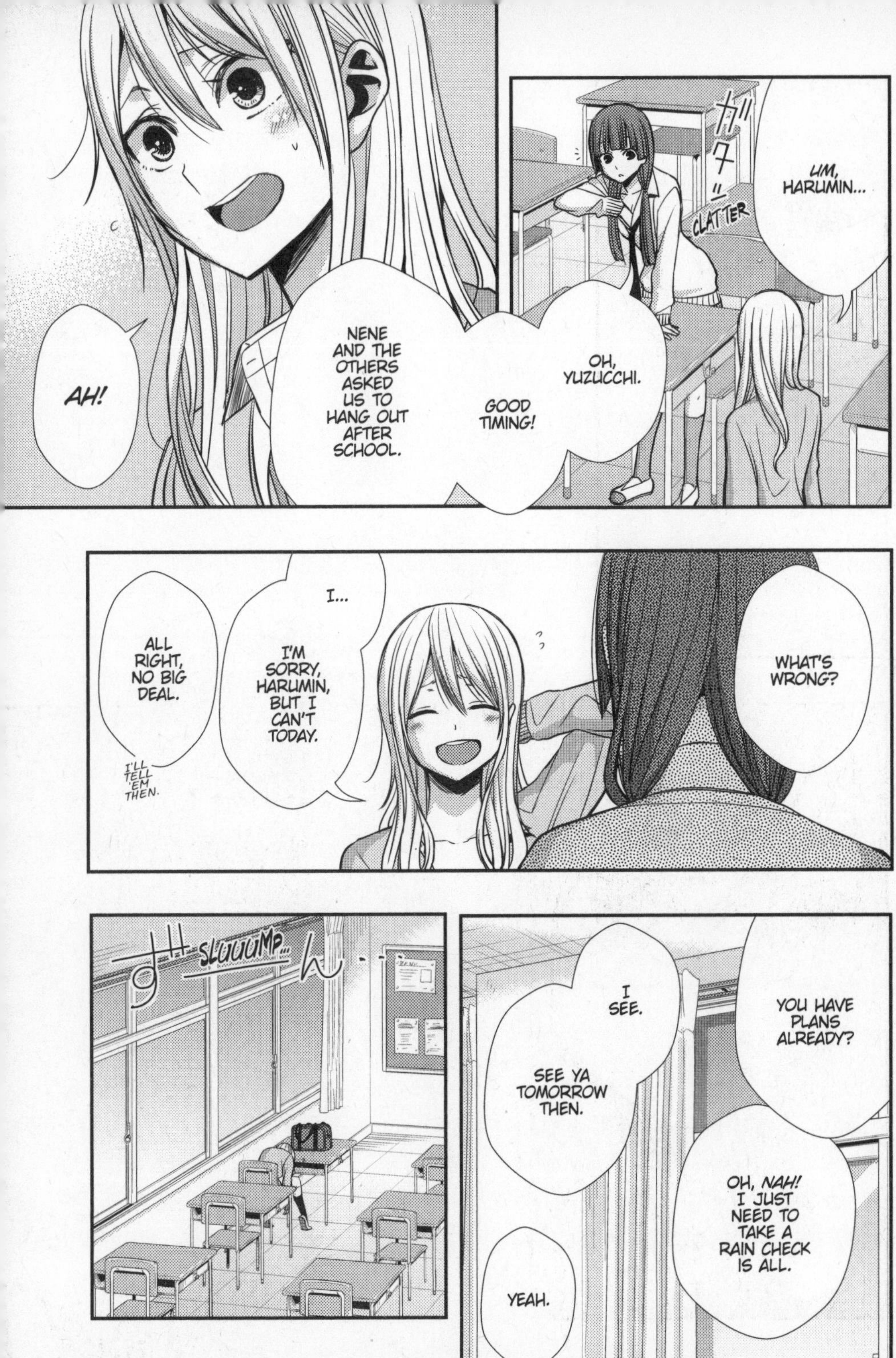
UM, HARUMIN...
CLATTER
OH, YUZUCCHI.
GOOD TIMING!
NENE AND THE OTHERS ASKED US TO HANG OUT AFTER SCHOOL.
AH!
WHAT'S WRONG?
I...
I'M SORRY, HARUMIN, BUT I CAN'T TODAY.
ALL RIGHT, NO BIG DEAL.
I'LL TELL 'EM THEN.
YOU HAVE PLANS ALREADY?
I SEE.
OH, NAH! I JUST NEED TO TAKE A RAIN CHECK IS ALL.
SEE YA TOMORROW THEN.
YEAH.
SLUUUMP...

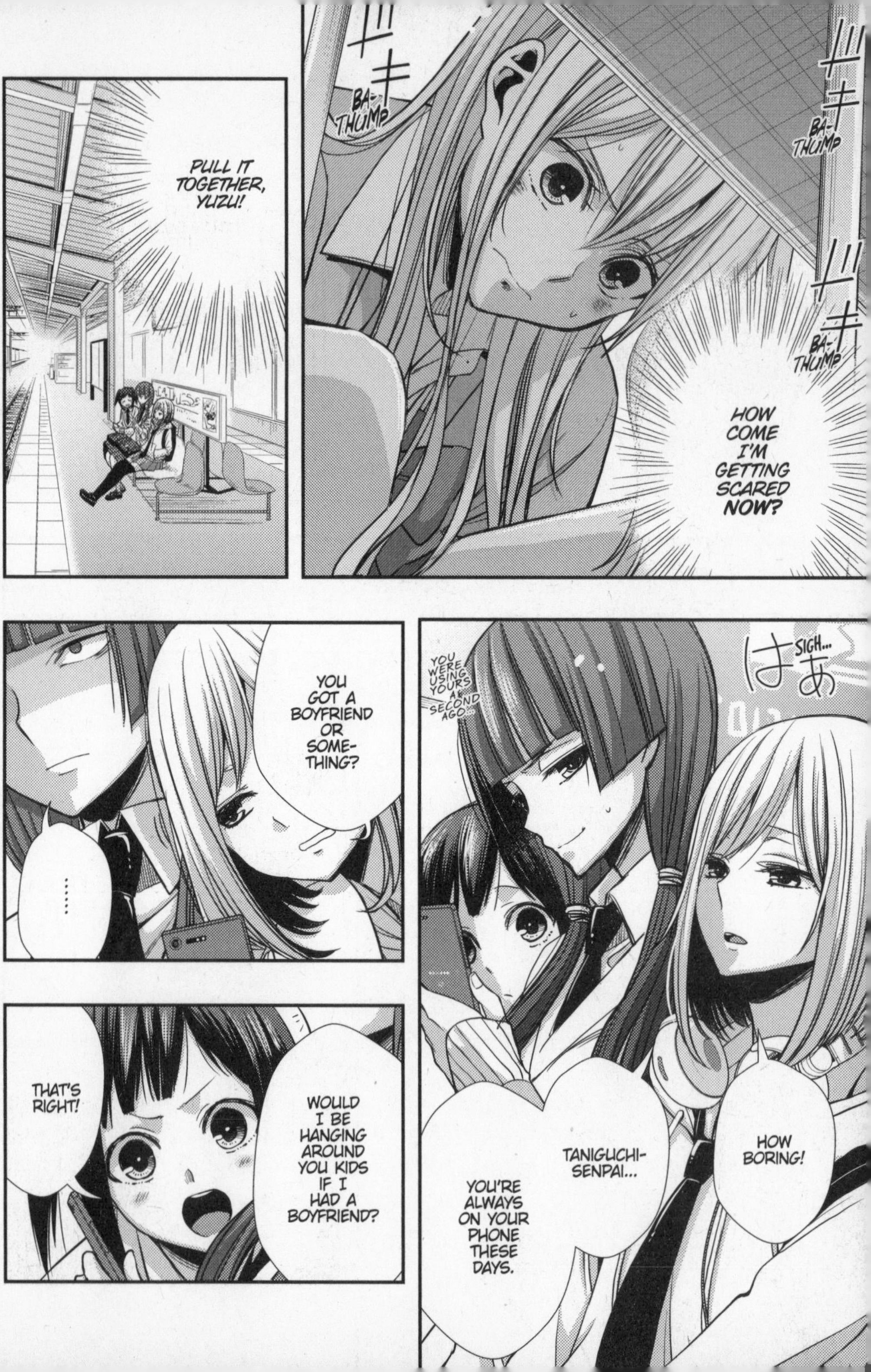

ドキ
BA-THUMP
ドキ
BA-THUMP
ドキ
BA-THUMP
HOW COME I'M GETTING SCARED NOW?
PULL IT TOGETHER, YUZU!
はあ
SIGH...
YOU WERE USING YOURS A SECOND AGO...
HOW BORING!
TANIGUCHI-SENPAI...
YOU'RE ALWAYS ON YOUR PHONE THESE DAYS.
YOU GOT A BOYFRIEND OR SOMETHING?
......
WOULD I BE HANGING AROUND YOU KIDS IF I HAD A BOYFRIEND?
THAT'S RIGHT!

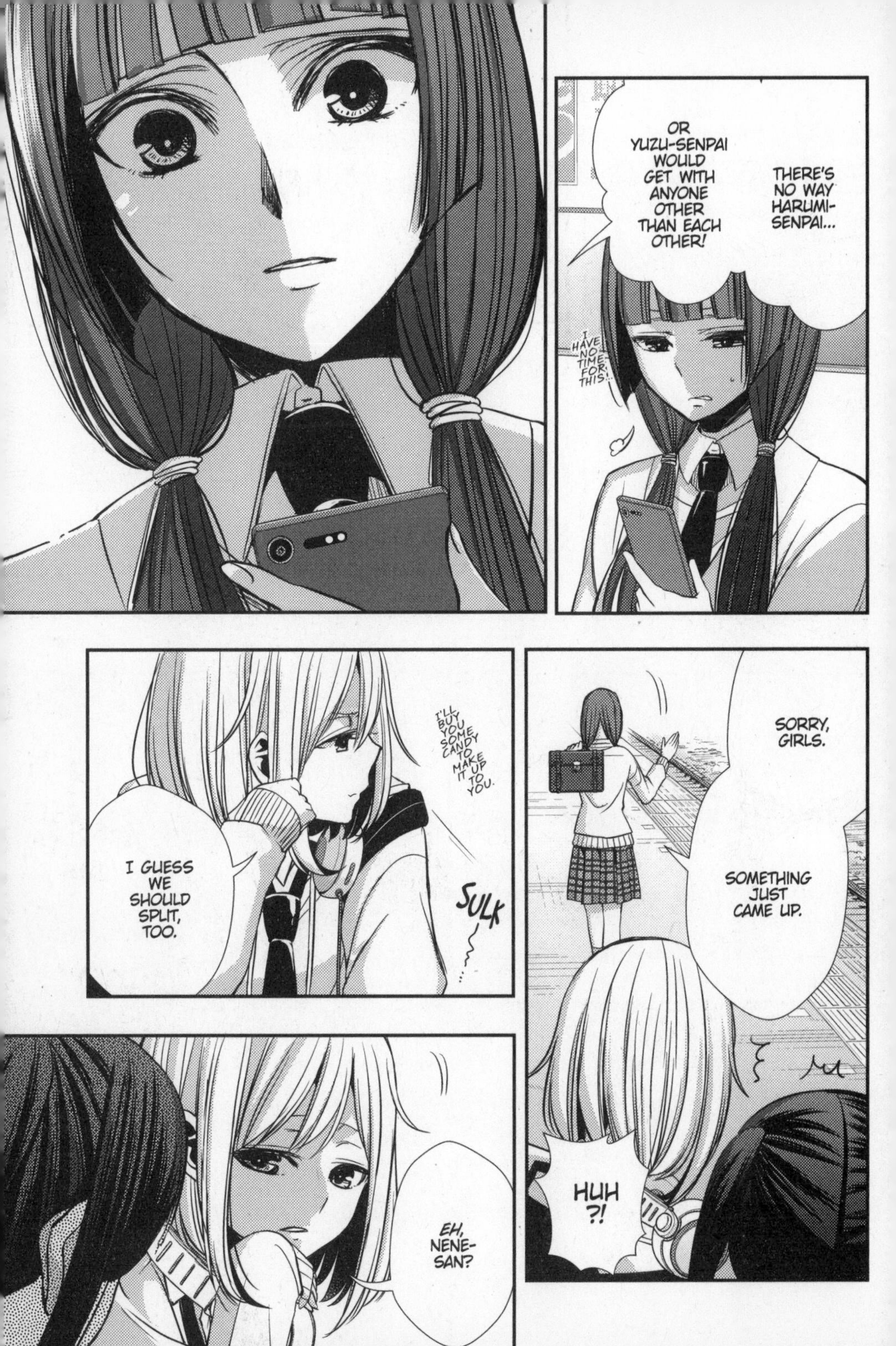
THERE'S NO WAY HARUMI-SENPAI...
OR YUZU-SENPAI WOULD GET WITH ANYONE OTHER THAN EACH OTHER!
I HAVE NO TIME FOR THIS...
SORRY, GIRLS.
SOMETHING JUST CAME UP.
HUH ?!
I'LL BUY YOU SOME CANDY TO MAKE IT UP TO YOU.
I GUESS WE SHOULD SPLIT, TOO.
SULK
EH, NENE-SAN?

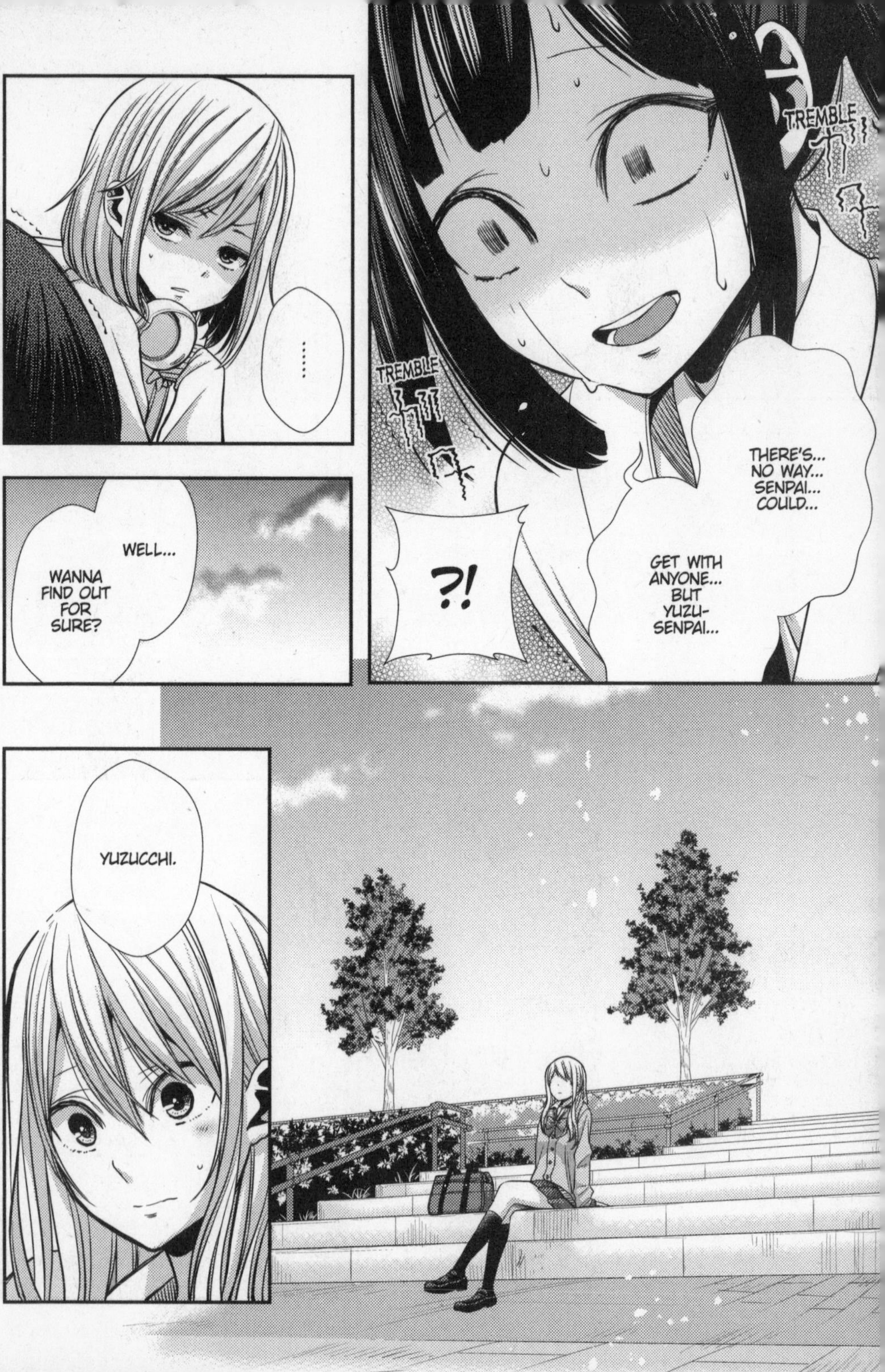
TREMBLE
TREMBLE
THERE'S... NO WAY... SENPAI... COULD...
GET WITH ANYONE... BUT YUZU-SENPAI...
?!
......
WELL... WANNA FIND OUT FOR SURE?
YUZUCCHI.

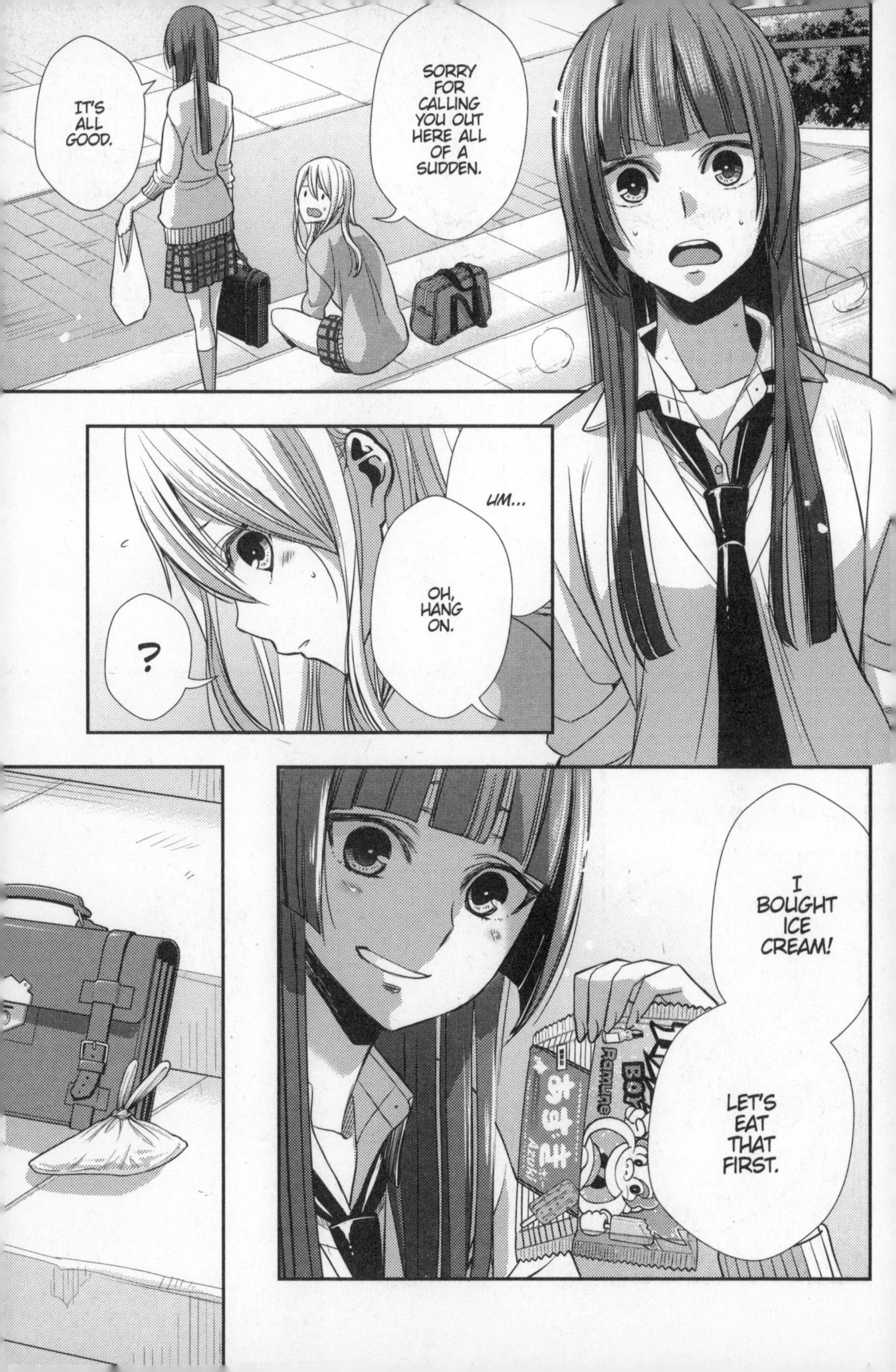
SORRY FOR CALLING YOU OUT HERE ALL OF A SUDDEN.
IT'S ALL GOOD.
UM...
OH, HANG ON.
?
I BOUGHT ICE CREAM!
LET'S EAT THAT FIRST.

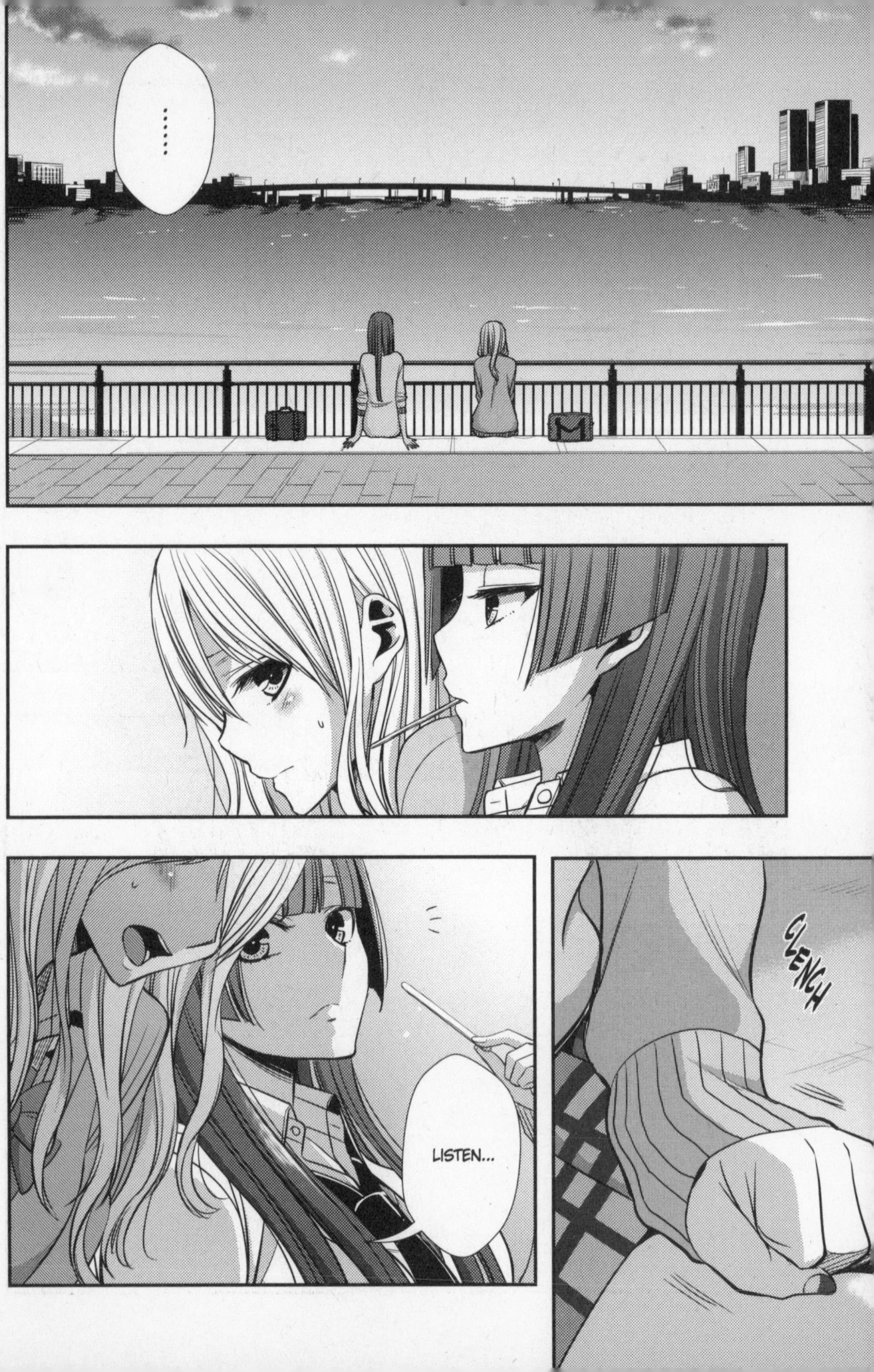
......
CLENCH
LISTEN...

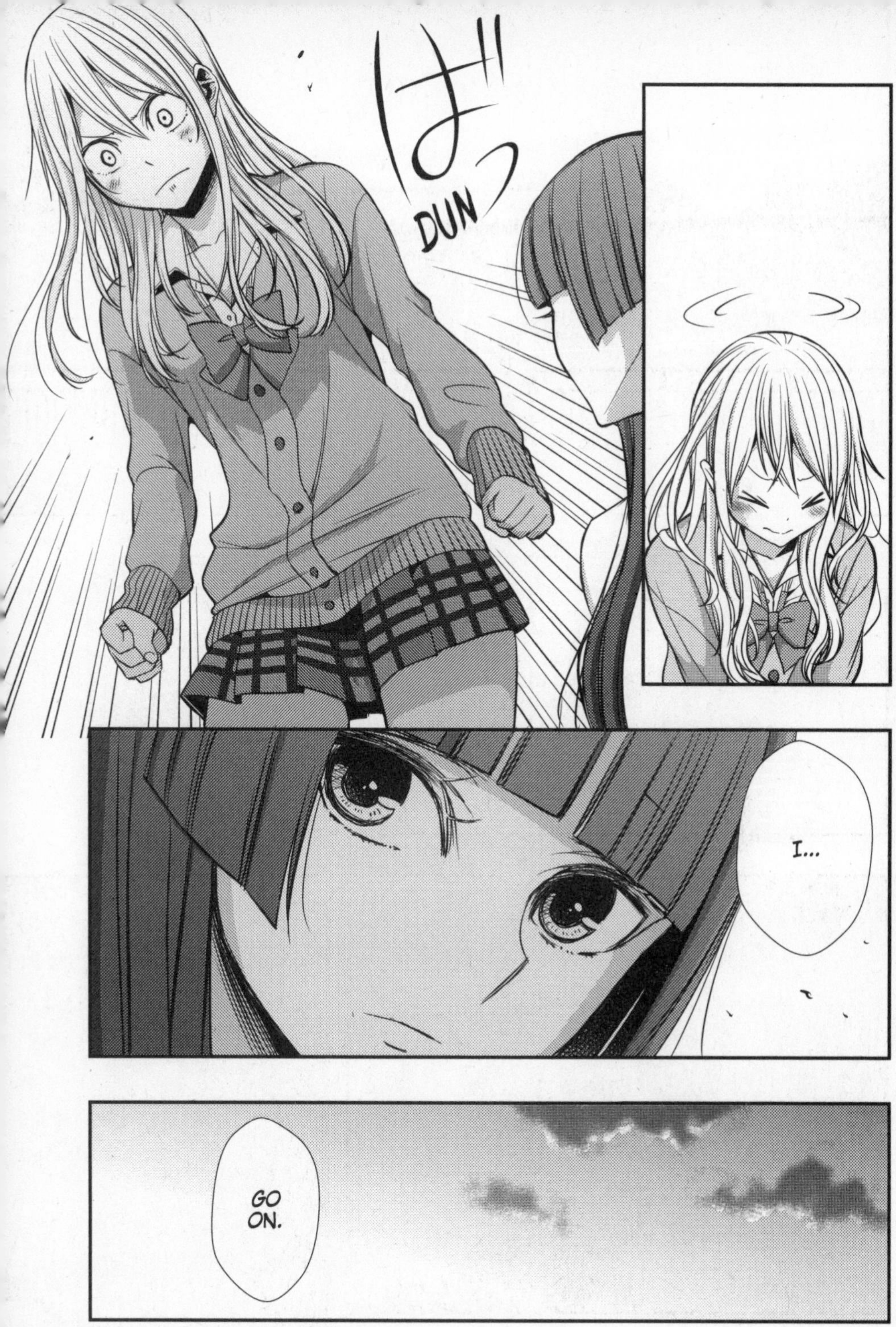
DUN
I...
GO ON.

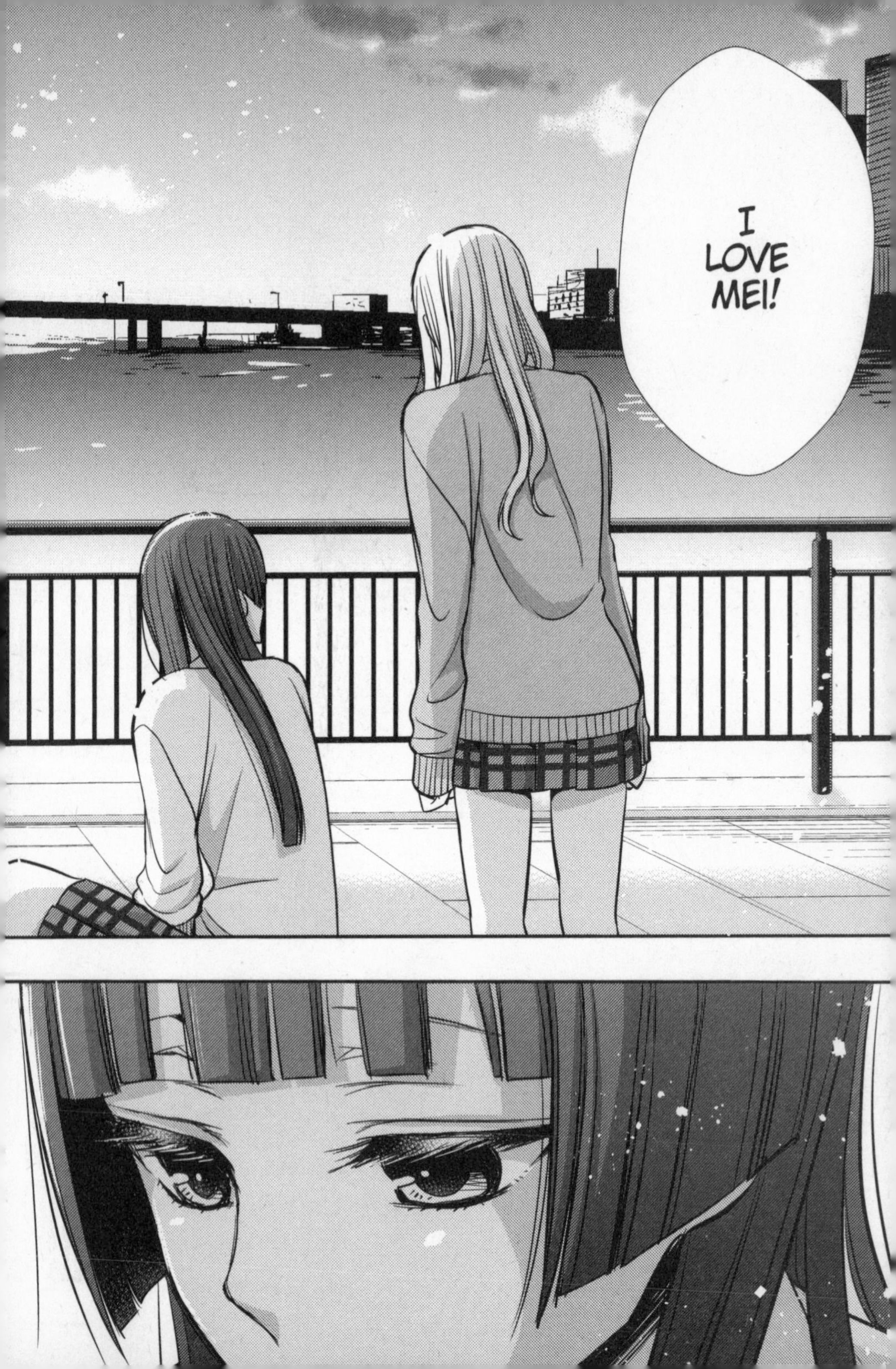
I LOVE MEI!

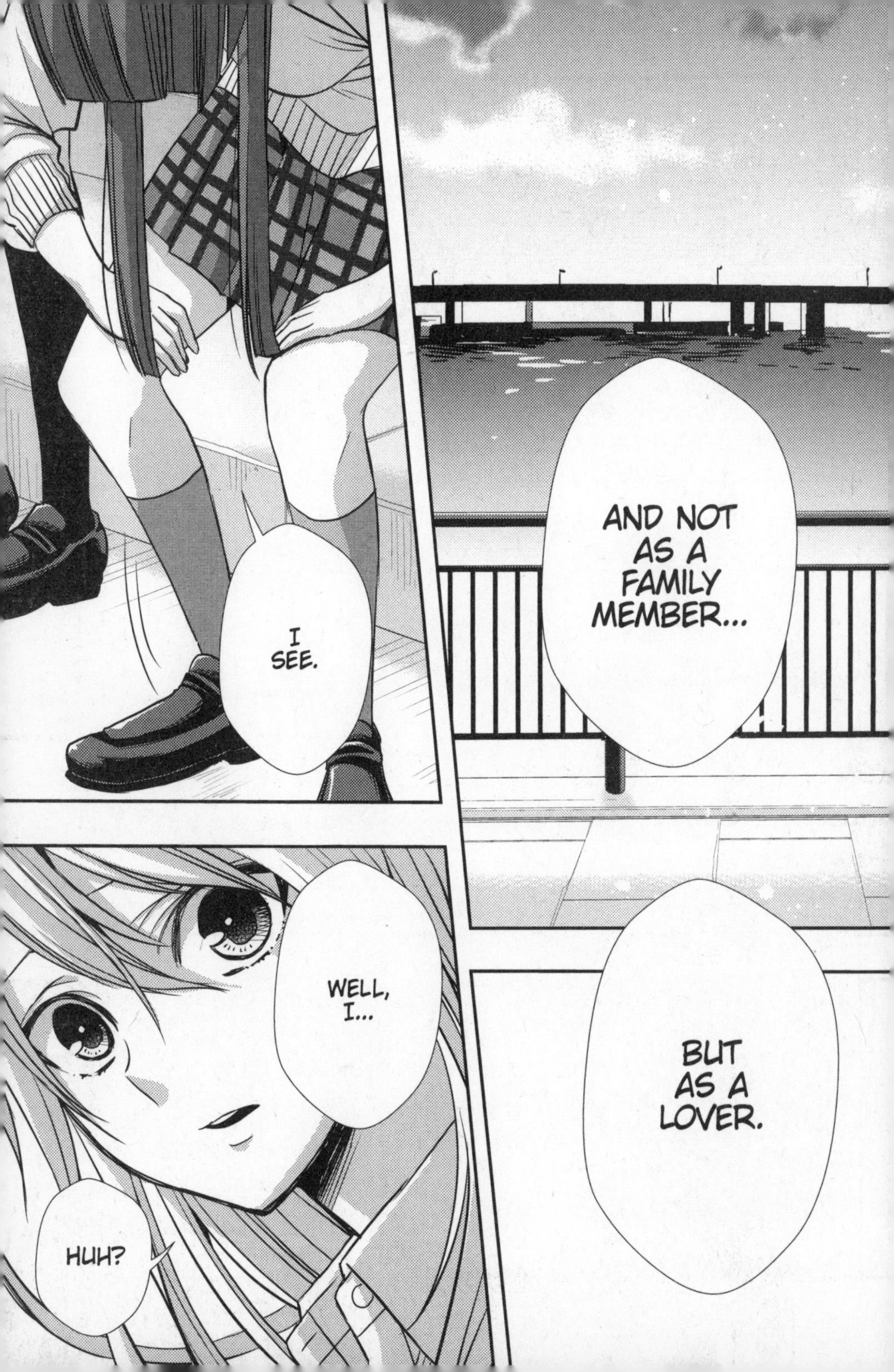
AND NOT AS A FAMILY MEMBER...
I SEE.
BUT AS A LOVER.
WELL, I...
HUH?

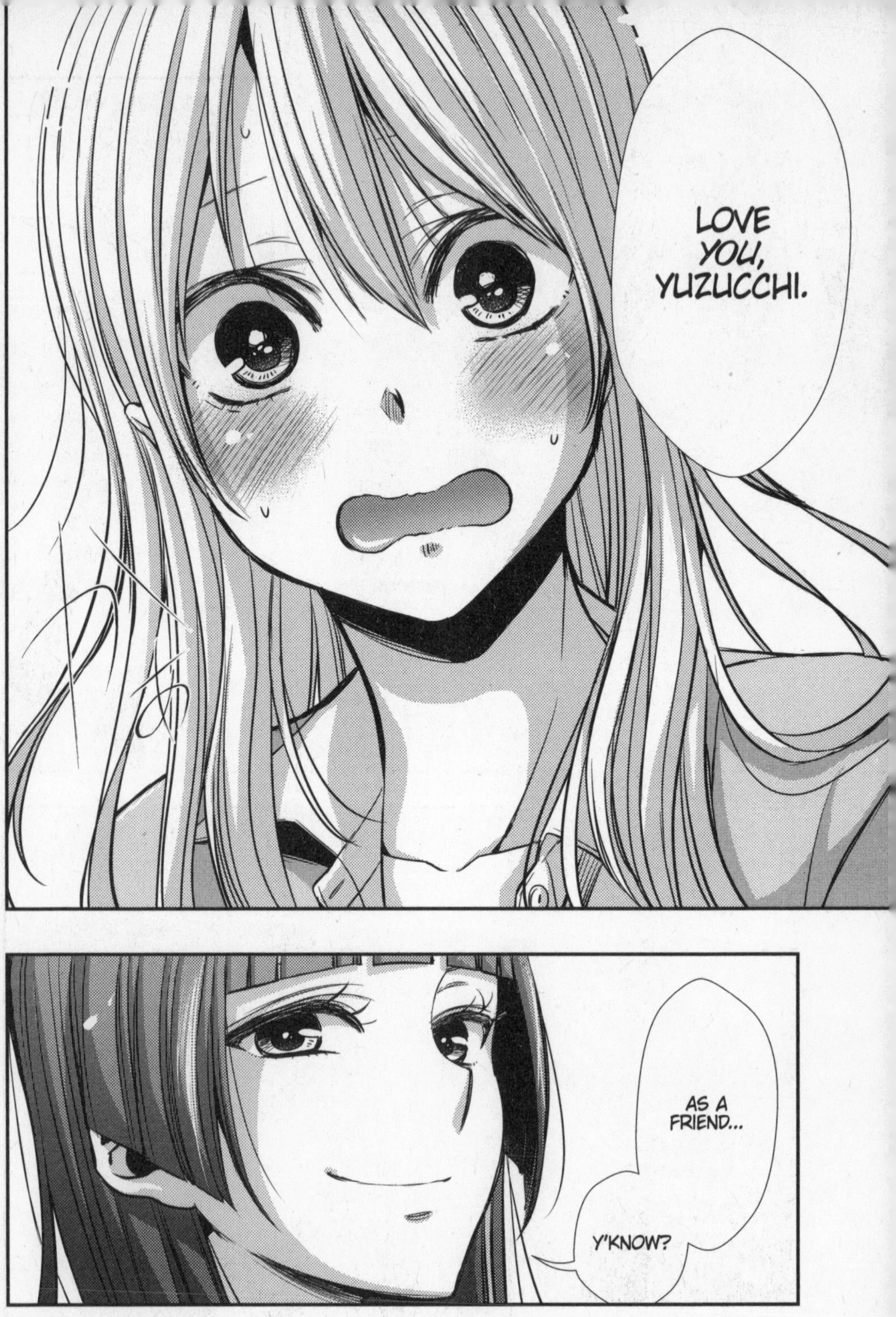
LOVE YOU, YUZUCCHI.
AS A FRIEND...
Y'KNOW?

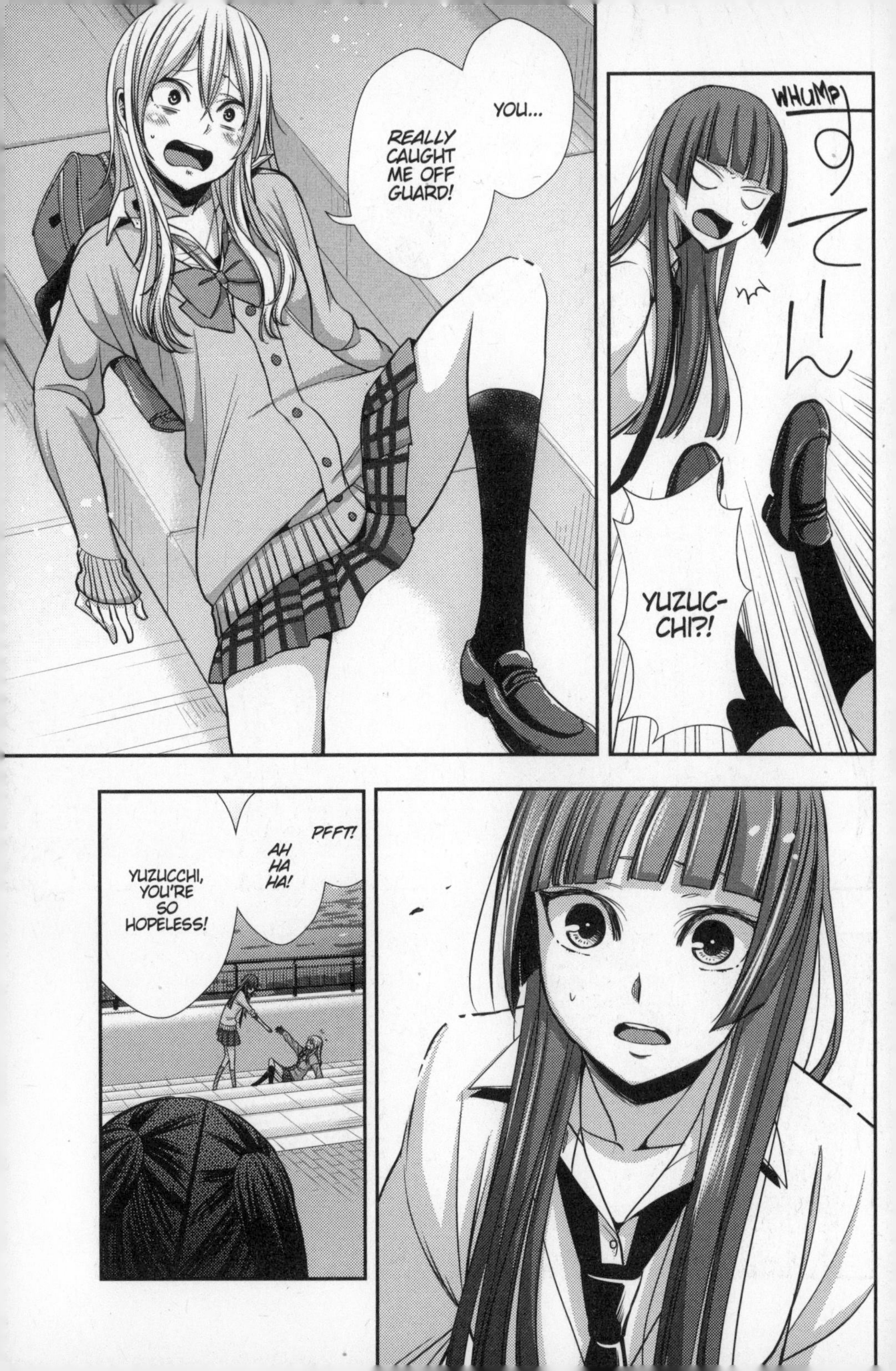
WHUMP
YUZUC-CHI?!
YOU...
REALLY CAUGHT ME OFF GUARD!
PFFT!
AH HA HA!
YUZUCCHI, YOU'RE SO HOPELESS!

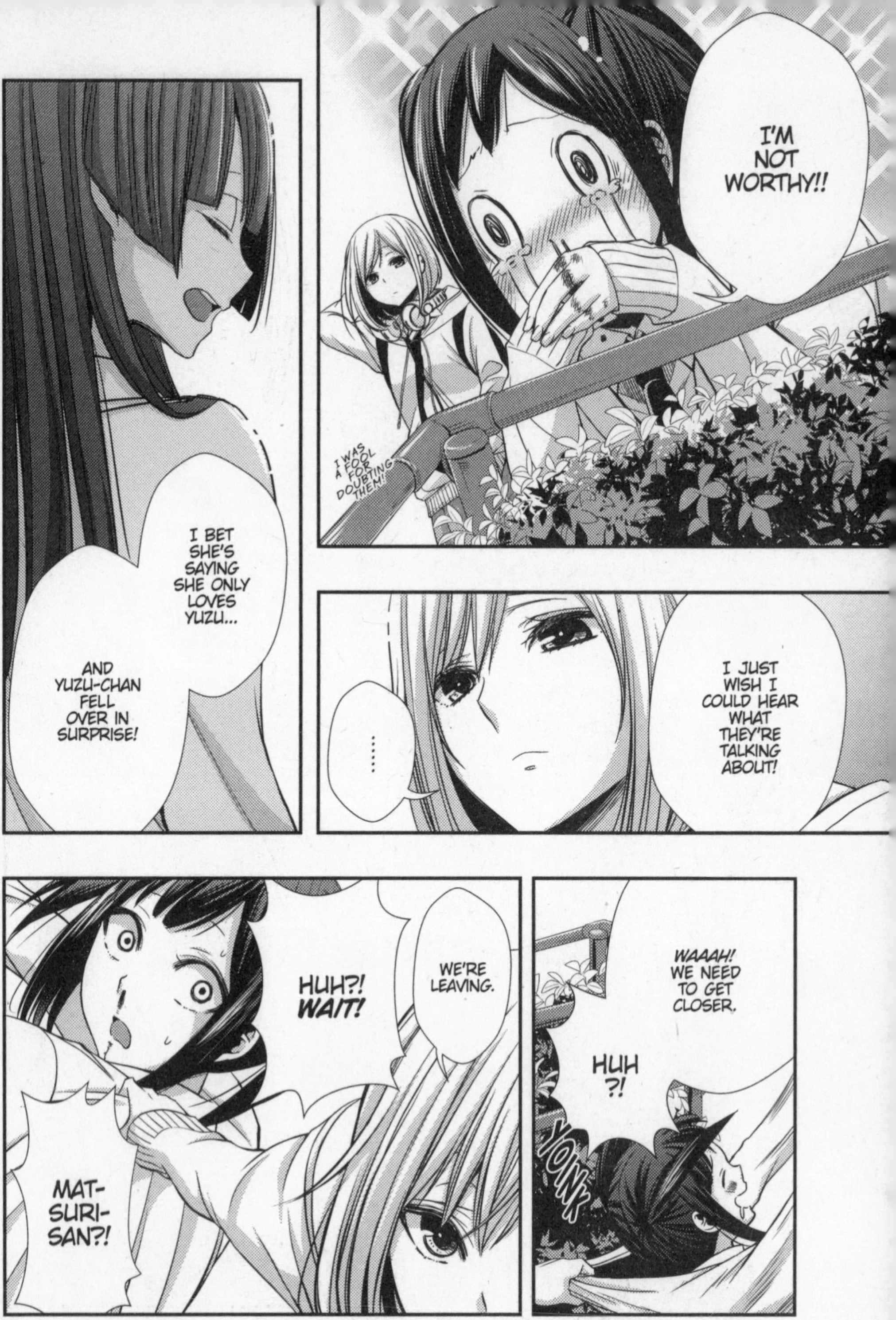
I'M NOT WORTHY!!
I WAS A FOOL FOR DOUBTING THEM!
I JUST WISH I COULD HEAR WHAT THEY'RE TALKING ABOUT!
......
I BET SHE'S SAYING SHE ONLY LOVES YUZU...
AND YUZU-CHAN FELL OVER IN SURPRISE!
WAAAH! WE NEED TO GET CLOSER.
HUH ?!
YONK
WE'RE LEAVING.
HUH?! WAIT!
MAT-SURI-SAN?!

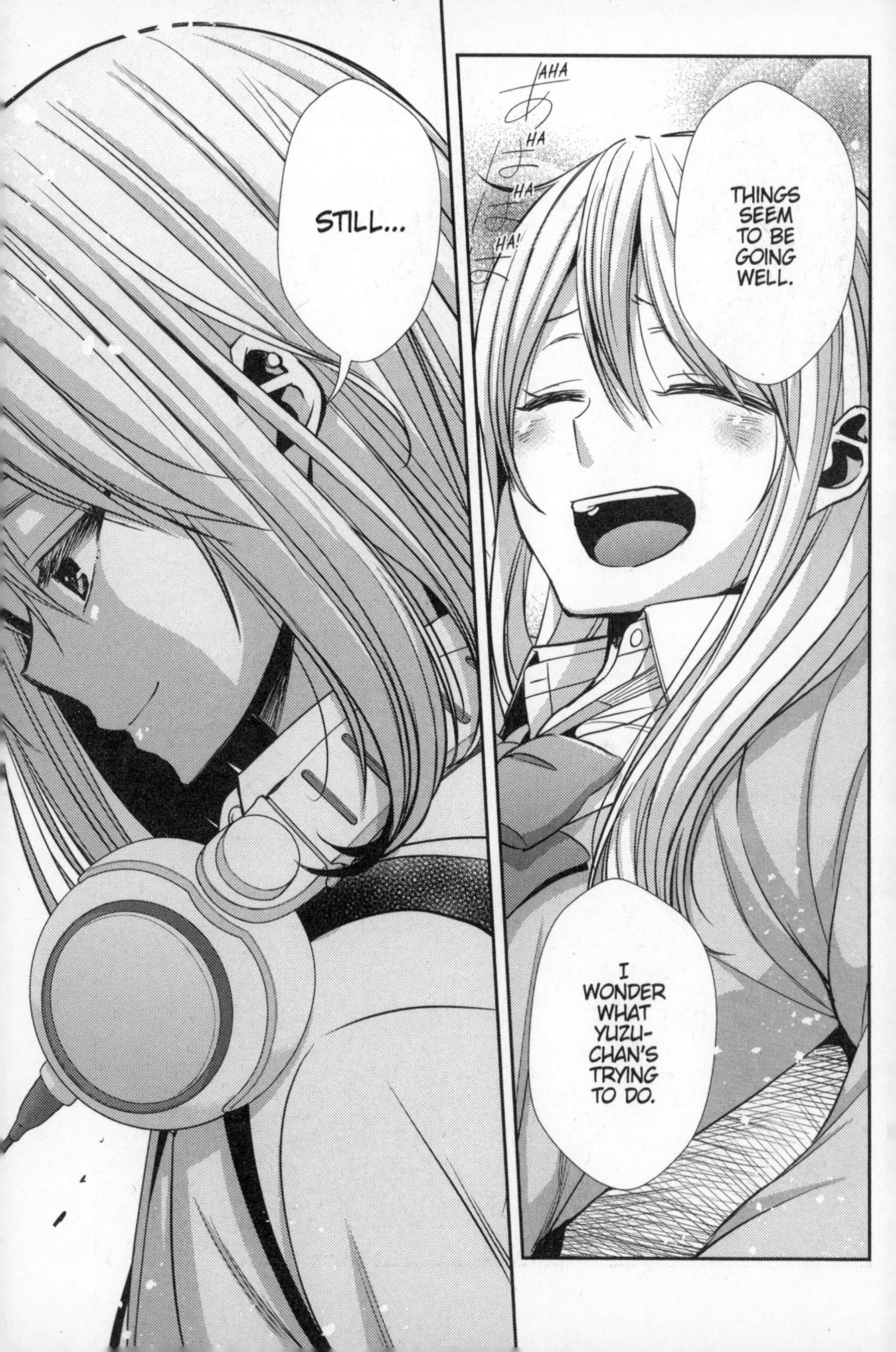
AHA HA HA HA!
THINGS SEEM TO BE GOING WELL.
I WONDER WHAT YUZU-CHAN'S TRYING TO DO.
STILL...

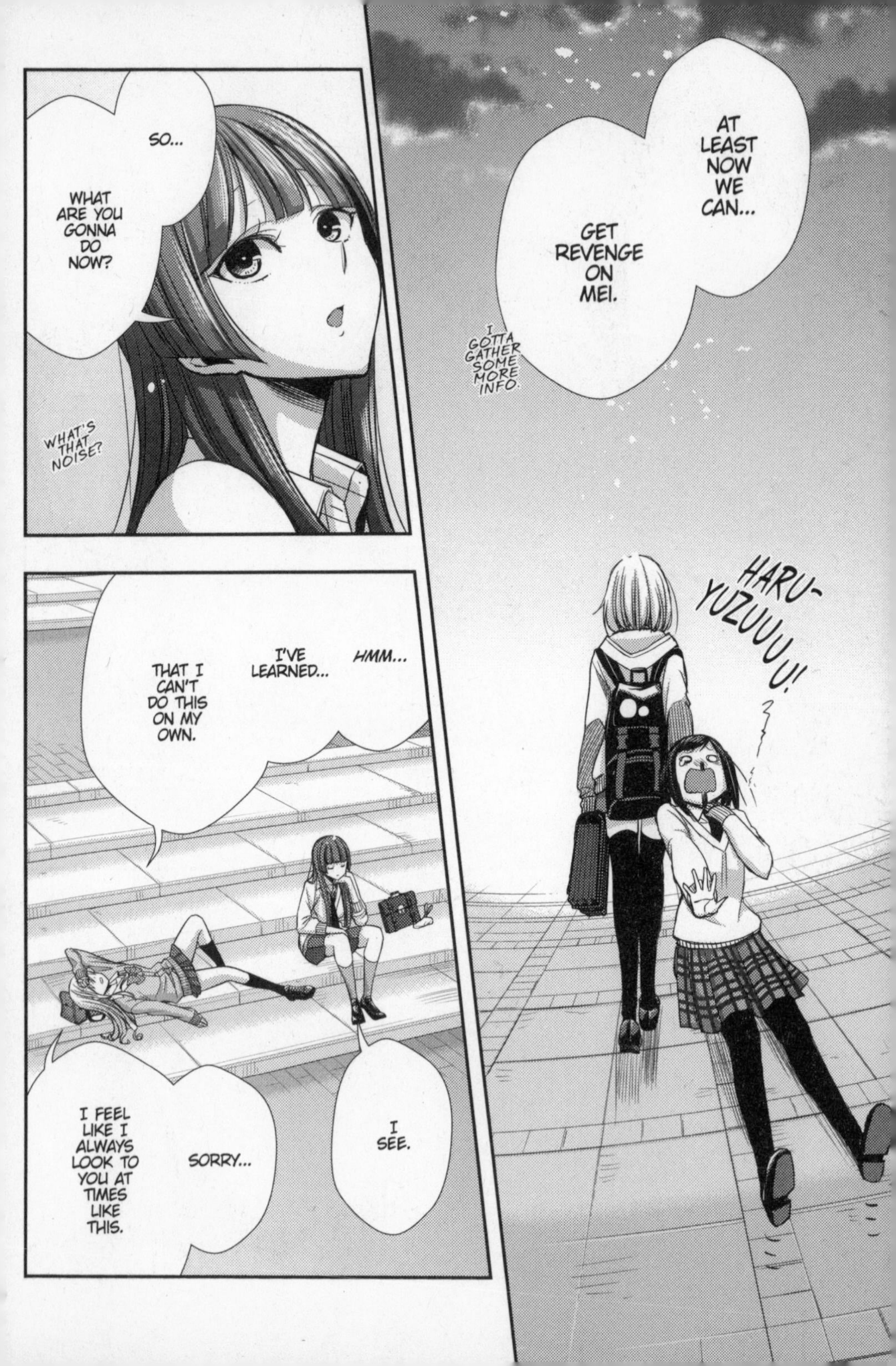
AT LEAST NOW WE CAN...
GET REVENGE ON MEI.
I GOTTA GATHER SOME MORE INFO.
HARU-YUZUUUUU!
SO...
WHAT ARE YOU GONNA DO NOW?
WHAT'S THAT NOISE?
HMM...
I'VE LEARNED...
THAT I CAN'T DO THIS ON MY OWN.
I SEE.
SORRY...
I FEEL LIKE I ALWAYS LOOK TO YOU AT TIMES LIKE THIS.

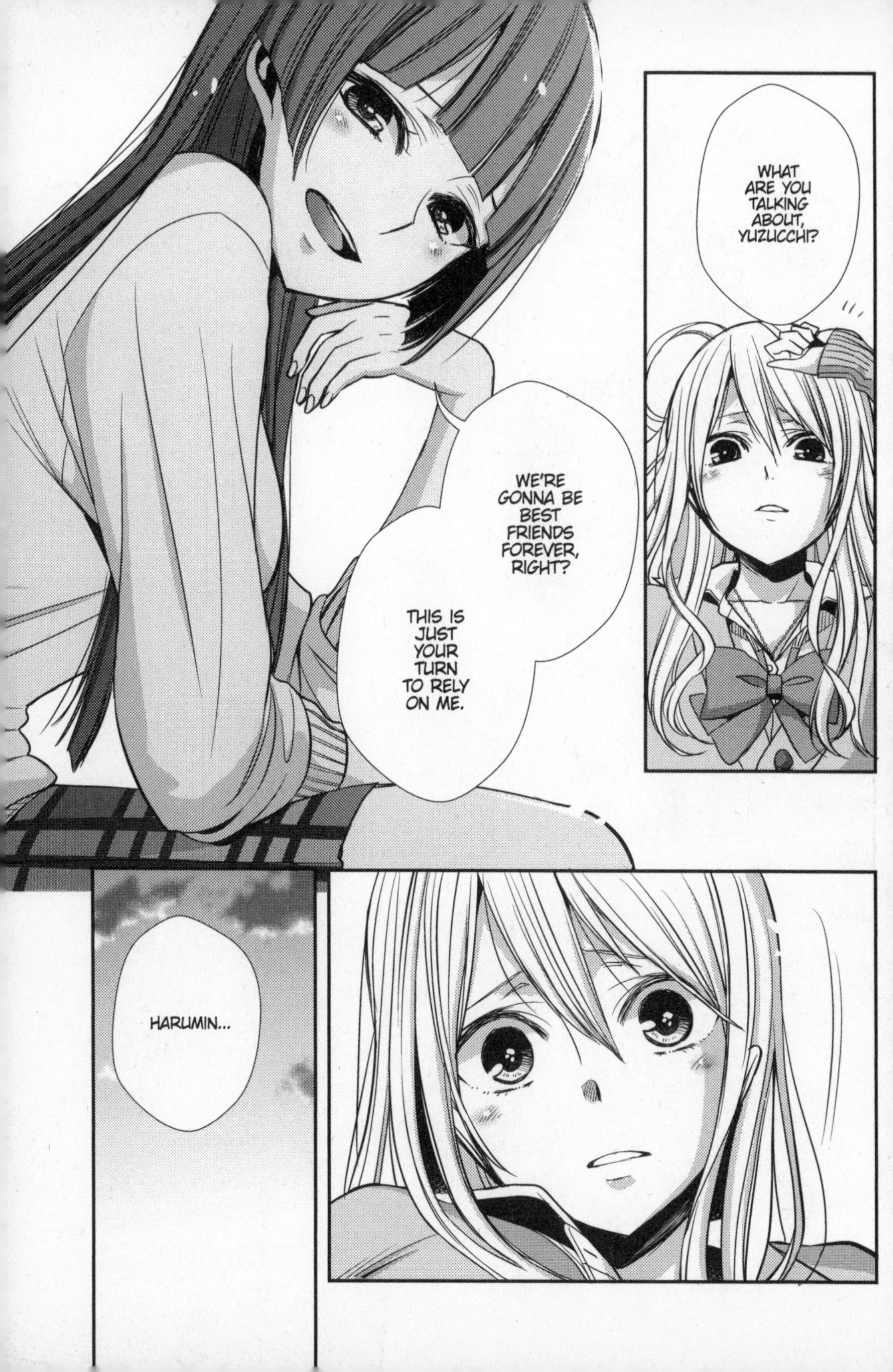
WHAT ARE YOU TALKING ABOUT, YUZUCCHI?
WE'RE GONNA BE BEST FRIENDS FOREVER, RIGHT?
THIS IS JUST YOUR TURN TO RELY ON ME.
HARUMIN...

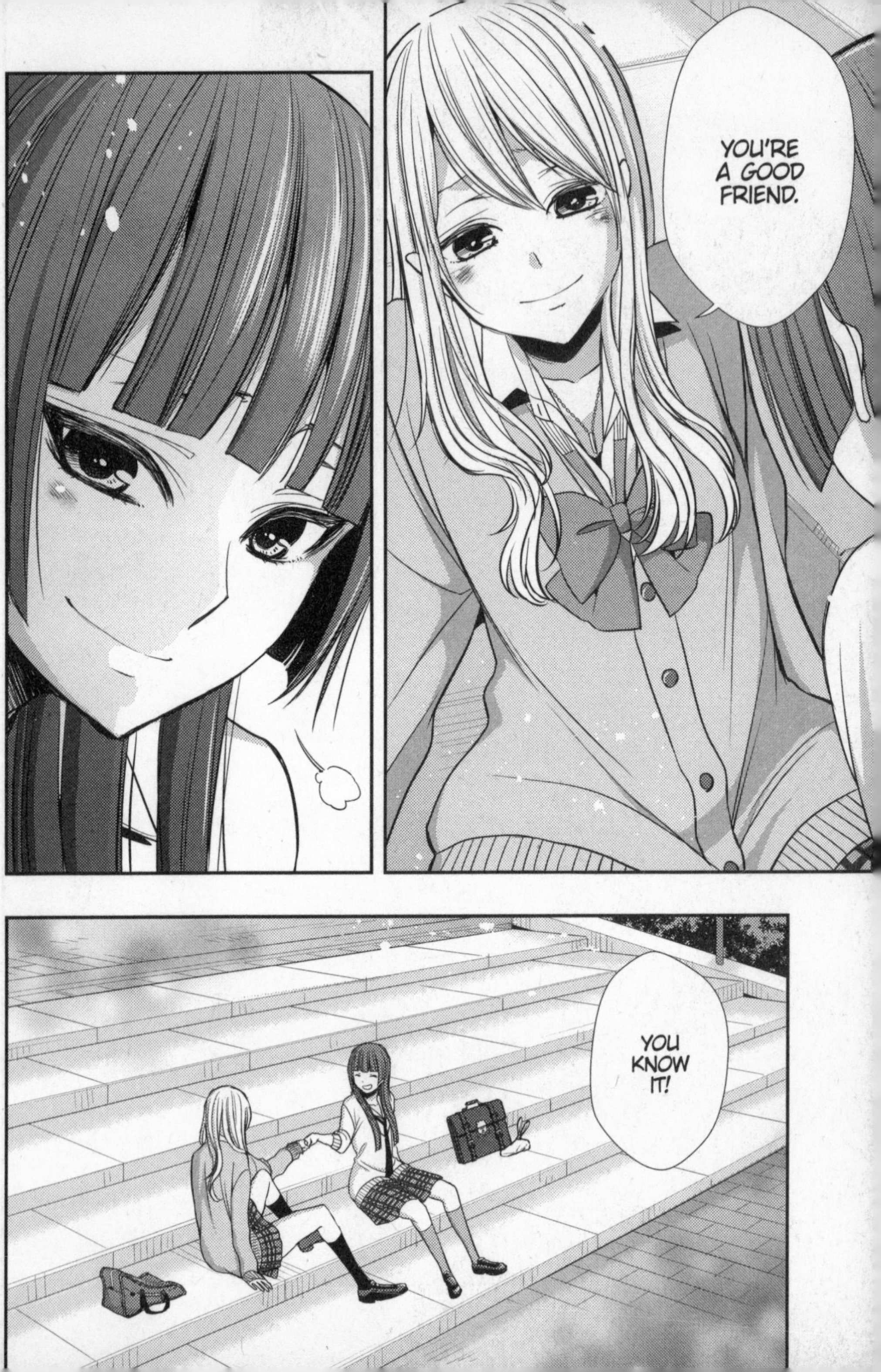
YOU'RE A GOOD FRIEND.
YOU KNOW IT!

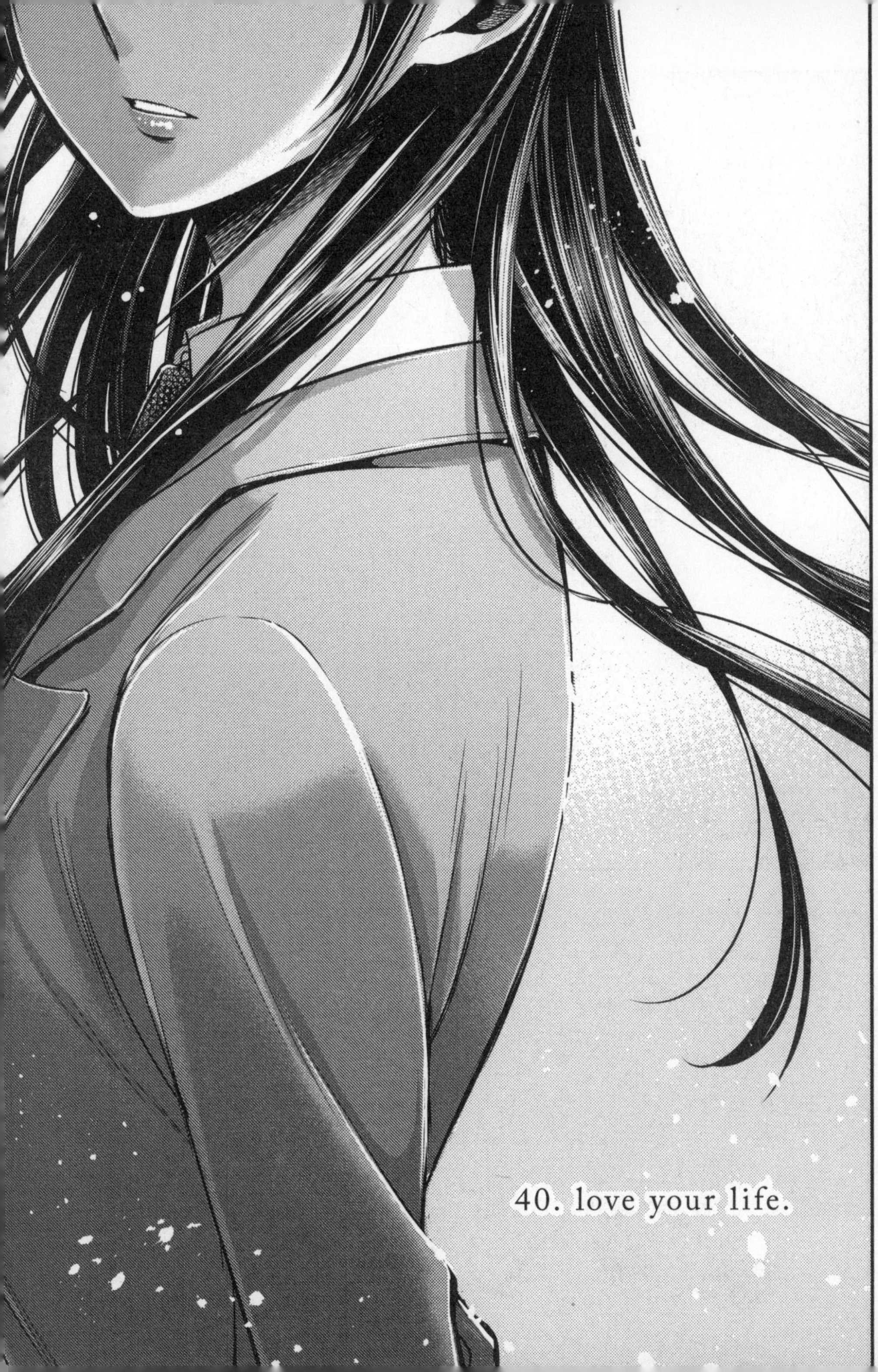
40. love your life.

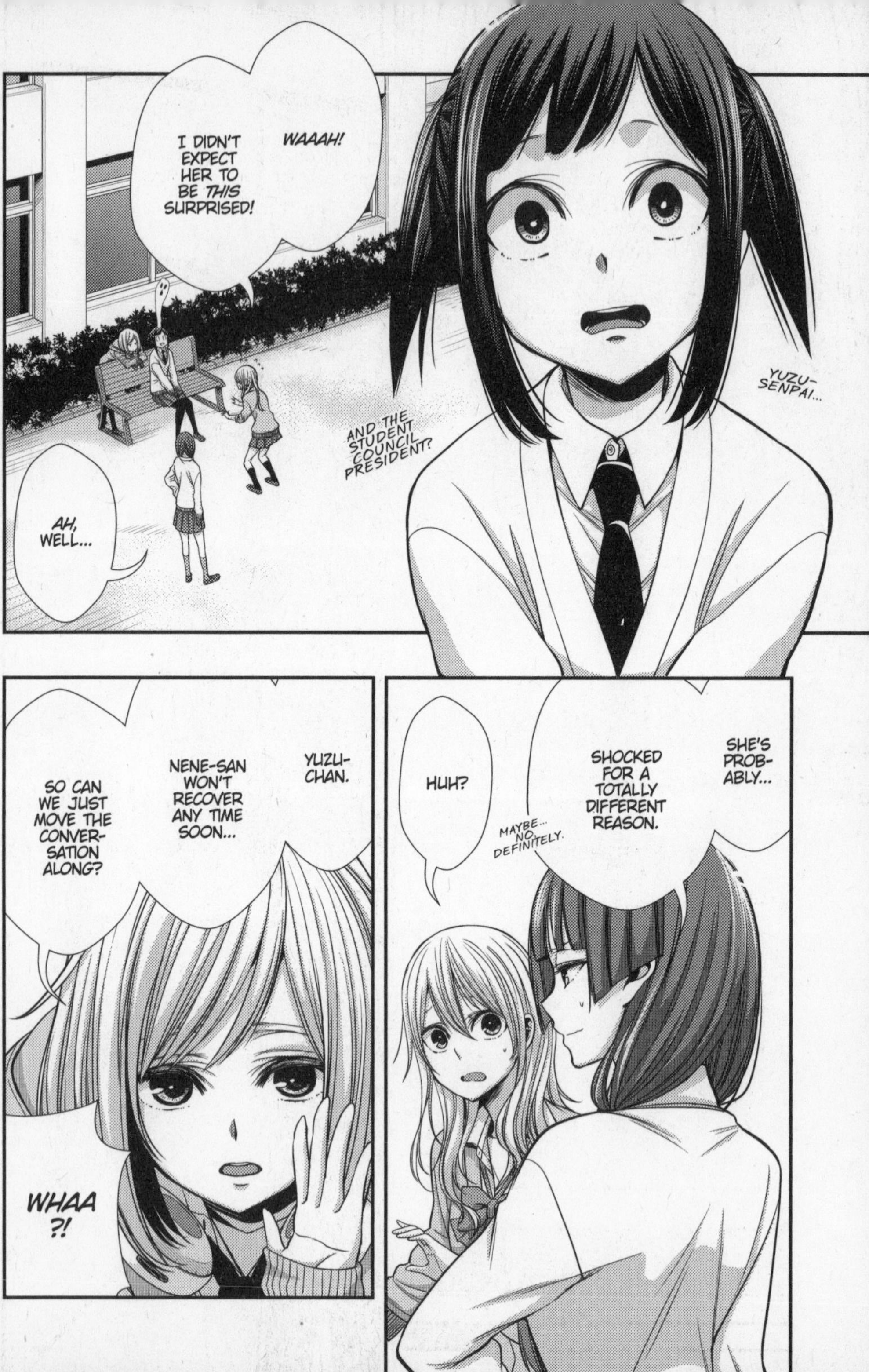
YUZU-SENPAI...
AND THE STUDENT COUNCIL PRESIDENT?
WAAAH!
I DIDN'T EXPECT HER TO BE *THIS* SURPRISED!
AH, WELL...
SHE'S PROBABLY...
SHOCKED FOR A TOTALLY DIFFERENT REASON.
HUH?
MAYBE... NO, DEFINITELY.
YUZU-CHAN.
NENE-SAN WON'T RECOVER ANY TIME SOON...
SO CAN WE JUST MOVE THE CONVERSATION ALONG?
WHAA ?!

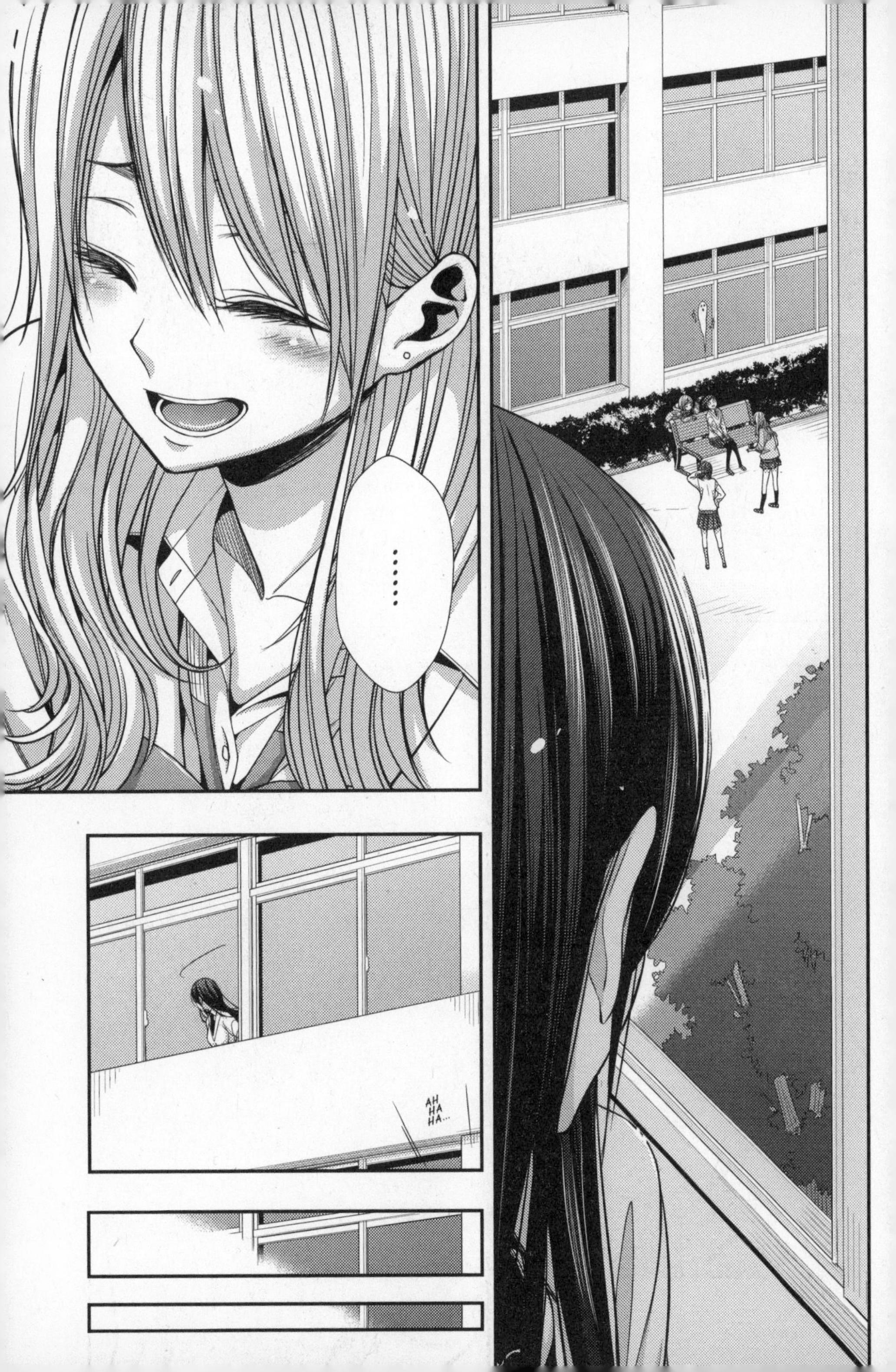
……
AH
HA
HA...

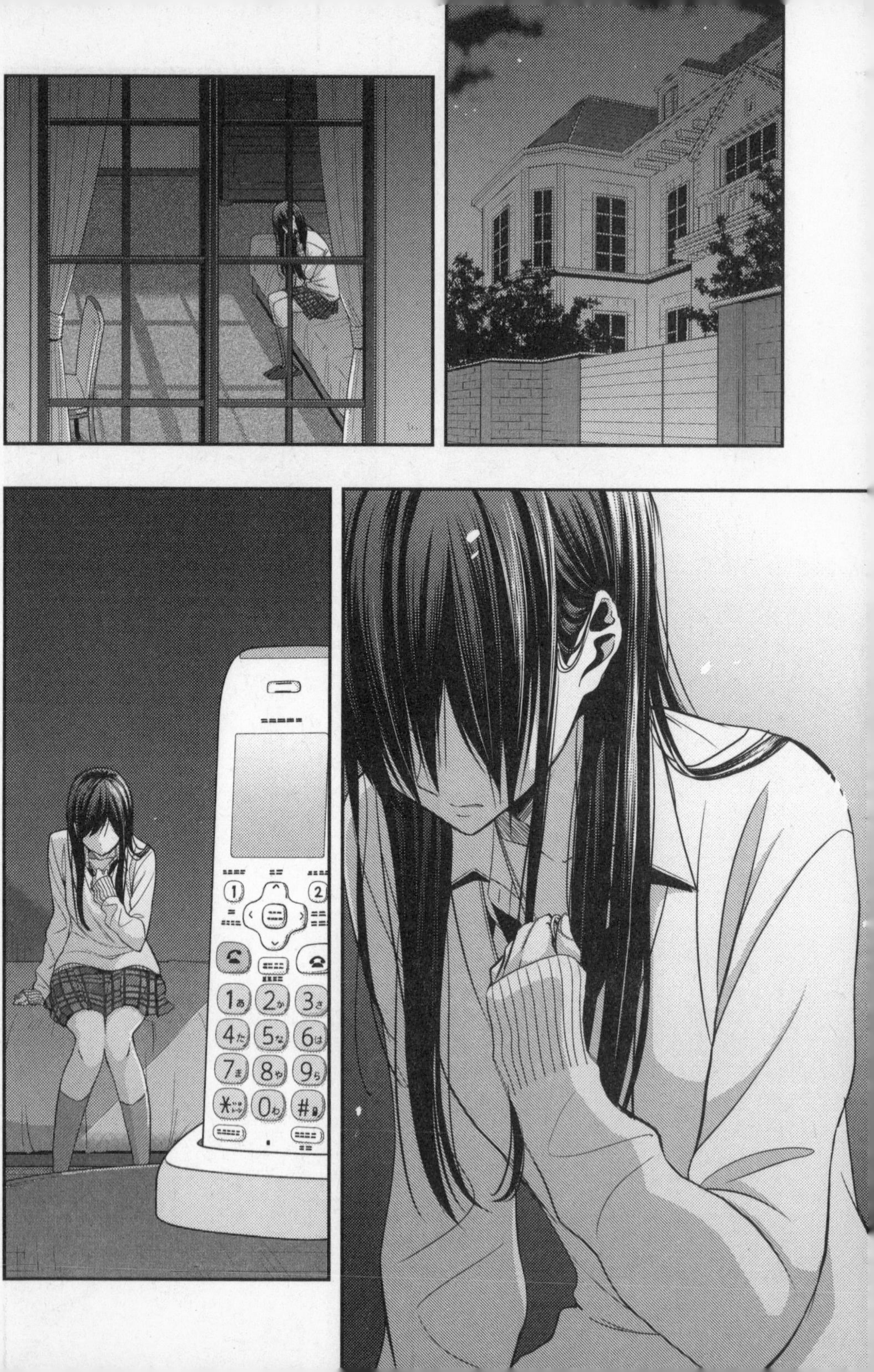

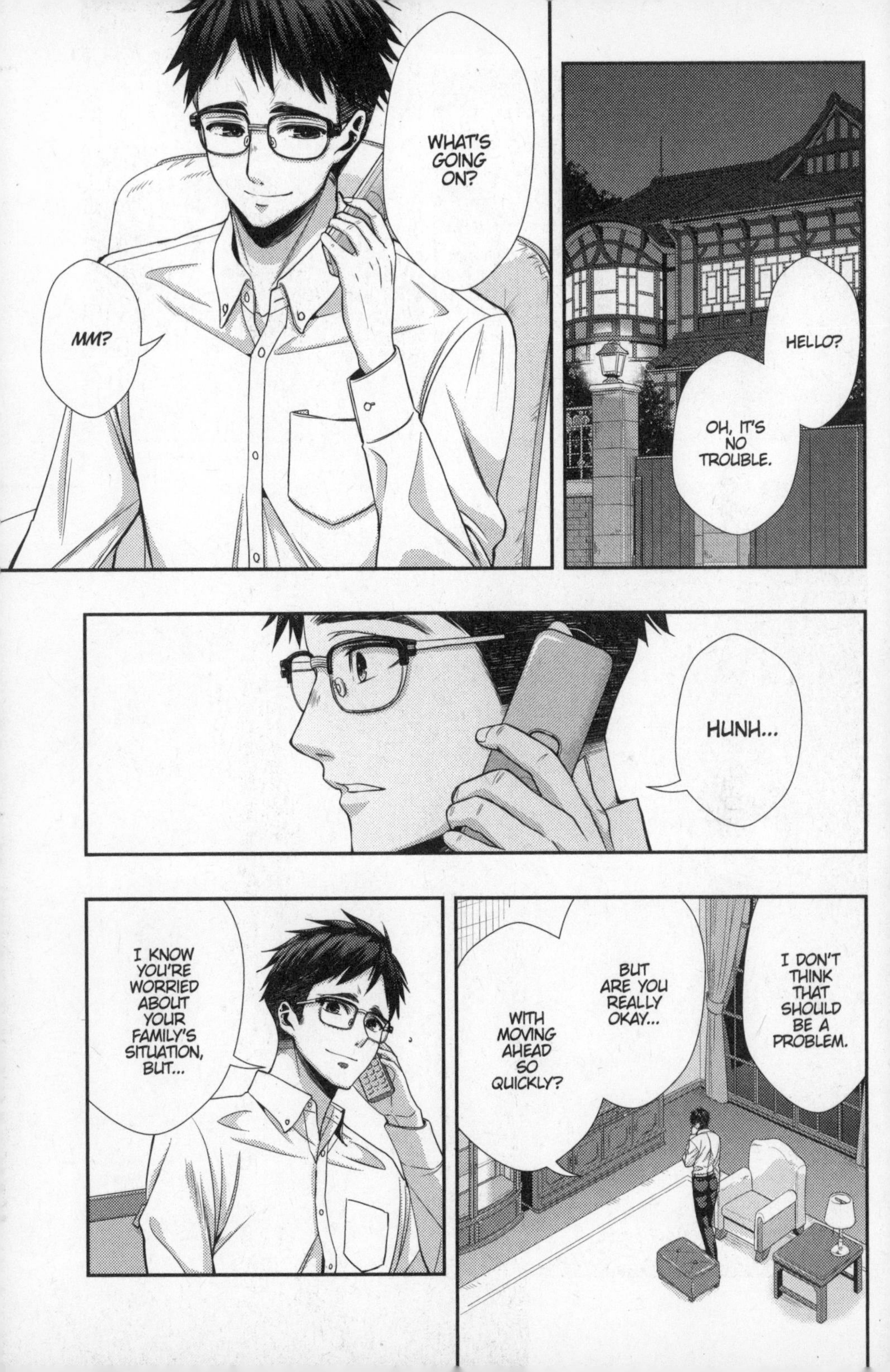
HELLO?
OH, IT'S NO TROUBLE.
WHAT'S GOING ON?
MM?
HUNH...
I DON'T THINK THAT SHOULD BE A PROBLEM.
BUT ARE YOU REALLY OKAY...
WITH MOVING AHEAD SO QUICKLY?
I KNOW YOU'RE WORRIED ABOUT YOUR FAMILY'S SITUATION, BUT...

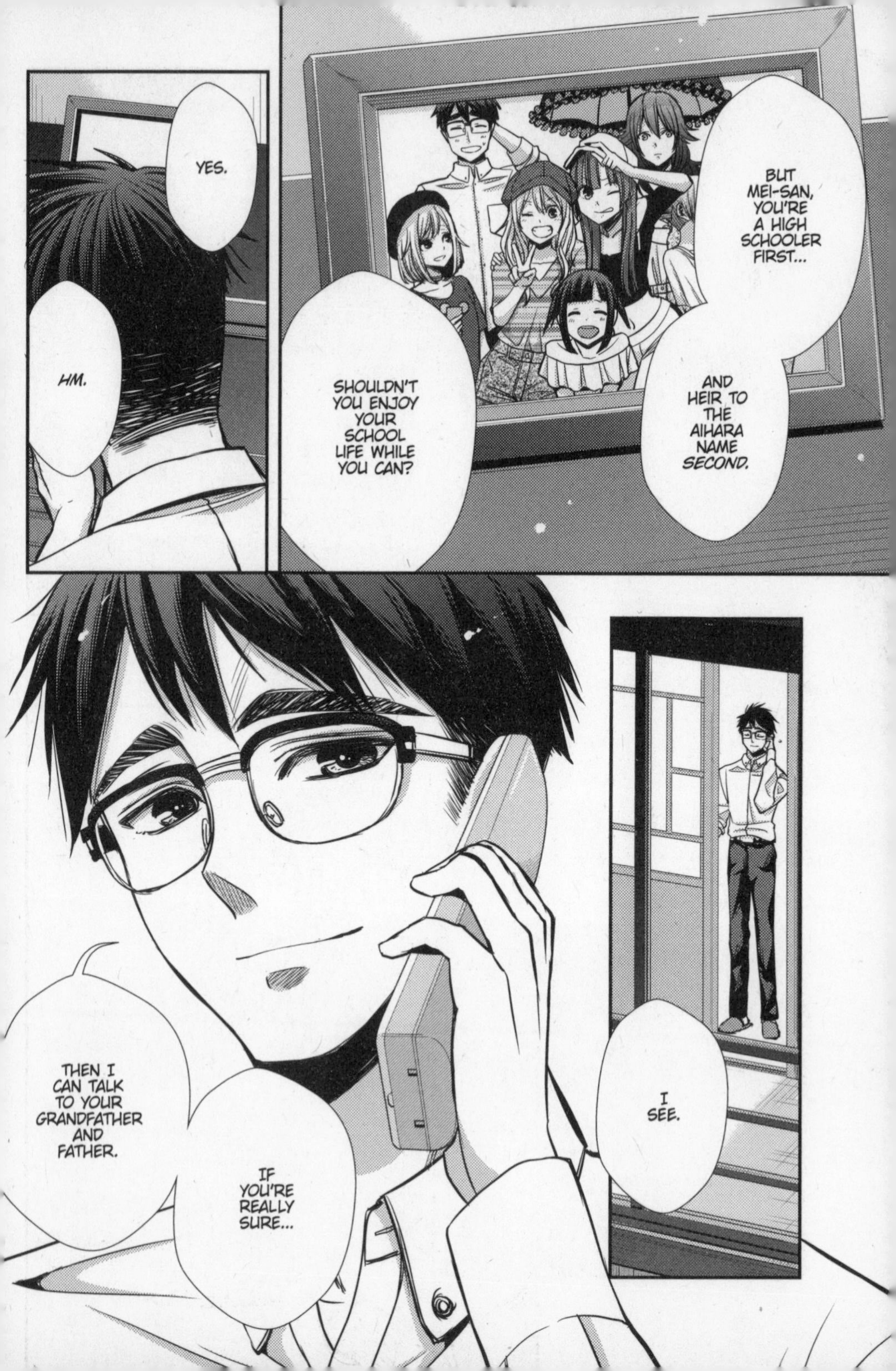
BUT MEI-SAN, YOU'RE A HIGH SCHOOLER FIRST...
AND HEIR TO THE AIHARA NAME SECOND.
SHOULDN'T YOU ENJOY YOUR SCHOOL LIFE WHILE YOU CAN?
YES.
HM.
I SEE.
IF YOU'RE REALLY SURE...
THEN I CAN TALK TO YOUR GRANDFATHER AND FATHER.

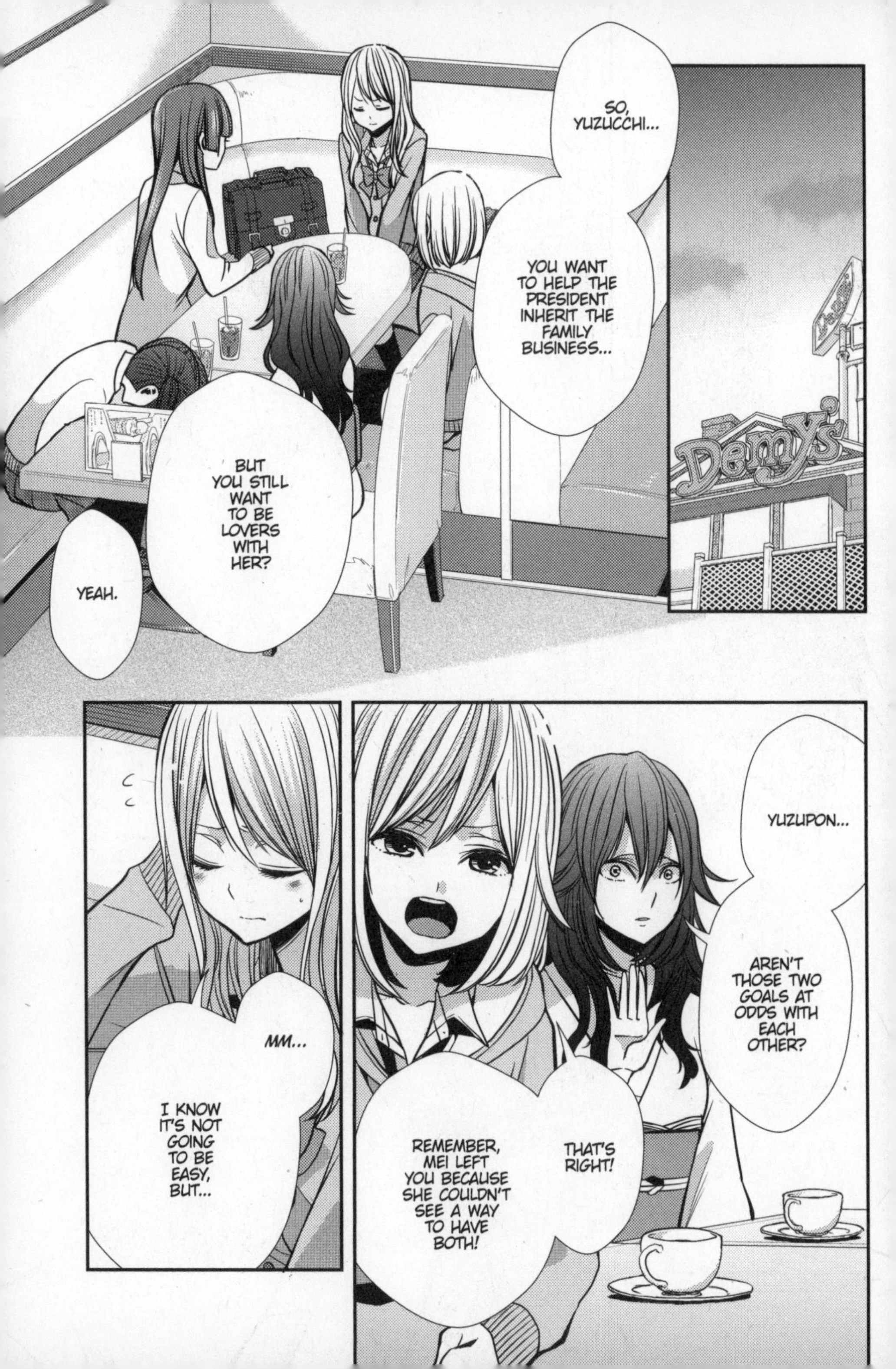
Demy's
SO, YUZUCCHI...
YOU WANT TO HELP THE PRESIDENT INHERIT THE FAMILY BUSINESS...
BUT YOU STILL WANT TO BE LOVERS WITH HER?
YEAH.
YUZUPON...
AREN'T THOSE TWO GOALS AT ODDS WITH EACH OTHER?
THAT'S RIGHT!
REMEMBER, MEI LEFT YOU BECAUSE SHE COULDN'T SEE A WAY TO HAVE BOTH!
MM...
I KNOW IT'S NOT GOING TO BE EASY, BUT...

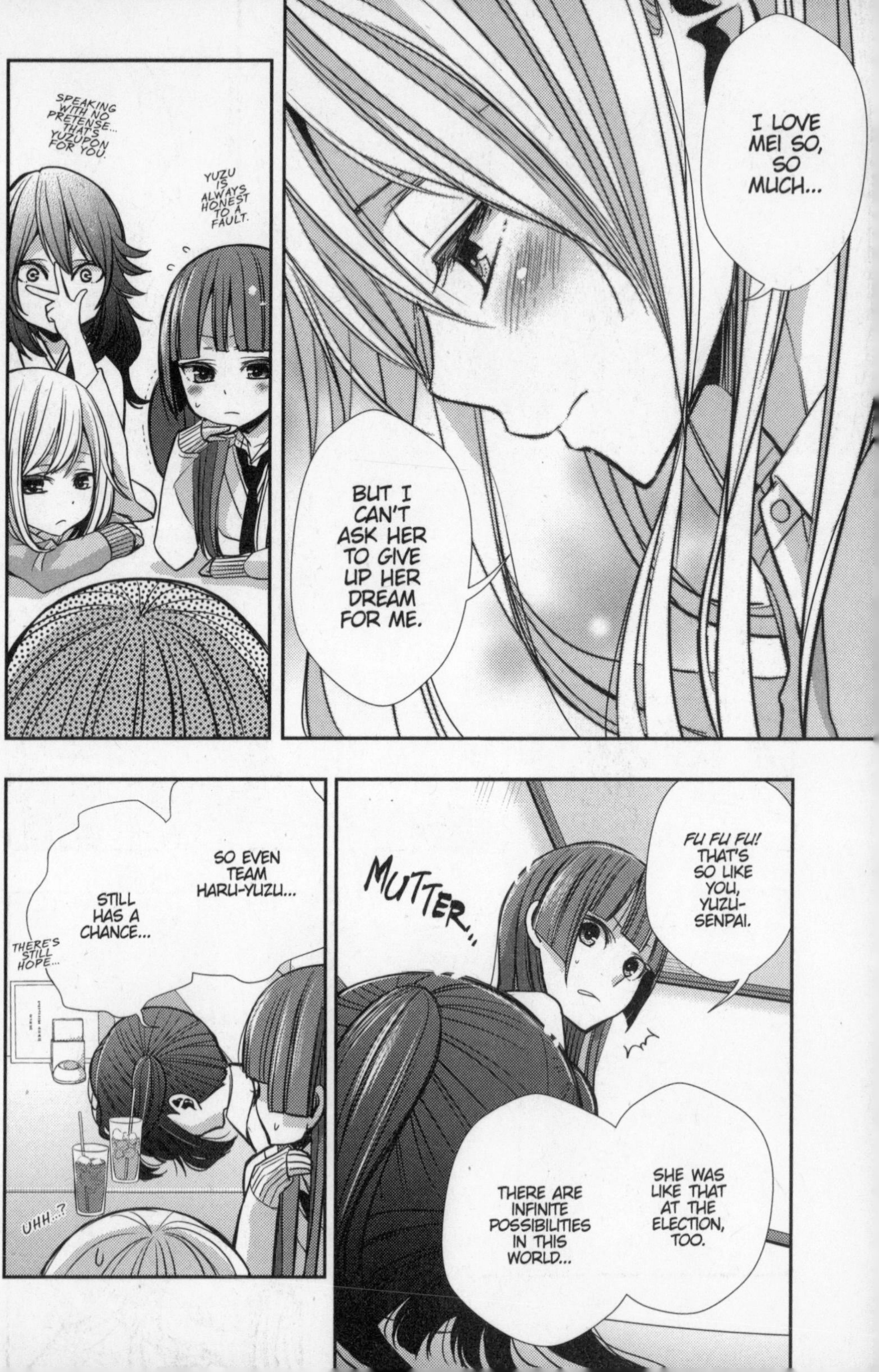
I LOVE MEI SO, SO MUCH...
BUT I CAN'T ASK HER TO GIVE UP HER DREAM FOR ME.
SPEAKING WITH NO PRETENSE... THAT'S YUZUPON FOR YOU.
YUZU IS ALWAYS HONEST TO A FAULT.
FU FU FU! THAT'S SO LIKE YOU, YUZU-SENPAI.
MUTTER...
SHE WAS LIKE THAT AT THE ELECTION, TOO.
THERE ARE INFINITE POSSIBILITIES IN THIS WORLD...
SO EVEN TEAM HARU-YUZU...
STILL HAS A CHANCE...
THERE'S STILL HOPE...
UHH..?

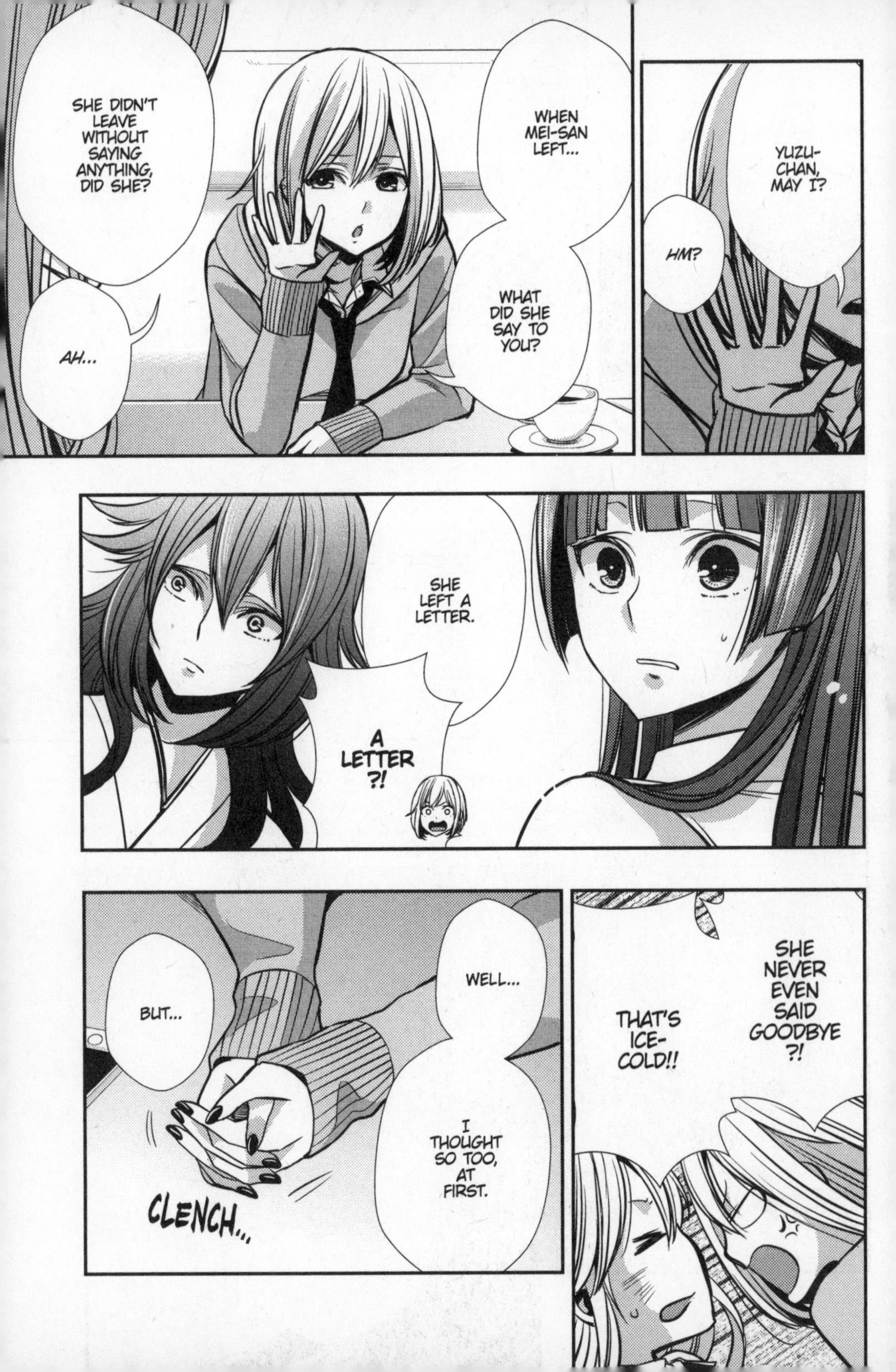
YUZU-CHAN, MAY I?
HM?
WHEN MEI-SAN LEFT...
WHAT DID SHE SAY TO YOU?
SHE DIDN'T LEAVE WITHOUT SAYING ANYTHING, DID SHE?
AH...
SHE LEFT A LETTER.
A LETTER?!
SHE NEVER EVEN SAID GOODBYE?!
THAT'S ICE-COLD!!
WELL...
I THOUGHT SO TOO, AT FIRST.
BUT...
CLENCH...

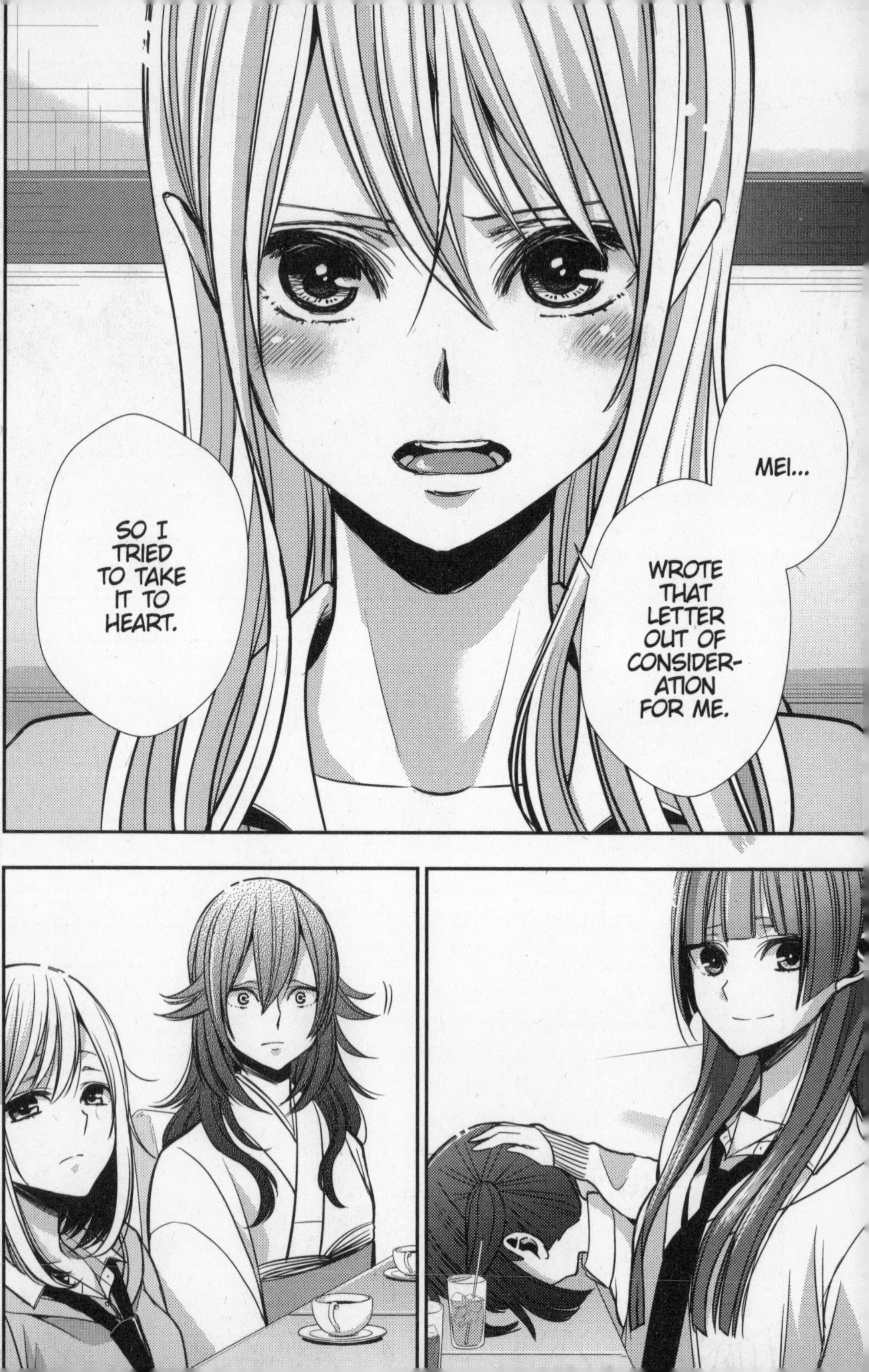
MEI...
WROTE THAT LETTER OUT OF CONSIDERATION FOR ME.
SO I TRIED TO TAKE IT TO HEART.

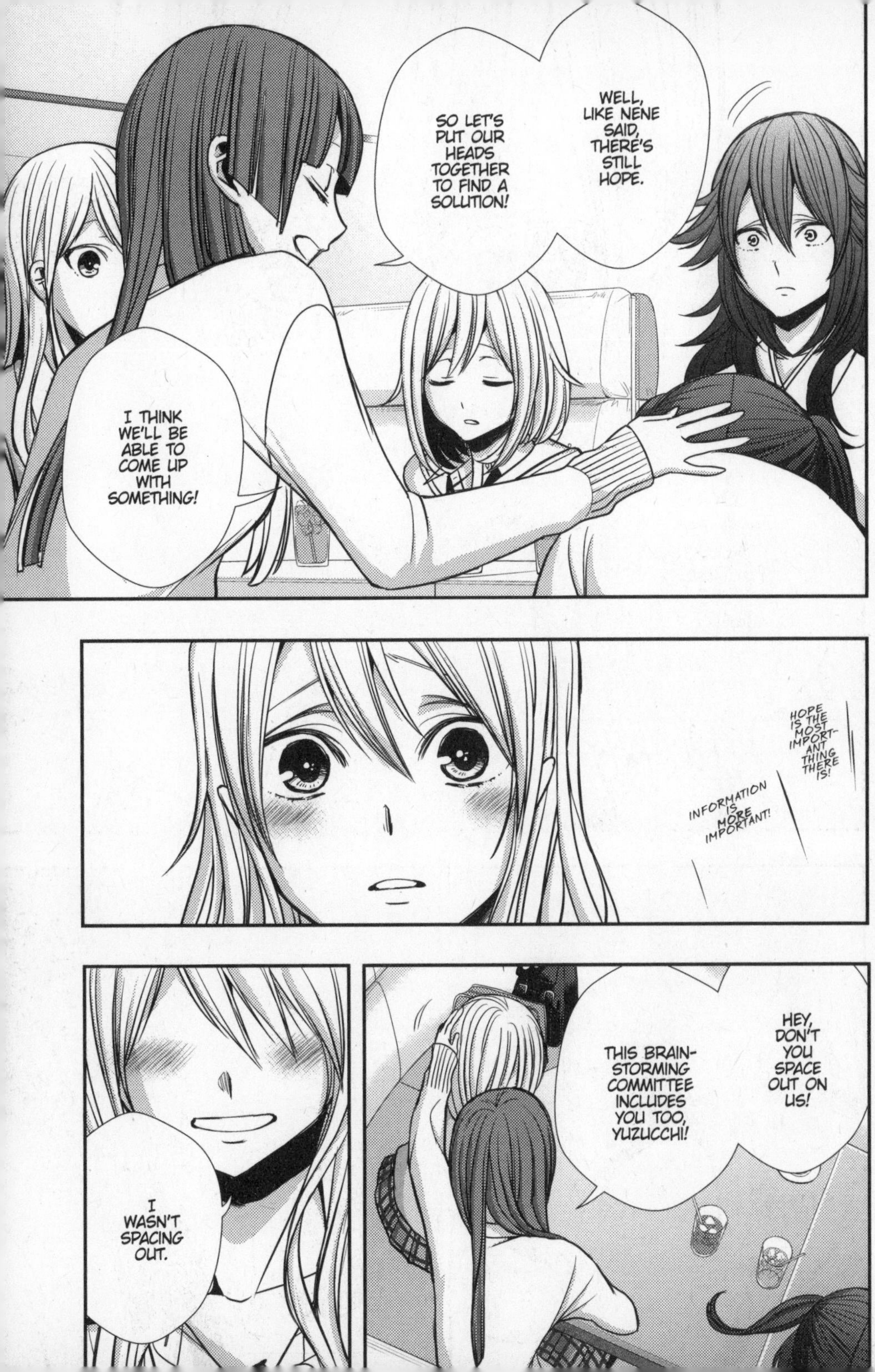
WELL, LIKE NENE SAID, THERE'S STILL HOPE.
SO LET'S PUT OUR HEADS TOGETHER TO FIND A SOLUTION!
I THINK WE'LL BE ABLE TO COME UP WITH SOMETHING!
HOPE IS THE MOST IMPORT-ANT THING THERE IS!
INFORMATION IS MORE IMPORTANT!
HEY, DON'T YOU SPACE OUT ON US!
THIS BRAIN-STORMING COMMITTEE INCLUDES YOU TOO, YUZUCCHI!
I WASN'T SPACING OUT.

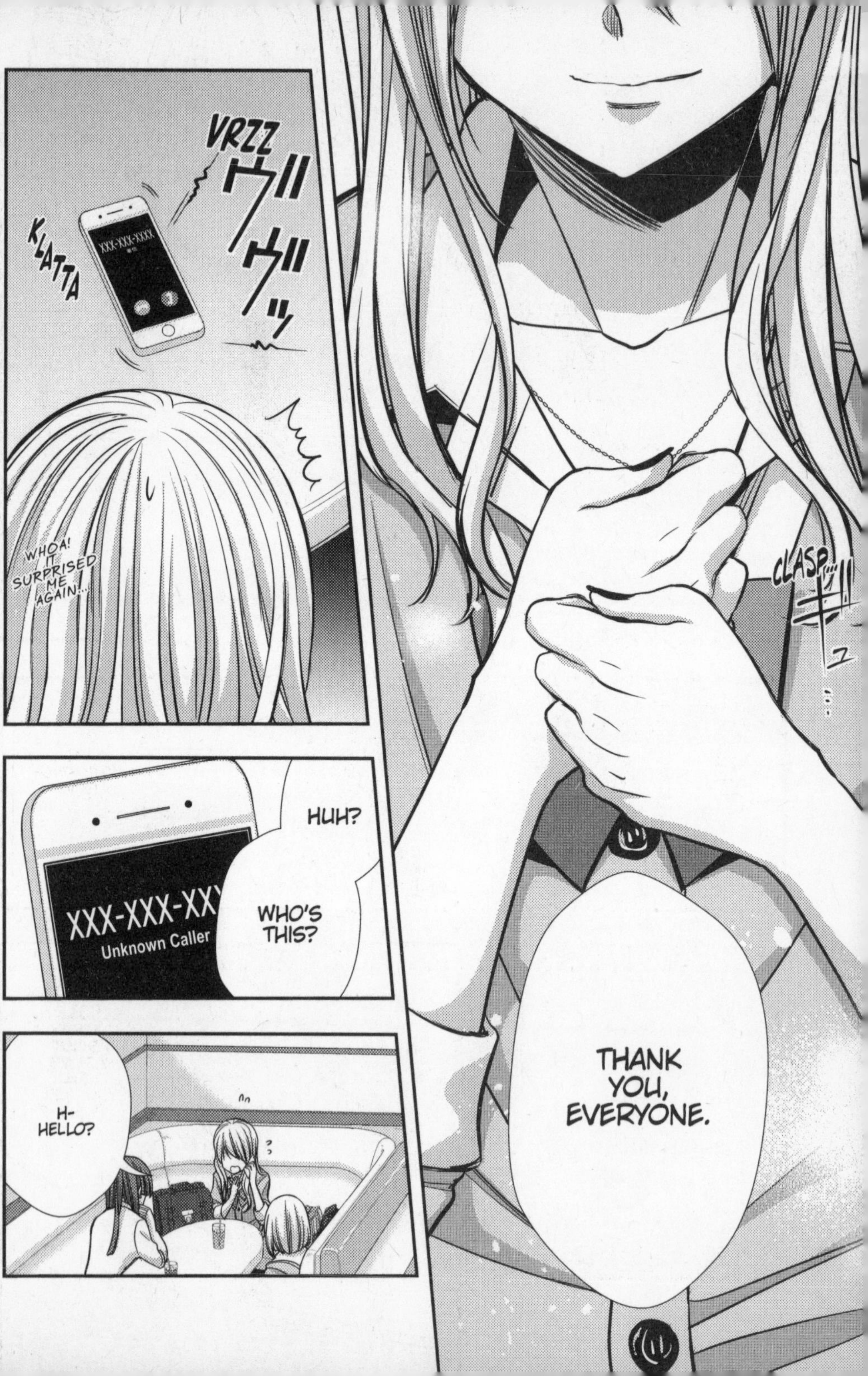
CLASP...!!
THANK YOU, EVERYONE.
VRZZ
KLATTA
WHOA! IT SURPRISED ME AGAIN...
HUH?
WHO'S THIS?
XXX-XXX-XX
Unknown Caller
H-HELLO?

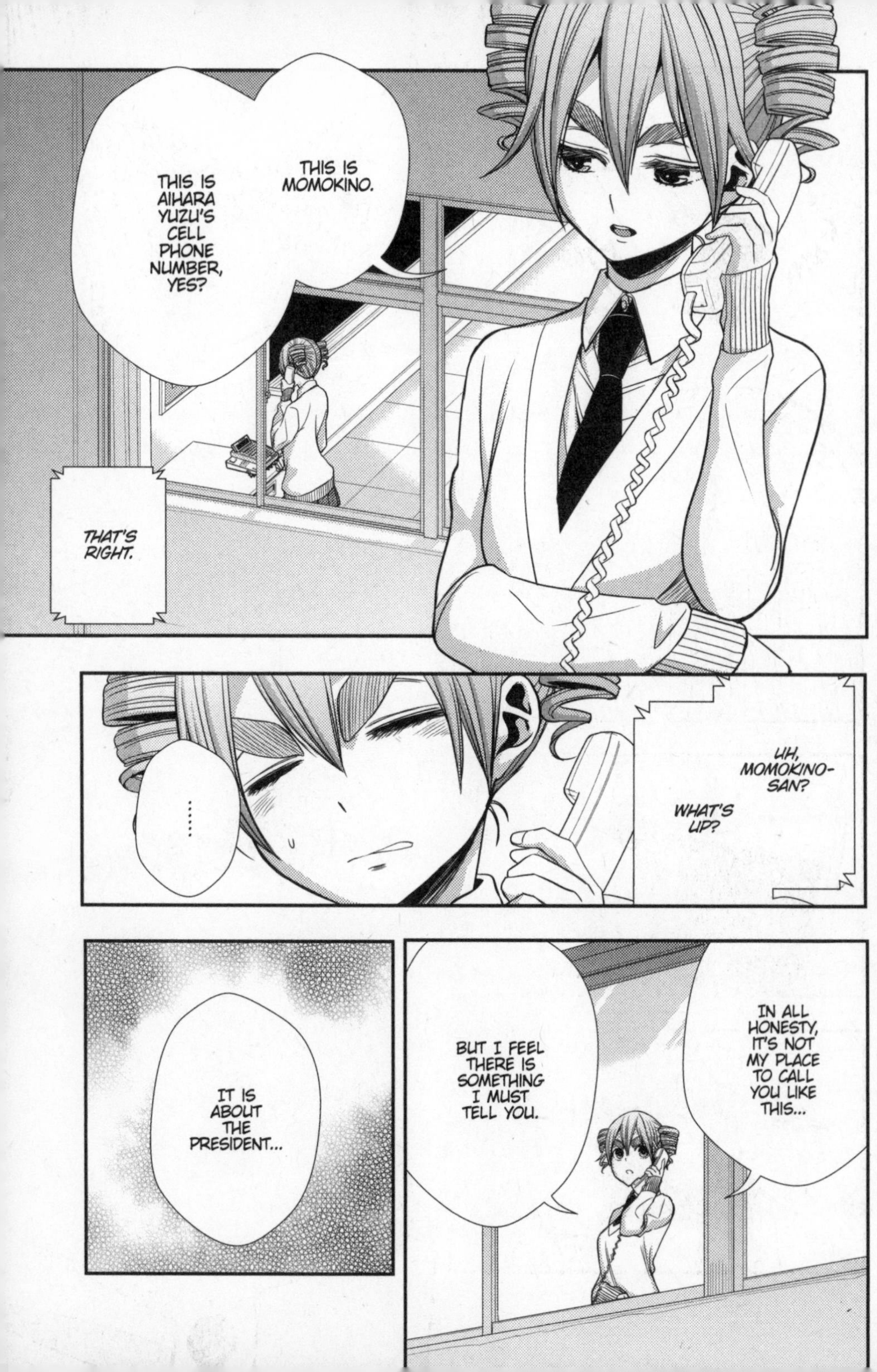
THIS IS MOMOKINO.
THIS IS AIHARA YUZU'S CELL PHONE NUMBER, YES?
THAT'S RIGHT.
UH, MOMOKINO-SAN?
WHAT'S UP?
......
IN ALL HONESTY, IT'S NOT MY PLACE TO CALL YOU LIKE THIS...
BUT I FEEL THERE IS SOMETHING I MUST TELL YOU.
IT IS ABOUT THE PRESIDENT...

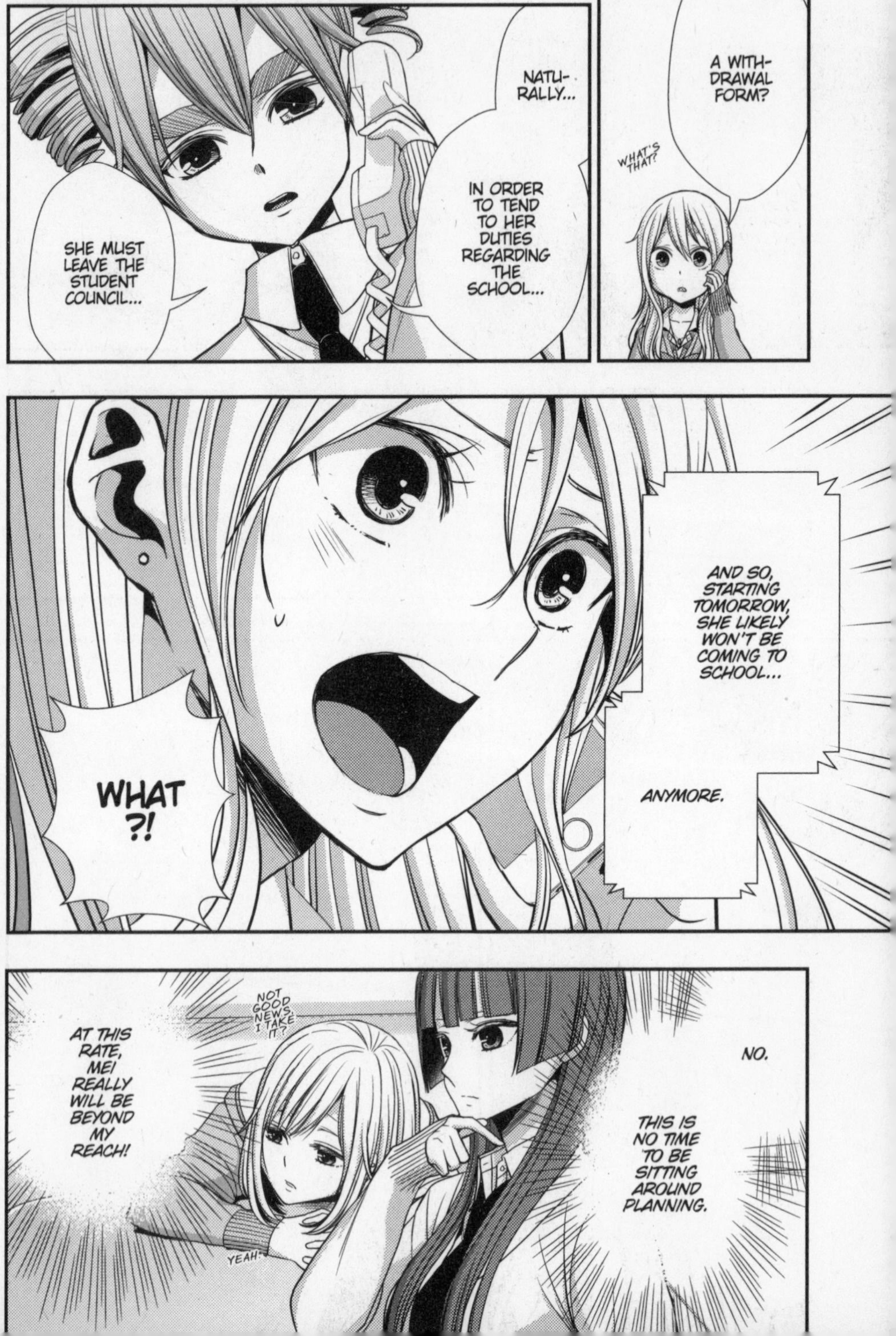
A WITHDRAWAL FORM?
WHAT'S THAT?
NATURALLY...
IN ORDER TO TEND TO HER DUTIES REGARDING THE SCHOOL...
SHE MUST LEAVE THE STUDENT COUNCIL...
AND SO, STARTING TOMORROW, SHE LIKELY WON'T BE COMING TO SCHOOL...
ANYMORE.
WHAT?!
NO.
THIS IS NO TIME TO BE SITTING AROUND PLANNING.
NOT GOOD NEWS, I TAKE IT?
AT THIS RATE, MEI REALLY WILL BE BEYOND MY REACH!
YEAH.

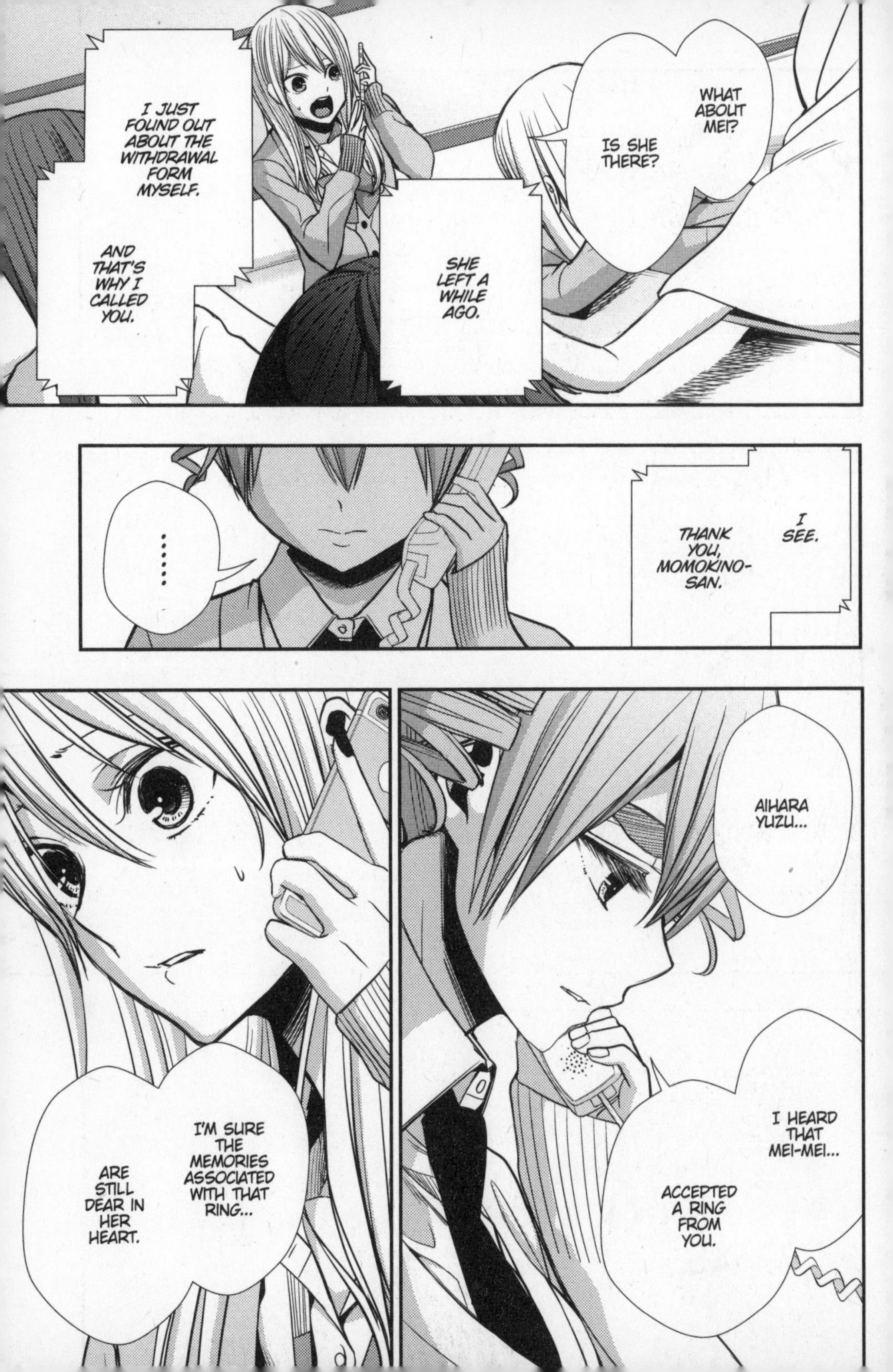
WHAT ABOUT MEI?
IS SHE THERE?
SHE LEFT A WHILE AGO.
I JUST FOUND OUT ABOUT THE WITHDRAWAL FORM MYSELF.
AND THAT'S WHY I CALLED YOU.
I SEE.
THANK YOU, MOMOKINO-SAN.
......
AIHARA YUZU...
I HEARD THAT MEI-MEI...
ACCEPTED A RING FROM YOU.
I'M SURE THE MEMORIES ASSOCIATED WITH THAT RING...
ARE STILL DEAR IN HER HEART.

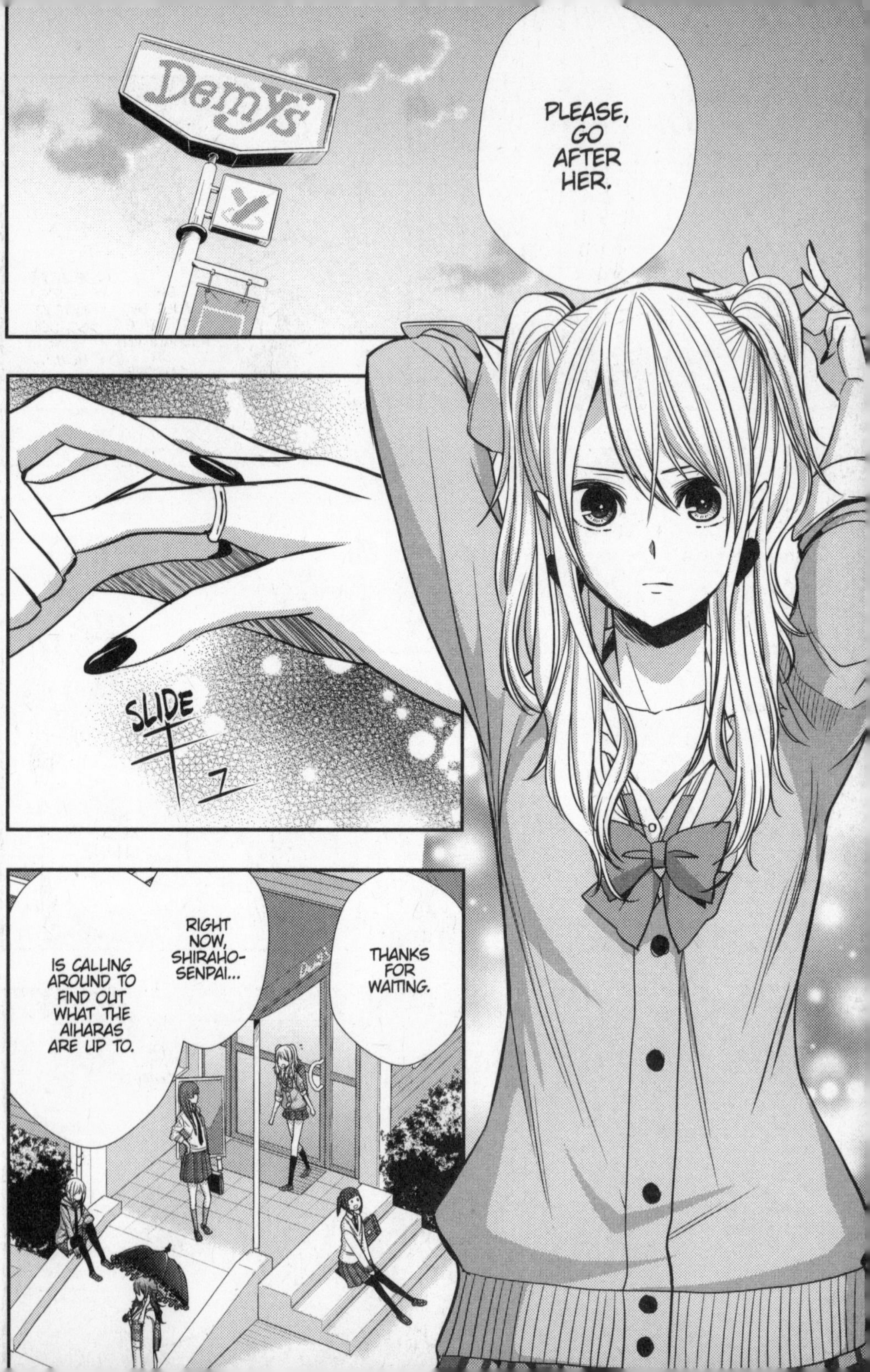
PLEASE, GO AFTER HER.
Demys'
SLIDE
THANKS FOR WAITING.
RIGHT NOW, SHIRAHO-SENPAI...
IS CALLING AROUND TO FIND OUT WHAT THE AIHARAS ARE UP TO.

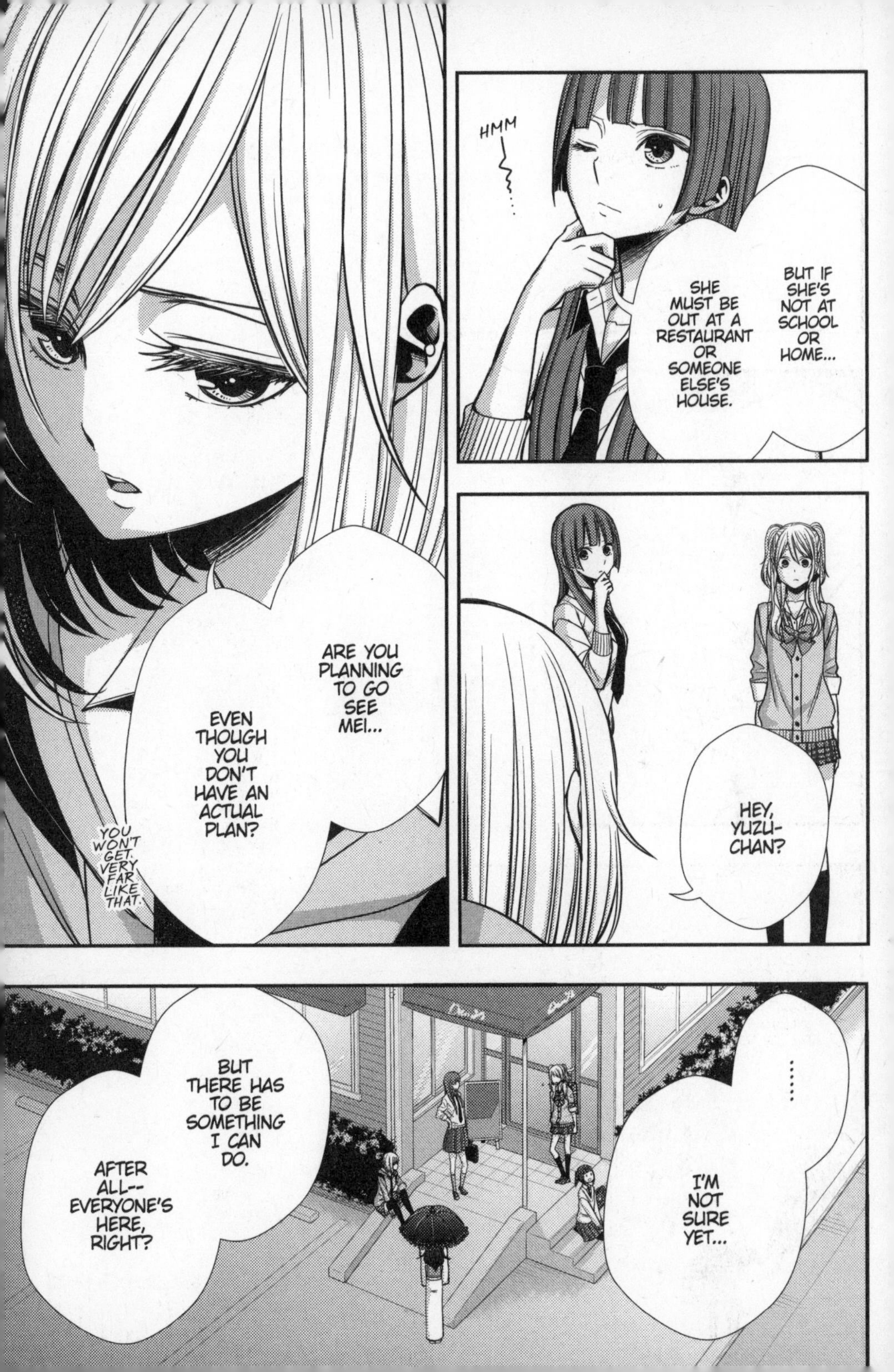
HMM...
BUT IF SHE'S NOT AT SCHOOL OR HOME...
SHE MUST BE OUT AT A RESTAURANT OR SOMEONE ELSE'S HOUSE.
HEY, YUZU-CHAN?
ARE YOU PLANNING TO GO SEE MEI...
EVEN THOUGH YOU DON'T HAVE AN ACTUAL PLAN?
YOU WON'T GET VERY FAR LIKE THAT.
......
I'M NOT SURE YET...
BUT THERE HAS TO BE SOMETHING I CAN DO.
AFTER ALL-- EVERYONE'S HERE, RIGHT?

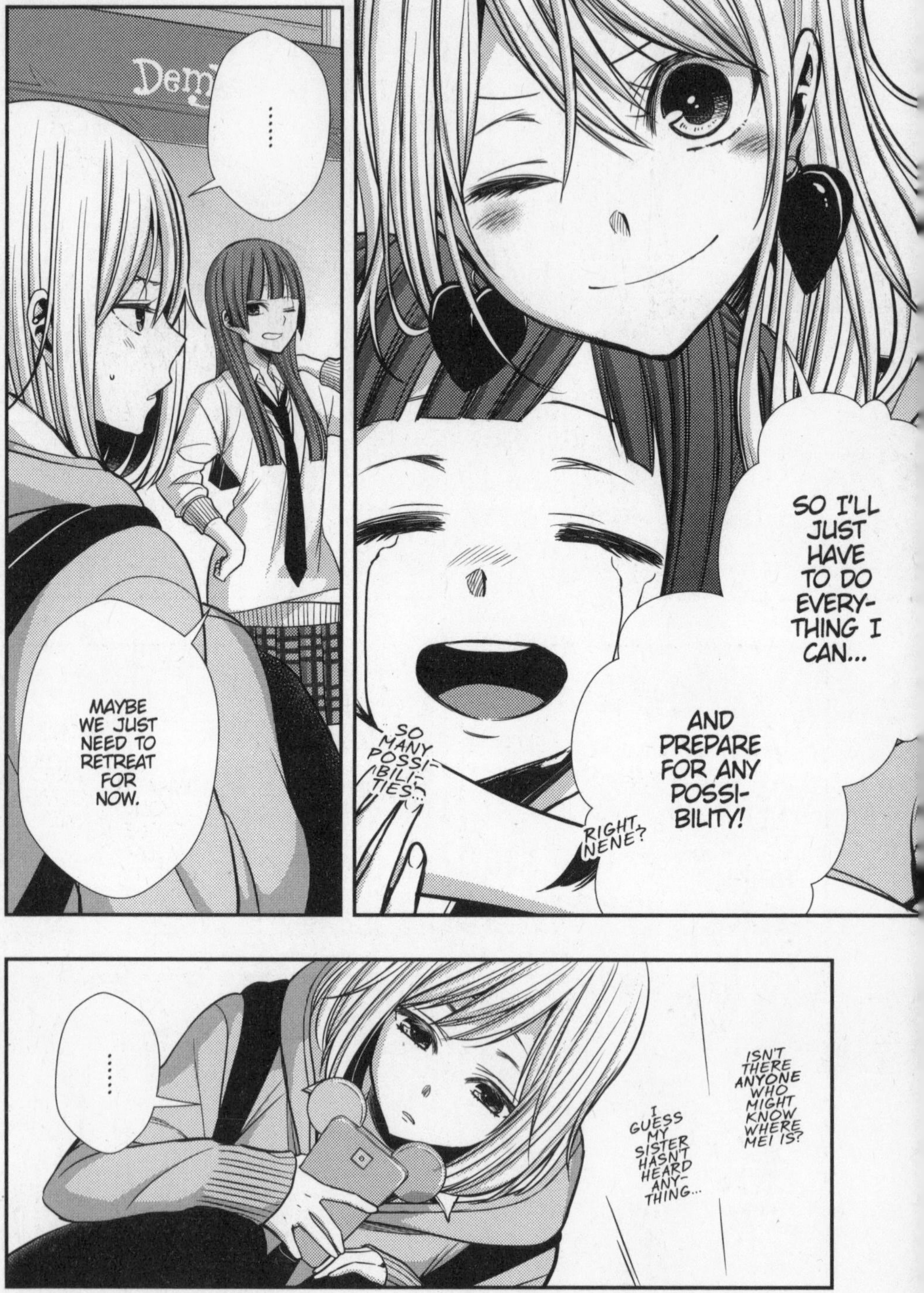
SO I'LL JUST HAVE TO DO EVERY-THING I CAN...
AND PREPARE FOR ANY POSSI-BILITY!
RIGHT, NENE?
SO MANY POSSI-BILI-TIES...
......
MAYBE WE JUST NEED TO RETREAT FOR NOW.
ISN'T THERE ANYONE WHO MIGHT KNOW WHERE MEI IS?
I GUESS MY SISTER HASN'T HEARD ANY-THING...
......

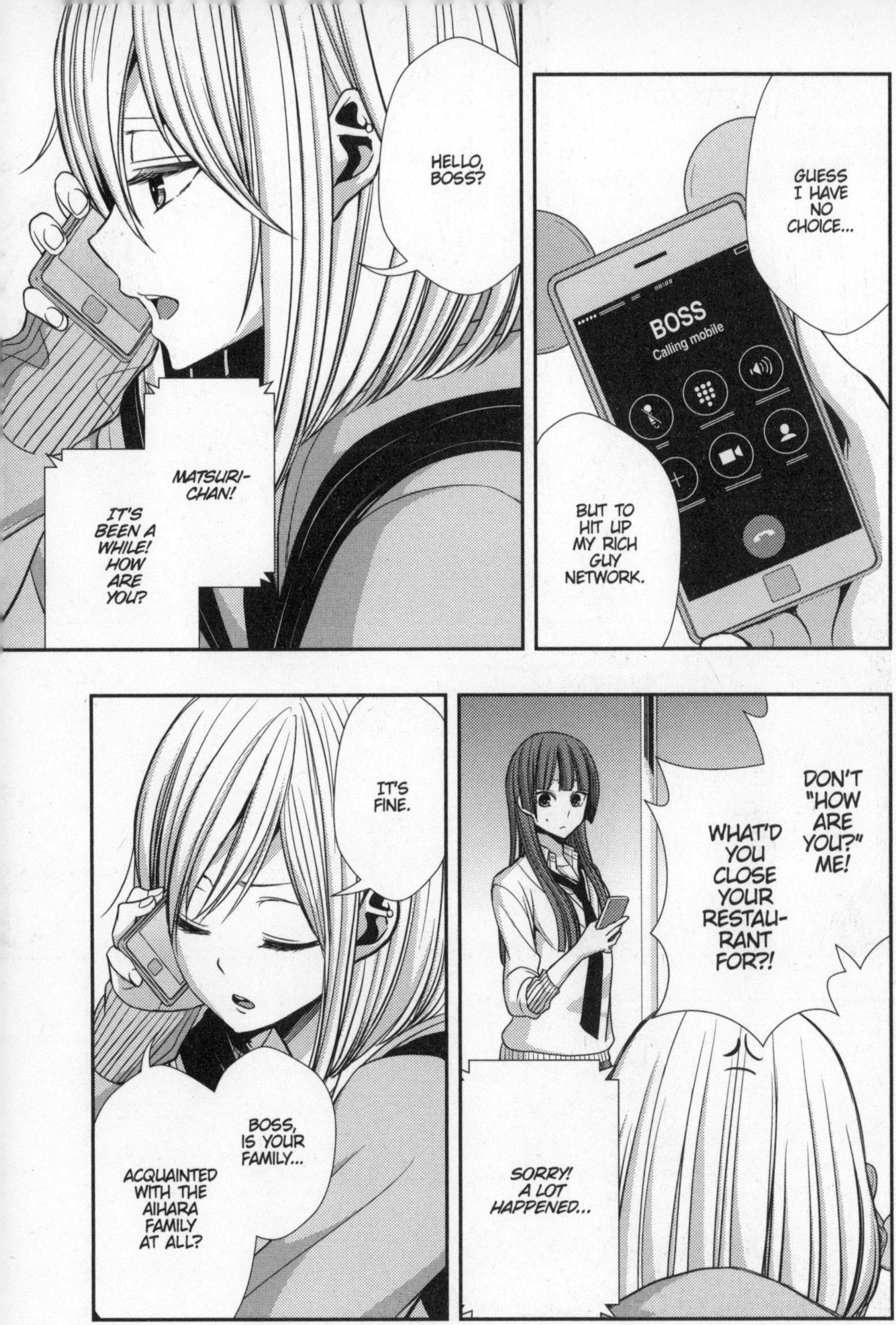

GUESS I HAVE NO CHOICE...
BOSS
Calling mobile
BUT TO HIT UP MY RICH GUY NETWORK.
HELLO, BOSS?
MATSURI-CHAN!
IT'S BEEN A WHILE! HOW ARE YOU?
DON'T "HOW ARE YOU?" ME!
WHAT'D YOU CLOSE YOUR RESTAU-RANT FOR?!
SORRY! A LOT HAPPENED...
IT'S FINE.
BOSS, IS YOUR FAMILY...
ACQUAINTED WITH THE AIHARA FAMILY AT ALL?

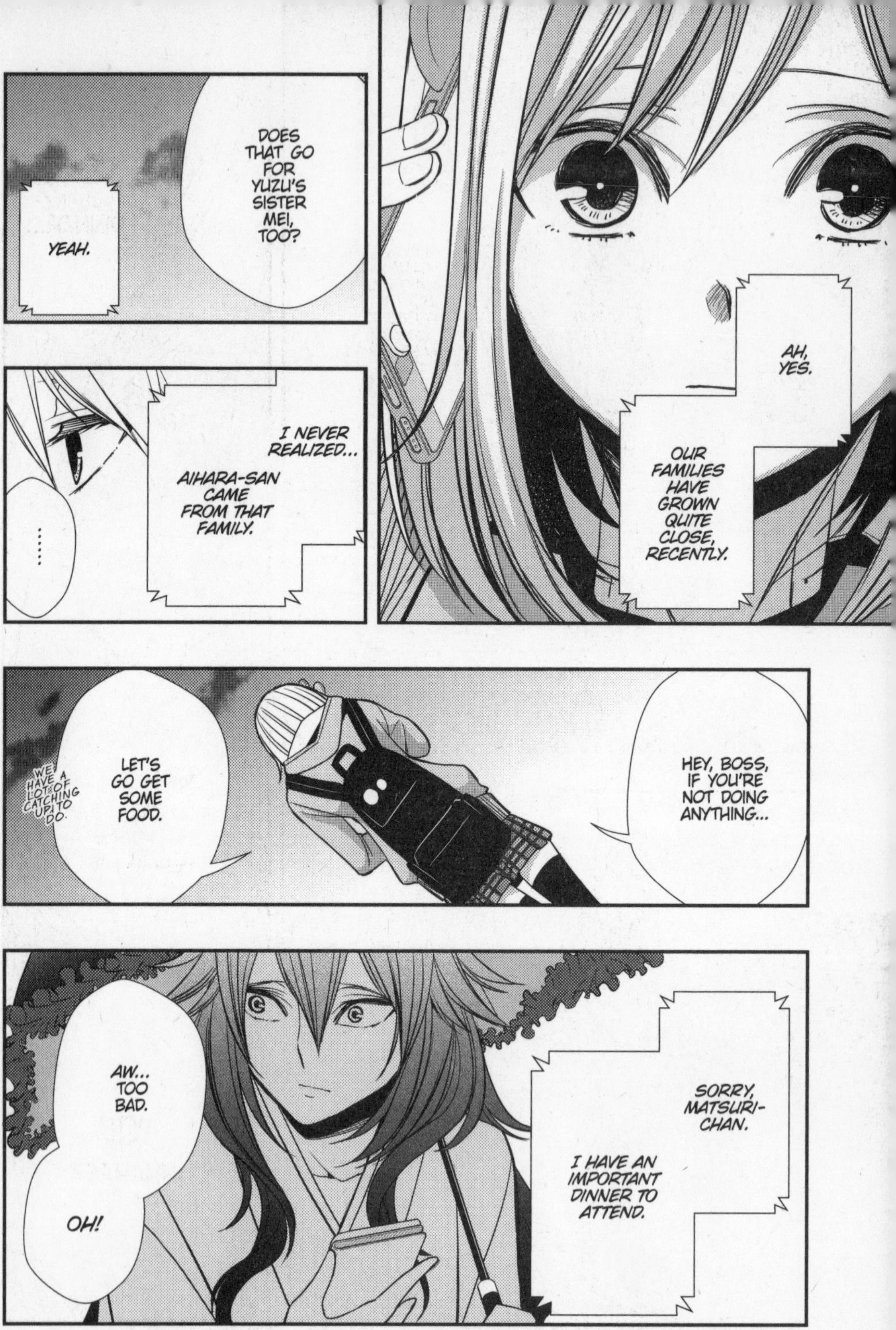
AH, YES.
OUR FAMILIES HAVE GROWN QUITE CLOSE, RECENTLY.
DOES THAT GO FOR YUZU'S SISTER MEI, TOO?
YEAH.
I NEVER REALIZED...
AIHARA-SAN CAME FROM THAT FAMILY.
......
HEY, BOSS, IF YOU'RE NOT DOING ANYTHING...
LET'S GO GET SOME FOOD.
WE HAVE A LOT OF CATCHING UP TO DO.
SORRY, MATSURI-CHAN.
I HAVE AN IMPORTANT DINNER TO ATTEND.
AW... TOO BAD.
OH!

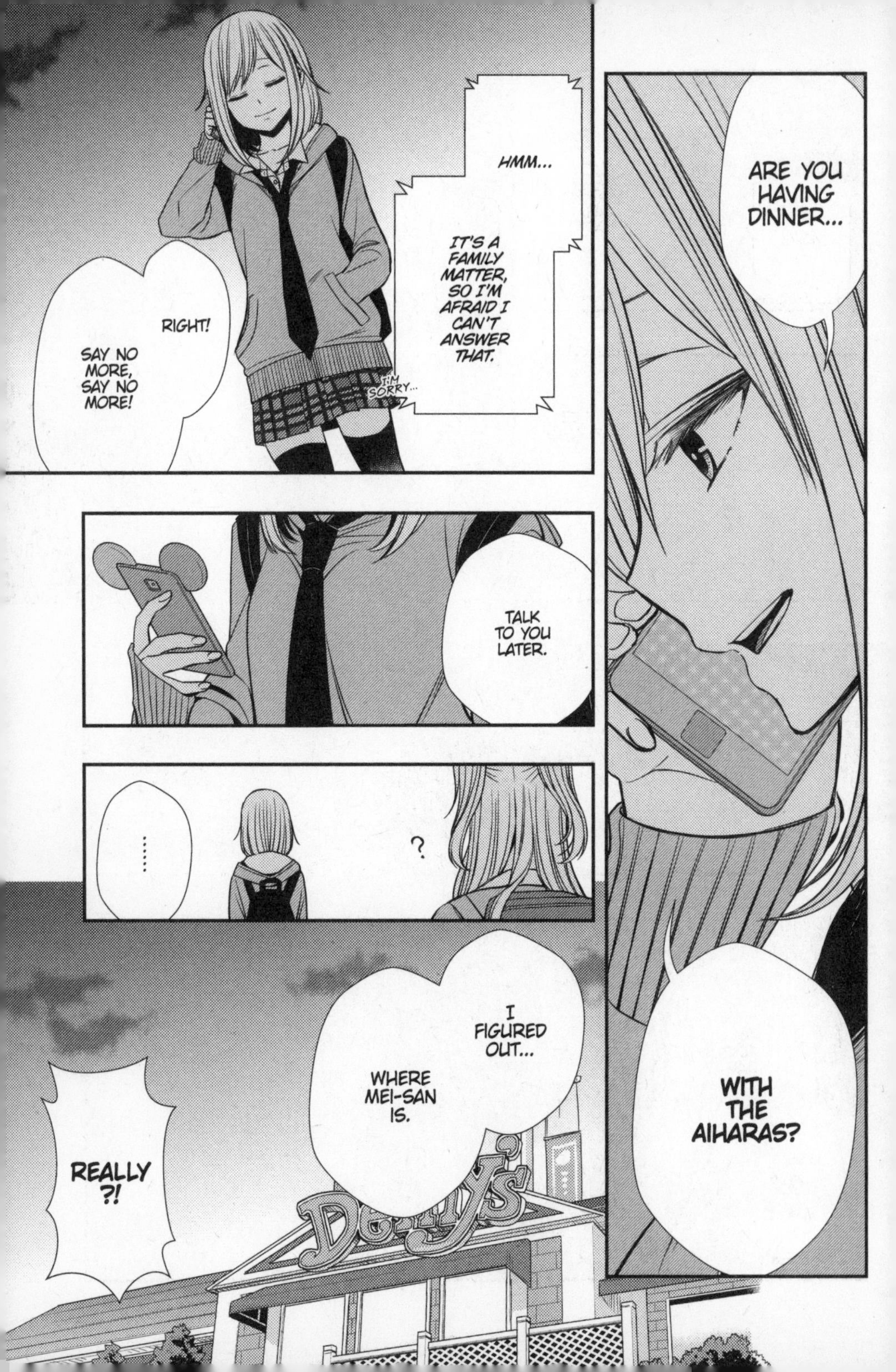

ARE YOU HAVING DINNER...
WITH THE AIHARAS?
HMM...
IT'S A FAMILY MATTER, SO I'M AFRAID I CAN'T ANSWER THAT.
I'M SORRY...
RIGHT!
SAY NO MORE, SAY NO MORE!
TALK TO YOU LATER.
?
......
I FIGURED OUT...
WHERE MEI-SAN IS.
REALLY?!

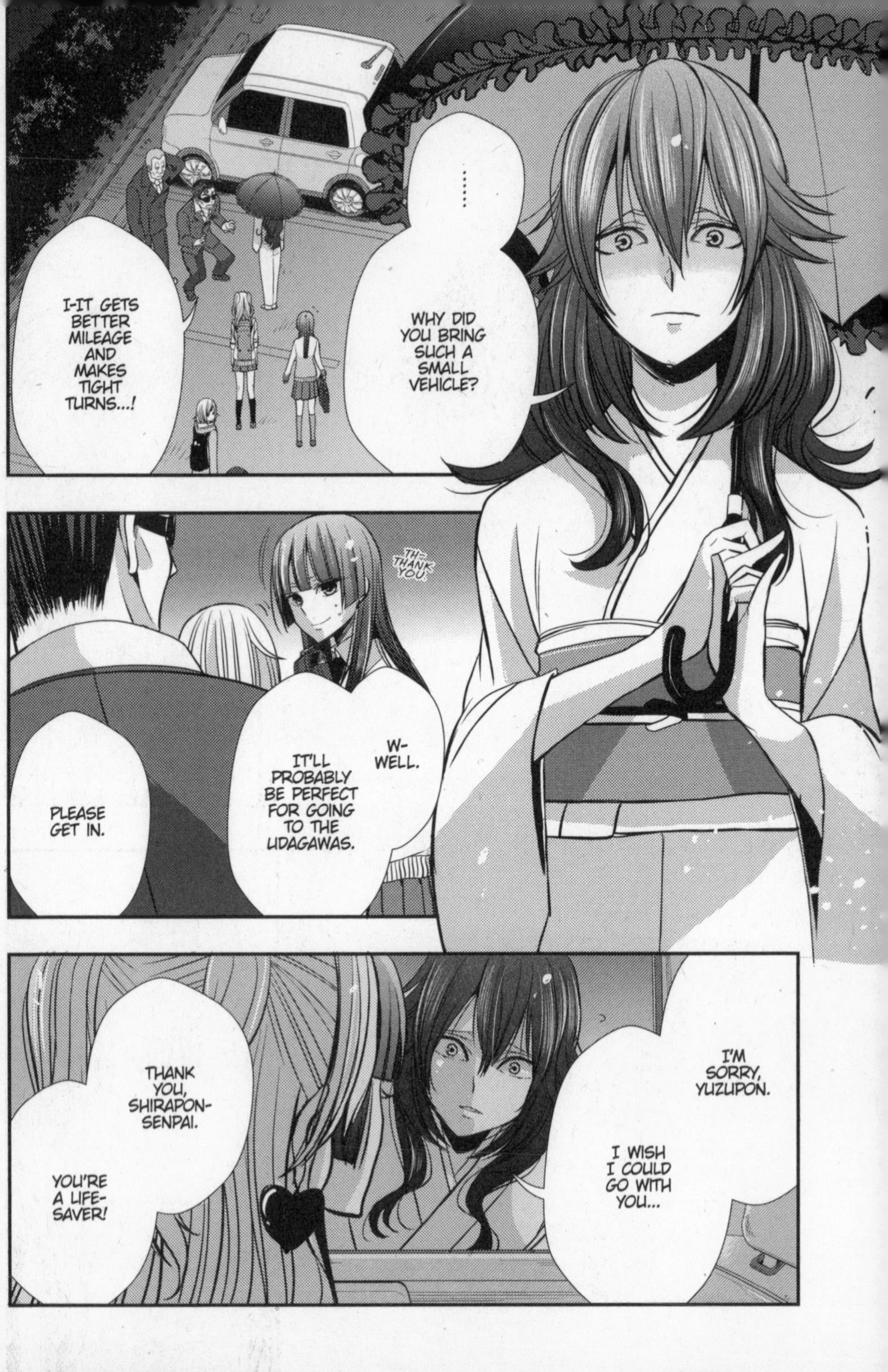
……
WHY DID YOU BRING SUCH A SMALL VEHICLE?
I-IT GETS BETTER MILEAGE AND MAKES TIGHT TURNS...!
TH-THANK YOU.
W-WELL.
IT'LL PROBABLY BE PERFECT FOR GOING TO THE UDAGAWAS.
PLEASE GET IN.
I'M SORRY, YUZUPON.
I WISH I COULD GO WITH YOU...
THANK YOU, SHIRAPON-SENPAI.
YOU'RE A LIFE-SAVER!

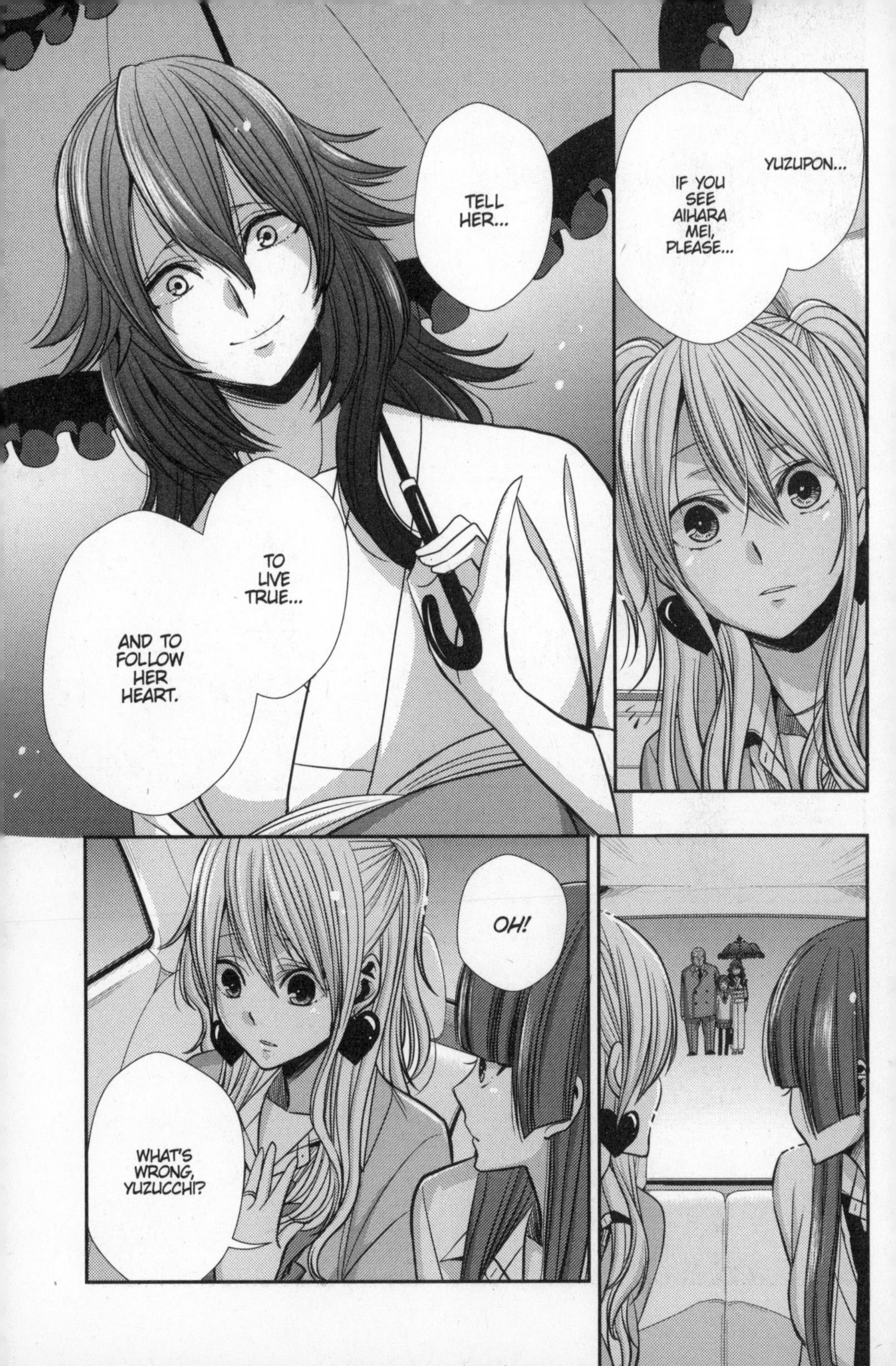
YUZUPON...
IF YOU SEE AIHARA MEI, PLEASE...
TELL HER...
TO LIVE TRUE...
AND TO FOLLOW HER HEART.
OH!
WHAT'S WRONG, YUZUCCHI?

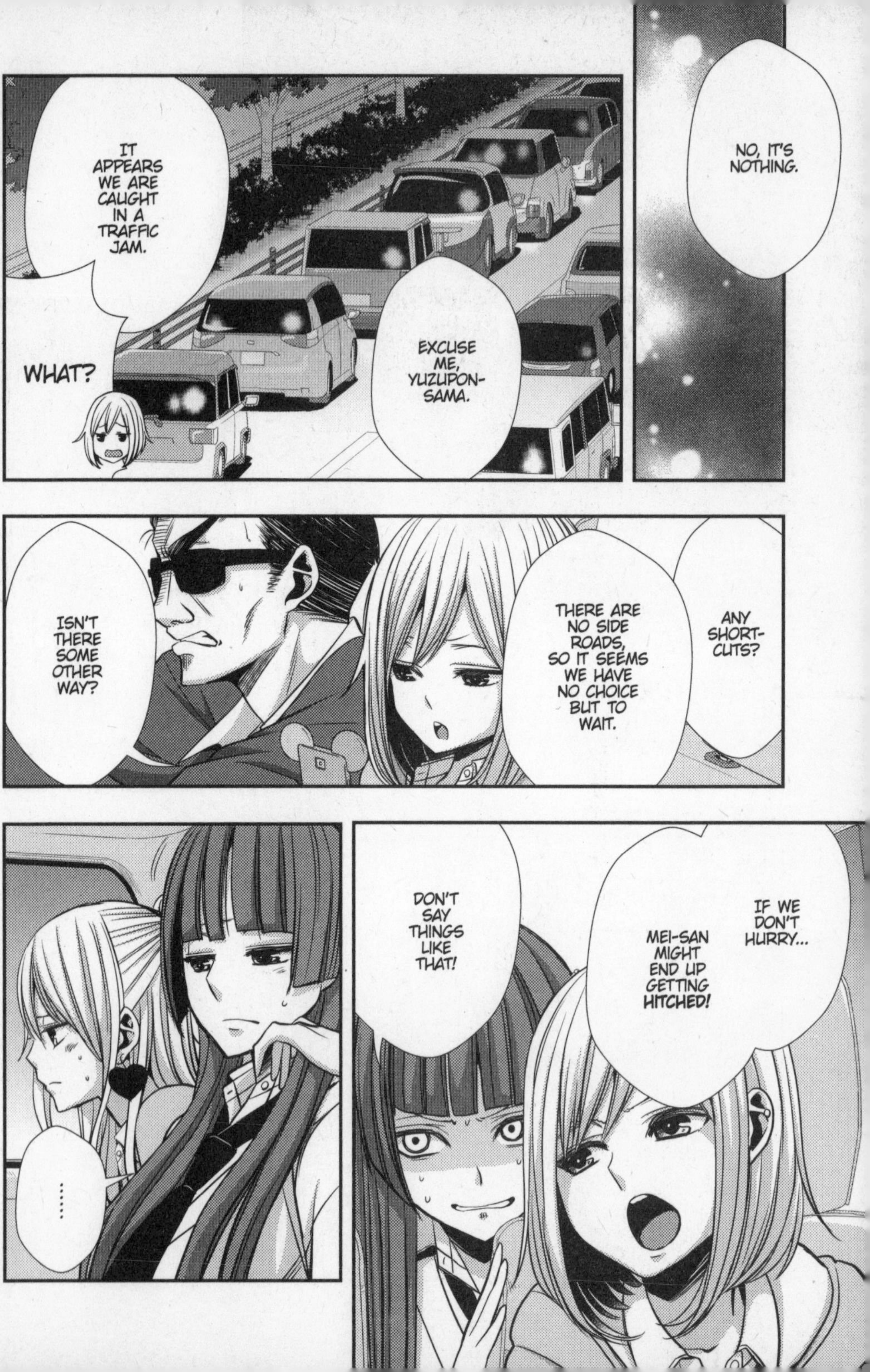
NO, IT'S NOTHING.
EXCUSE ME, YUZUPON-SAMA.
IT APPEARS WE ARE CAUGHT IN A TRAFFIC JAM.
WHAT?
ANY SHORT-CUTS?
THERE ARE NO SIDE ROADS, SO IT SEEMS WE HAVE NO CHOICE BUT TO WAIT.
ISN'T THERE SOME OTHER WAY?
IF WE DON'T HURRY...
MEI-SAN MIGHT END UP GETTING HITCHED!
DON'T SAY THINGS LIKE THAT!
......

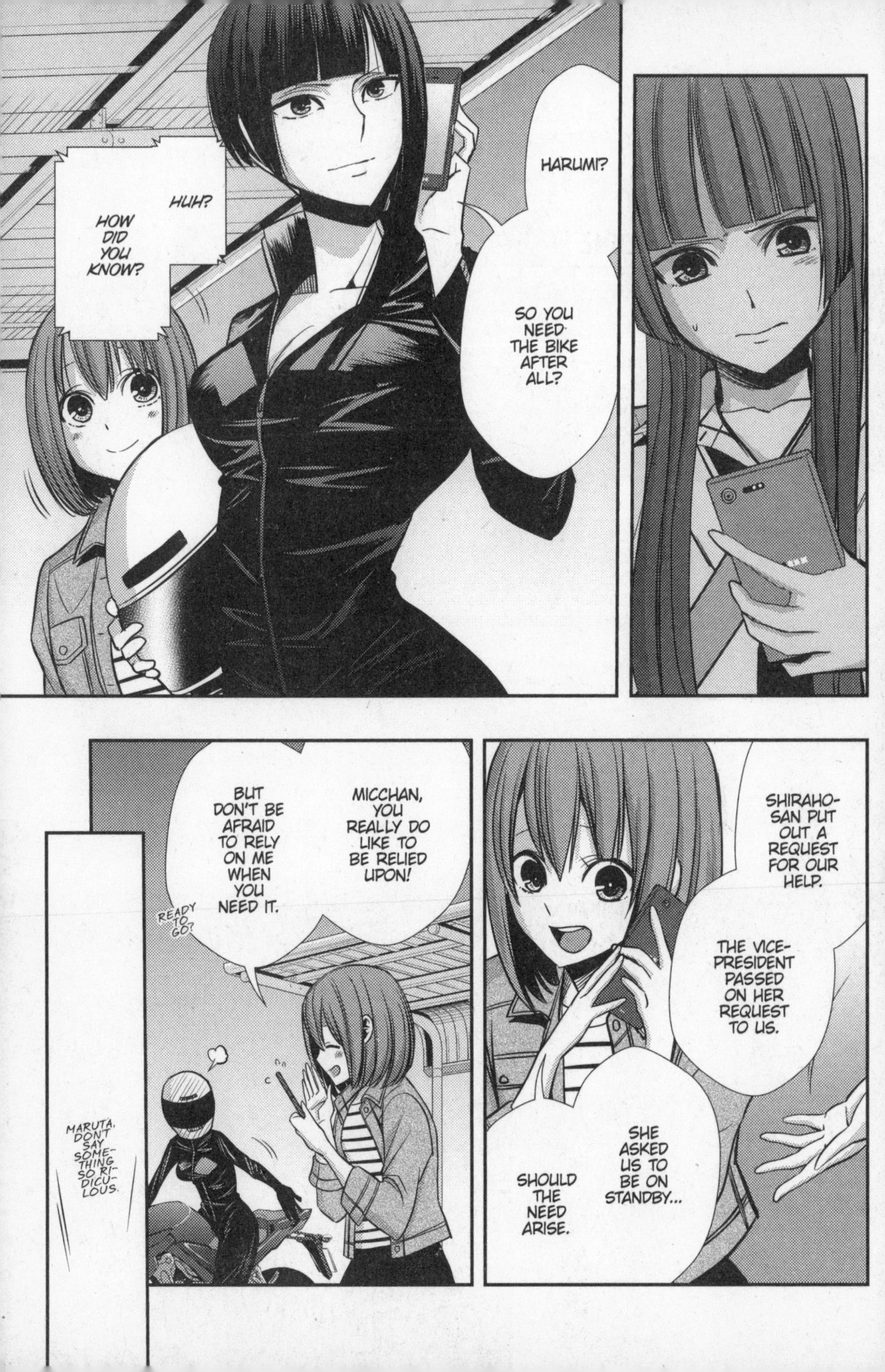
HARUMI?
SO YOU NEED THE BIKE AFTER ALL?
HUH? HOW DID YOU KNOW?
SHIRAHO-SAN PUT OUT A REQUEST FOR OUR HELP.
THE VICE-PRESIDENT PASSED ON HER REQUEST TO US.
SHE ASKED US TO BE ON STANDBY...
SHOULD THE NEED ARISE.
MICCHAN, YOU REALLY DO LIKE TO BE RELIED UPON!
BUT DON'T BE AFRAID TO RELY ON ME WHEN YOU NEED IT.
READY TO GO?
MARUTA, DON'T SAY SOMETHING SO RIDICULOUS.

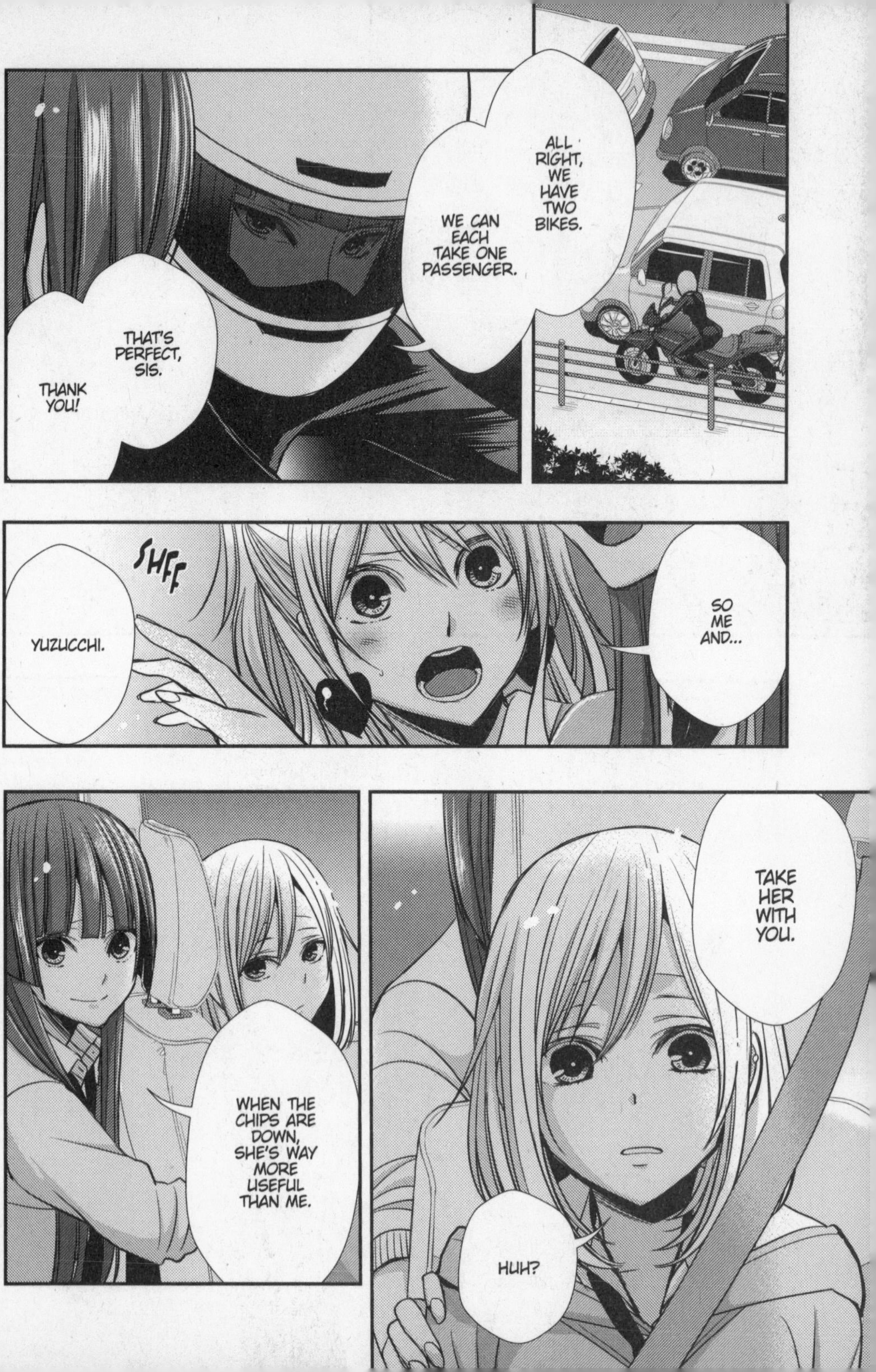
ALL RIGHT, WE HAVE TWO BIKES.
WE CAN EACH TAKE ONE PASSENGER.
THAT'S PERFECT, SIS.
THANK YOU!
SO ME AND...
SHFF
YUZUCCHI.
TAKE HER WITH YOU.
HUH?
WHEN THE CHIPS ARE DOWN, SHE'S WAY MORE USEFUL THAN ME.

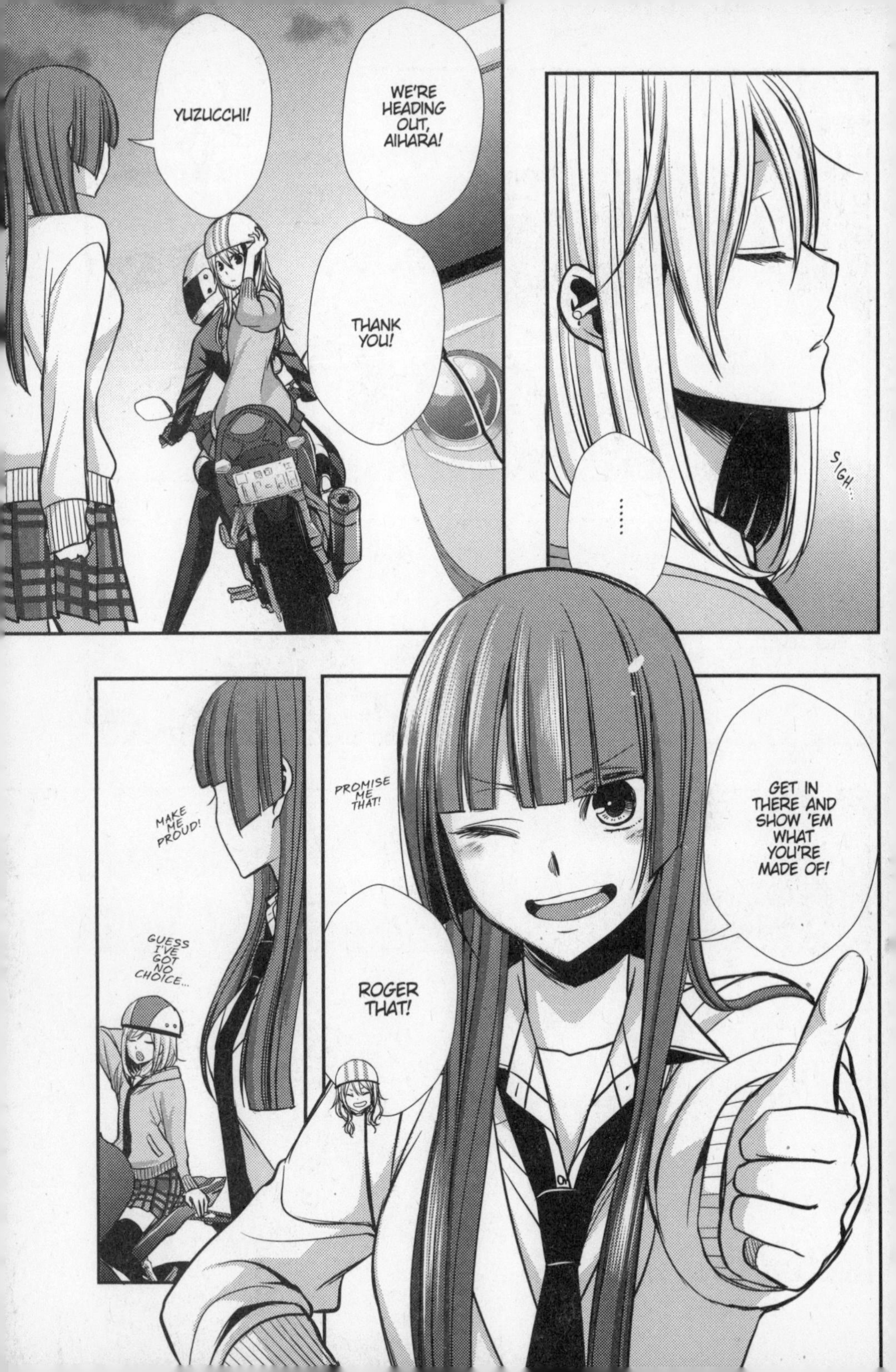
......
SIGH...
WE'RE HEADING OUT, AIHARA!
THANK YOU!
YUZUCCHI!
GET IN THERE AND SHOW 'EM WHAT YOU'RE MADE OF!
ROGER THAT!
PROMISE ME THAT!
MAKE ME PROUD!
GUESS I'VE GOT NO CHOICE...

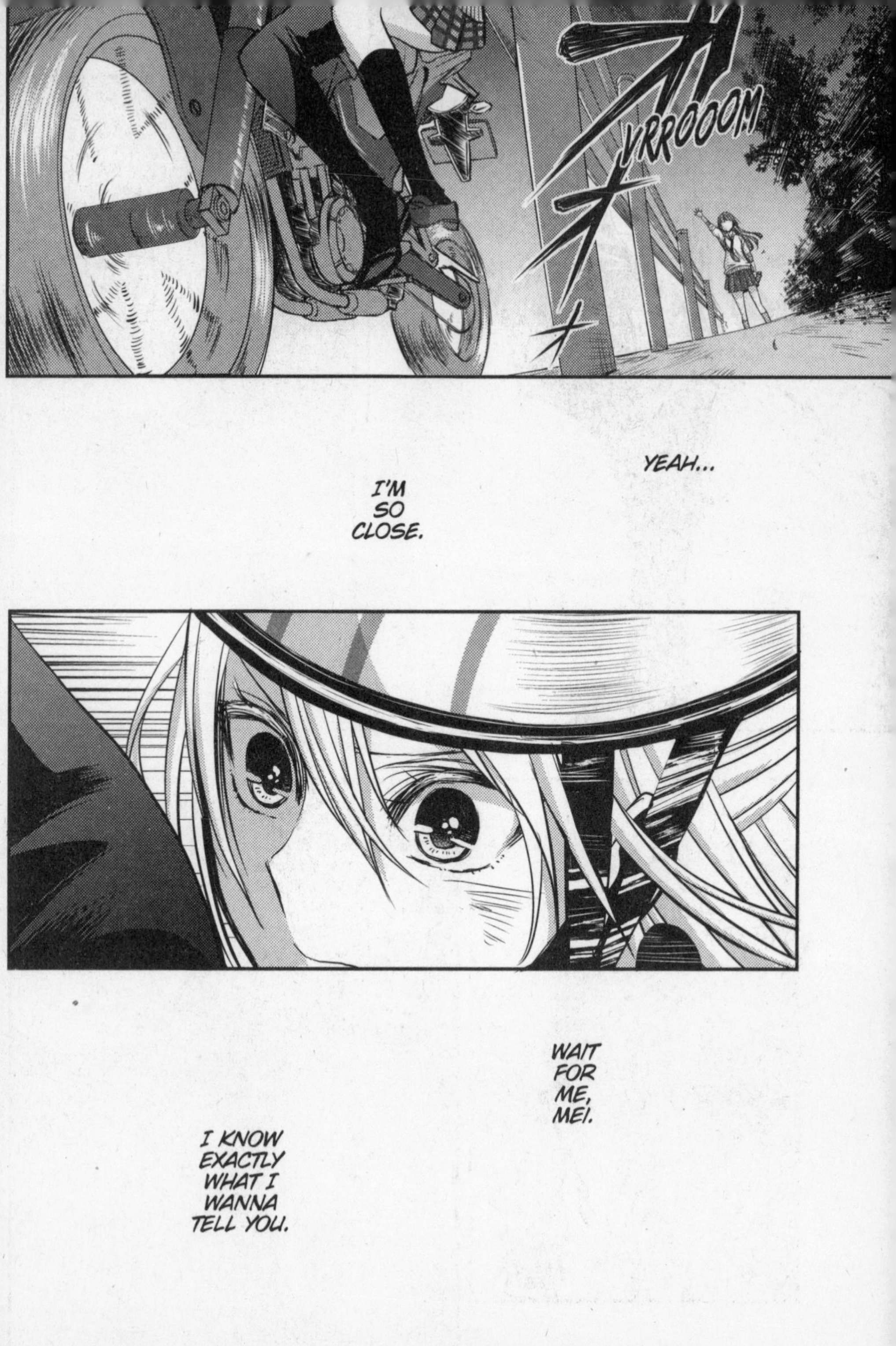
VRROOOM
YEAH...
I'M SO CLOSE.
WAIT FOR ME, MEI.
I KNOW EXACTLY WHAT I WANNA TELL YOU.

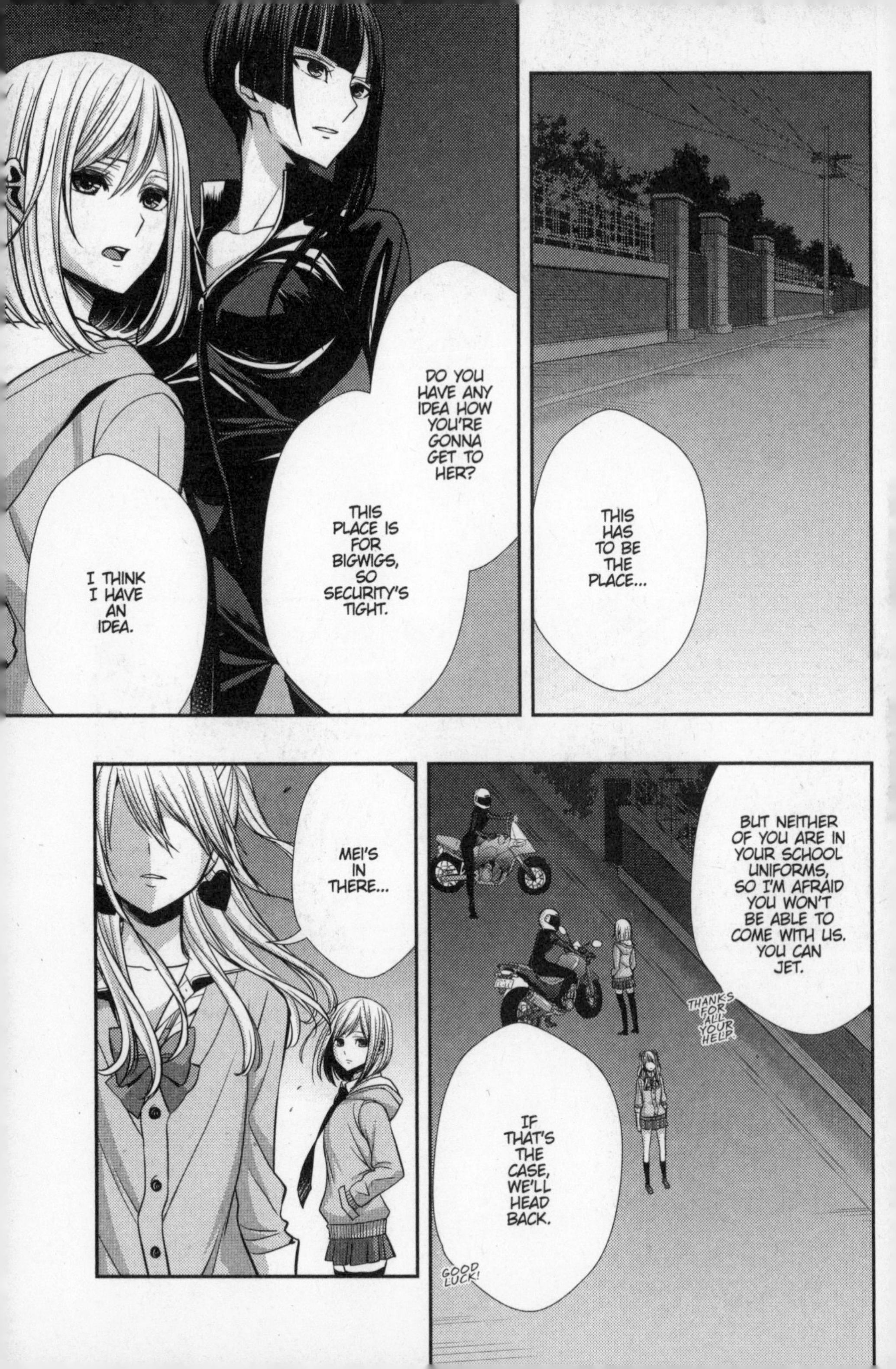
THIS HAS TO BE THE PLACE...
DO YOU HAVE ANY IDEA HOW YOU'RE GONNA GET TO HER?
THIS PLACE IS FOR BIGWIGS, SO SECURITY'S TIGHT.
I THINK I HAVE AN IDEA.
BUT NEITHER OF YOU ARE IN YOUR SCHOOL UNIFORMS, SO I'M AFRAID YOU WON'T BE ABLE TO COME WITH US. YOU CAN JET.
THANKS FOR ALL YOUR HELP.
IF THAT'S THE CASE, WE'LL HEAD BACK.
GOOD LUCK!
MEI'S IN THERE...

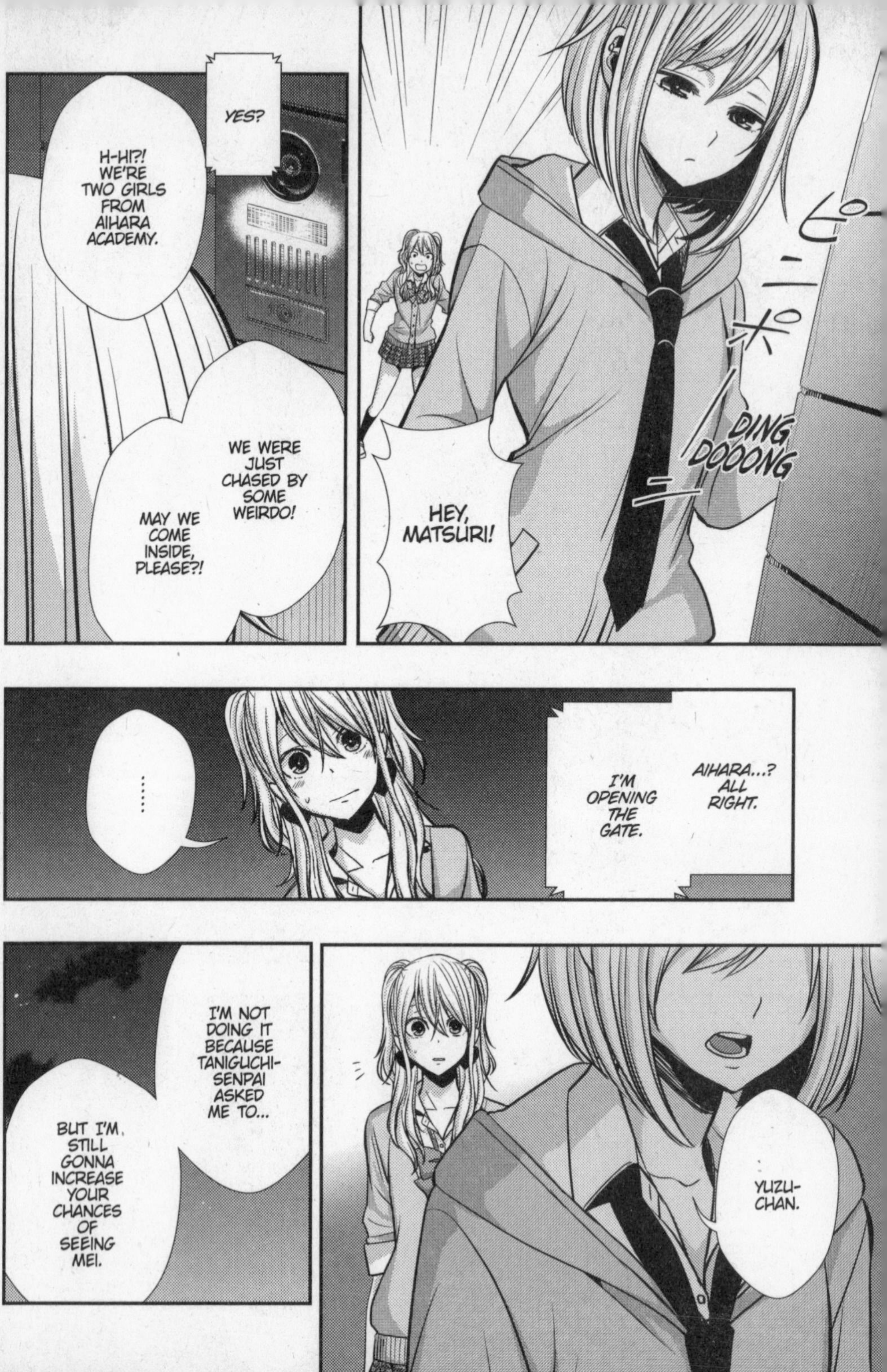
ピーンポーン
DING DOOOONG
HEY, MATSURI!
YES?
H-HI?! WE'RE TWO GIRLS FROM AIHARA ACADEMY.
WE WERE JUST CHASED BY SOME WEIRDO!
MAY WE COME INSIDE, PLEASE?!
AIHARA...? ALL RIGHT.
I'M OPENING THE GATE.
......
YUZU-CHAN.
I'M NOT DOING IT BECAUSE TANIGUCHI-SENPAI ASKED ME TO...
BUT I'M STILL GONNA INCREASE YOUR CHANCES OF SEEING MEI.

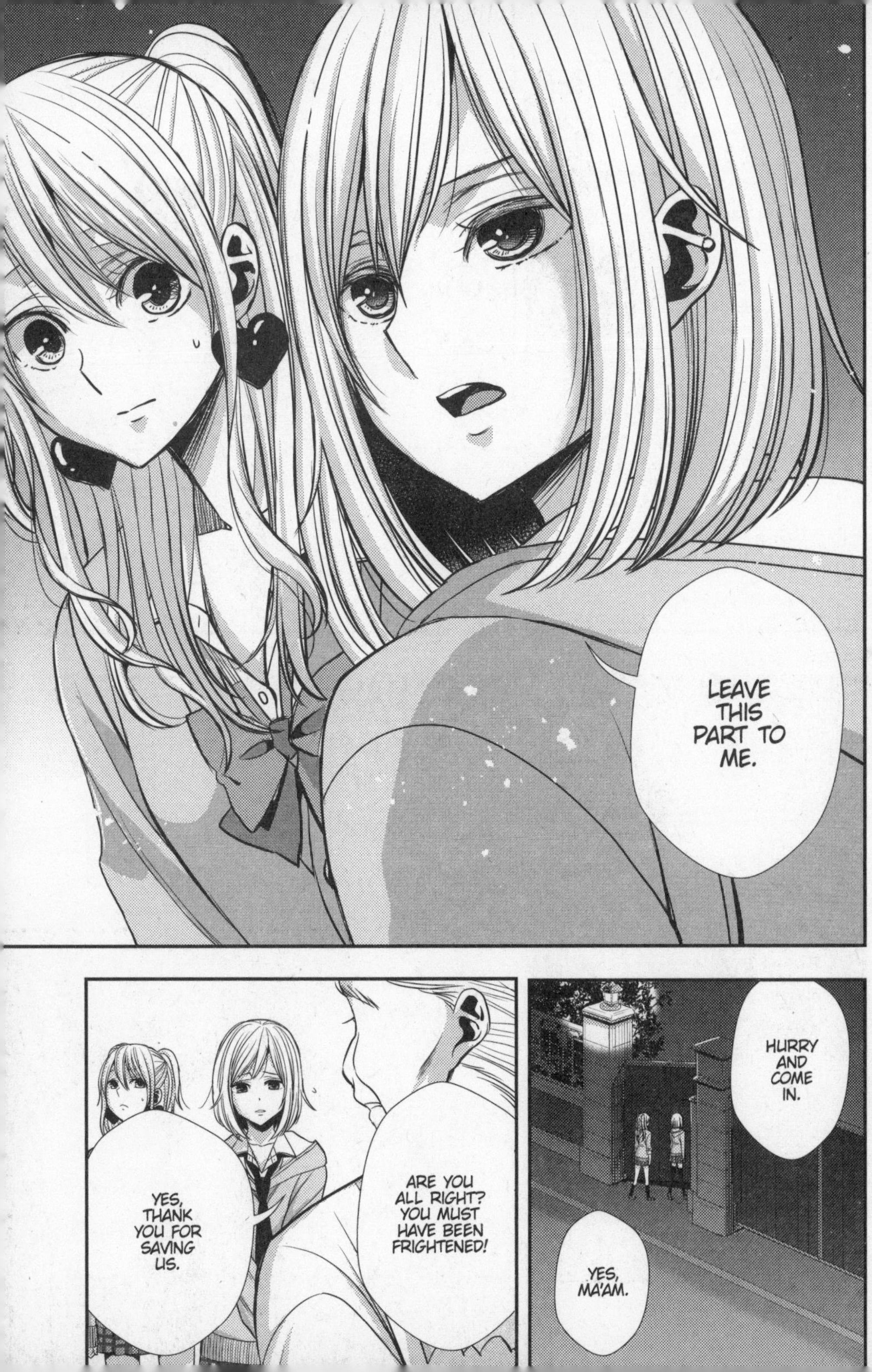
LEAVE THIS PART TO ME.
HURRY AND COME IN.
YES, MA'AM.
ARE YOU ALL RIGHT? YOU MUST HAVE BEEN FRIGHTENED!
YES, THANK YOU FOR SAVING US.

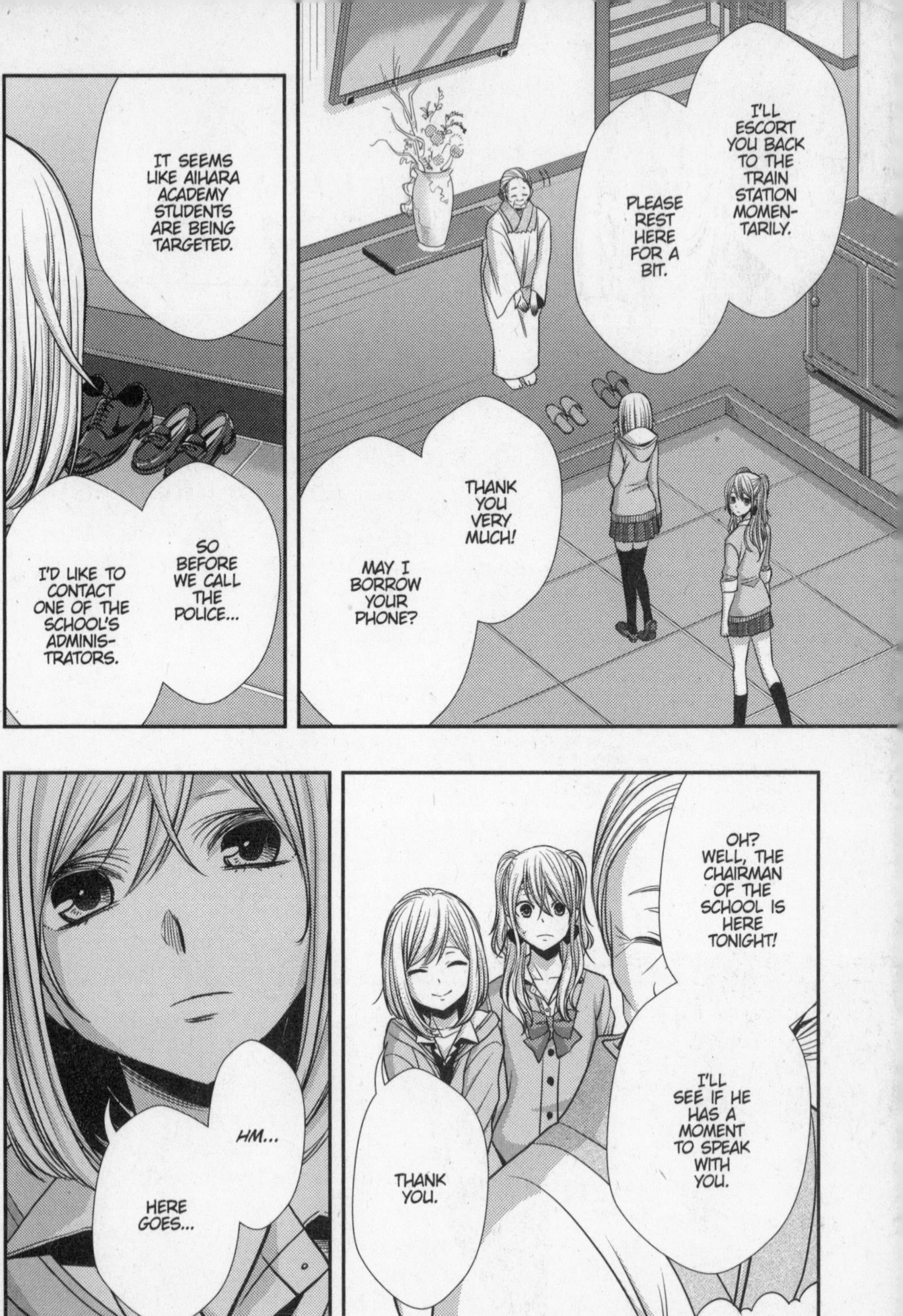
I'LL ESCORT YOU BACK TO THE TRAIN STATION MOMENTARILY.
PLEASE REST HERE FOR A BIT.
THANK YOU VERY MUCH!
MAY I BORROW YOUR PHONE?
IT SEEMS LIKE AIHARA ACADEMY STUDENTS ARE BEING TARGETED.
SO BEFORE WE CALL THE POLICE...
I'D LIKE TO CONTACT ONE OF THE SCHOOL'S ADMINISTRATORS.
OH? WELL, THE CHAIRMAN OF THE SCHOOL IS HERE TONIGHT!
I'LL SEE IF HE HAS A MOMENT TO SPEAK WITH YOU.
THANK YOU.
HM...
HERE GOES...

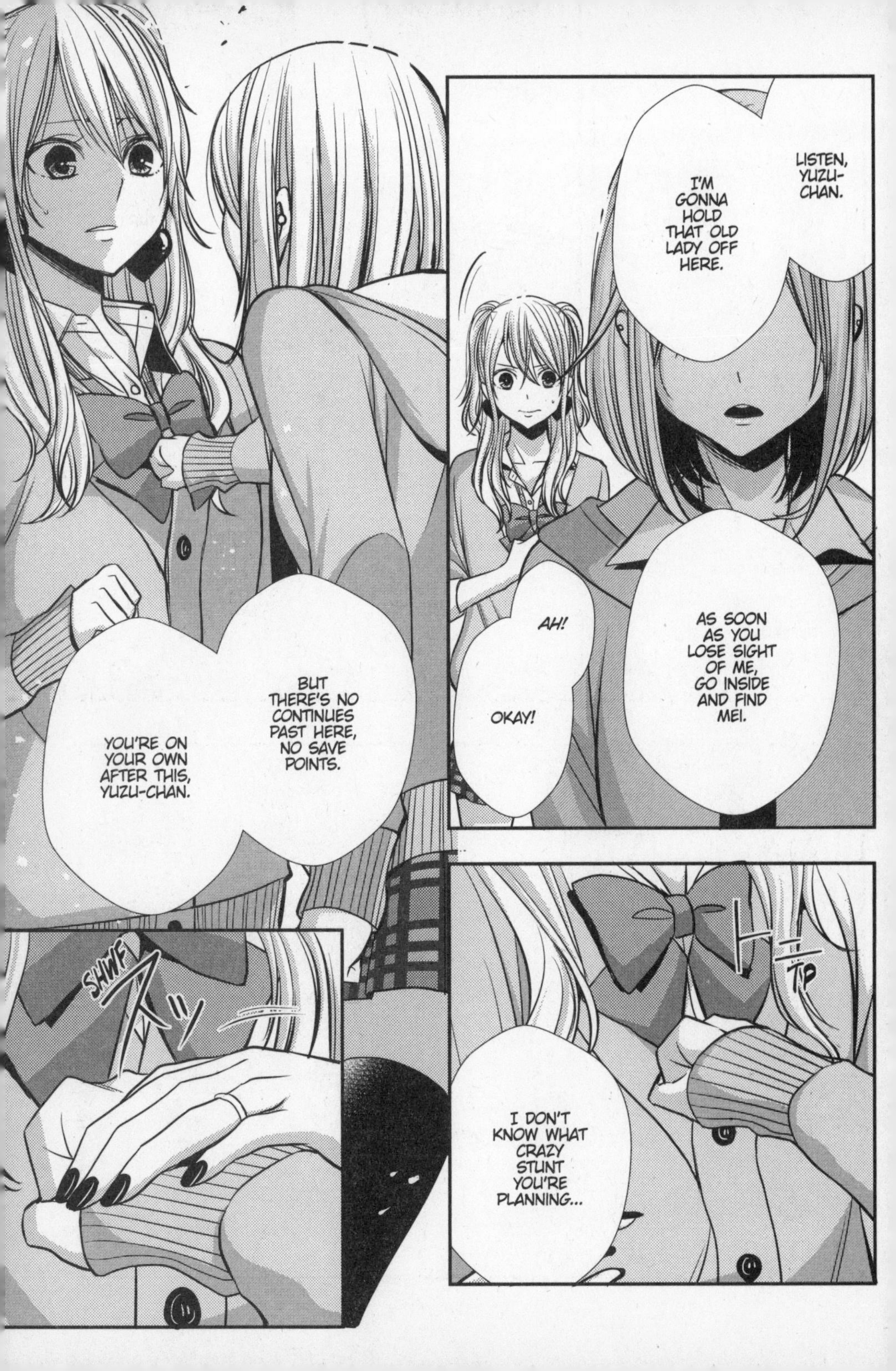
LISTEN, YUZU-CHAN.
I'M GONNA HOLD THAT OLD LADY OFF HERE.
AS SOON AS YOU LOSE SIGHT OF ME, GO INSIDE AND FIND MEI.
AH!
OKAY!
BUT THERE'S NO CONTINUES PAST HERE, NO SAVE POINTS.
YOU'RE ON YOUR OWN AFTER THIS, YUZU-CHAN.
TIP
I DON'T KNOW WHAT CRAZY STUNT YOU'RE PLANNING...
SHWF

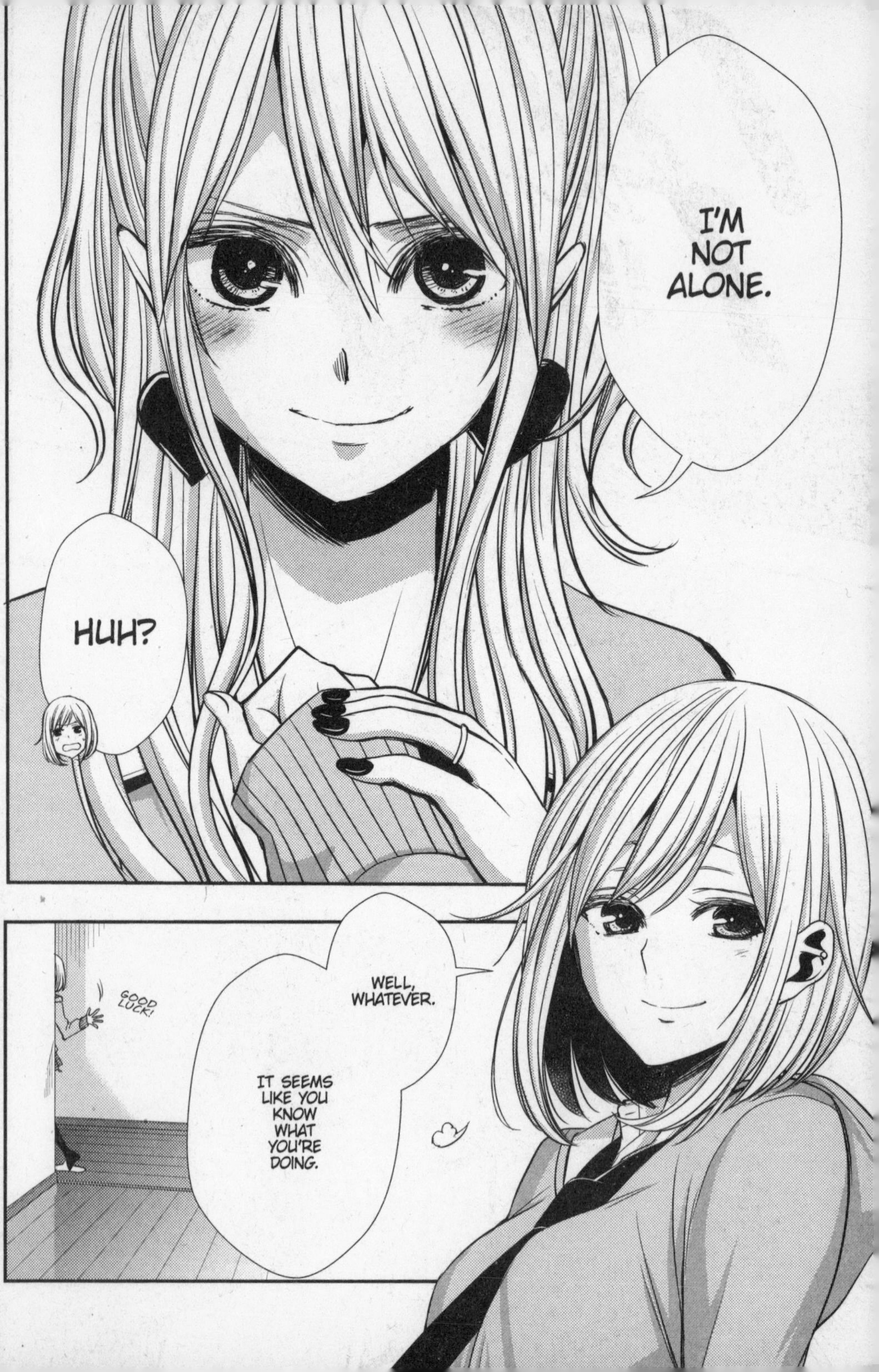
I'M NOT ALONE.
HUH?
WELL, WHATEVER.
IT SEEMS LIKE YOU KNOW WHAT YOU'RE DOING.
GOOD LUCK!

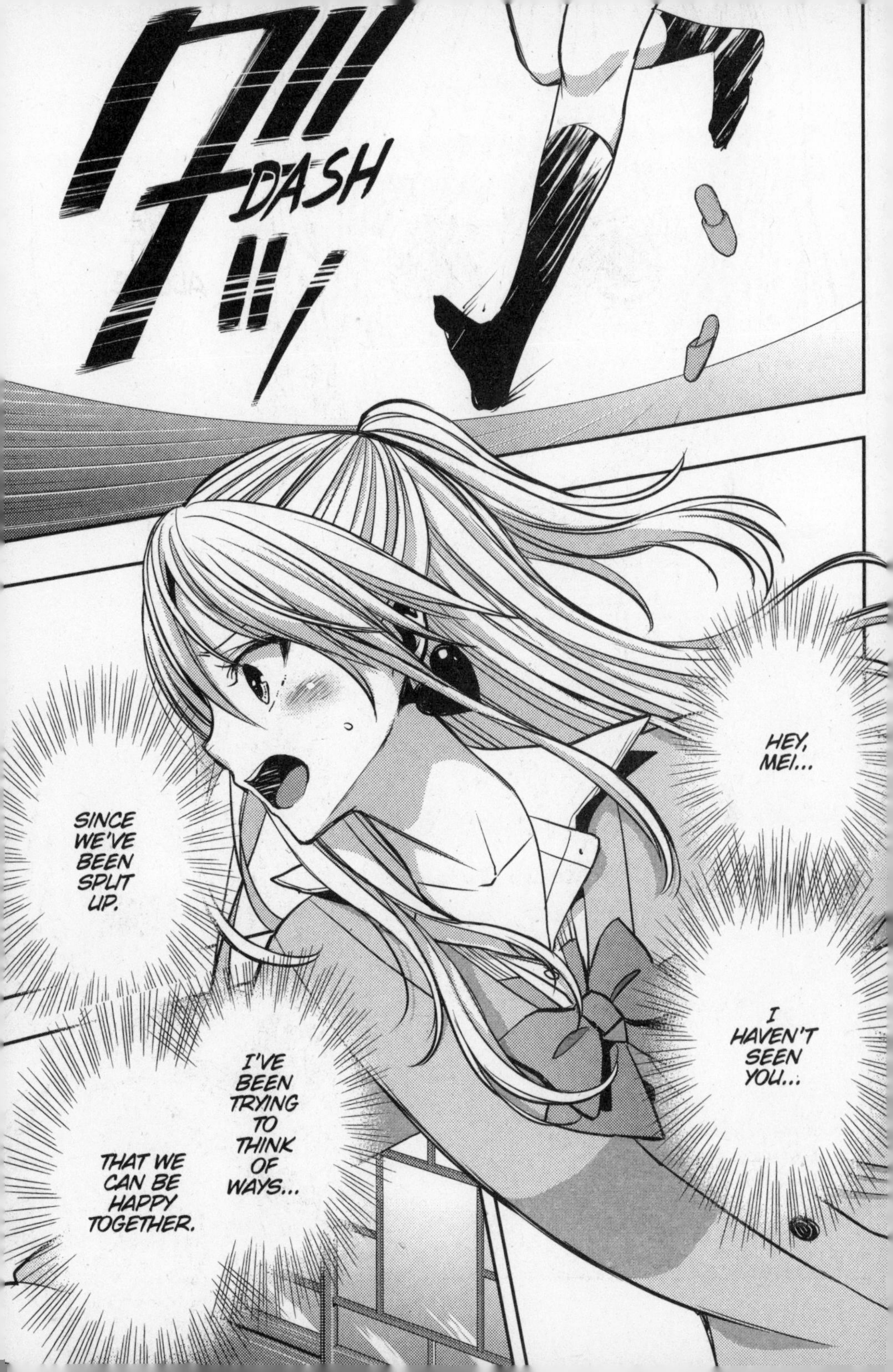
DASH
HEY, MEI...
I HAVEN'T SEEN YOU...
SINCE WE'VE BEEN SPLIT UP.
I'VE BEEN TRYING TO THINK OF WAYS...
THAT WE CAN BE HAPPY TOGETHER.

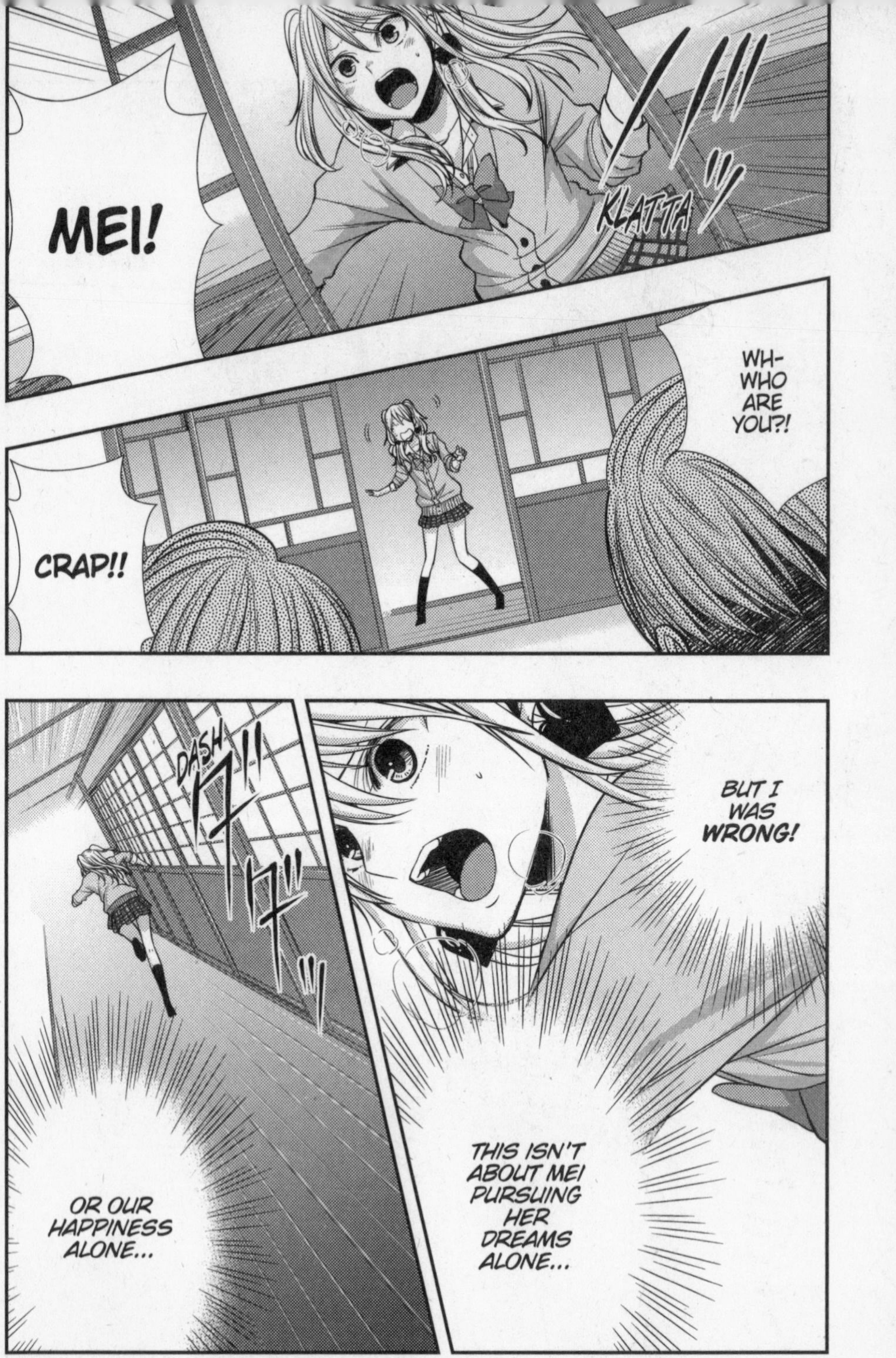
KLATTA
MEI!
WH-WHO ARE YOU?!
CRAP!!
BUT I WAS WRONG!
THIS ISN'T ABOUT MEI PURSUING HER DREAMS ALONE...
DASH
OR OUR HAPPINESS ALONE...

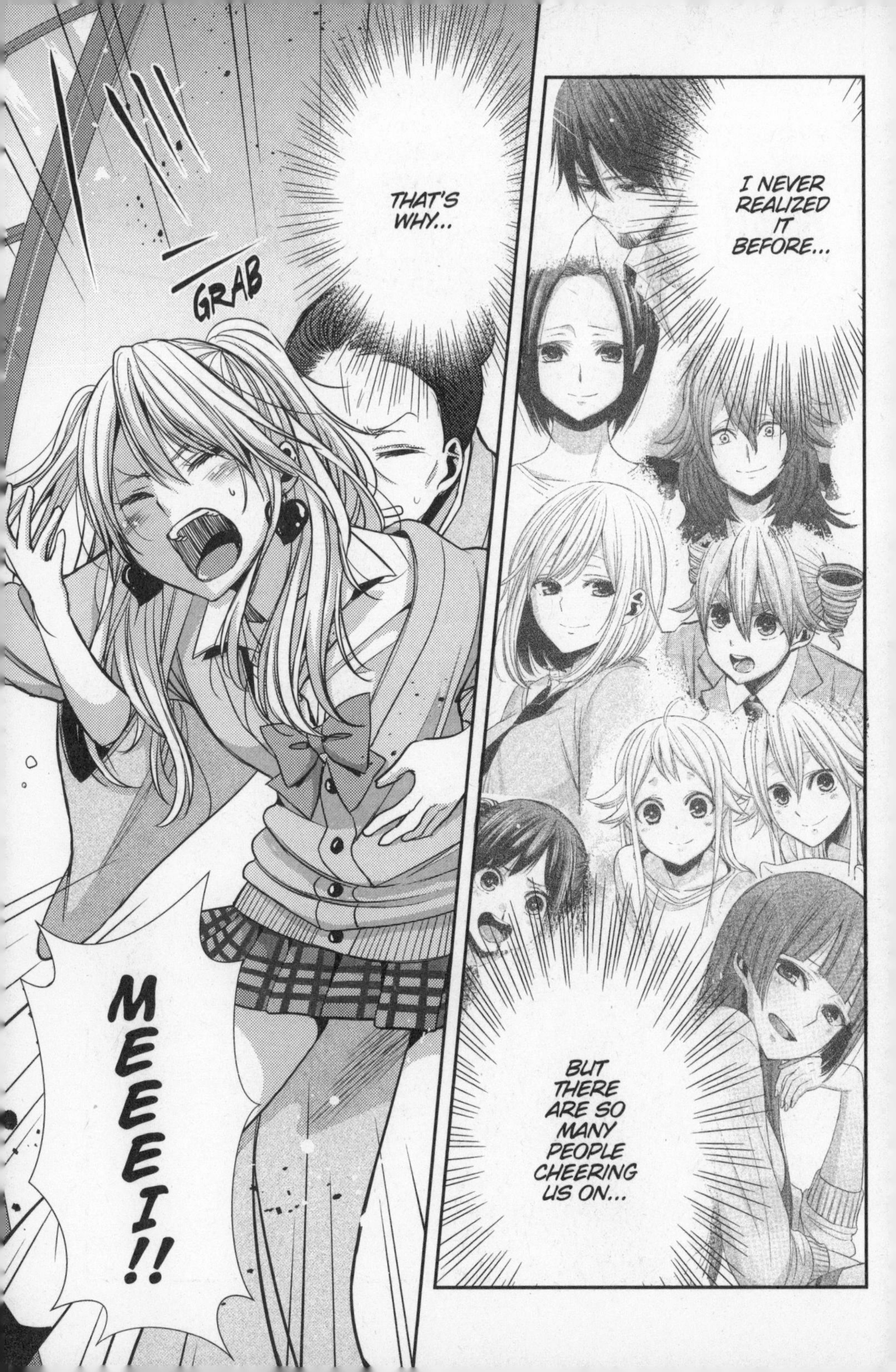
I NEVER REALIZED IT BEFORE...
BUT THERE ARE SO MANY PEOPLE CHEERING US ON...
THAT'S WHY...
GRAB
MEEEI!!

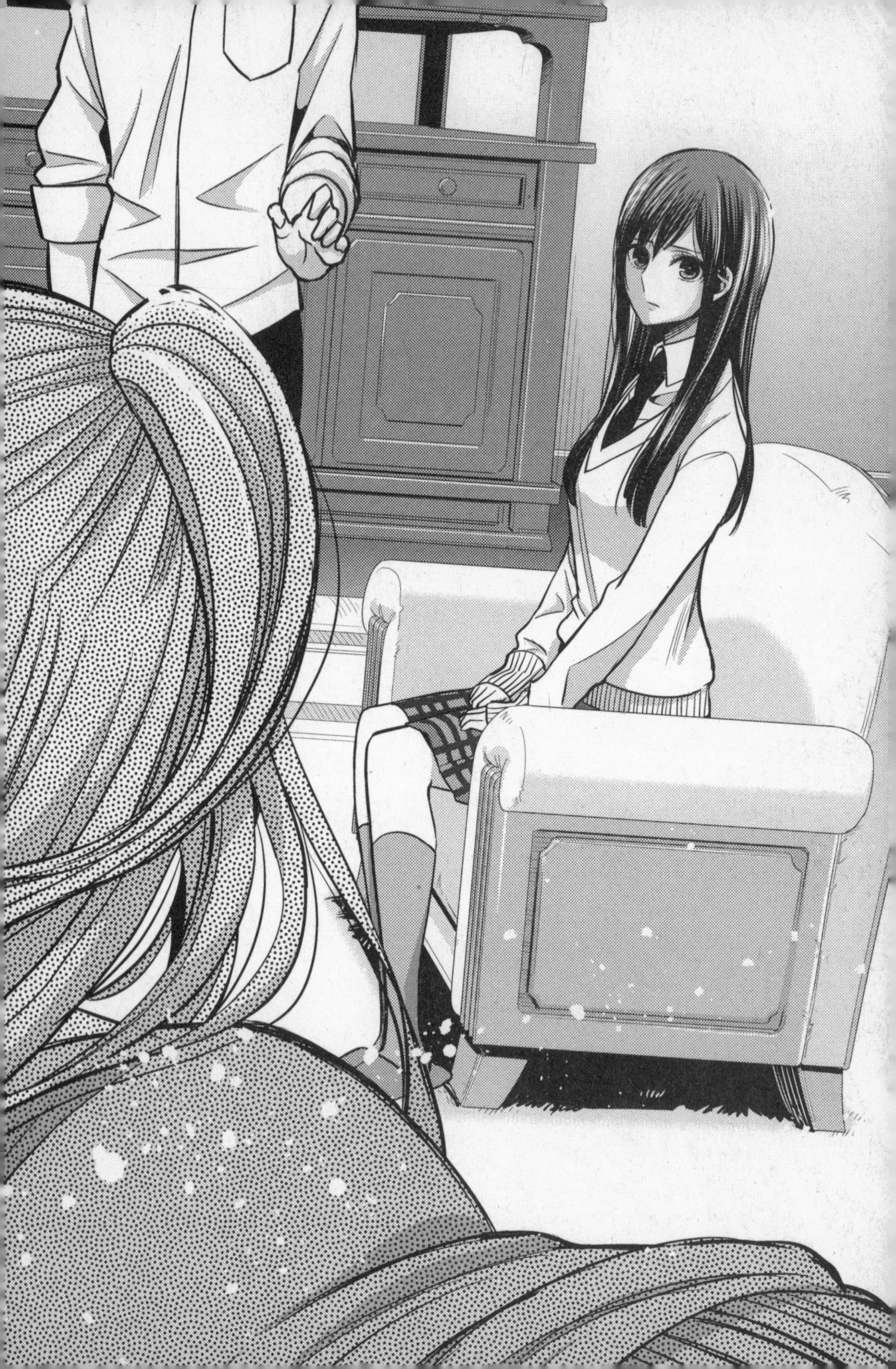

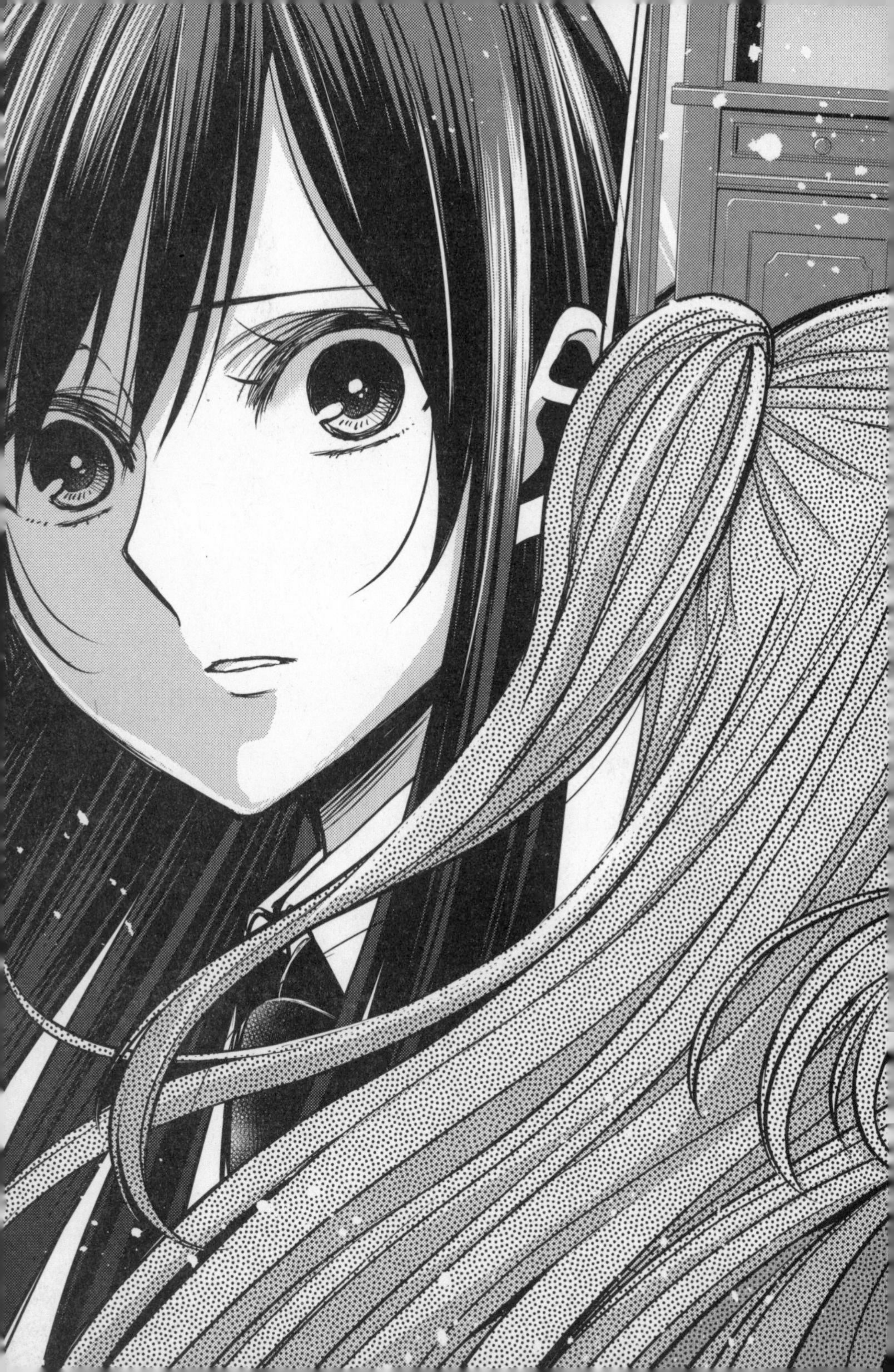

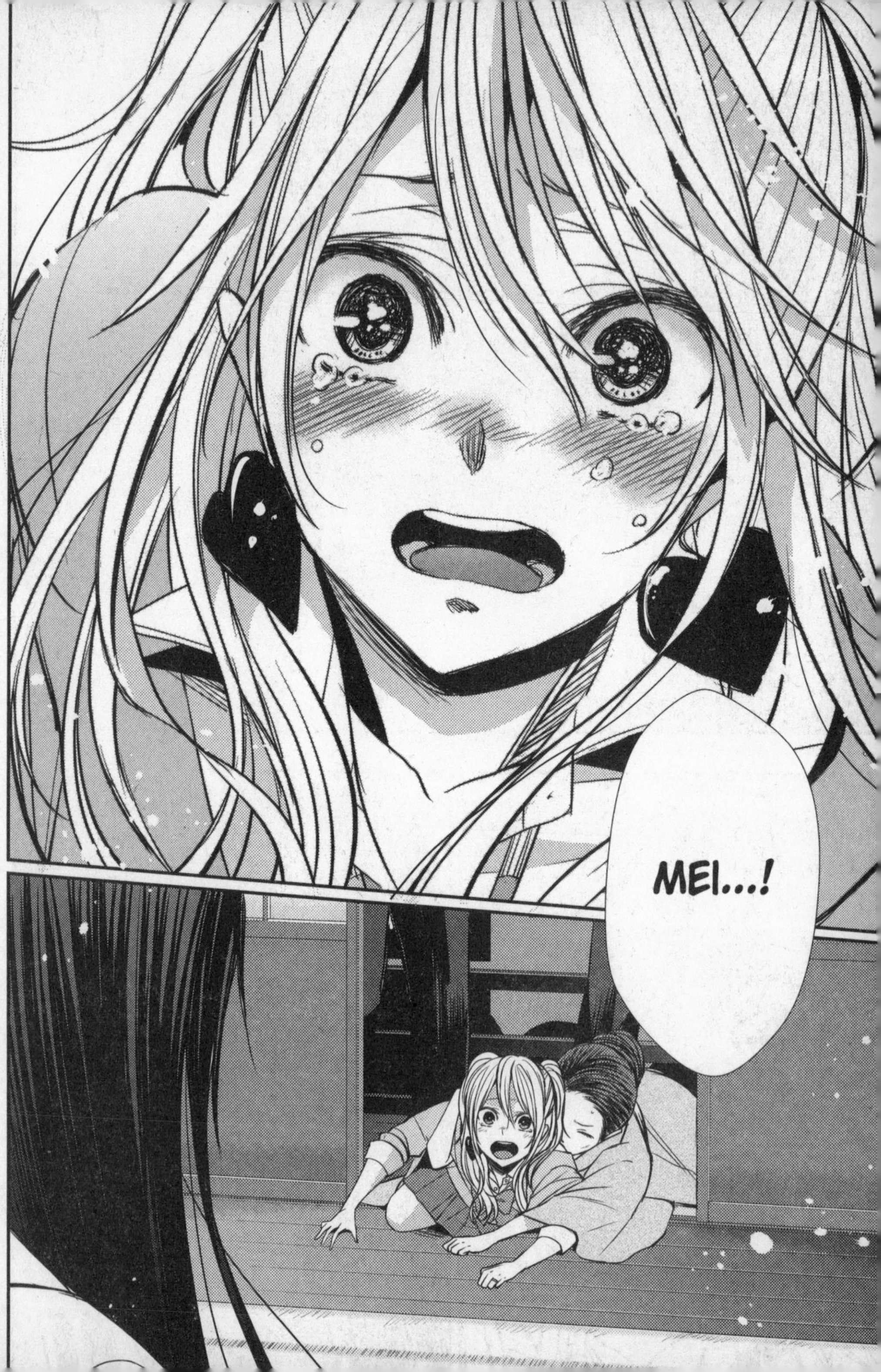
MEI...!

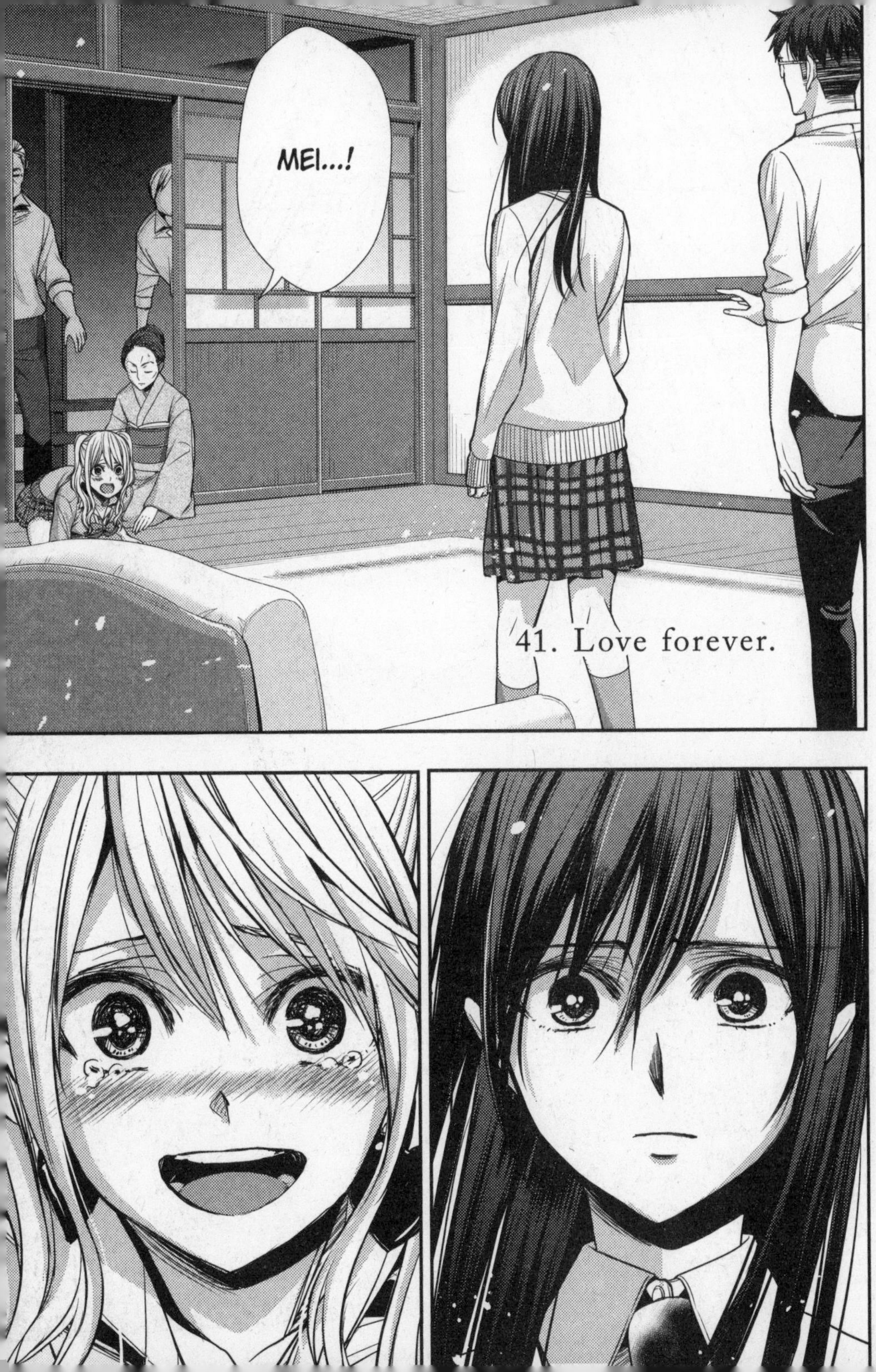
MEI...!
41. Love forever.

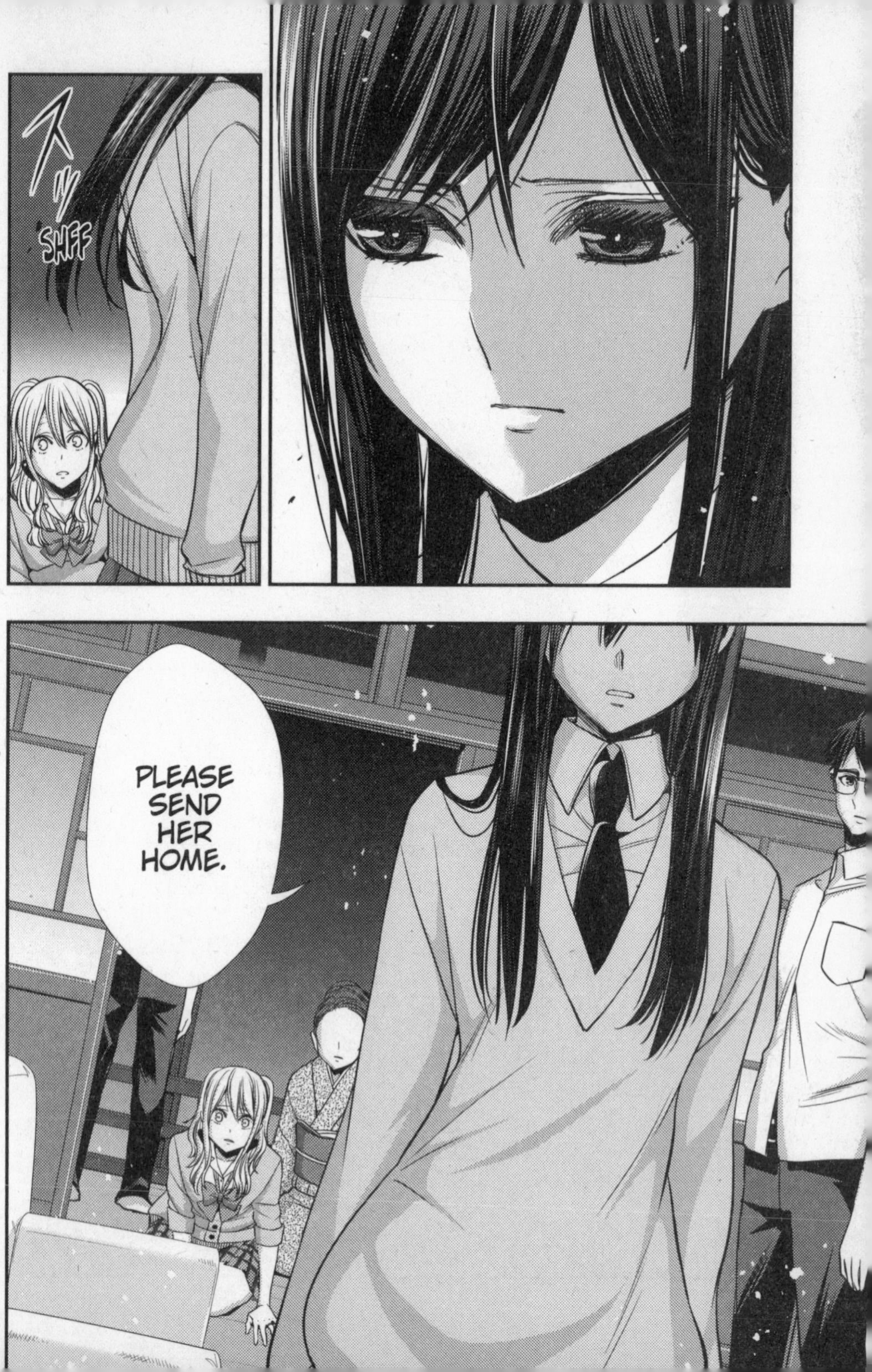
スッ
SHFF
PLEASE SEND HER HOME.

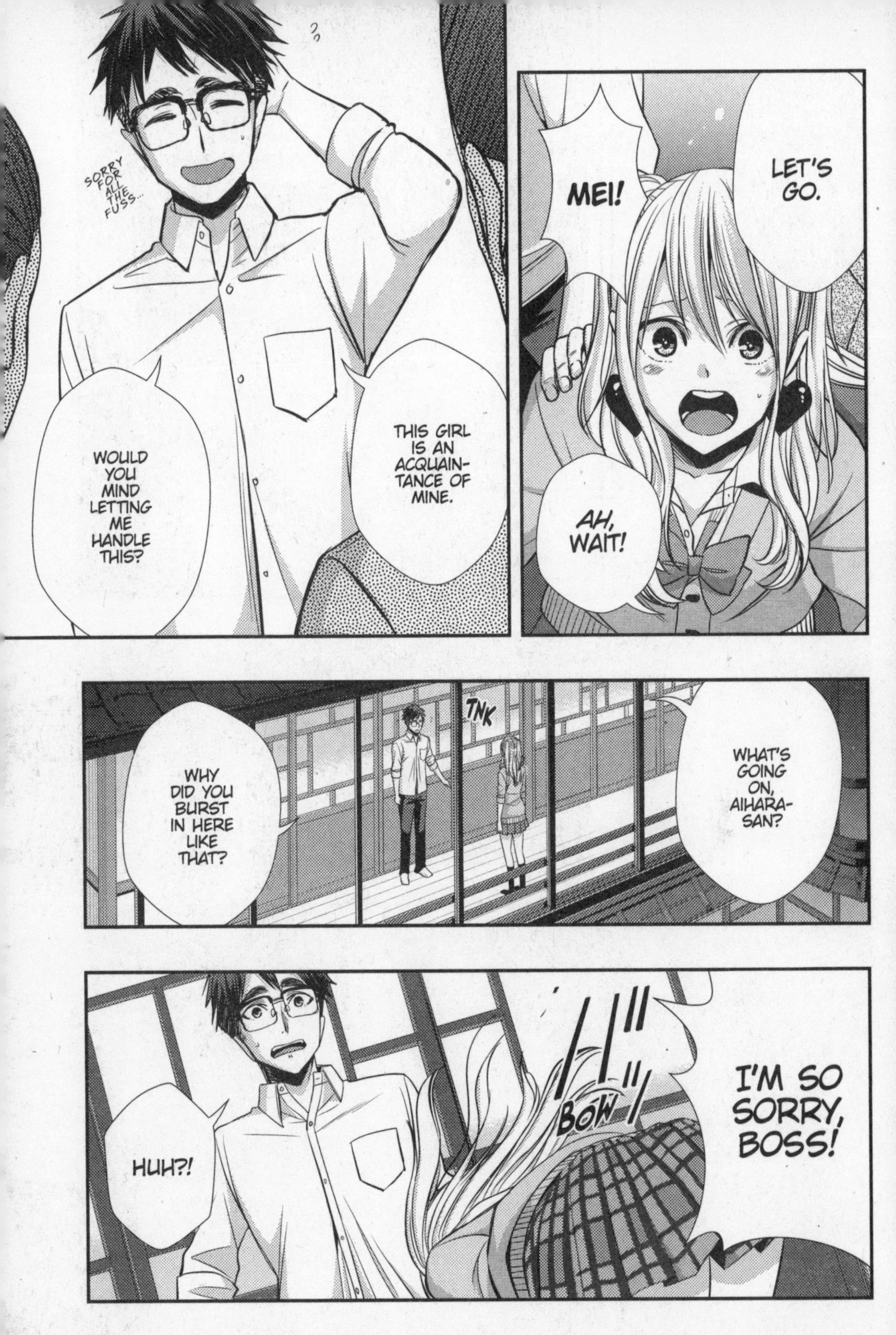
LET'S GO.
MEI!
AH, WAIT!
SORRY FOR ALL THE FUSS...
THIS GIRL IS AN ACQUAINTANCE OF MINE.
WOULD YOU MIND LETTING ME HANDLE THIS?
WHAT'S GOING ON, AIHARA-SAN?
TNK
WHY DID YOU BURST IN HERE LIKE THAT?
I'M SO SORRY, BOSS!
BOW
HUH?!

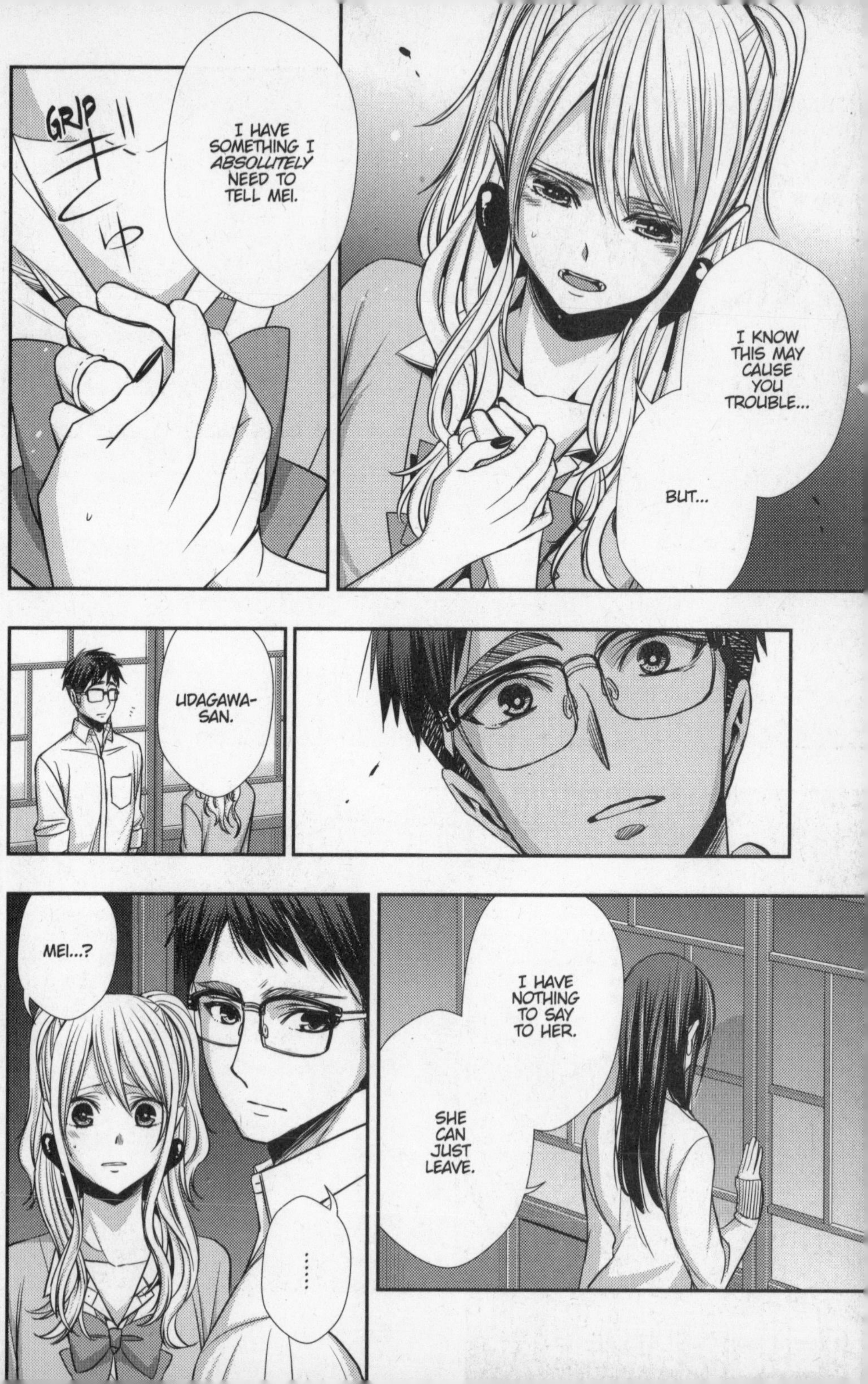
I KNOW THIS MAY CAUSE YOU TROUBLE...
BUT...
GRIP
I HAVE SOMETHING I ABSOLUTELY NEED TO TELL MEI.
UDAGAWA-SAN.
I HAVE NOTHING TO SAY TO HER.
SHE CAN JUST LEAVE.
MEI...?
......

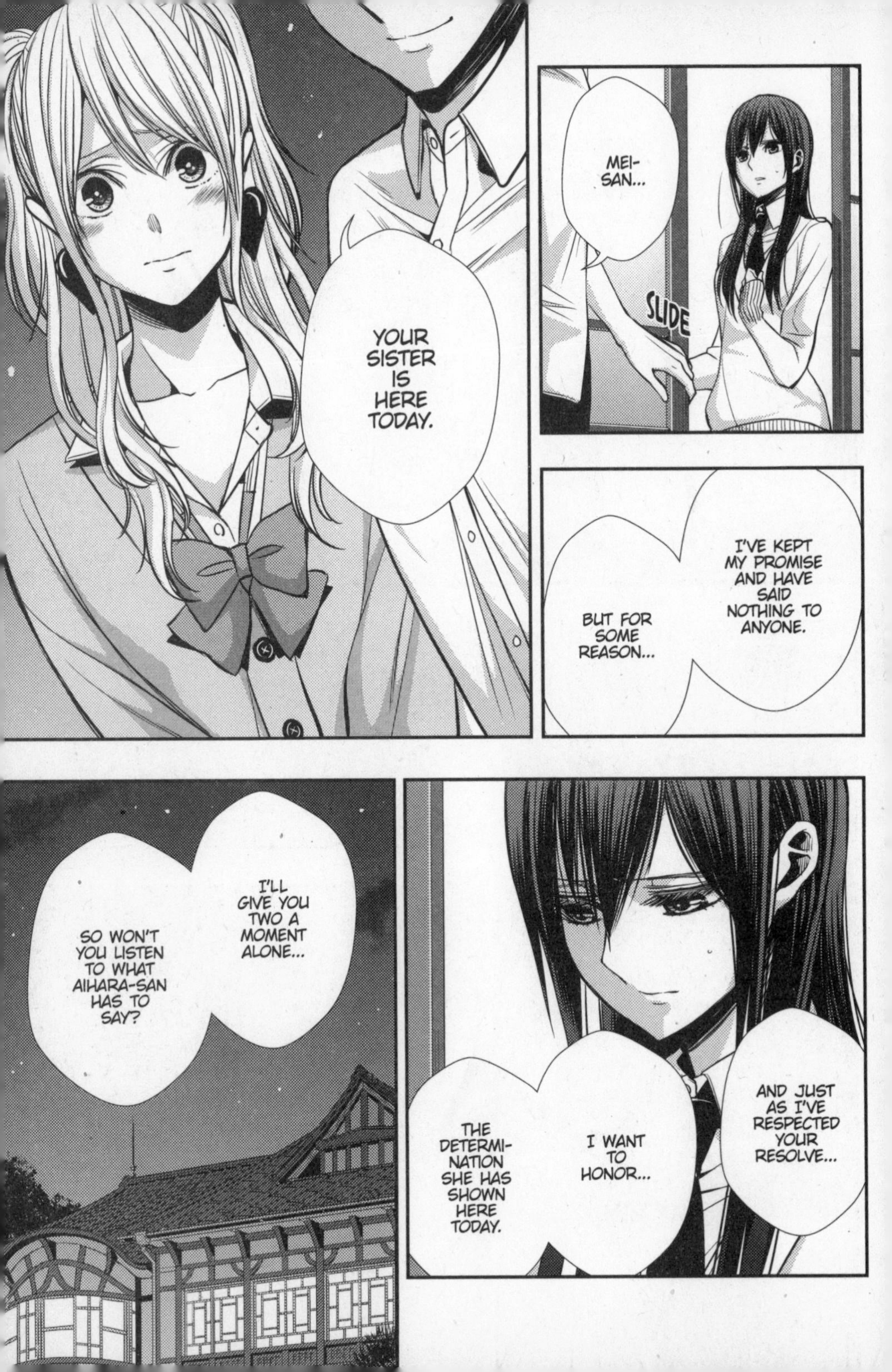
MEI-SAN...
SLIDE
I'VE KEPT MY PROMISE AND HAVE SAID NOTHING TO ANYONE.
BUT FOR SOME REASON...
YOUR SISTER IS HERE TODAY.
AND JUST AS I'VE RESPECTED YOUR RESOLVE...
I WANT TO HONOR...
THE DETERMINATION SHE HAS SHOWN HERE TODAY.
I'LL GIVE YOU TWO A MOMENT ALONE...
SO WON'T YOU LISTEN TO WHAT AIHARA-SAN HAS TO SAY?

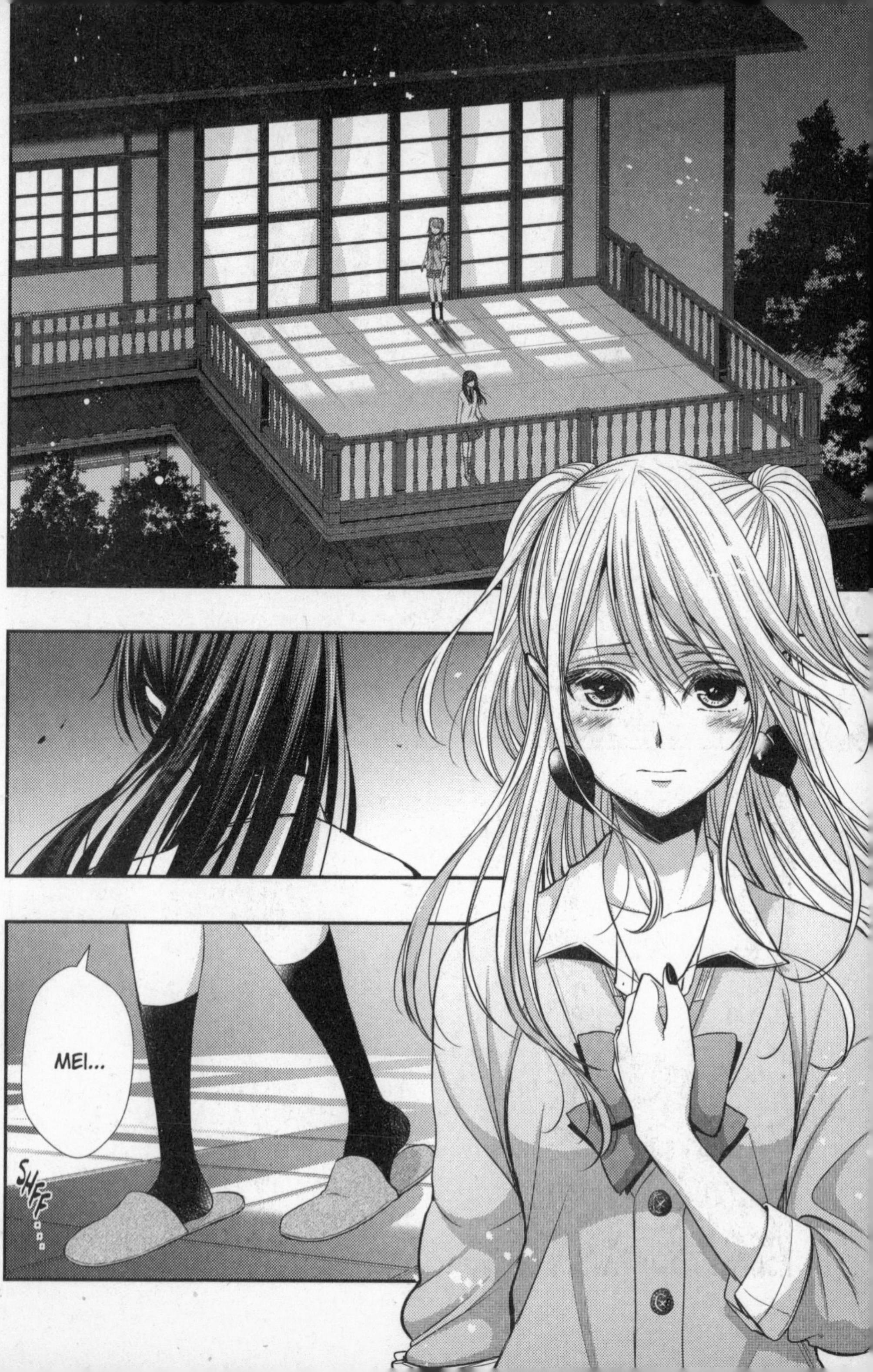
MEI...
SHFF...

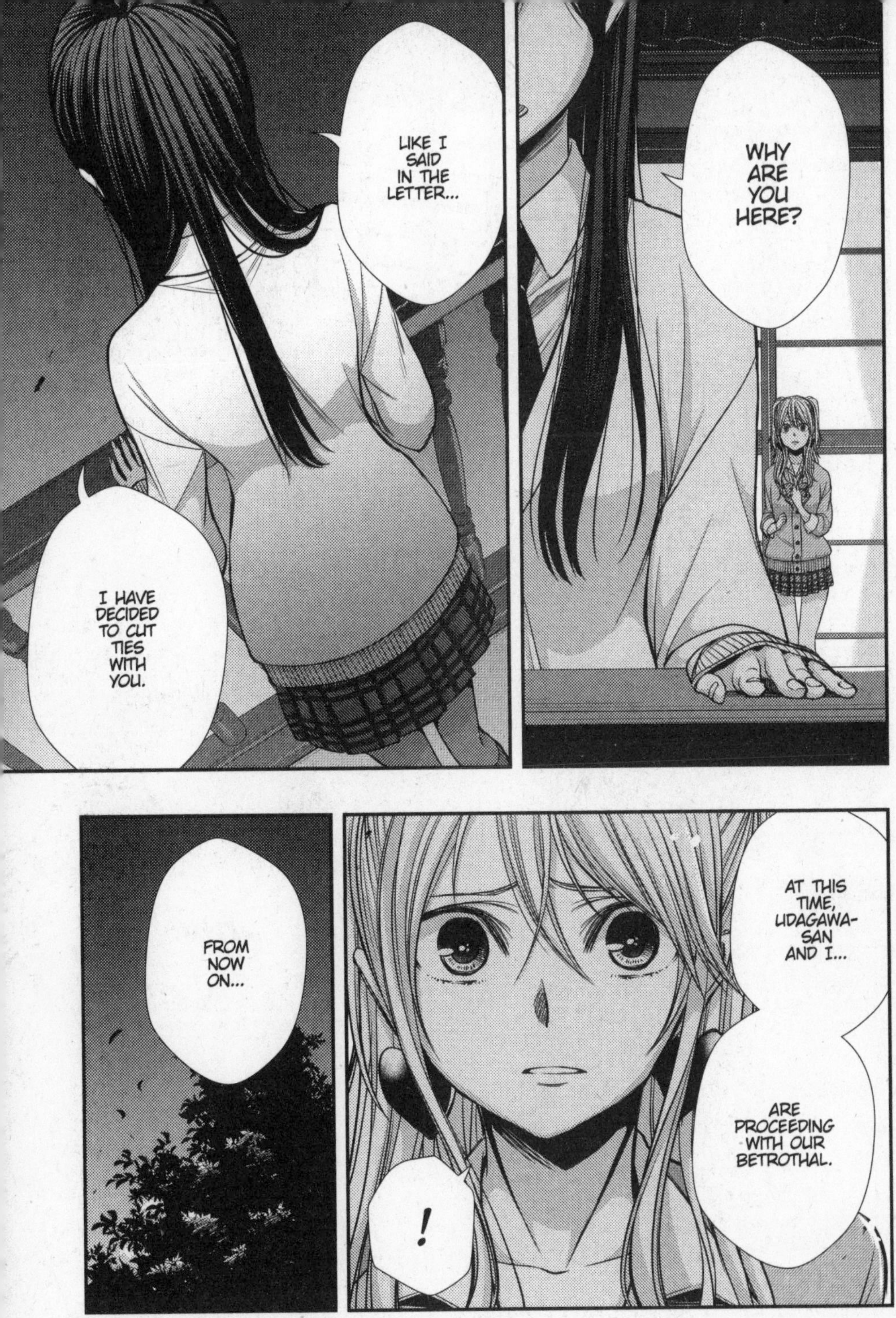
WHY ARE YOU HERE?
LIKE I SAID IN THE LETTER...
I HAVE DECIDED TO CUT TIES WITH YOU.
AT THIS TIME, UDAGAWA-SAN AND I...
ARE PROCEEDING WITH OUR BETROTHAL.
!
FROM NOW ON...

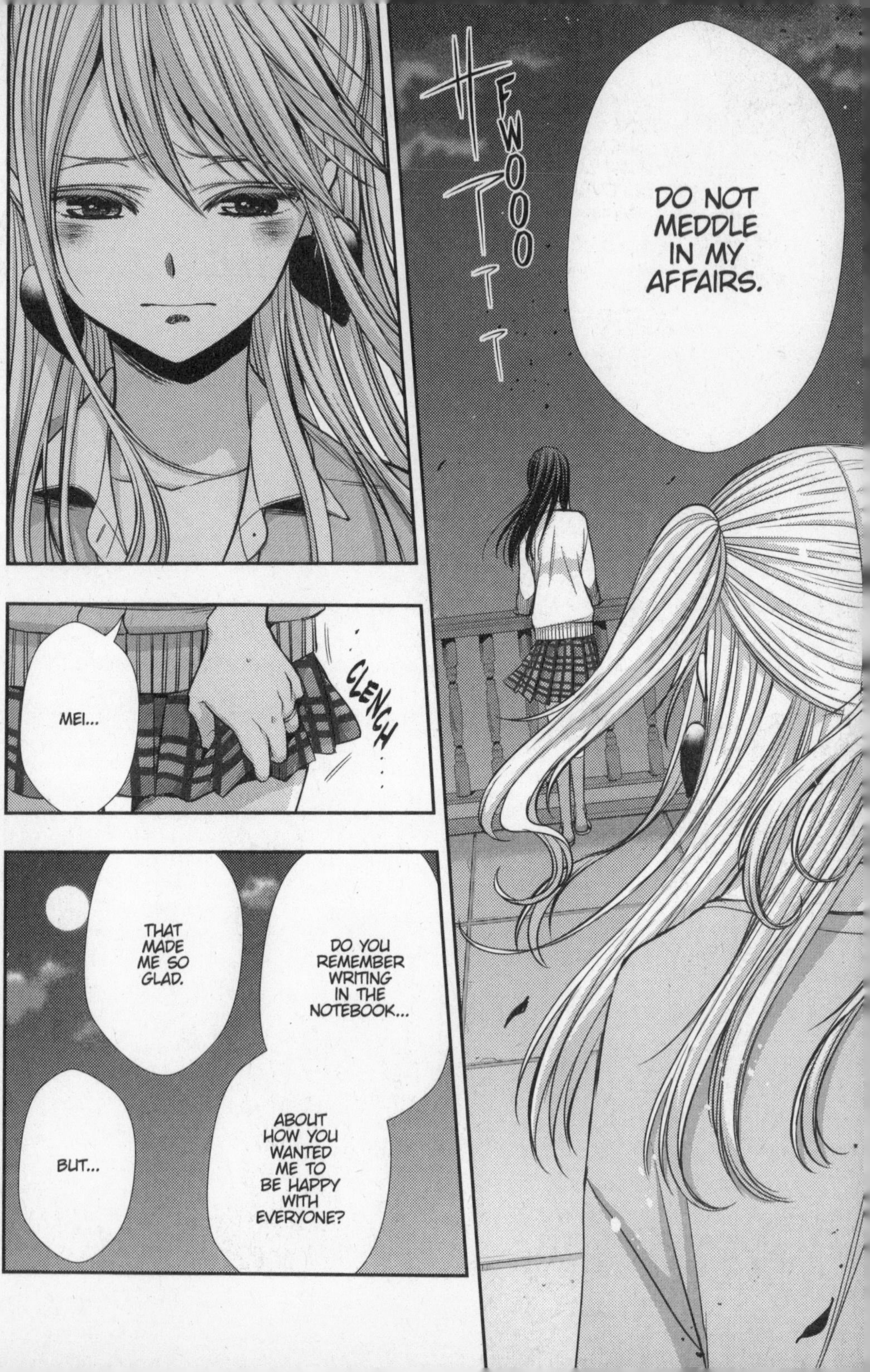
FWOOOT
DO NOT MEDDLE IN MY AFFAIRS.
CLENCH
MEI...
DO YOU REMEMBER WRITING IN THE NOTEBOOK...
ABOUT HOW YOU WANTED ME TO BE HAPPY WITH EVERYONE?
THAT MADE ME SO GLAD.
BUT...

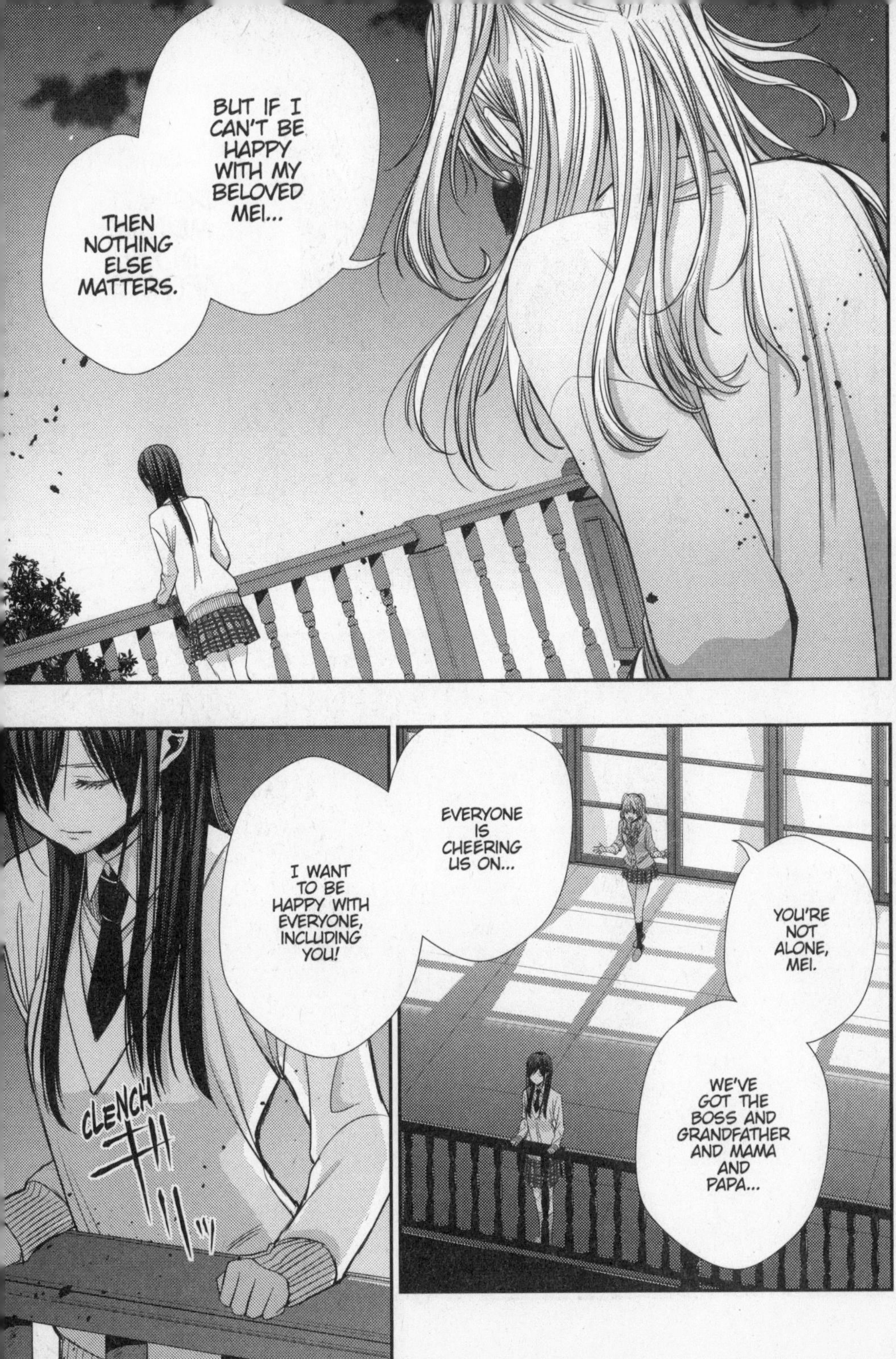
BUT IF I CAN'T BE HAPPY WITH MY BELOVED MEI...
THEN NOTHING ELSE MATTERS.
YOU'RE NOT ALONE, MEI.
WE'VE GOT THE BOSS AND GRANDFATHER AND MAMA AND PAPA...
EVERYONE IS CHEERING US ON...
I WANT TO BE HAPPY WITH EVERYONE, INCLUDING YOU!
CLENCH

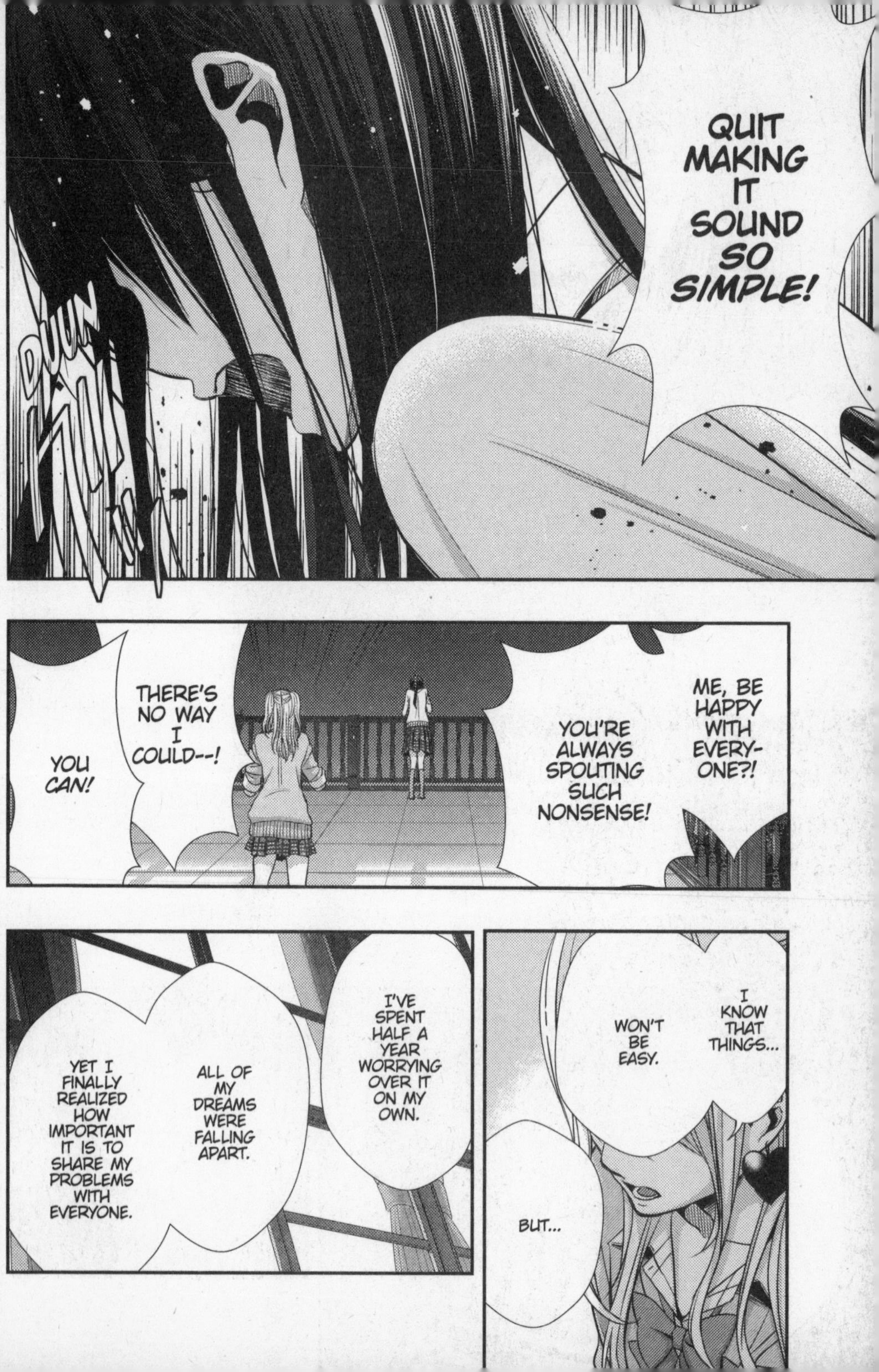
QUIT MAKING IT SOUND SO SIMPLE!
DUUN
ME, BE HAPPY WITH EVERY-ONE?!
YOU'RE ALWAYS SPOUTING SUCH NONSENSE!
THERE'S NO WAY I COULD--!
YOU CAN!
I KNOW THAT THINGS...
WON'T BE EASY.
BUT...
I'VE SPENT HALF A YEAR WORRYING OVER IT ON MY OWN.
ALL OF MY DREAMS WERE FALLING APART.
YET I FINALLY REALIZED HOW IMPORTANT IT IS TO SHARE MY PROBLEMS WITH EVERYONE.

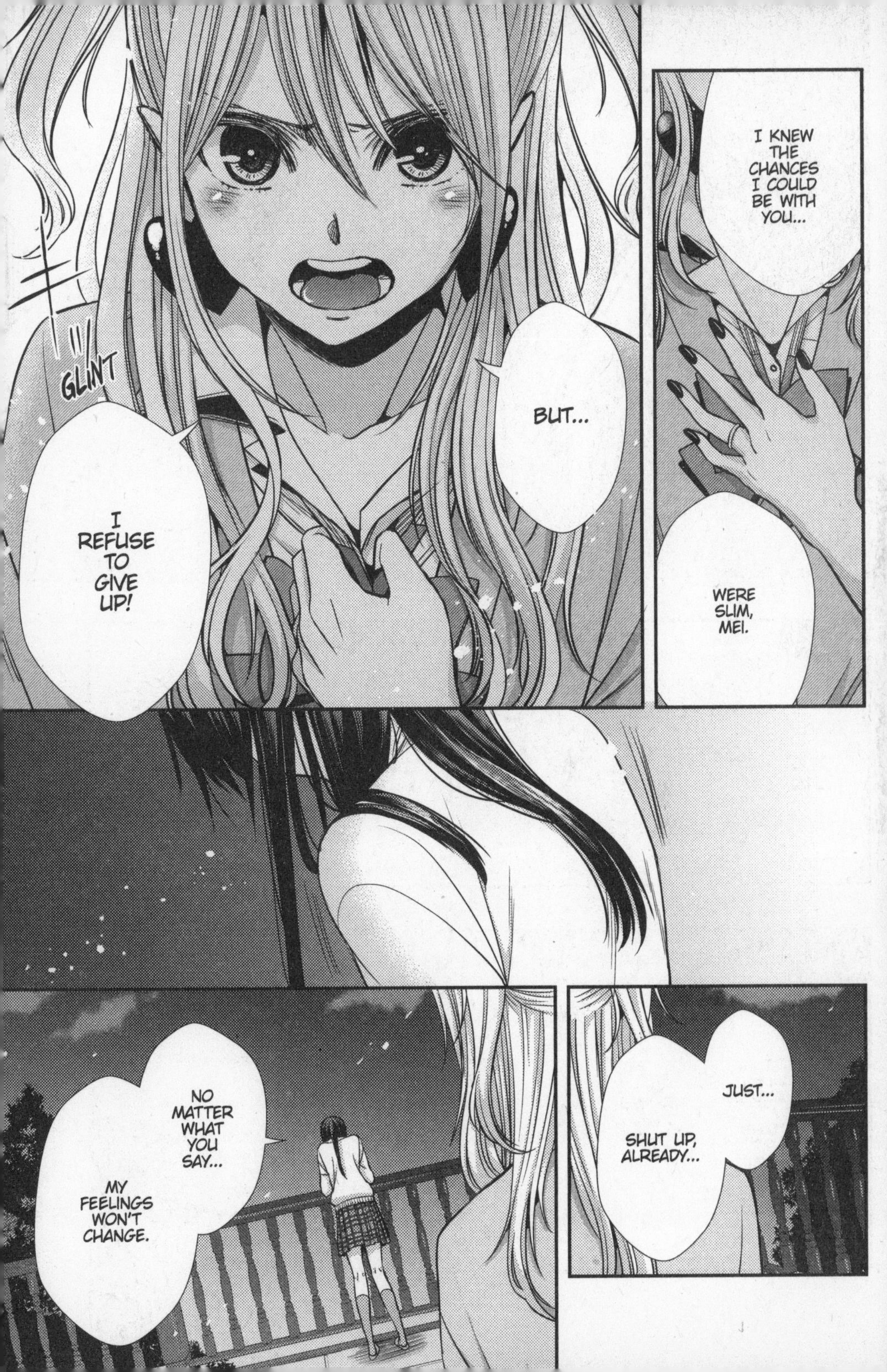
I KNEW THE CHANCES I COULD BE WITH YOU...
WERE SLIM, MEI.
BUT...
I REFUSE TO GIVE UP!
GLINT
JUST...
SHUT UP, ALREADY...
NO MATTER WHAT YOU SAY...
MY FEELINGS WON'T CHANGE.

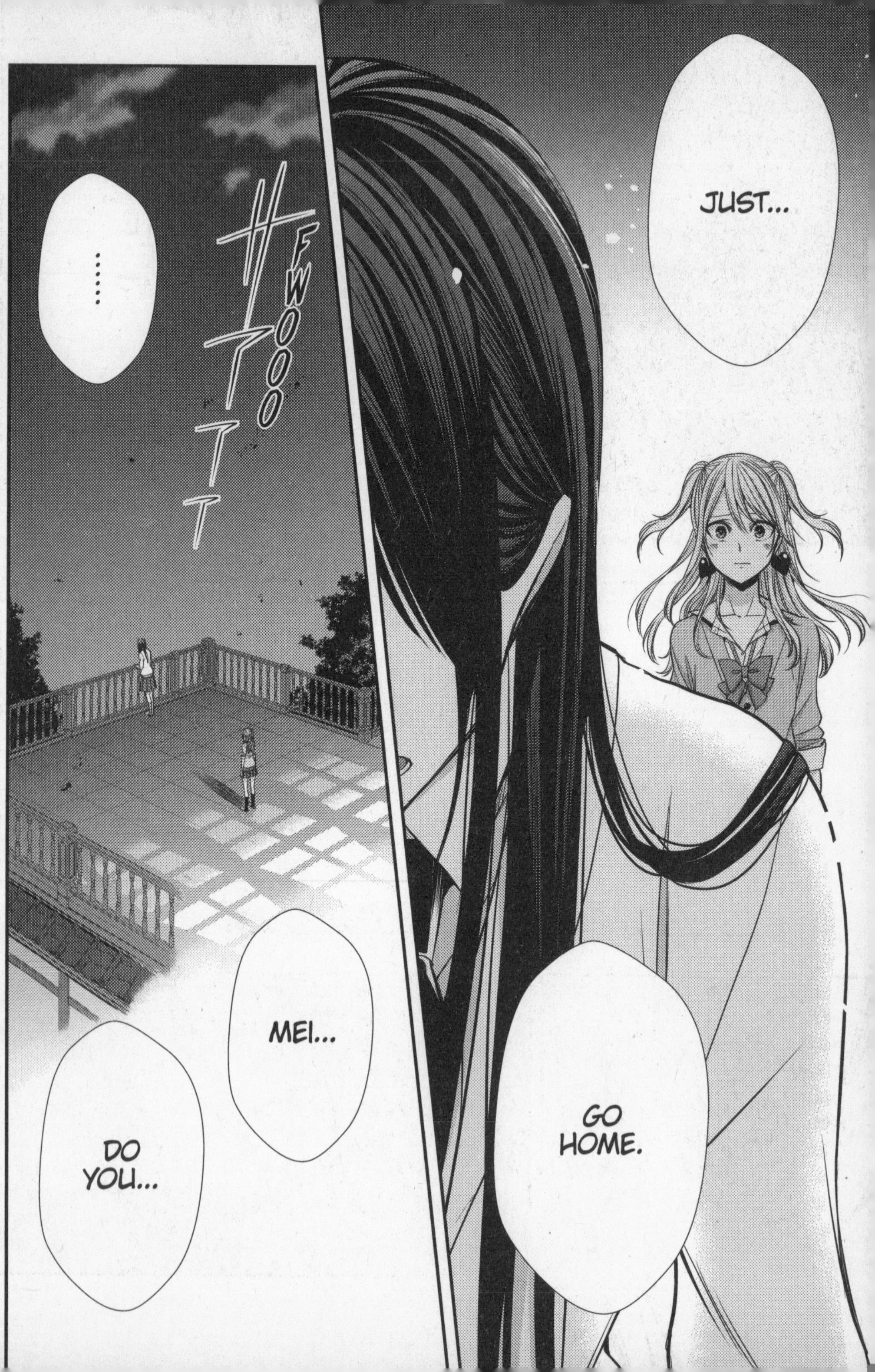
JUST...
GO HOME.
......
FWOOO
MEI...
DO YOU...

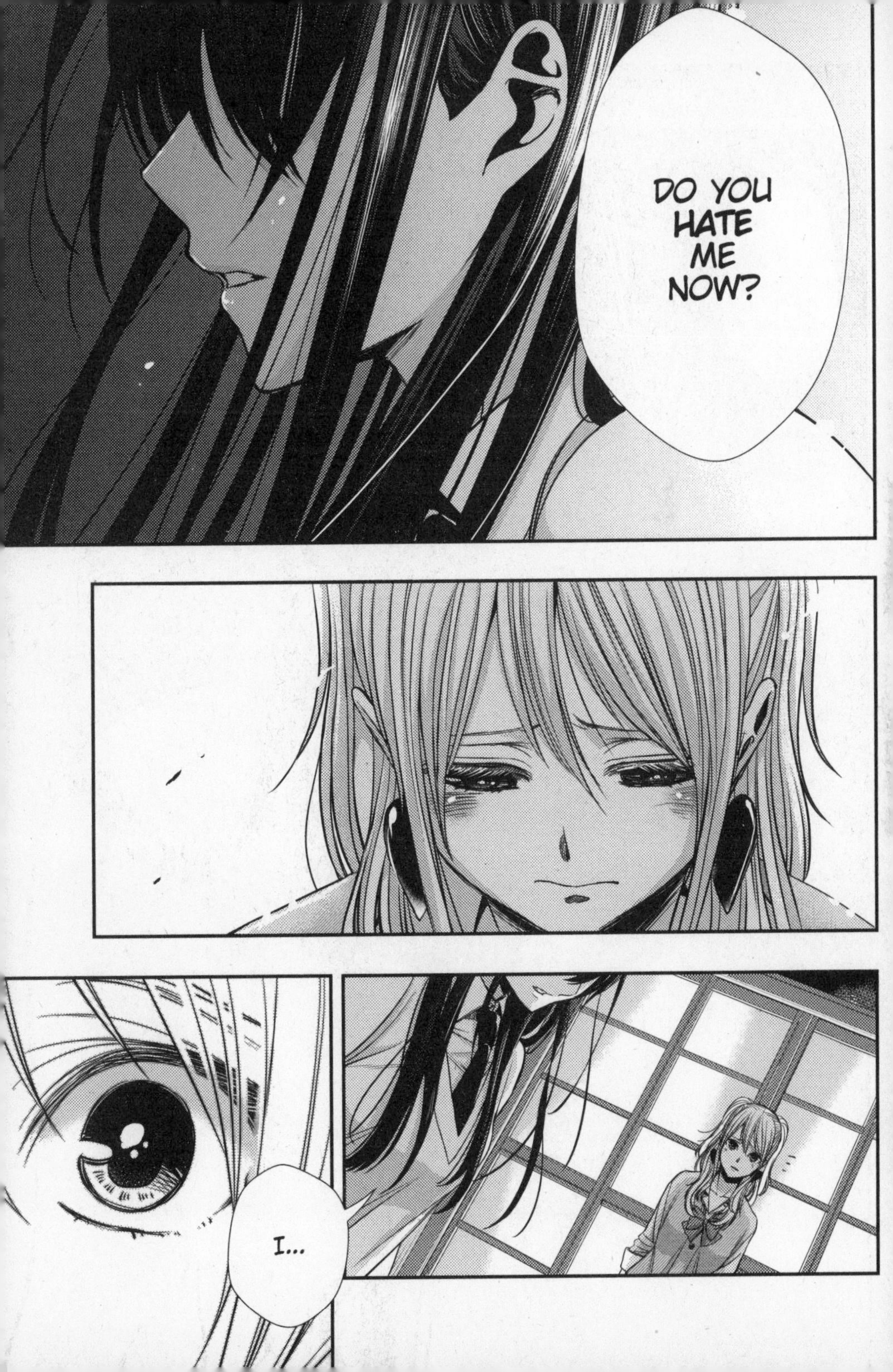
DO YOU HATE ME NOW?
I...

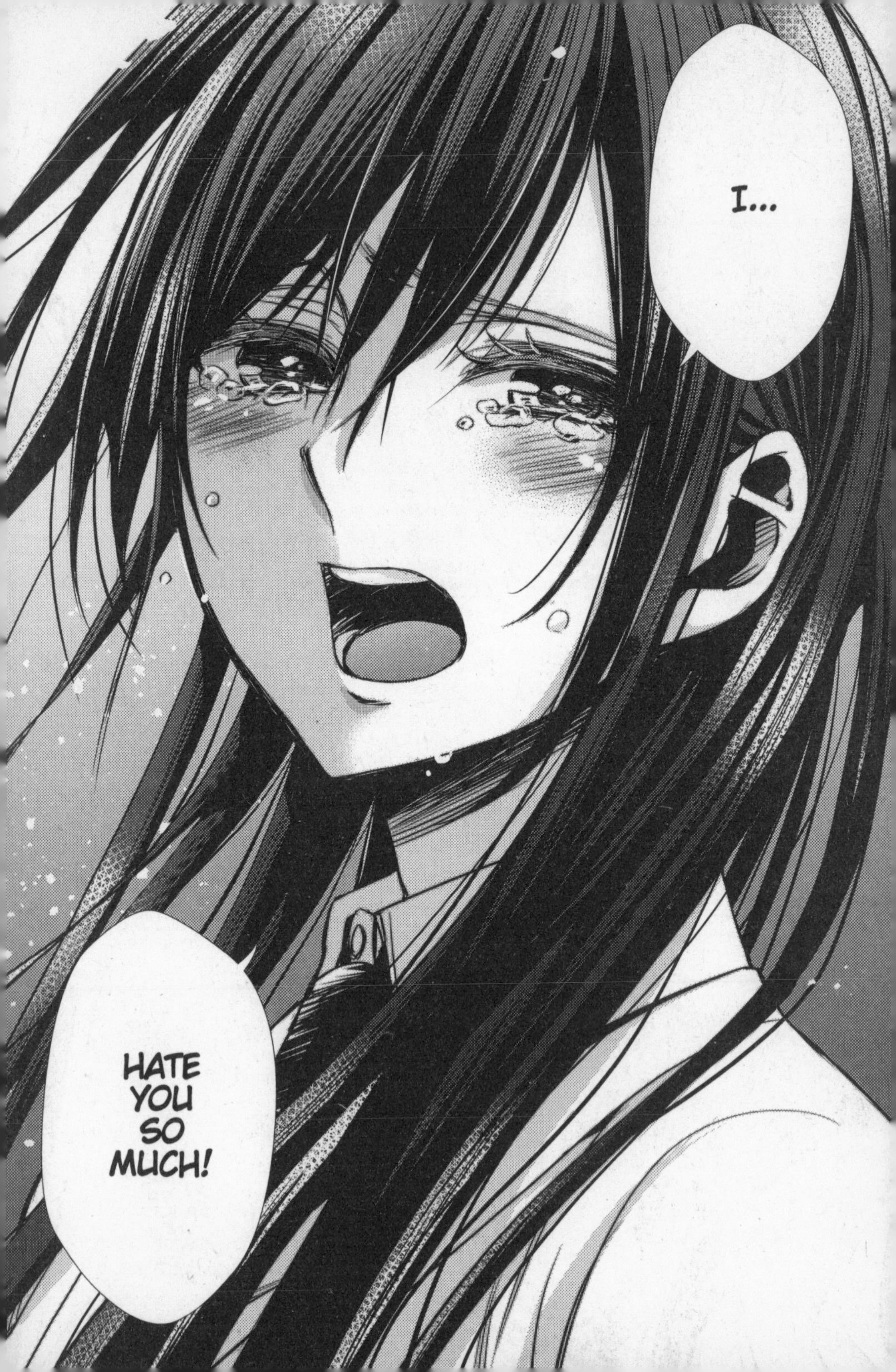
I...
HATE YOU SO MUCH!

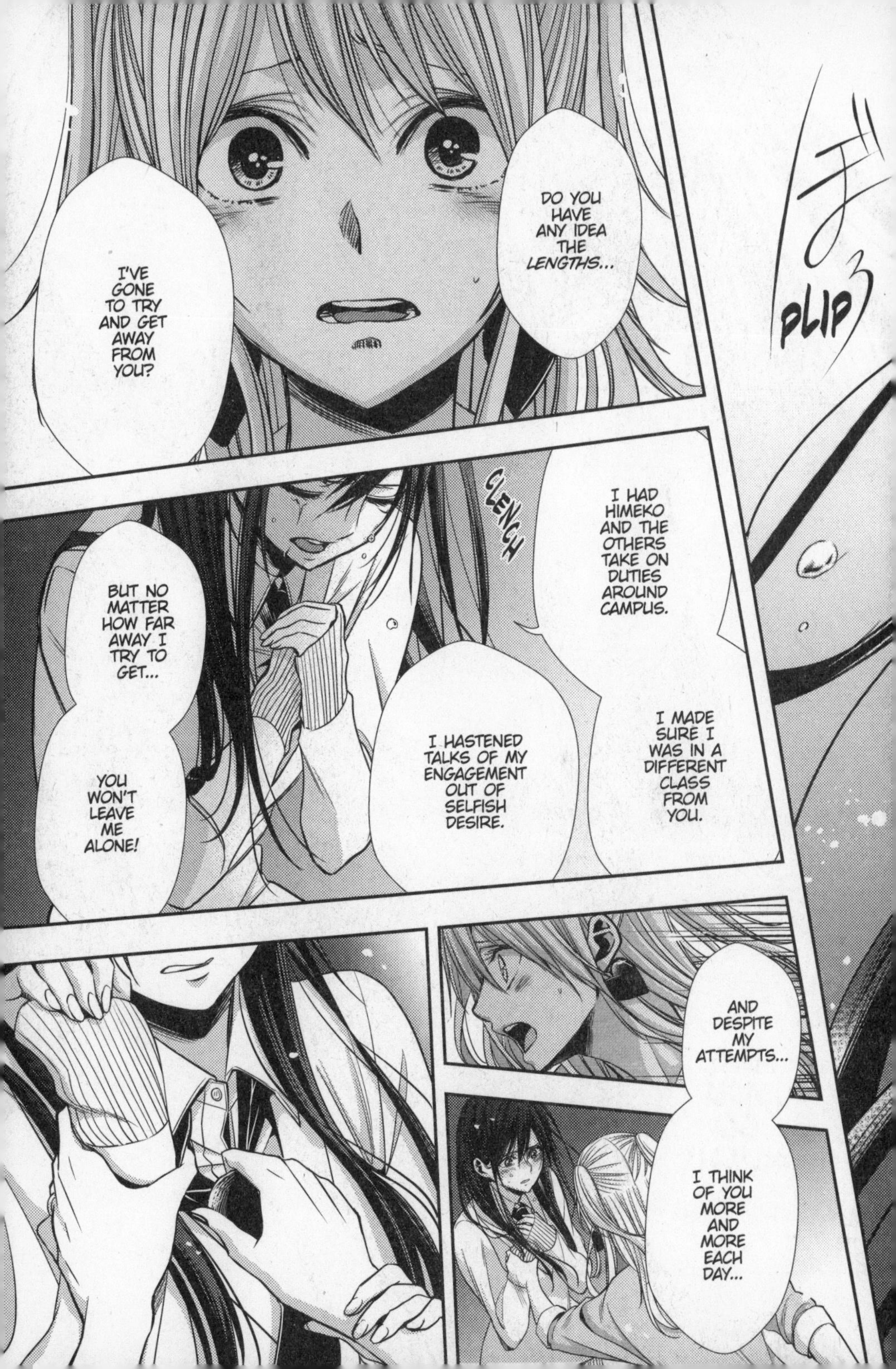
PLIP
DO YOU HAVE ANY IDEA THE LENGTHS...
I'VE GONE TO TRY AND GET AWAY FROM YOU?
I HAD HIMEKO AND THE OTHERS TAKE ON DUTIES AROUND CAMPUS.
CLENCH
I MADE SURE I WAS IN A DIFFERENT CLASS FROM YOU.
I HASTENED TALKS OF MY ENGAGEMENT OUT OF SELFISH DESIRE.
BUT NO MATTER HOW FAR AWAY I TRY TO GET...
YOU WON'T LEAVE ME ALONE!
AND DESPITE MY ATTEMPTS...
I THINK OF YOU MORE AND MORE EACH DAY...

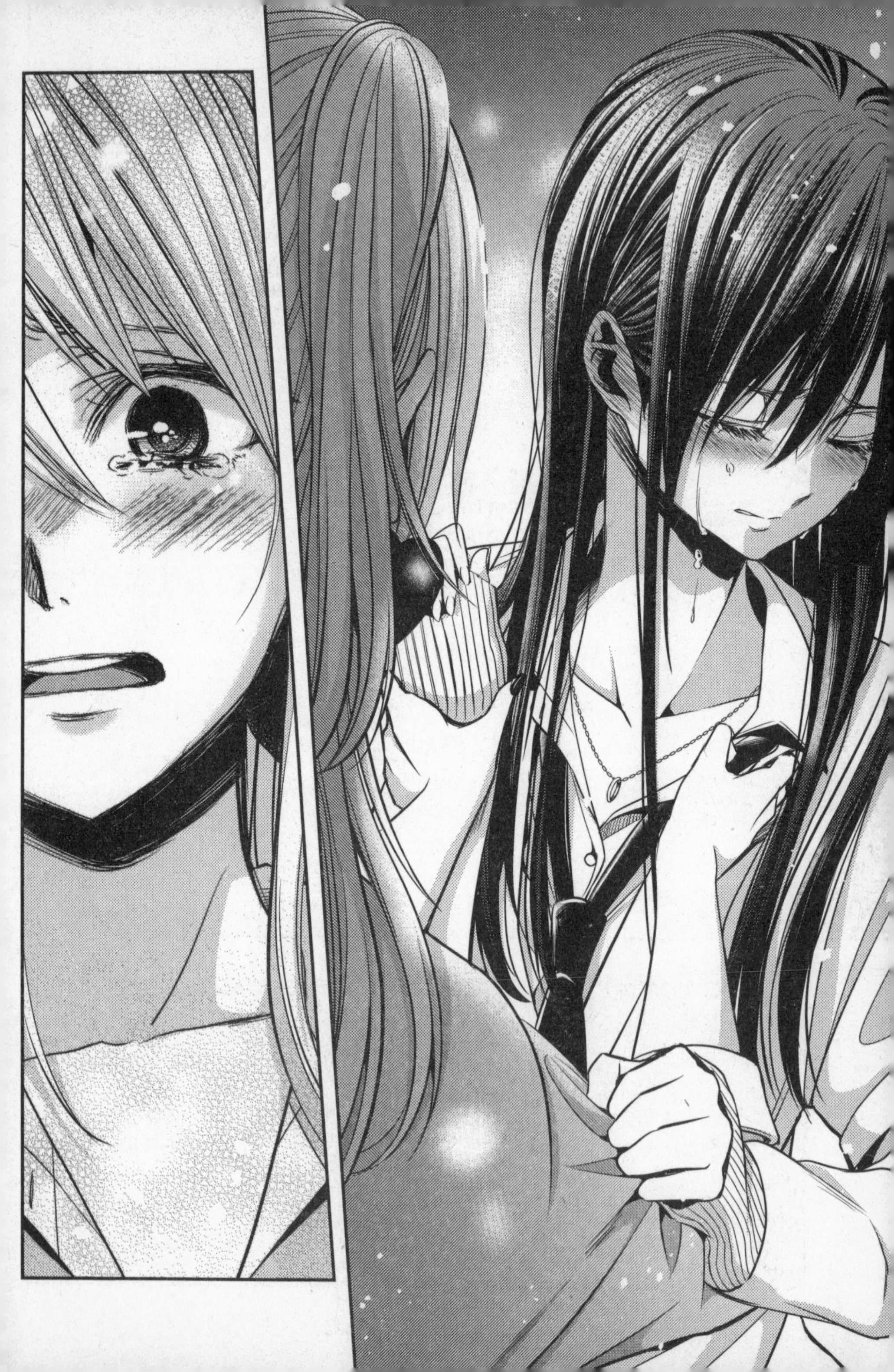

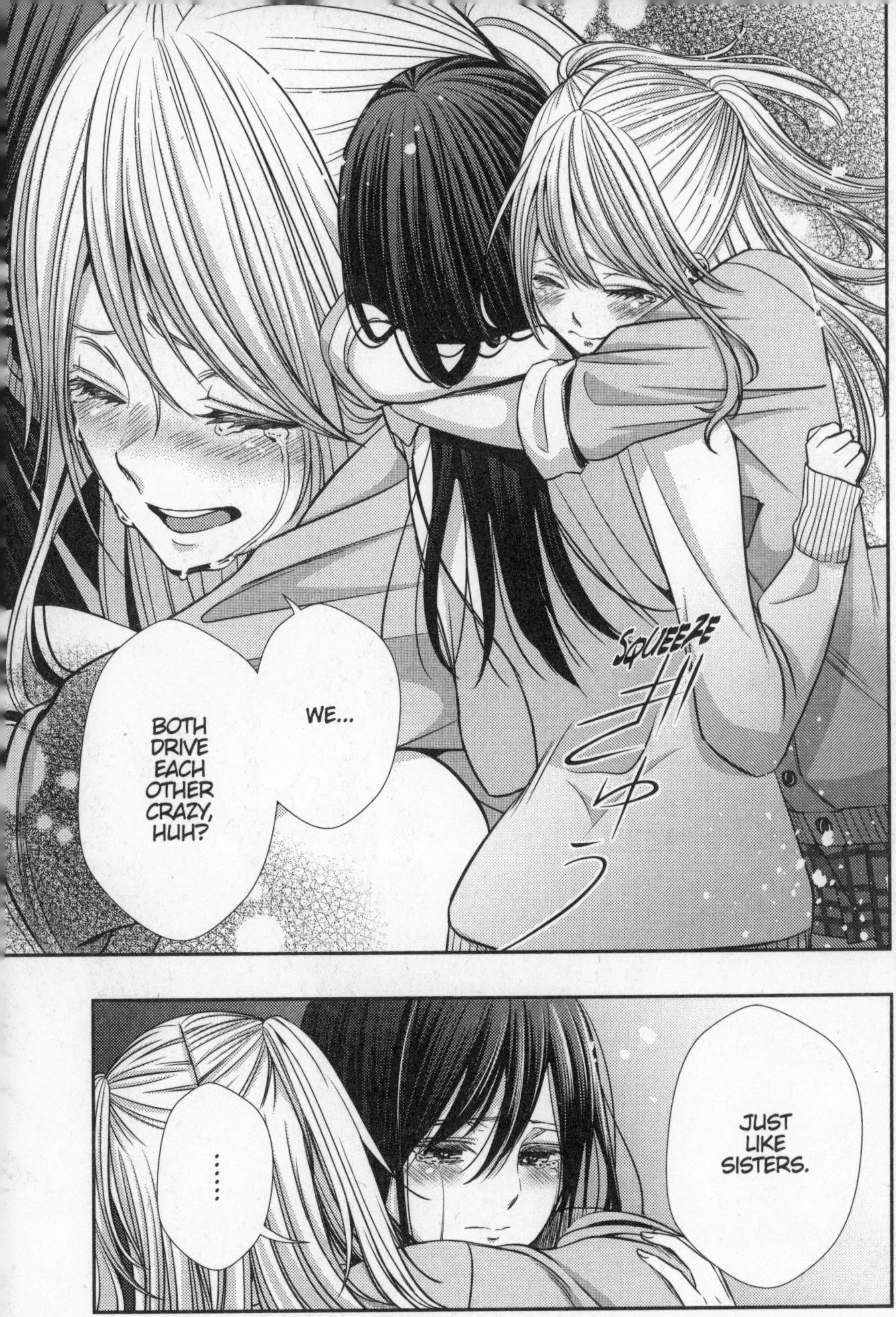
WE...
BOTH DRIVE EACH OTHER CRAZY, HUH?
SQUEEZE
ぎゅう
JUST LIKE SISTERS.
......

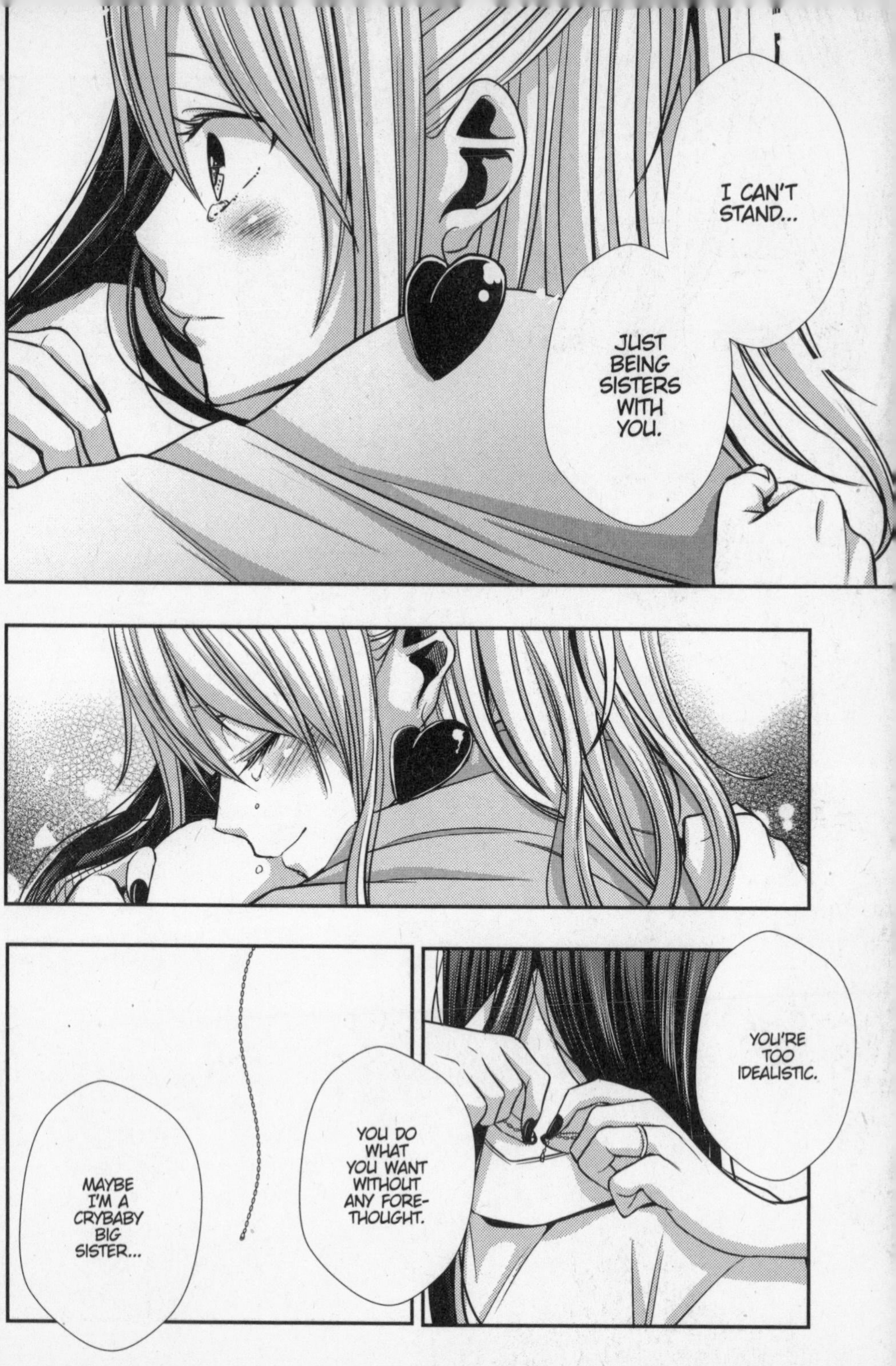
I CAN'T STAND...
JUST BEING SISTERS WITH YOU.
YOU'RE TOO IDEALISTIC.
YOU DO WHAT YOU WANT WITHOUT ANY FORE-THOUGHT.
MAYBE I'M A CRYBABY BIG SISTER...

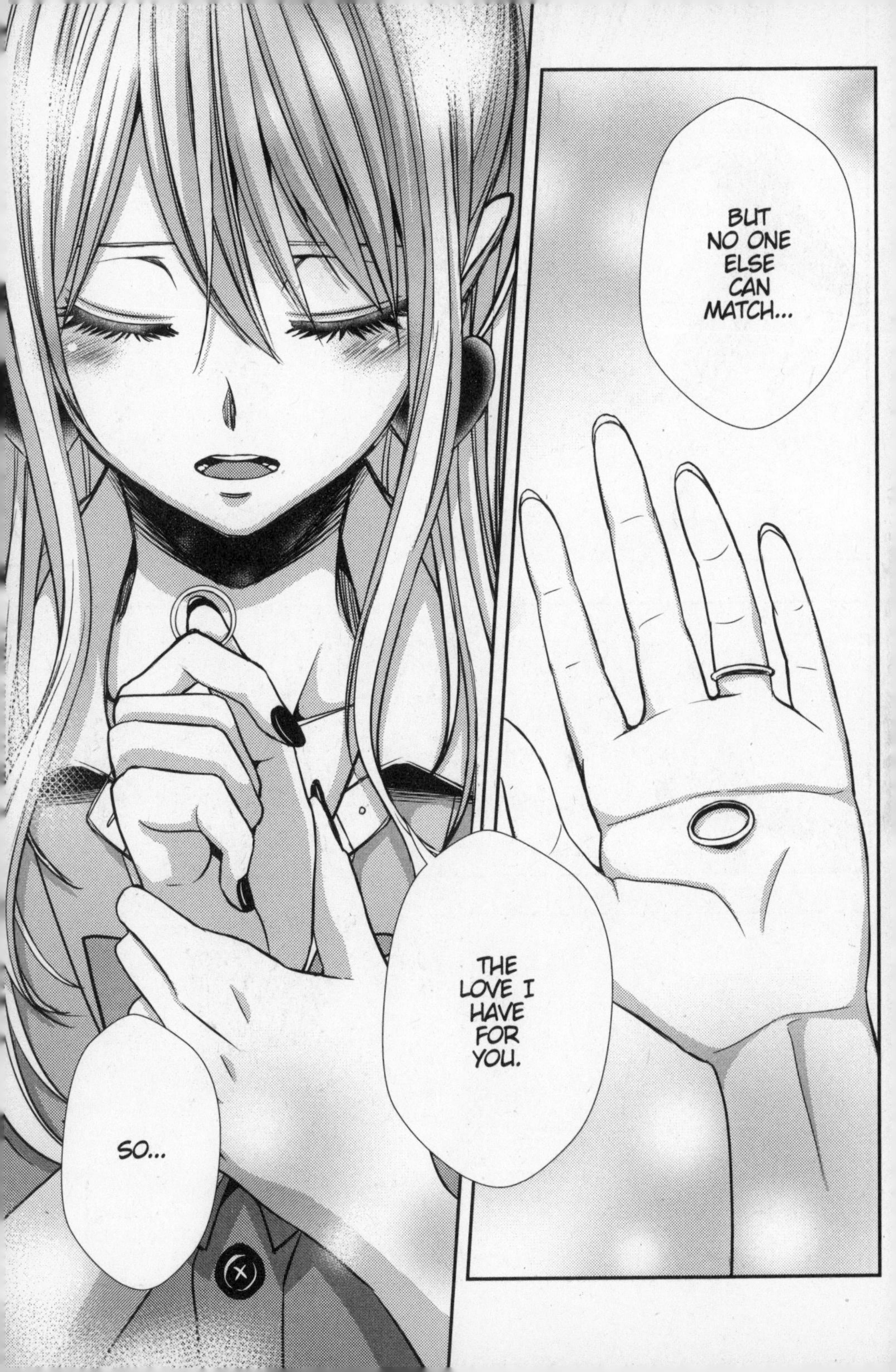
BUT NO ONE ELSE CAN MATCH...
THE LOVE I HAVE FOR YOU.
SO...

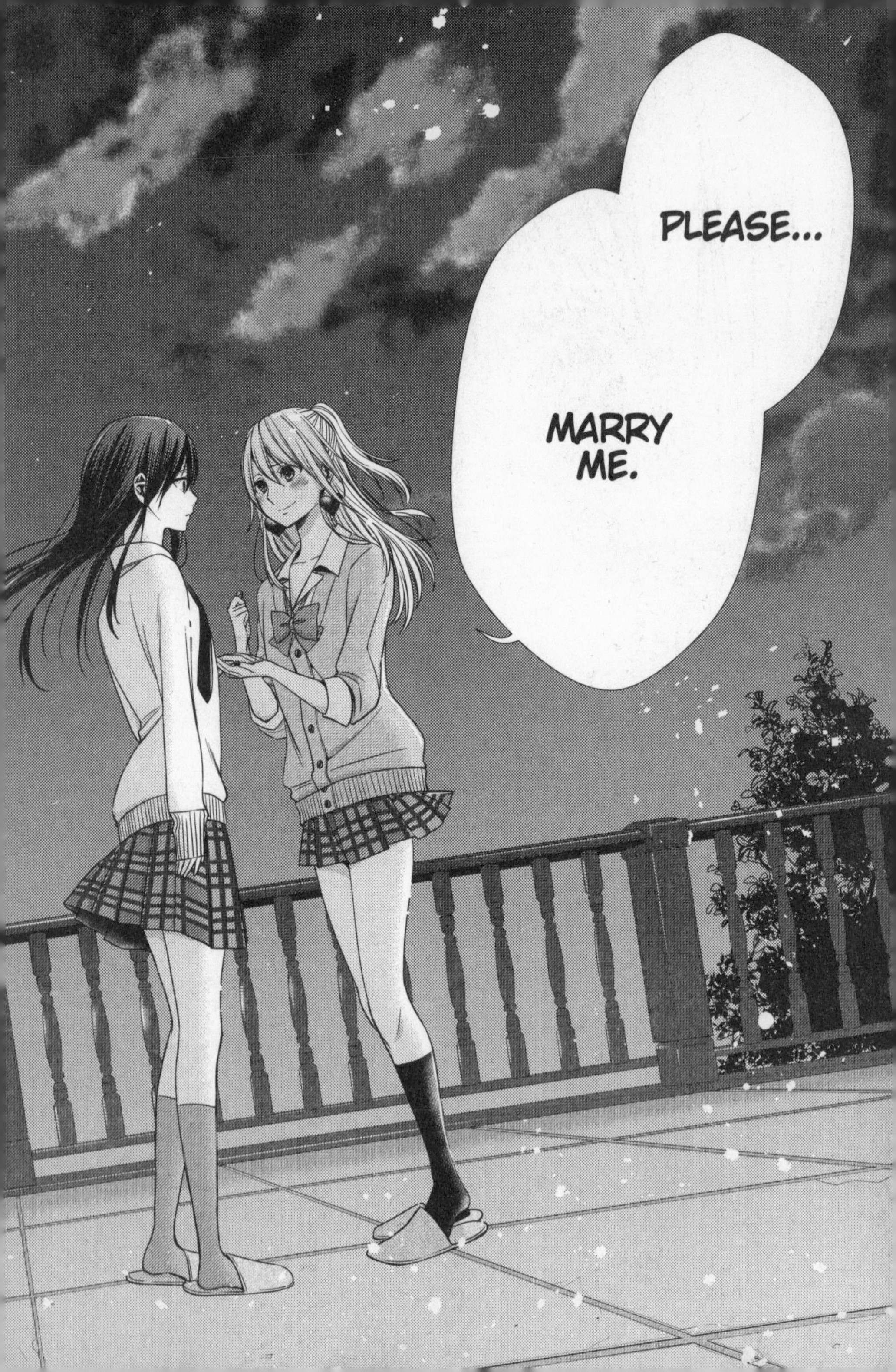
PLEASE...
MARRY ME.

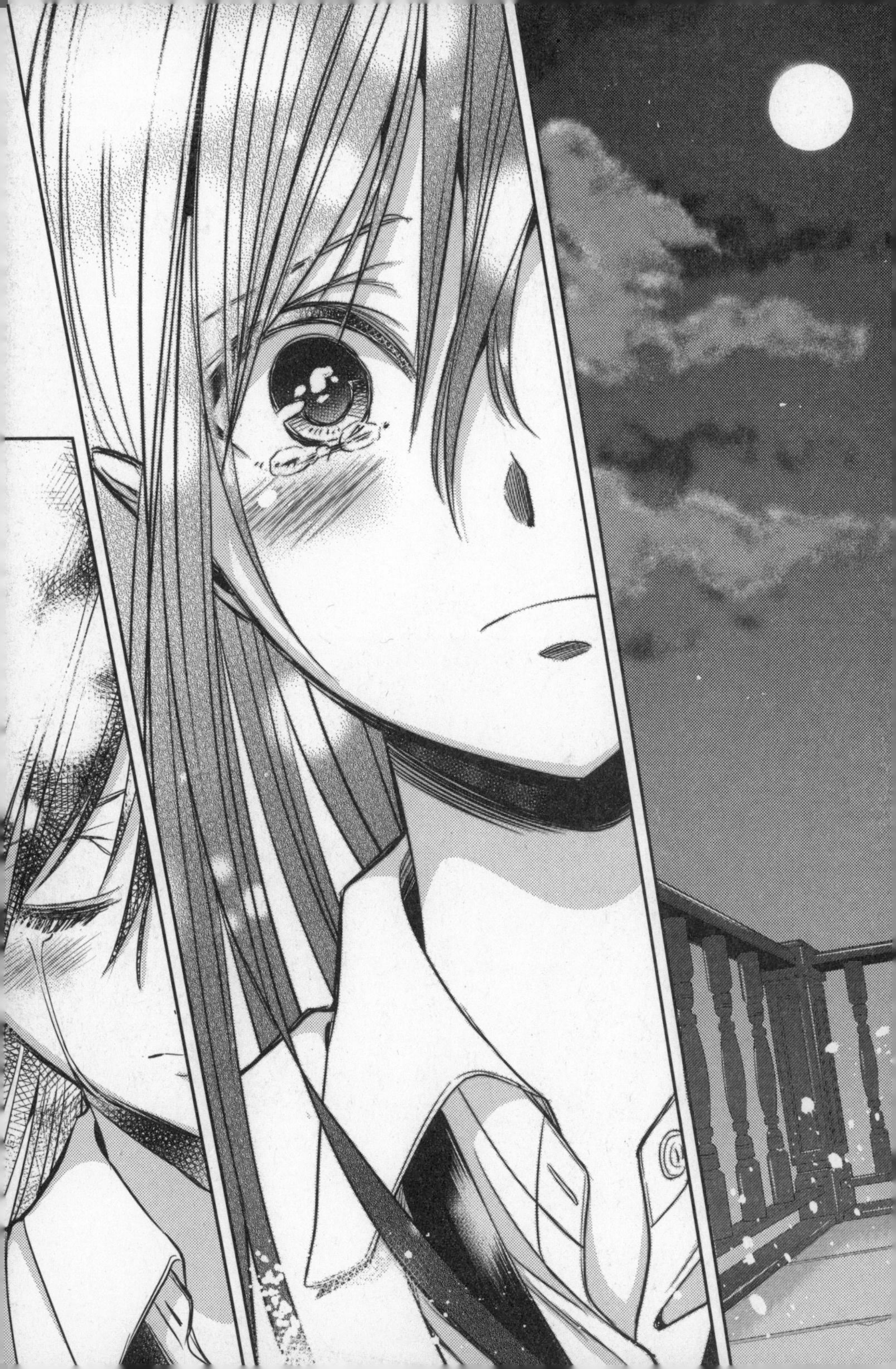

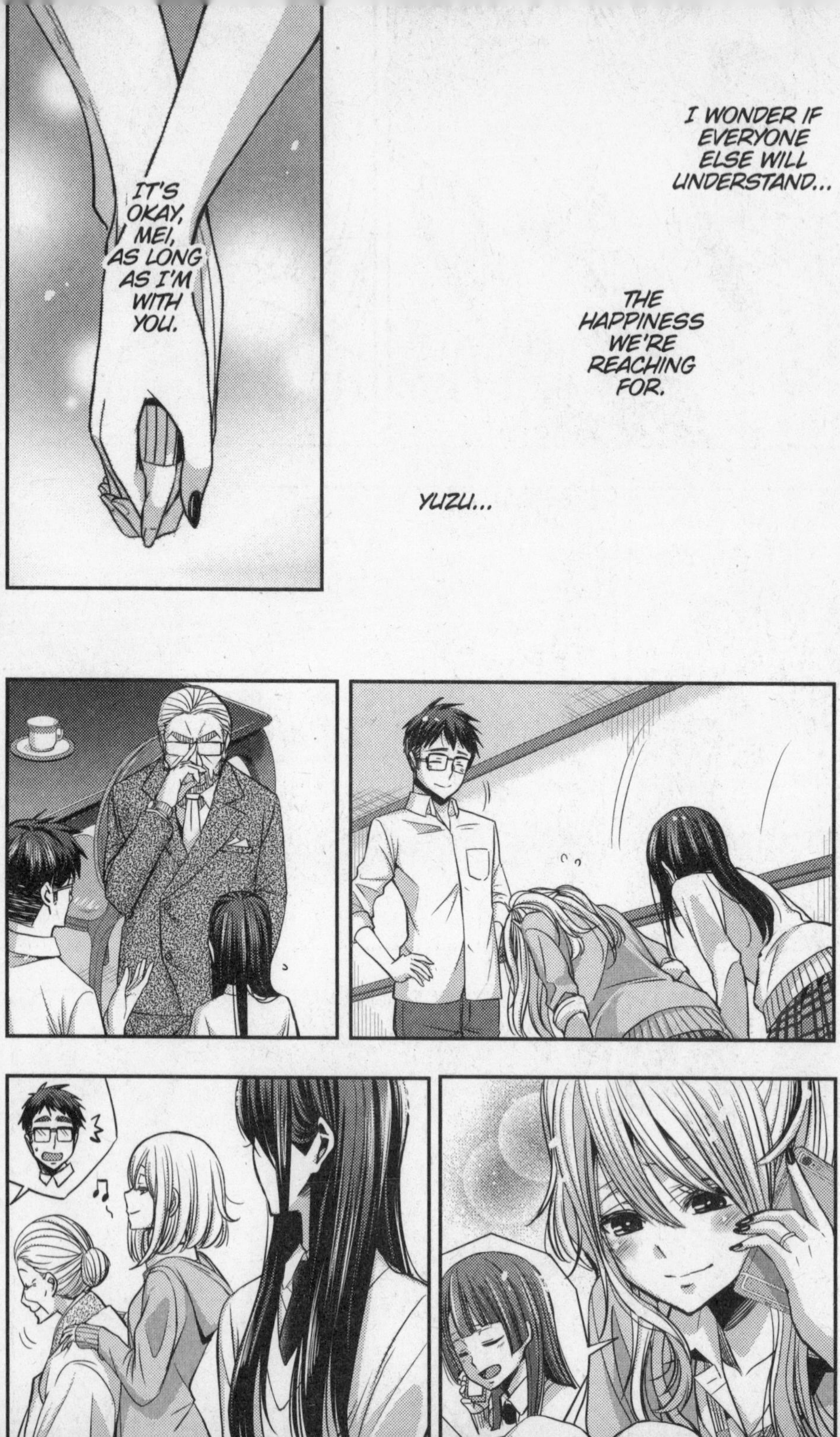
I WONDER IF EVERYONE ELSE WILL UNDERSTAND...
THE HAPPINESS WE'RE REACHING FOR.
YUZU...
IT'S OKAY, MEI, AS LONG AS I'M WITH YOU.

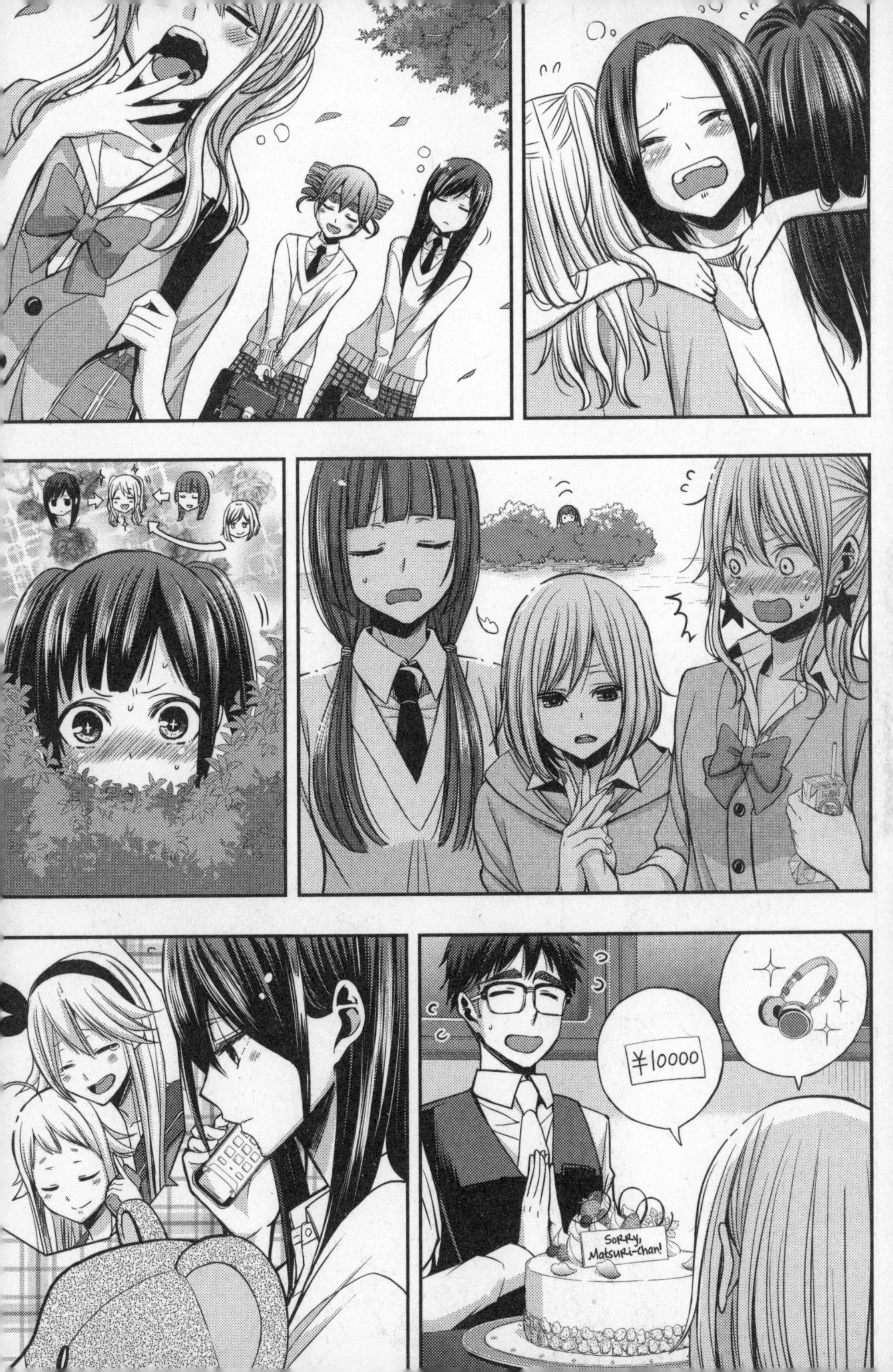
¥10000
SORRY, MATSURI-CHAN!

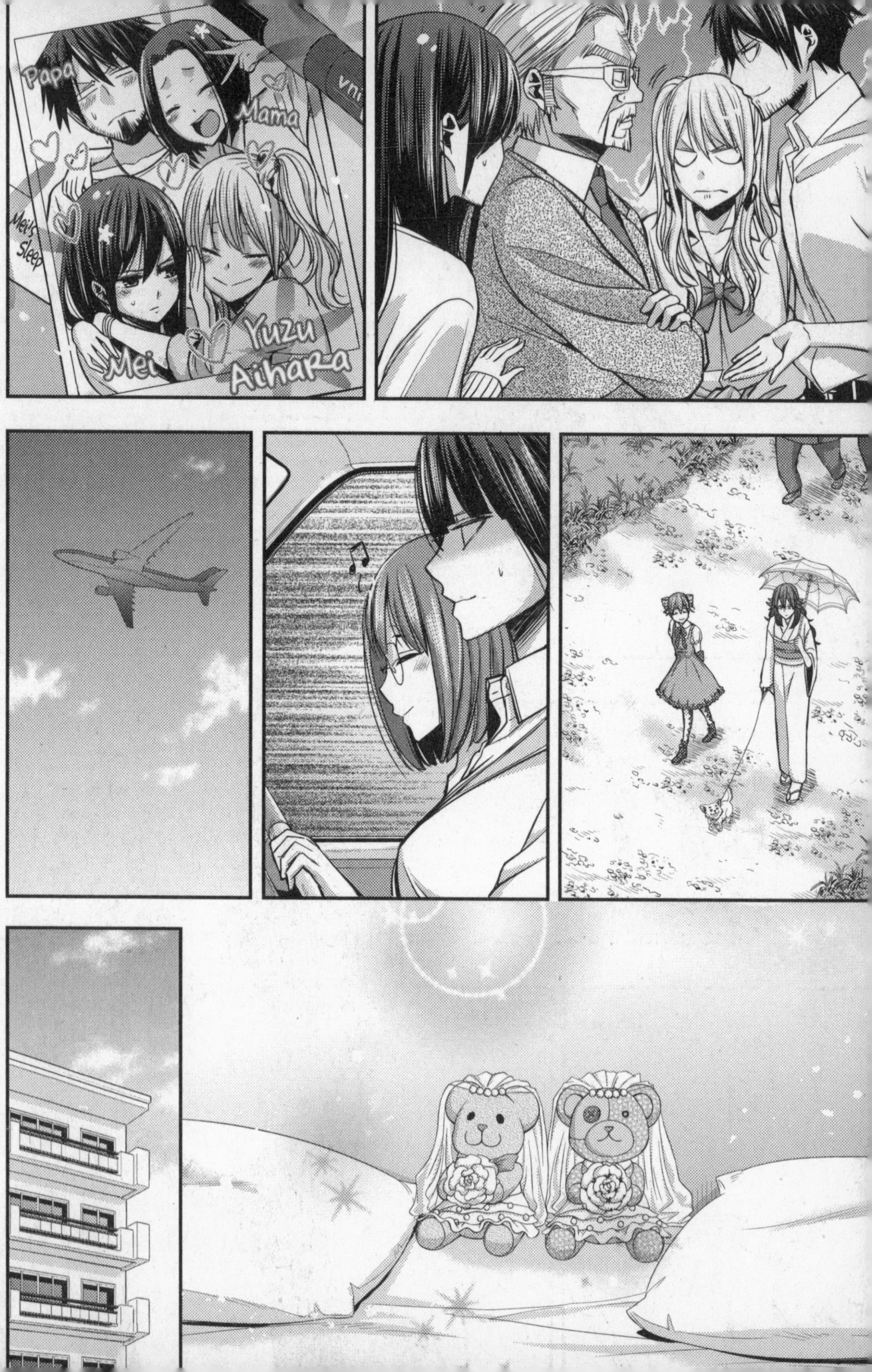
Papa
Mama
Mei's Sleep
Yuzu Aihara
Mei

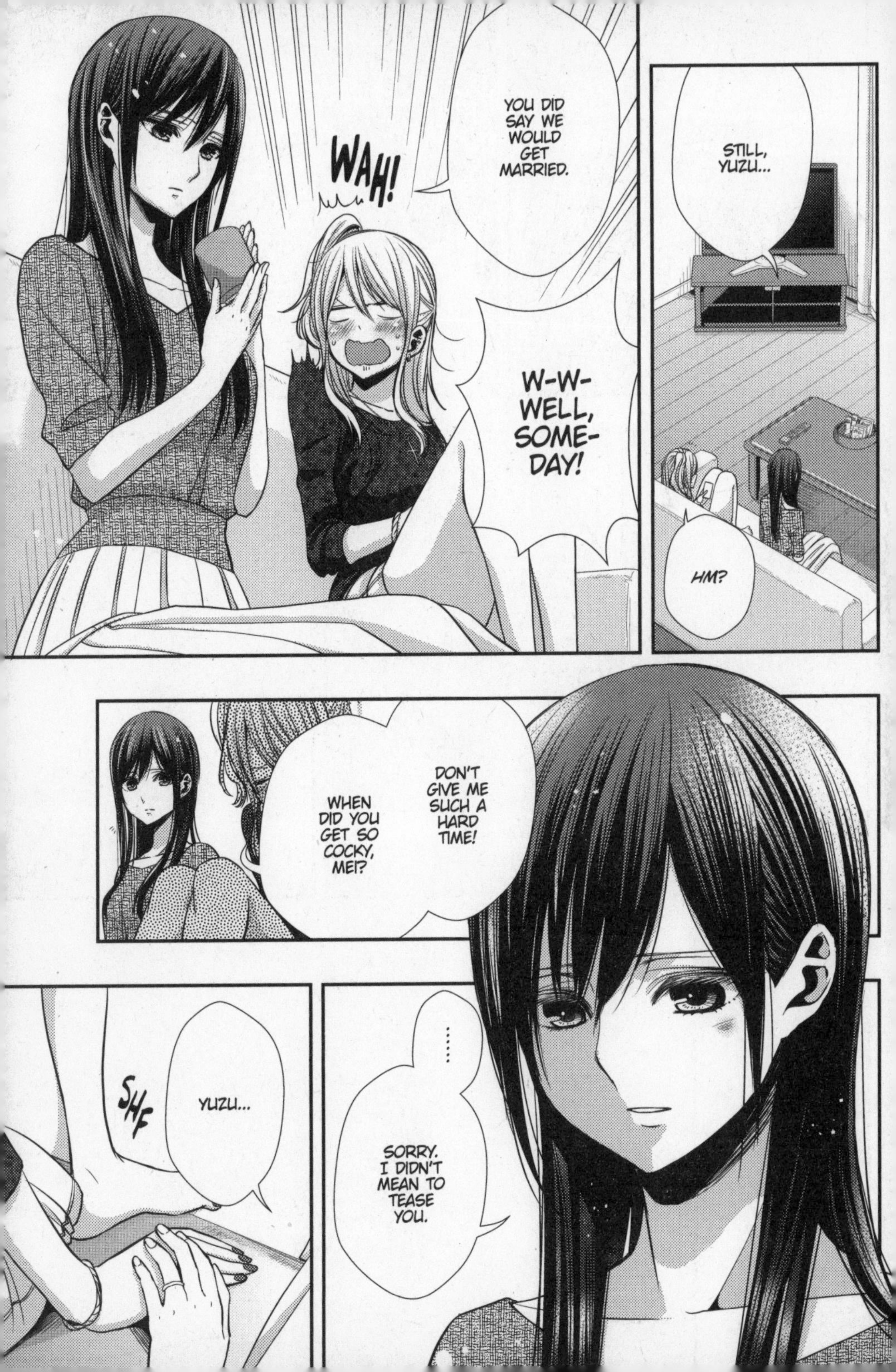
STILL, YUZU...
HM?
YOU DID SAY WE WOULD GET MARRIED.
WAH!
W-W-WELL, SOME-DAY!
DON'T GIVE ME SUCH A HARD TIME!
WHEN DID YOU GET SO COCKY, MEI!?
......
SORRY. I DIDN'T MEAN TO TEASE YOU.
SHF
YUZU...

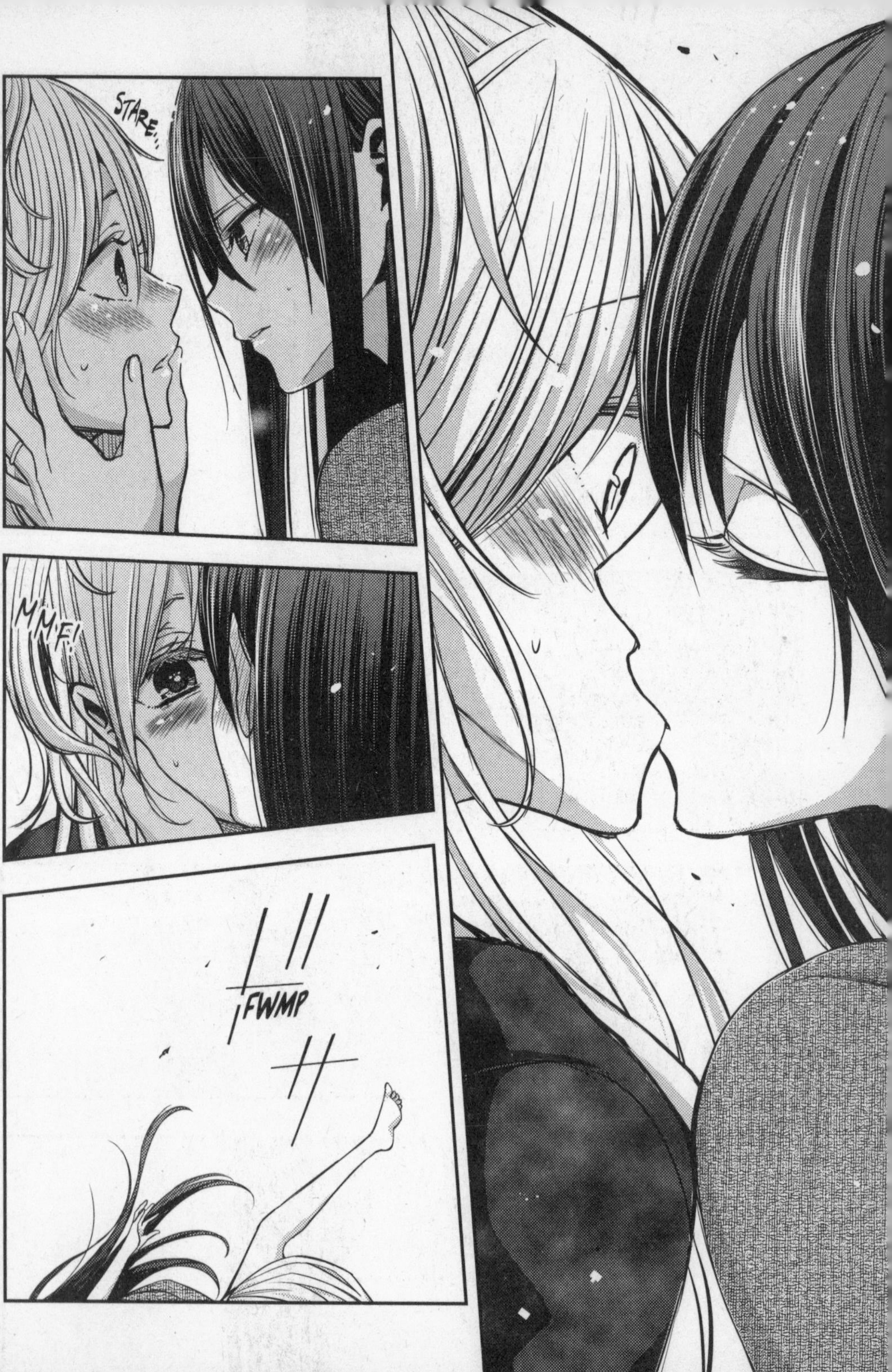
STARE...
MMF!
FWMP

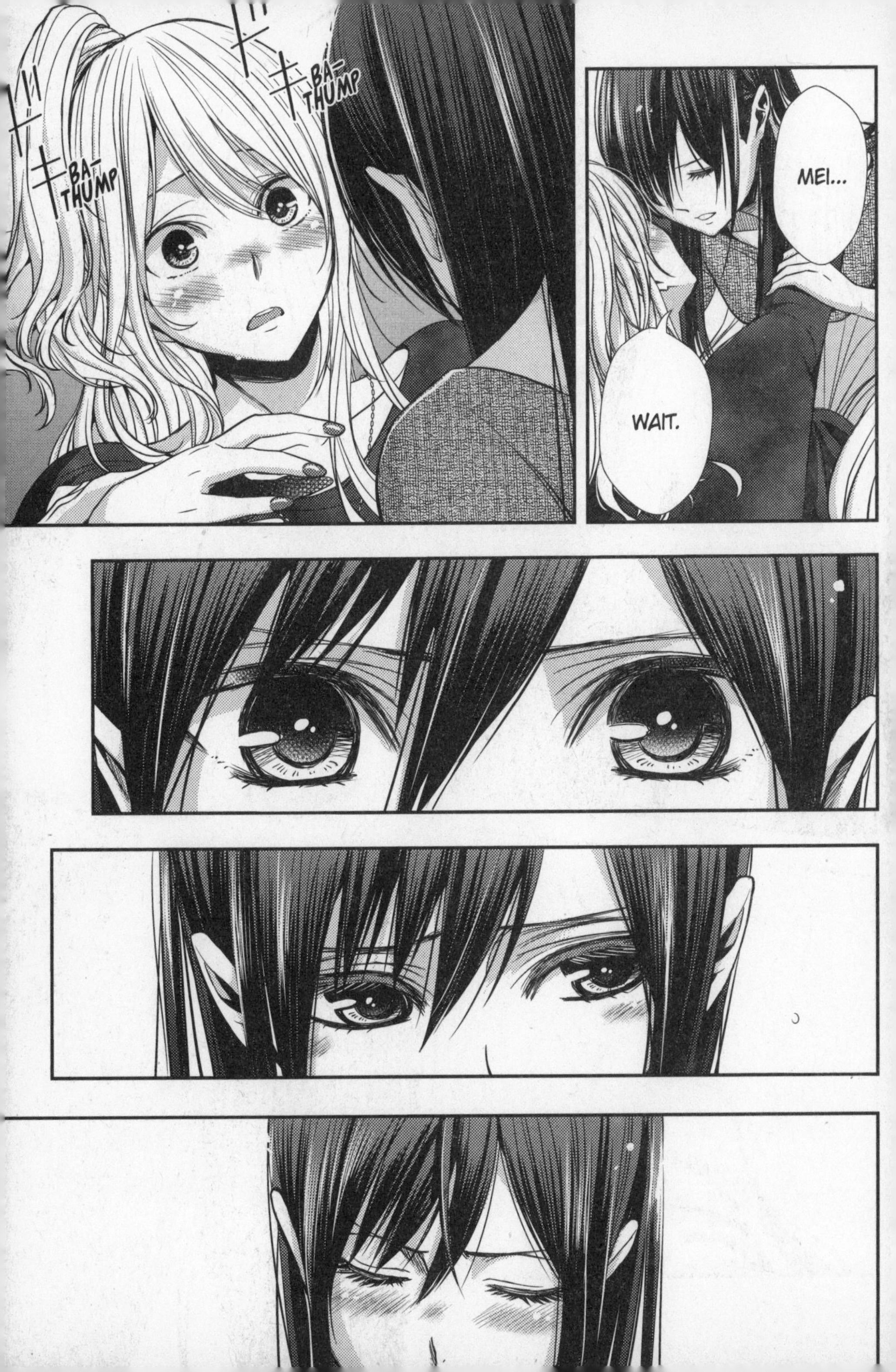
MEI...
WAIT.
BA-THUMP
BA-THUMP

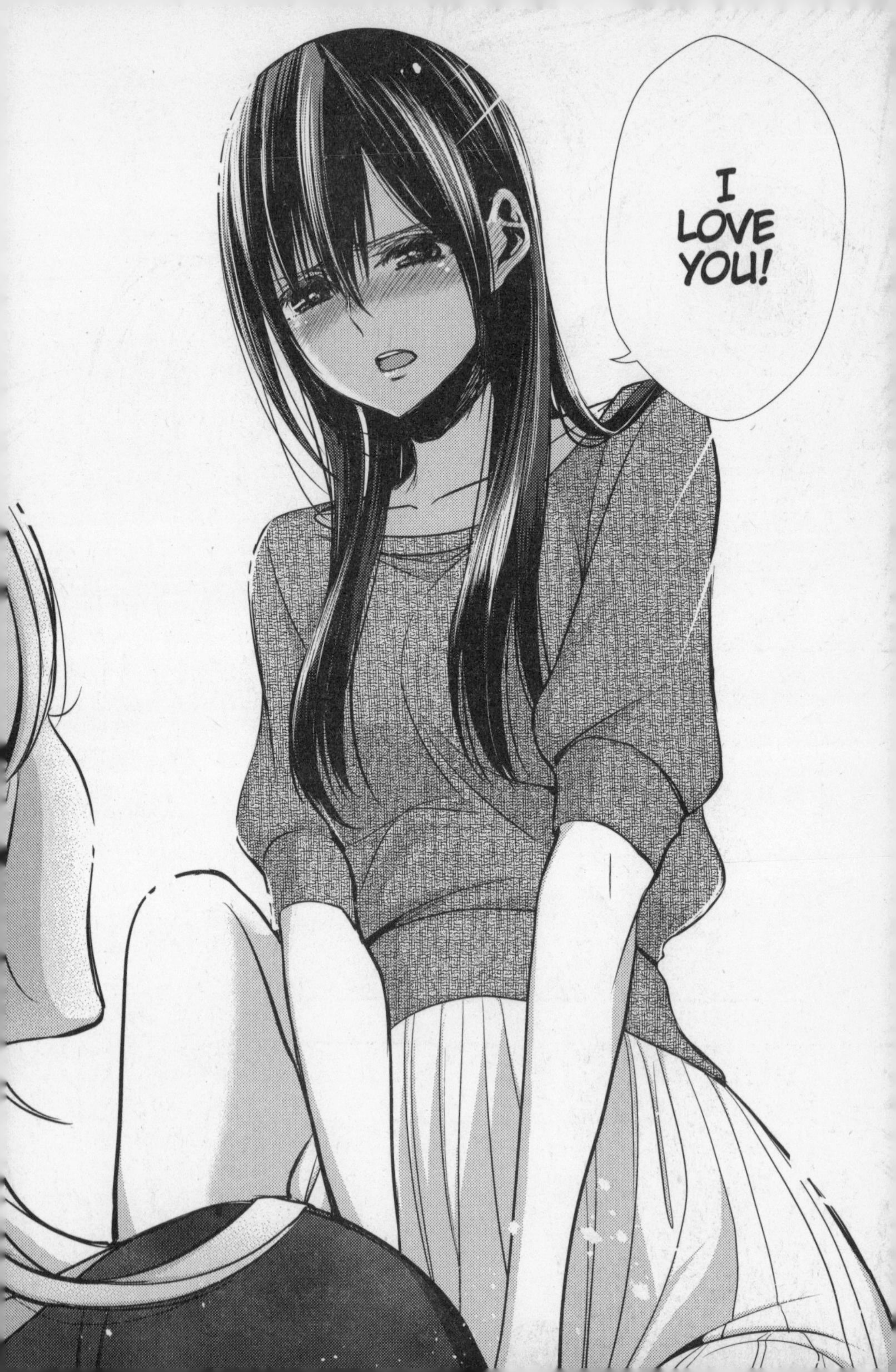
I LOVE YOU!

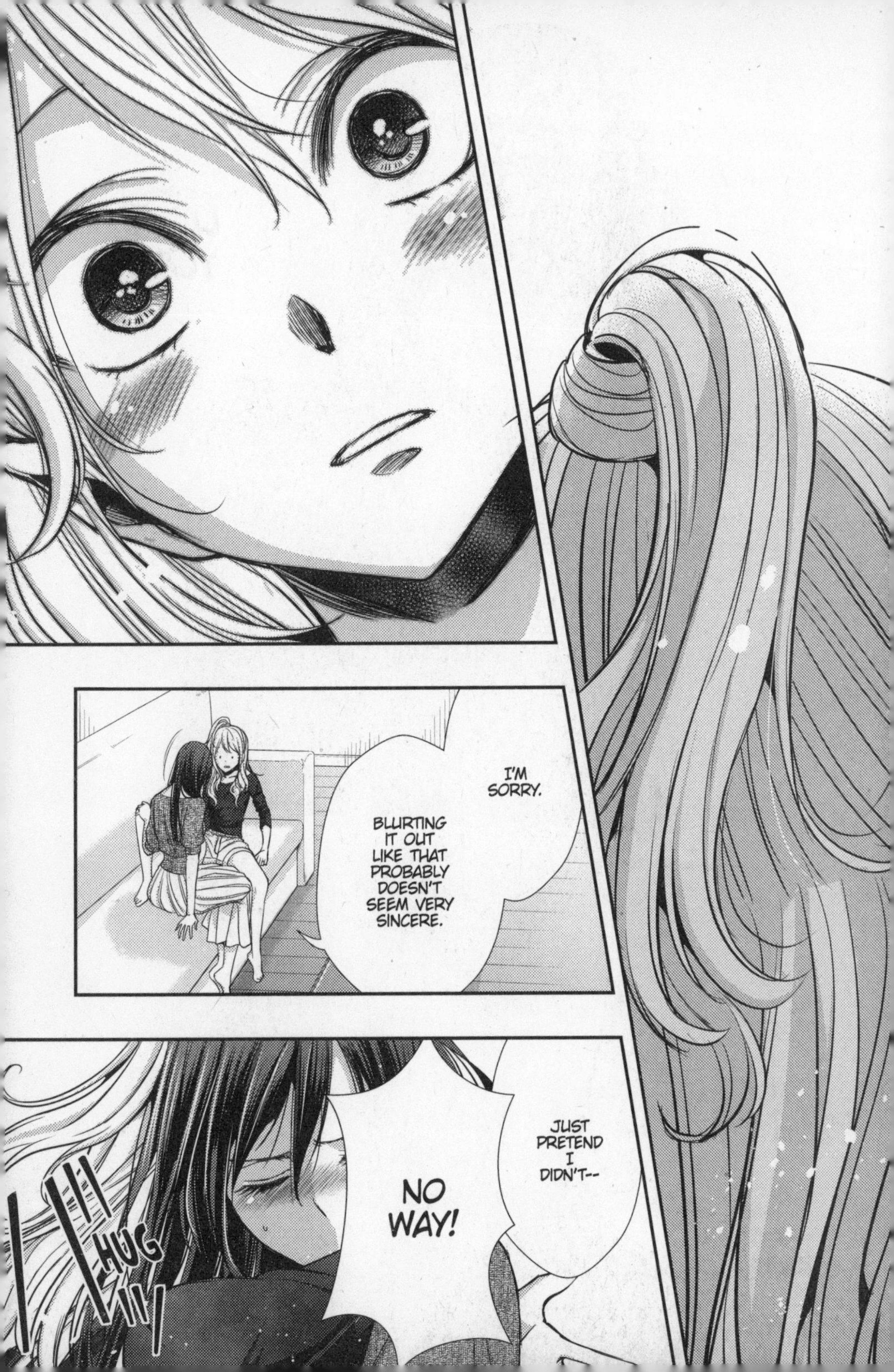
I'M SORRY.
BLURTING IT OUT LIKE THAT PROBABLY DOESN'T SEEM VERY SINCERE.
JUST PRETEND I DIDN'T--
NO WAY!
HUG

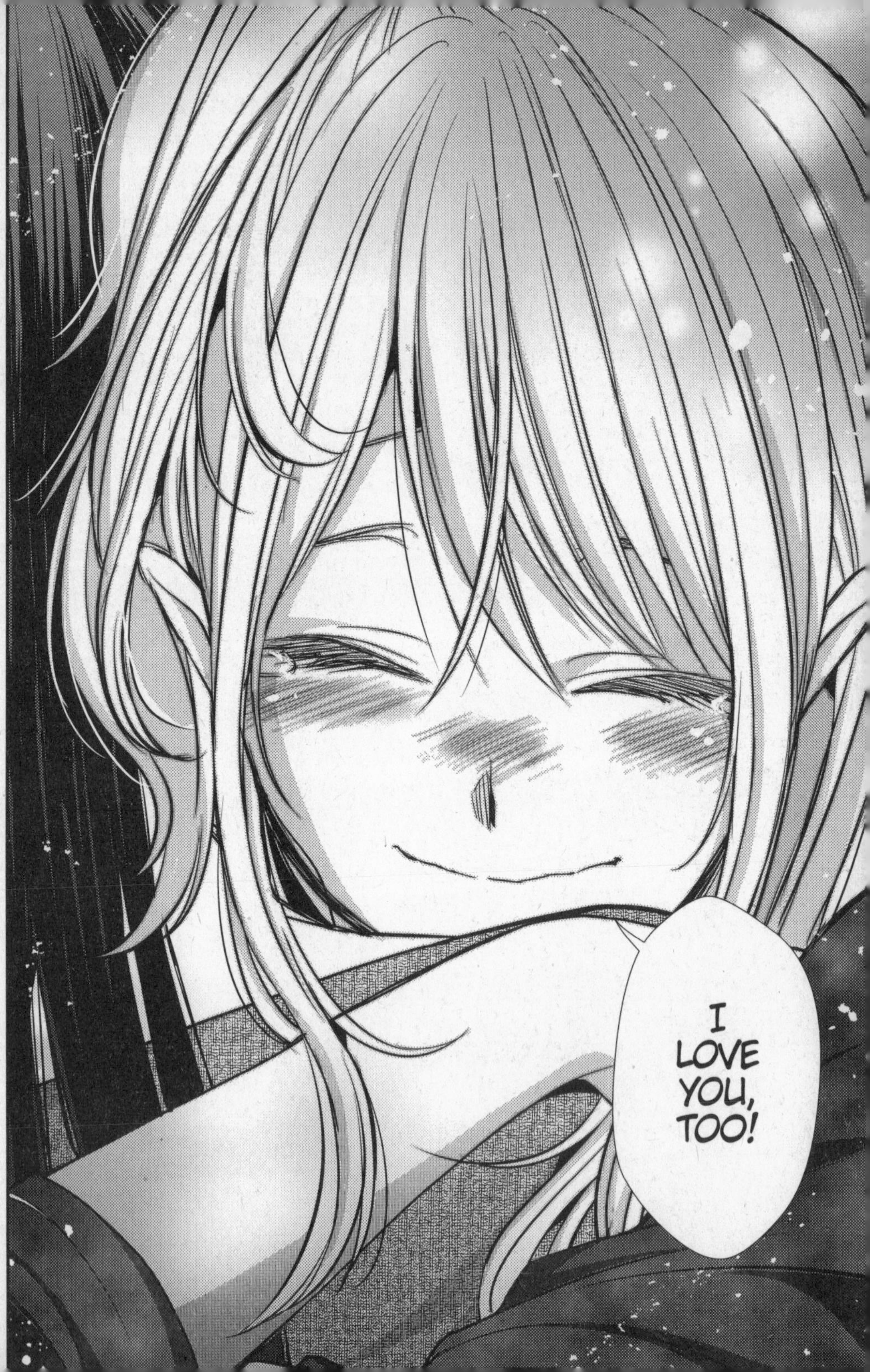
I LOVE YOU, TOO!

citrus

[シトラス]

SECRET LOVE AFFAIR WITH SISTER

SEVEN SEAS ENTERTAINMENT PRESENTS

citrus

story & art by SABUROUTA   VOLUME 10

TRANSLATION
Amber Tamosaitis

ADAPTATION
Shannon Fay

LETTERING AND RETOUCH
Roland Amago
Bambi Eloriaga-Amago

COVER DESIGN
Nicky Lim

PROOFREADER
Stephanie Cohen

EDITOR
Jenn Grunigen

PRODUCTION MANAGER
Lissa Pattillo

MANAGING EDITOR
Julie Davis

EDITOR-IN-CHIEF
Adam Arnold

PUBLISHER
Jason DeAngelis

CITRUS VOLUME 10
© SABUROUTA 2018
First published in Japan in 2018 by ICHIJINSHA Inc., Tokyo.
English translation rights arranged with ICHIJINSHA Inc., Tokyo, Japan.

No portion of this book may be reproduced or transmitted in any form without written permission from the copyright holders. This is a work of fiction. Names, characters, places, and incidents are the products of the author's imagination or are used fictitiously. Any resemblance to actual events, locales, or persons, living or dead, is entirely coincidental.

Seven Seas press and purchase enquiries can be sent to Marketing Manager Lianne Sentar at press@gomanga.com. Information regarding the distribution and purchase of digital editions is available from Digital Manager CK Russell at digital@gomanga.com.

Seven Seas and the Seven Seas logo are trademarks of Seven Seas Entertainment. All rights reserved.

ISBN: 978-1-64275-103-1

Printed in Canada

First Printing: July 2019

10 9 8 7 6 5 4 3 2 1

FOLLOW US ONLINE: www.sevenseasentertainment.com

READING DIRECTIONS

This book reads from *right to left*, Japanese style. If this is your first time reading manga, you start reading from the top right panel on each page and take it from there. If you get lost, just follow the numbered diagram here. It may seem backwards at first, but you'll get the hang of it! Have fun!!

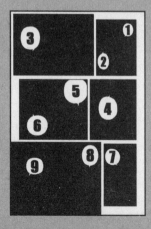

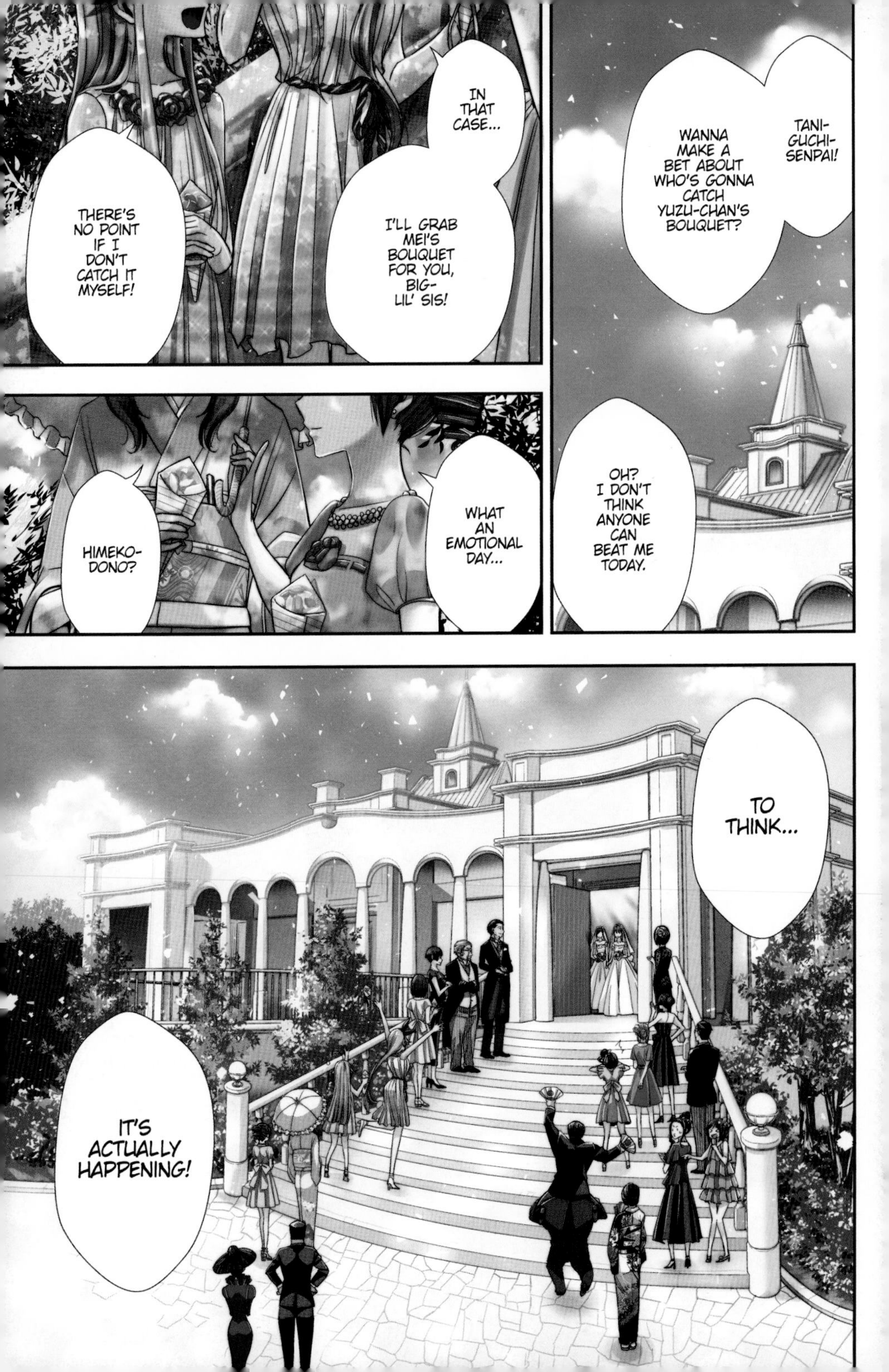
TANI-GUCHI-SENPAI!
WANNA MAKE A BET ABOUT WHO'S GONNA CATCH YUZU-CHAN'S BOUQUET?
OH? I DON'T THINK ANYONE CAN BEAT ME TODAY.
IN THAT CASE...
I'LL GRAB MEI'S BOUQUET FOR YOU, BIG-LIL' SIS!
THERE'S NO POINT IF I DON'T CATCH IT MYSELF!
WHAT AN EMOTIONAL DAY...
HIMEKO-DONO?
TO THINK...
IT'S ACTUALLY HAPPENING!

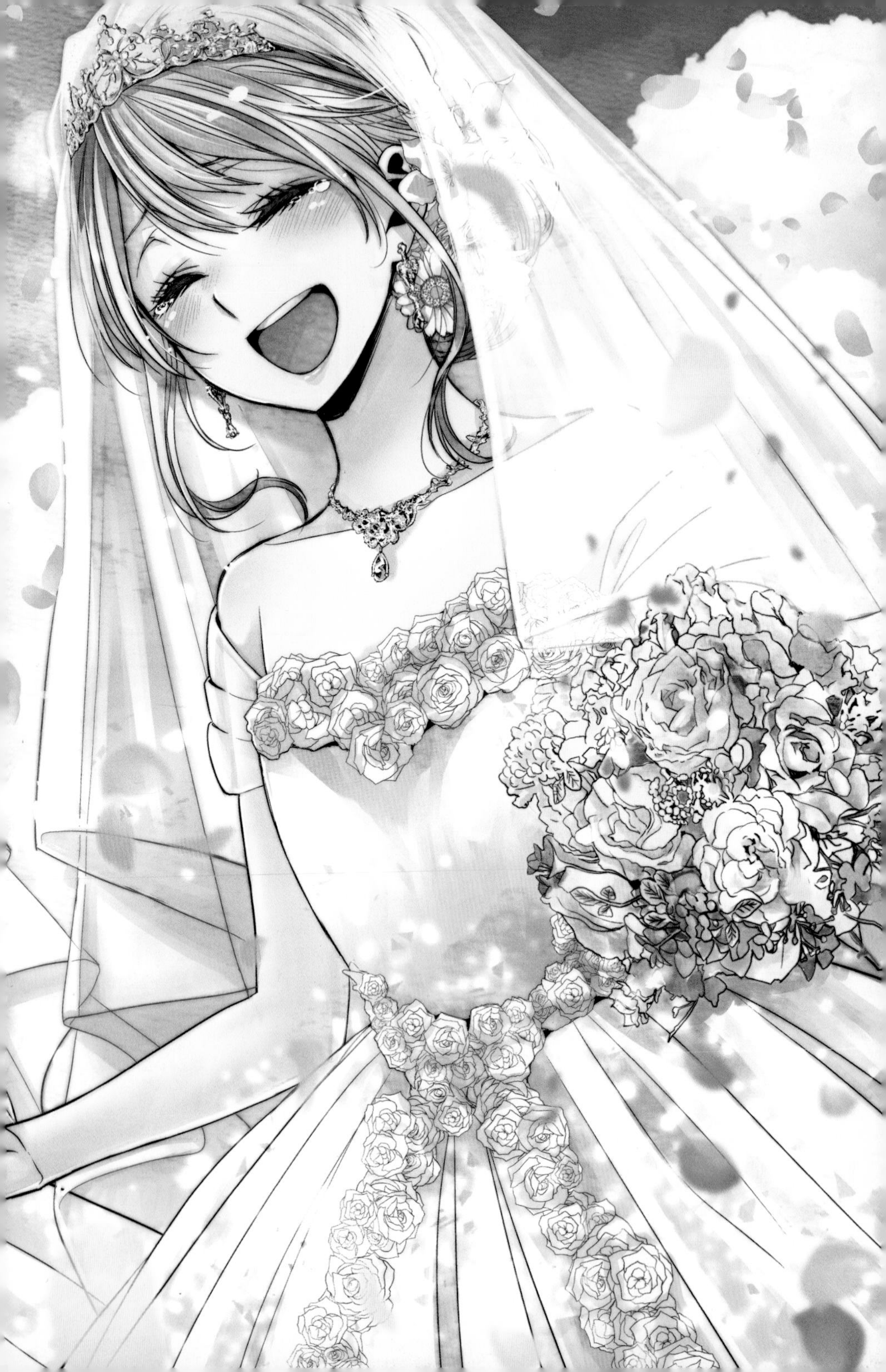

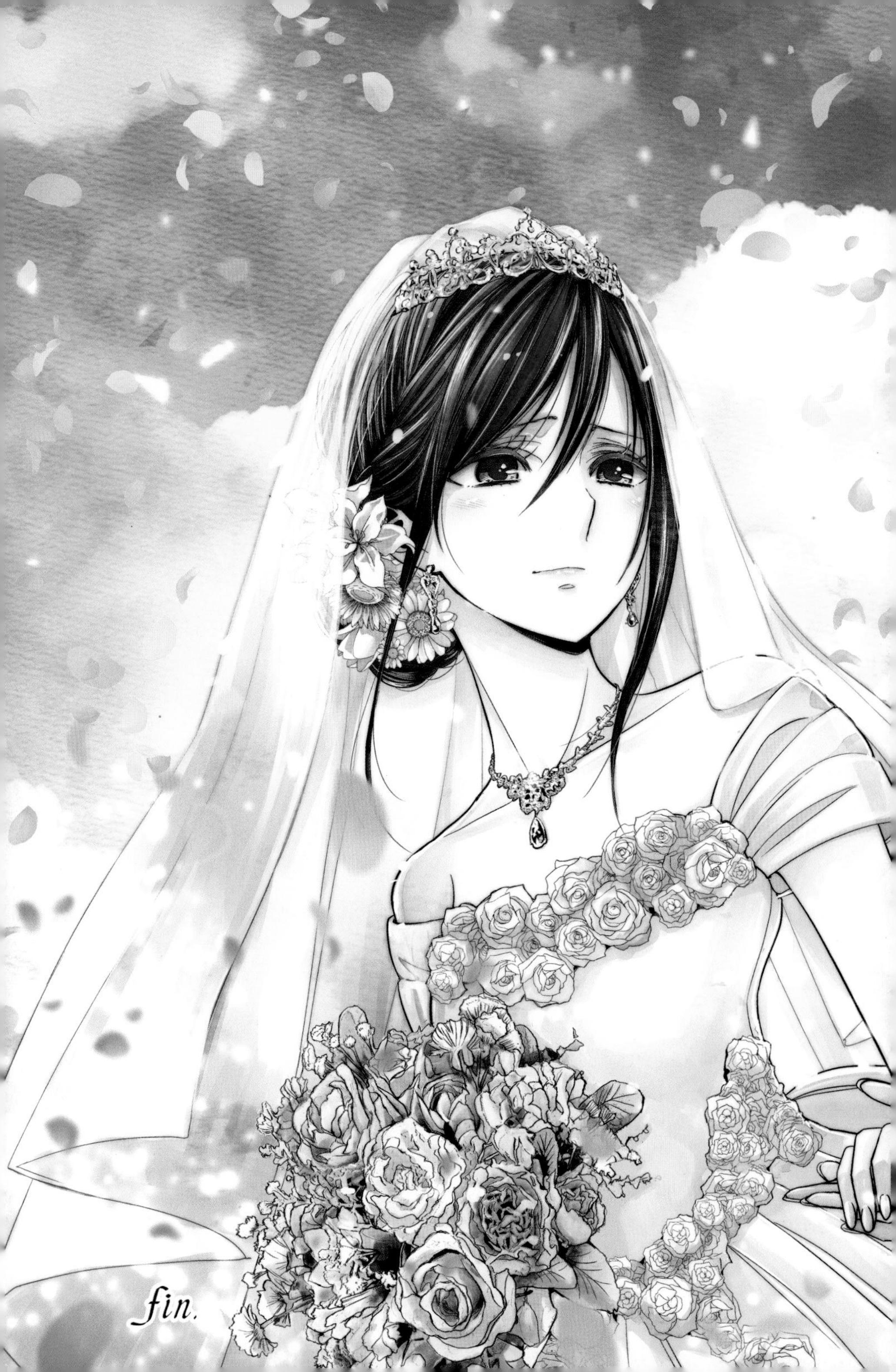
fin.

Thank you for reading Volume 10 of Citrus!!

{ WE'VE FINALLY REACHED THE FINAL VOLUME...!! }

THE PAST SIX YEARS HAVE BEEN A LONG ROAD, YET THEY SEEM
TO HAVE PASSED IN THE BLINK OF AN EYE--
A GLOWING EXPERIENCE SIMILAR TO GOING THROUGH THE SCHOOL YEARS.

IT'S BEEN A TIME FULL OF LAUGHTER, WORRIES, HEARTACHE, AND STRENGTH.
I DON'T THINK I COULD HAVE REACHED THIS HAPPY ENDING
WITHOUT EVERYONE'S HELP.

TO ALL THE PEOPLE WHO SUPPORTED ME: MY MANAGING EDITOR IKAI-SAMA AND THE
EDITORS, BOOKSELLERS, AND ASSISTANTS, AND TO EVERYONE WHO GENTLY KEPT
WATCH OVER YUZU AND MEI FOR TEN WHOLE VOLUMES...

THANKS FOR ALLOWING ME TO DRAW THE SAME STORY FOR SO LONG...
AND FOR LETTING ME GUIDE THESE TWO TO THEIR HAPPILY EVER AFTER.

THIS WORK HAS BROUGHT SUCH UNENDING HAPPINESS.
I THANK YOU ALL FROM THE BOTTOM OF MY HEART. HONESTLY,
THANK YOU SO MUCH!

AND JUST AS YUZU WISHES IN THIS VOLUME FOR EVERYONE'S HAPPINESS,
IF THIS WORK HAS BROUGHT JOY TO EVEN ONE PERSON, I WILL BE HAPPY.

OH, AND, AND!!
FOR THOSE MOMENTS OF THEIR HAPPINESS THAT DIDN'T FIT INTO THE MAIN STORY,
{ THERE'S CITRUS+! }

I HOPE YOU ALL ARE ABLE TO ENJOY IT AS MUCH AS THE MAIN STORYLINE.

I AM SO HAPPY I COULD DRAW MORE OF MEI AND YUZU. THANK YOU! THANK YOU!

WELL THEN...MAY WE MEET AGAIN IN THEIR HAPPY FUTURE...!!

2018.10.18   SABUROUTA

Special Thanks

UMEDZU-SAMA KAWATANI DESIGNS •
EVERYONE AT COMIC YURI HIME
THE FOREIGN PUBLISHERS • FUJIHARA-SAMA
WATANABE-SAMA • SAKATA-SAMA
OSUSHI
AND EVERYONE THAT SUPPORTED CITRUS!

Information on Citrus can be found here ☆

Saburouta's Twitter → @ saburouta
Citrus Hashtag → #citrus

Up-to-date as of October 2018